BASILICA OF THE ASSUMPTION OF THE BLESSED VIRGIN MARY

Baltimore, Maryland

BAPTISMS 1854-1870

T. Ridgeway Trimble

Colonial Roots
Millsboro, Delaware
2016

ISBN 978-1-68034-058-7

Printed January 2016

CONTENTS

Image: 19th century sketch of the Basilica of the Assumption of the Blessed Virgin Mary, Baltimore, Maryland. See Howard, George W., *The Monumental City—It's Past History and Present Resources* (Baltimore: J.D. Ehlers & Co. Engravers & Steam Book Printers, 1873), p. 34.

Acknowledgements

I am grateful to Francis P. O'Neill of the Maryland Historical Society, an author of a number of volumes, who made my task so much easier with his good counsel and his seemingly endless knowledge of Maryland history. Thanks, too, go to Kay R. King, a fellow Maryland Historical Society volunteer and author, for her excellent suggestions and encouragement. I am also grateful to Dr. Trisha T. Pyne, Director of the Associated Archives of St. Mary's Seminary & University, who very kindly helped me fill in some gaps in my research.

TRT

Introduction

The baptismal entries in this volume were transcribed from the 1977 microfilm copy produced by the Maryland State Archives of the original records.[1] I also reviewed a few pages of the 1854-1870 Baptismal Register on microfilm in the archives of the Archdiocese of Baltimore.[2] While the original entries were handwritten in chronological order, I have transcribed the records alphabetically and included an alphabetical list of maiden names. Researchers are cautioned to review various possible spellings of a surname.

Although most of the 1854 -1870 Baptismal Register entries are in English, pages 509 – 517 are written in Latin. When translating these entries into English I was mindful that certain Latin names can sometimes be translated in several ways—such as Mary or Maria for the Latin, *Maria,* or Ellen or Helen for the Latin, *Helena.*

My transcription includes pertinent information concerning a baptism, however, occasionally you will find that I have included a priest's name. While all handwritten entries include the name of the officiating priest, I chose to include the priest's name only if there was some commentary, such as "conditionally baptized" etc. In the case of an adult baptism, I noticed the handwritten entry may have included the phrase "received his (or her) profession of faith"; however, I did not transcribe this phrase just as I did not include the

---

[1] Maryland State Archives (1977) microfilm - "Basilica of the Assumption of the Blessed Virgin Mary Collection, MSA SC2702 SCM 1513-1 Baptisms 1854 -1870". A copy of this microfilm is in the collection of the Maryland Historical Society (microfilm reel #3177).

[2] These records are housed at the Associated Archives at Saint Mary's Seminary & University in Baltimore, Maryland.

officiating priest's name after every entry. I reasoned that once a researcher found the name in the book he/she was looking for, he/she would want to read the original handwritten entry.

Should you wish to review the text of a specific handwritten record, please refer to the "p" number at the end of the entry. This number designates the actual page number in the Baptismal Registry. (See footnote #1.)

TRT

A Brief History
of
The Minor Basilica of the Assumption of the Blessed Virgin Mary

The Basilica of the Assumption of the Blessed Virgin Mary in Baltimore, Maryland, the oldest Roman Catholic Cathedral in the United States, had its modest beginnings in St. Peter's Chapel, consecrated in 1775. Located at "Little Sharp" and Saratoga Streets, the original structure was quite small. To better serve the needs of the growing Catholic community it was enlarged two times in the late 1700s and was eventually known as St. Peter's Pro-Cathedral.[3]

Baltimore was established as a Roman Catholic "See" in 1789. The Rev. John Carroll, a Jesuit priest, was consecrated in 1790 as its first Bishop. Bishop Carroll determined that Baltimore needed a much larger church to serve as a Cathedral and eventually purchased high land at Saratoga and Charles Streets in 1805 for his church. The cathedral's cornerstone was laid the following year, but actual construction did not begin in earnest until 1809. To design the new edifice Bishop Carroll engaged Benjamin Henry Latrobe, the architect of the American Capitol. Of course, Bishop Carroll (appointed Archbishop in 1808) needed to find the money to finance the cathedral's construction and did so

---

[3] Cuyler, The Rev. Cornelius M., S. S., *The Baltimore Co-Cathedral - Minor Basilica of the Assumption of the Blessed Virgin Mary: It's History and Description* (Baltimore: Litz Printing Co., 1951, 1961?). The pages are unnumbered.

by raising funds through donations and lottery funds over a number of years.[4]

The Basilica was dedicated in 1821, a year after Henry Latrobe's death and six years after Archbishop Carroll's death. Craftsmen and artisans continued to decorate the interior spaces of the cathedral in the years following the consecration and additional exterior construction included two towers (1830s) and a portico (1863).[5] Most recently, the Basilica underwent a two-year renovation in 2004 and damage from an earthquake in 2011 necessitated additional repairs.

The Basilica's predecessor - St. Peter's Pro-Cathedral - was closed in 1841, and the Basilica continued to serve as Baltimore's only Roman Catholic cathedral until a new one, The Cathedral of Mary Our Queen, was consecrated in 1959. Today, the landmark Minor Basilica of the National Shrine of the Assumption of the Blessed Virgin Mary, the mother church of Roman Catholicism in the United States, continues to serve the Baltimore Roman Catholic community as a Co-Cathedral.

---

[4] Riordan, Rev. M. J., *Cathedral Records From the Beginning of Catholicity in Baltimore to the Present Time* (Baltimore: The Catholic Mirror Pub. Co., 1906) p25.

[5] Cuyler, *op. cit.*

Abbreviations

Archb = Archbishop
b = born
Balt. = Baltimore
bp = baptismal date
(c) = black
c/o = child of
ed. note = transcriber's note
g = godparent
lc/o = lawful child of
ic/o = illegitimate child of
nc = natural child
nc/o = natural child of
ndg = no date or day given
nmg = no month given
p = page
spr = sponsor(s)
[?] = no surname recorded
w = witness
______ (an underline) designates a possible spelling, (or portion thereof), or the name is illegible/missing

Basilica of the Assumption of the Blessed Virgin Mary
Baptisms 1854-1870

[?] - Carlene, "parents unknown" bp 30 Jun 1856 spr Jane Hammond p88

[?] - Margaret _____, "age about 24 years" bp 2 Apr 1855 "baptized conditionally" H. B. Coskery, priest [*ed. note: faint record*] p41

[?] - Mary Anne, b 12 Aug 1850 "parents unknown" bp 29 Apr 1855 spr Jane R_____ [*ed. note: faint record*] p45

[?] – George, "about 4 months old" "a foundling" bp 17 Oct 1864 spr Ellen Boswell p342

[?] – George, b 4 Sep 1865 lc/o _____ _____ & Ann Riley bp 7 Oct 1865 p366

[?] – Lucy Ann, b *ndg* bp 19 Dec 1858 "baptized privately" Thos. Foley, priest p177

[?] – Margaret Ellen, "about 3 weeks old" "a foundling" bp 31 Aug 1865 Thos. Foley, priest p363

[?] – Mary Josephine, "about middle of Oct 1856" "parents unknown" bp 10 Feb 1857 spr Mary Currace p110

[?] – Mary Margaret, "30 years old" bp 19 Aug 1869 spr Sister Mary Joseph, S. S. p480

[?] – Mary Rose, "5 years old" bp 19 Aug 1869 spr Sister Mary Joseph, S. S. p480

[?] – Mary Virginia (c), b *ndg* nc "belonging to Dr. Tubman" bp 21 Jan 1860 spr Mary Tubman p212

[?] – Oliver, b 18 May *ndg* "parents unknown" bp 21 May 1867 spr Amelia Enh___ p413

[?] – Wm. Isaac, b 20 Oct 1854 "foundling" bp 18 Jan 1855 spr Ann Phipps p35

ABELL – Helen Marie, b 9 Dec 1856 lc/o Arounah S. Abell & Mary Campbell "(born Fox)" bp 12 Dec 1856 spr Margaret Fox p104

ABELL – Margaret, b 19 Jan1859 lc/o Arounah S. Abell & Mary Campbell "(born Fox)" bp 26 Jan 1859 spr Margaret Fox p179

ABELL – Mary Anna Florine, b 30 May 1855 lc/o Aronnah S. Abell & Mary Fox (Campbell) bp 6 Jun 1855 spr Rosa Abell p48

ABELL – William Slicer, b 18 Dec 1861 lc/o William Abell & Margaret Stanton bp 20 Feb 1862 spr Mary Cox p275

ADAMS – Edward Gayner, b 13 Oct 1855 lc/o Captain George Adams & Adelaide Bousquet bp 3 Jun 1856 spr Lydia Adams p84

ADAMS – Elizabeth Catherine Adams, "age about 22 years" bp 29 Jun 1855 "baptized conditionally" H. B. Coskery, priest p50

ADAMS – Horatio Francis, "about 7 years old" lc/o Hemsley Adams & Harriet Lecompte (c) bp 16 Sep 1861 spr Ann Williamson p260

ADAMS – John, b 15 May 1858 lc/o Capt. Jno. Adams, USA & Georgiana McDougal bp 19 Jun 1858 spr Dr. Rich. McShe___ & Augusta Lusby p160

ADAMS – John Carroll, b 1 Mar 1864 lc/o John A. Adams & Sarah E. Carroll bp 10 Mar 1864 spr Mary E. Carroll p328

ADAMS – Louis Alexander, b 6 Aug 1859 lc/o Hensley Adams & Harriet Lecompte (c) bp 29 Aug 1859 spr Elizabeth Colbert p199

ADAMS – Mary Elizabeth (c), b 16 Mar 1870 lc/o John Adams & Eliza Cole bp 20 Mar 1870 spr Henrietta Smith p496

ADAMS – Thomas Patton, b 19 Nov 1856 lc/o Capt. John Adams, USA & Georgiana McDougal bp 30 Dec 1856 spr Lt. Theodore Talbot, USA & Eliza Nunes p106

ADDISON – Charles, b 20 Nov 1846 lc/o Dennis Addison & Patricia Rose (c) bp 4 Feb 1857 spr C______ Addison, Frances Castor & Ellen Taylor p109

ADDISON – Joseph, 22 May 1847 lc/o Dennis Addison & Patricia Rose (c) bp 4 Feb 1857 spr C______ Addison, Frances Castor & Ellen Taylor p109

ADDISON – Rebecca, b 22 Jan 1844 lc/o Dennis Addison & Patricia Rose (c) bp 4 Feb 1857 spr C______ Addison, Frances Castor & Ellen Taylor p109

ADDISON – Rich., b 2 Oct 1867 lc/o Thos. Addison & Rose Campbell bp 29 Oct 1867 spr Rose Gantley p425

ADREAN – Pearson John, b 5 Mar 1822 bp 9 Apr 1858 g John Brady p153

ADRIEN – Joseph Thomas, b 6 Nov 1857 lc/o Pearson Adrien & Catherine A. Murphy bp 21 Mar 1858 spr John Brady & Margaret Brady p151

ADVENT – Mary Advent, "4 weeks old" "a foundling" bp 20 Dec 1862 spr Mary A. Kilduff p298

AGNEW – Mary Aloysius, b 21 Jun [*ed. note: year not written, probably 1868*] lc/o John D. Agnew & Lizzie C. Bryne bp 4 Jul 1868 spr John Hoover, "proxy for Mary A. Hoover" p448

AGNEW – Theresa, b 20 May 1855 lc/o Thomas Agnew & Mary Dunn bp 23 May 1855 spr James Dunn & Ann Boyle p47

AGNEW – Veronica Magdellena, b 20 Jul 1857 lc/o Thomas Agnew & Mary M. Dunn bp 20 Jul 1857 spr Nora Cahill p128

AHER – Mary Aher, "4 yrs old" lc/o Edwin Aher bp 26 Sep 1867 "baptized privately" Thos. Foley, priest p422

AIREY – Ann Airey, "aged 18" bp 24 Apr 1867 "baptized conditionally" Thos. Foley, priest p411

ALBERT – Charles Francis (c), b 24 Jul 1865 lc/o Frisby Albert & Mary <u>Barton</u> bp 1 Aug 1865 spr Hannah <u>Barton</u> p361

ALBERT – Eugene Leon Albert, b 19 Aug 1869 lc/o Henry J. Albert & Victorine May Guerard bp 26 Aug 1869 spr Eugene Francis Guerard & Eugenie Guerard p481

ALBERT – Eva Nila Josephine, b 4 Dec 1866 lc/o Henry J. Albert & Victorine Mary Guerand bp 15 Dec 1866 spr Francis Guerand & Josephine Guerand p402

ALDRIDGE – John Henry Aldridge, b *ndg* 1832 lc/o Andrew & Ann Aldridge bp 14 Feb 1860 "baptized conditionally" Thos. Foley, priest p215

ALICE – Mary Ann, b 6 Apr 1859 lc/o John Alice & Mary Wallis bp 5 May 1859 spr Mary Christina Kries p188

ALLEN – Henry Ambrose, b 23 Feb 1854 bp 18 Feb 1857 "baptized privately" Thos. Foley, priest p111

ALLEN – William Wallace Allen, "aged about 22 years" bp 14 Mar 1866 spr John M. McCafferty & Josephine Cropper "baptized conditionally" James Gibbons, priest p378

AMBROSE – Samuel, b 23 Jun 1860 lc/o John Ambrose & Ellen Gaines bp 28 Oct 1860 spr Mary A. Murray p233

AMES – Joseph Aloysius, b 28 Jan 1854 nc/o Susan Ames (c) bp 26 Apr 1854 p11

ANDERSON – Abraham Anderson (c) b 20 Feb 1863 bp 27 Feb 1863 "baptized privately" Thos. Foley, priest p302

ANDERSON – Charles Horace, b 24 Mar 1849 lc/o Charles Anderson & Eliza Jane Franklin bp 11 Apr 1855 spr Susanna Margaret Daley p43

ANDERSON – Charles McHenry, b 7 Feb 1863 lc/o Jerome Anderson & Eliza Patterson (c) bp 29 Apr 1863 spr Lavinia Anderson p306

ANDERSON – Eliza Jane Anderson "(born Franklin)", "34 years of age" bp 4 June 1857 spr Susanna Daley p123

ANDERSON – Emily, b 10 Jul 1859 c/o Sarah Anderson bp 8 Sep 1859 spr Emily Roach p199

ANDERSON – George Francis, b 21 Jan 1858 lc/o Charles Anderson & Eliza Jane Franklin bp 22 Mar 1858 spr Susanna Daley p151

ANDERSON – James Franklin Daley, b 8 Aug 1862 lc/o Charles Anderson & Eliza Jane Franklin bp 8 Sep 1862 spr Cecilia Daley p289

ANDERSON – Johanna Augustus, b 28 Aug 1865 lc/o Charles Anderson & Eliza Jane Franklin bp 25 Sep 1865 spr Susan Trumbi p365

ANDERSON – John Edward, b 28 Nov 1855 lc/o Charles Anderson & Eliza I. Franklin bp 31 Mar 1856 spr Susanna Daley p78

ANDERSON – John Nelson, b 27 Feb 1866 lc/o William F. Anderson & Margaret De Swan bp 22 Jul 1866 spr Philip De Swan & Anne Hannah p390

ANDERSON – Joseph Dorsey, b 17 May 1847 lc/o Charles Anderson & Eliza Jane Franklin bp 11 Apr 1855 spr Susanna Margaret Daley p43

ANDERSON – Mary Clara, b 4 May 1863 lc/o Thomas M. Anderson & Rose Campbell bp 17 May 1863 spr Bernard Campbell & Bridget Kelly p307

ANDERSON – Sarah Anderson (c), "aged about 27 years" bp 7 Sep 1859 spr Margt. Glenn "baptized conditionally" H. B. Coskery, priest p199

ANDERSON – Sarah Elizabeth, b 8 Jul 1860 lc/o Charles Anderson & Eliza Jane Franklin bp 18 Jul 1860 spr Susanna Daley p227

ANDERSON – Thomas, b 6 Oct 1861 lc/o Thomas Anderson & Rose Campbell bp 20 Oct 1861 spr John Gately & Rose Gately p264

ANDERSON – William John, b 29 Mar *ndg* lc/o Thomas Anderson & Rose Campbell bp 1 Apr 1855 [*ed. note: faint record*] p41

ANDREW – Benjamin Franklin, b *ndg* Oct 1868 lc/o Benjamin Franklin Andrew & Catharine D. Daley bp 1 Dec 1868 spr Catharine Lambert p459

ANDREWS – Agnes, b 16 Feb 1863 lc/o William A. Andrews & Mary Morgan bp 14 Apr 1863 spr Mary R. Andrews p306

ANDREWS – Catharine Dumaris, b 2 Nov 1860 lc/o Benjamin Andrews & Catharine Demaris bp 30 Nov 1860 spr Cecilia Daley p236

ANDREWS – Catharine, b 21 Nov 1860 lc/o William A. Andrews & Mary Morgan bp 25 Mar 1861 spr Mary Rose Andrews p247

ANDREWS – Elizabeth, b 10 Sep 1856 lc/o William A. Andrews & Mary Ann Martin bp 11 Nov 1856 spr Catherine Andrews p101

ANDREWS – Ella, b 2 Jan 1865 lc/o William A. Andrews & Mary Rose Morgan bp 17 Feb 1865 spr Mary R. Andrews p351

ANDREWS – James Robert, b 5 Feb 1858 lc/o Benjamin Andrews & Domeria Daily bp 13 May 1858 spr Cecilia Daily p155

ANDREWS – Mary Grady, b 28 Jan 1870 lc/o William A. Andrews & Mary Morgan bp 19 Mar 1870 spr Frank Andrews & Lizzie Andrews p496

ANDREWS – Mary Rebecca, b 3 Jul 1855 lc/o Benjamin Andrews & Catherine de Mays Daley bp 29 Jan 1856 spr Catherine Philips p71

ANDREWS – Mary Rosa, b 2 Mar 1854 lc/o William Andrews & Mary Morgan bp 2 May 1854 spr Martha Quilan p11

ANDREWS – Robert Allen, b 12 Aug 1867 lc/o William Allen Andrews & Marie Morgan bp 21 Sep 1867 spr Charles Andrews & Mary R. Andrews p421

ANDREWS – Susanna Agnes, b 9 Aug 1864 lc/o Benjamin Franklin Andrews & Cath. Daly bp 7 Sep 1864 spr Susanna Daly p339

ANDREWS – William Franklin, b 14 Aug 1858 lc/o William Alter Andrews & Mary Morgan bp 28 Oct 1858 spr Mary F. Quinlin p172

ANGEL – Flora Catharine, b 1 April 1867 lc/o Abner Angel & Catharine Medairy bp 15 Dec 1868 spr Johanne Foley & Hannah Daley p460

ANGEL – Mary Belle, b 10 Aug 1868 lc/o Abner Angel & Catharine Medairy bp 15 Dec 1868 spr Johanne Foley & Hannah Daley p460

ANGELERIE – Mary Theresa, b 6 Jul 1870 lc/o Jules Angelerie & Marie Antonnelie bp 24 Aug 1870 spr Alexendrine & Emile Jean Michel Laroque p507

ANWELL – John Thomas, b 21 Jul 1859 lc/o Edward Anwell & Mary Kirker bp 13 May 1860 spr Maria Sheran p221

ANZMANN – Francis Anzmann "(born Seymour)", "aged 21 years" bp 16 Nov 1865 "baptized conditionally" Thos. Foley, priest p369

APPOLD – Ella, "18 months old" lc/o George & Mary Appold bp 24 May 1867 "baptized privately" Thos. Foley, priest p413

ARCHER – Lelia Phillips, b 2 Sep 1856 lc/o James Archer & Catherine Ellen Brown bp 3 Sep 1856 spr Serena Spencer & Francis Patrick, Archb. Balt. p94

ARCHER – Mary, b 8 Sep 1854 lc/o James P. Archer & Catherine A. Brown bp 16 Sep 1854 spr James Conroy & U. Vict. Page p23

ARCHER – Thomas Stevenson, b 26 Sep 1861 lc/o James P. Archer & Catharine E. Brown bp 9 Oct 1861 spr Thos. Foley & Mary La___ p263

ARDIN – Mary Amelia Philomena, b 9 Apr 1841 lc/o David Ardin & Amelia "(decd)" bp 12 May 1865 spr Elizabeth Foudriat "baptized conditionally" Thos. Foley, priest p356

ARGENTI – Jerome John Baptist, b 5 Dec 1860 lc/o Tullio Argenti & Ellen Kelly bp 18 Dec 1860 spr Andrew Ghia & Theresa Bonner p238

ARGENTI – Jullio Pompio Nicholas, b 22 Feb 1863 lc/o Jullio Argenti & Ellen Kelly bp 5 Apr 1863 spr Nicholas Dobroslunish & Margaret Scott p305

ARMOR – Charles Lee Armor, "about 27 years of age" lc/o James & Catherine Armor bp 30 Nov 1855 spr John Doyle & J. McSherry _____ Dobnes p67

ARMSTRONG – Mary Martina, b 2 Dec 1855 lc/o John Armstrong & Mary Kelly bp 10 Feb 1856 spr Henrietta Armstrong p72

ARMSTRONG – Sarah Georgiana, b 28 Mar 1854 lc/o John C.Armstrong & Nancy Kelly bp 23 Apr 1854 spr Ellen Mary Kelly [*ed. note: entry for Sarah Georgiana Kelly is listed as being baptized on the same date- baptized name of child could have been incorrectly entered*] p11

AROL – Francis, "now in sixth year" lc/o Henry Arol & Susanna Davis bp 13 Oct 1856 spr May J. Davis "I supplied the ceremonies of baptism…privately baptized by Rev. Jas. Dolan" Thos. Foley, priest p99

AROL – Samuel, b 24 Nov 1855 lc/o Henry Arol & Susan Davis bp 5 Mar 1856 spr Ellen Welch p74

ARRIGHI – Mary Angeline Adelaide, b 2 Feb 1860 lc/o Zephyr Arrighi & Catharine Chilsa bp 11 Feb 1861 spr Peter Molinari & Angeline Cerrighini p243

ARTHUR – Margaret, b 1 Jan 1859 c/o Albert & "somebody else" [sic] bp 14 Mar 1859 spr Elizabeth Stewart p184

ASHTON – George Ferendina, b 3 Feb 1870 lc/o George Ashton & Sarah Ann Smith bp 6 Mar 1870 spr C. Ferendina & Bernardina Rankie p495

ATKINSON – Ellen, b 7 Jul 1854 lc/o Dr. Thomas C. Atkinson & Ellen McNally bp 8 Aug 1854 spr Henry McNally & Minnie Wilson p19

ATKINSON – Harriet Ann Atkinson (c) "aged about 13 years" bp 11 Jun 1857 "I supplied the ceremonies" "baptized by me 11 years ago" H. B. Coskery, priest p123

ATKINSON – Mary Ann Caroline, b 4 Nov 1857 lc/o Robert Atkinson & Maria Michel bp 30 Nov 1857 spr Charles Atkinson & Louisa Atkinson p142

ATWELL – Hannah Atwell, "aged about 30 years" bp 23 Mar 1868 p437

AUBRY – Sarah Julianna, "aged about 15 years" bp 31 Jan 1865 p349

AUGUSTUS – Adele, b 6 Mar 1865 lc/o Victor Augustus & Adele Borrigus (all c) bp 3 Sep 1865 spr Ann Brown (c) p364

AUGUSTUS – Charles Pulaski, b 3 Nov 1869 lc/o Victor Augustus & Adele Barragus (c) bp 9 Jan 1870 spr Elizabeth Johnson p491

AUGUSTUS – Clara Virginia, b 6 Jun 1863 lc/o Victorine Augustus & Adele Barragas (c) bp 31 Aug 1865 spr Elizabeth Johnston p314

AUSTIN – Alba Mary Austin, "20 years old" bp 14 Jul 1858 spr Claudia C. Cuminsky p163

BACON – Mary Catherine Bacon, "about 16 years old" "servant of Mrs. Juliette Garesche (St. Louis, Mo)" bp 13 May 1857 spr Mary McLane p120

BADGER – Emma Elizabeth Badger, b 27 Sep 1833 bp 15 Feb 1863 p301

BAFSON – Charles William, b 21 Sep 1864 lc/o James W. Bafson & Mary Catharine Brady bp 9 Oct 1864 spr Chs. Reubens & Mary Brady p341

BAILEY – Agnes V. (c), b 23 Feb 1870 lc/o Ephraim Bailey & Mary Smith bp 6 Apr 1870 spr Jane Thompson p499

BAILEY – Ann Bailey, "age about sixty five years" bp 27 Dec 1854 "baptized conditionally" H. B. Coskery, priest p32

BAILEY – Catherine Henrietta, b 31 Aug 1858 lc/o Edwin Bailey & Lucinda Hewitt bp 22 Sep 1858 spr Henry McShane & Catherine McShane p169

BAILEY – Edwin Bailey, "aged 30 years" bp 16 Aug 1857 spr Mary A. Ryan "I supplied the ceremonies to Lucinda Hewitt, "his wife" Thos. Foley, priest p130

BAILEY – Grace Ann Bailey (c), "aged about 26 years" bp 26 Jul 1860 spr Mary Berry "I baptized conditionally" H. B. Coskery, priest p228

BAKER – Clara Gertrude, b 1 Feb 1865 lc/o Alexander & Frances (Hahn) Baker bp 27 Feb 1865 spr Sylvester Hahn & Louis Hahn p352

BAKER – Frances Teresa, b 14 Mar 1861 c/o George Alexander Baker & Mary Frances Kuhn, "his lawful wife" bp 2 May 1861 spr Andrea Palladio Caldwell & Mary Philomena Kuhn p250

BAKER – Susan, b 19 Aug 1836 lc/o David & Sarah Baker bp 18 Oct 1856 spr Adele Langue p99

BAKER – Valesca Maria Antoinette, b 8 May 1854 lc/o Samuel E. Baker & Valesca Arens bp 22 July 1854 spr Lucy Antoi. Arens & Mary Mullan p18

BALL – Anna Belle Sella, b 15 Mar 1861 lc/o John Ball & Kate Carr bp 24 Mar 1861 spr James Carr & Ann Quinn p246

BALL – Clara Teresa, b 14 Dec 1862 lc/o John Ball & Catharine Carr bp 4 Jan 1863 spr Francis Henry Carr & Jane Simpson p299

BALL – John Francis, b 22 Jul 1864 lc/o John Ball & Catharine Carr bp 31 Jul 1864 spr Hugh King & Bridget King p337

BALL – Lydia Elizabeth, b 22 Jul 1867 lc/o John H. Ball & Catharine Carr bp 2 Apr 1867 spr Helena Eliz. Sneider p418

BALL – Rose, b 5 Jul 1870 lc/o John H. Ball & Catharine Carr bp 27 Jul 1870 spr Mary E. Townsend p506

BALLARD – Ellen Cynthia, b 6 Sep 1853 lc/o Frederick Ballard & Mary Dolan bp 21 Oct 1855 spr Ellen Dolan p62

BALLARD – James Franklin, b 6 Sep 1853 l/co Frederick Ballard & Mary Dolan bp 21 Oct 1855 spr Margaret Rush p62

BALLARD – Mary Louisa, b 11 May 1870 lc/o Byren Ballard & Addie Gill bp 13 May 1870 spr Mrs. O'Meara "baptized privately" John Doughtery, priest p501

BALLARD – William Scott, b 20 Jun 1861 lc/o James Ballard & Sarah Woods bp 21 Jul 1861 spr John & Mary Thompson p257

BALLOD – Mary Jane, b 19 Nov 1858 lc/o James Ballod & Sarah Woods bp 30 Jan 1859 spr Daniel Caul & Anna Caul p180

BAMBERGER – Joseph Wenceslaus, b 28 Sep 1859 lc/o Joseph C. Bamberger & Elizabeth Buckley bp 23 Jan 1860 spr Fanny Rooney p212

BAMBERGER – Thomas Wright, b 10 Oct 1862 lc/o Joseph Bamberger & Elizabeth Buckley bp 12 Apr 1863 spr Chs. Cellery & Fanny Hirst p305

BANE – Charles William, b 1 Jan 1854 lc/o Charles Bane & Mary A. Williams bp 8 Jan 1854 spr Elizabeth Behan p2

BANKS – Francis Joseph, b 29 Jul 1868 c/o Charles Wm. Banks & Emily Maulsby bp 3 Sep 1869 spr Mary Lucinda Banks Fitch p482

BANKS – James, b 16 Jan 1858 lc/o James Banks & Ellen, "his wife" bp 9 Jun 1858 spr Ann Phipps (c) p159

BANKS – Jane, b 22 Jan 1867 c/o Charles Wm. Banks & Emily Maulsby bp 3 Sep 1869 spr Mary Isabel Banks p482

BANKS – Marian Emily Sewell, b 14 Oct *ndg* [*ed. note: most likely 1870*] c/o Carol Banks "of Baltimore" & Emily Maulsby "of Harford County" bp 22 Oct 1870 spr Mary Phipps & Carol Vahler p515

BANNON – Jno. Patk., b 5 Apr 1855 lc/o John Bannon & Maria Tansey bp 11 May 1855 spr Mich. & Rosa Bannon p46

BANNON – William Thomas, b 15 Nov 1856 lc/o Hugh Bannon & Ann Connelly bp 16 Nov 1856 spr Wm. Connelly & Mary Bannon p101

BANON – Mark, b 25 Apr 1858 lc/o James Banon & Mary Wall bp 7 Jun 1858 spr Eliza Hayden p158

BARBIERI – Teresa, b 9 Sep 1862 c/o Joseph Barbieri & Celtine Rappeti, "his wife" bp 11 Sep 1862 spr Francis Barbieri & Teresa Conia p289

BARDON – Edward Michael, b 1 Feb 1861 lc/o Michael Bardon & Martha Spalding "(born Breed)" bp 3 Feb 1861 spr Martha Spalding p242

BARLOW – Mary Ann Barlow "an orphan", b *ndg* 1854 bp 8 May 1854 spr Mary Gilland p11

BARNES – Clara Ellen Sophia (c), b 15 Nov 1861 c/o Jesse Wilson & Margaret Barnes (c) bp 18 Nov 1862 spr Mary Brown p295

BARNES – Mary Ann, b 15 Mar 1870 lc/o Richard Barnes & Catharine McElvey bp 27 Mar 1870 spr Hugh McElvey & Lizzie Cassidy p498

BARRANGER – Lewis John, b 28 Dec 1864 lc/o Louis Barrenger & Delia Gibbons bp 18 Jan 1865 spr George Barrenger & Mary Carlin p348

BARRANGER – Mary Helen Lee, b 19 Mar 1863 lc/o Lewis Barranger & Delia E. Gibbons bp 27 Mar 1863 spr Henry C. Barranger & Alice Sweeney p304

BARREDA– Maria Elvira Manuela Thomasa de la Santissima Trinidad, b 18 Sep 1854 lc/o Frederick Lucien Barreda & Matilda Laverrie Barreda "both born in Seville, Spain" bp 19 Sep 1854 spr Felipe Barreda & Manuela Laverrie p24

BARRENGER – George Peter Coskery, b 21 Oct 1868 lc/o Louis L. Barrenger & Lydia E. Givens bp 5 Nov 1868 spr Lewis [sic] L. Barrenger, Jr. & Barbara Elizabeth Barrenger p457

BARRENGER – Isabella, b 24 May 1867 lc/o Lewis L. Barrenger & Delia Gibbons bp 5 Jun 1867 spr John Barranger & Isabella Smith p414

BARRETT – Catharine, b 9 Jun 1867 lc/o James J. Barrett & Catharine Carroll bp 3 Jul 1867 spr James Carroll & Ann Mary "of A. Carroll" p416

BARRETT – Eleanor, b 25 Aug 1850 lc/o John N. & Eleanor Barrett bp 4 Sep 1857 spr Virginia S. Barrett p133

BARRETT – Francis Marion, b 1 Nov 1856 lc/o John Barrett & Eleanor Barrett bp 14 Oct 1857 spr Virginia S. Barrett p138

BARRETT – James, b 30 May 1865 lc/o James Barrett & Catharine Carroll bp 22 Jun 1865 spr Bridget Carroll p358

BARRETT – John, b 11 Mar 1870 lc/o James J. Barrett & Catharine Carroll bp 21 Mar 1870 spr Rev. John Foley, D. D. & Catharine Barrett p497

BARRETT – John, b 19 Nov 1857 lc/o John Barrett & Kate Connor bp 21 Nov 1857 spr Eliza Connor p141

BARRETT – Laurence Clinton, b 10 Aug 1860 lc/o Thomas H. Barrett & Emily M. During bp 23 Dec 1860 spr Marg Regelin p238

BARRETT – Mary Amelia, b 9 Aug 1868 lc/o Chas. Barrett & Ann O'Brien bp 16 Aug 1868 spr Edwd. & Mary O'Brien p451

BARRETT – Mary, b 24 Mar 1864 lc/o James Barrett & Catharine Carroll bp 27 Mar 1864 spr Fanny Wheeler p329

BARRETT – Virginia Tyler, b 1 Aug 1839 lc/o John N. & Eleanor Barrett bp 28 Aug 1857 spr Bel McLanahan p132

BARRETT – Walter Joseph, b 2 Nov 1863 lc/o Thomas Barrett & Emily Deuring bp 3 Dec 1863 spr Laura Virginia Trulty p321

BARRINGER – Andrew Jackson, b 27 Jul 1853 lc/o Andrew Barringer & Sarah Lettinger bp 27 Aug spr Patk. & Cecilia Murray p21

BARRINGER – Laura Virginia, b 12 Jun 1861 lc/o George Barringer & Susan Burrows bp 10 Jul 1861 spr Mary Randalls p255

BARRINGER – Mary Louisa, b 25 Oct 1869 lc/o Charles Barrenger & Mary Sullivan bp 19 Dec 1869 spr Ann Flannigan p489

BARROLL – Elizabeth, b 18 Aug 1857 lc/o James M. Barroll & Ann Ellen Jenkins bp 20 Aug 1857 spr W. Kennedy Jenkins & Sallie Kennedy p131

BARROLL – Francis, b 4 Oct 1854 lc/o James W. Barroll & Amelia Ann Henderson bp 8 Oct 1854 spr Emma Wycoff p25

BARRON – Ann, "11 days old" lc/o James Barron & Mary Wall bp 9 Jul 1855 spr Ellen Walsh p52

BARRY – Anna Hilliard, b 2 Jun 1857 lc/o John S. Barry & Rosa C. Hilliard bp 27 Jun 1857 spr Julia McManus, "proxy for Jane Barry" p125

BARRY – Denis, b 1 Sep 1854 lc/o James Barry & Honora Smith bp 17 Sep 1854 spr Patk. Killel & Mary Brennan p23

BARRY – Henry Aloysius, b 8 Jun 1863 c/o John S. Barry & Rosalie L. C. Hilliard bp 28 Jun 1863 spr David & Ida Mary Barry p310

BARRY – Ida Mary, 21 Dec 1854 lc/o John S. Barry & Rose L. C. Hilliard bp 30 Jan 1855 spr Mary Barry p36

BARRY – James, b 27 Aug 1869 lc/o James Barry & Lydia Donnelly bp 20 Sep 1869 spr Ann Dougherty p484

BARRY – John Andrew, b 10 Jun 1858 lc/o James Barry & Honora Smith bp 20 Jun 1858 spr Luke Burns & Bridget Brannon p160

BARRY – John S., b 16 Dec 1860 lc/o John S. Barry & Rosa L. C. Hilliard bp 19 Jan 1861 spr Ann Brande p240

BARRY – Margaret Jane, b 8 Dec 1853 lc/o William Barry & Catherine Murphy bp 8 Jan 1854 spr Wm. Leahy & Ellen Welch p1

BARRY – Robt. McKeen, b 18 Nov 1869 lc/o Robert C. Barry & Johanna McKeen bp 24 Dec 1869 spr Hon. T. P. Scott & Kate Barry p490

BARRY – Rosalie Clayborne, b 25 Oct 1858 lc/o John S. Barry & Rosalie C. Hillaide bp 18 Nov 1858 spr Cecilia Barry p174

BARRY- Thomas, b 13 Jan 1854 lc/o Peter Barry & Rose Bradley bp 15 Jan 1854 spr Nell Flanigan & Sarah A. Sheridan p2

BART – Charles Mary, b 31 May 1858 lc/o Charles Lewis Bart & Agnes Brady bp 3 Aug 1858 "I supplied the ceremonies of baptism" "baptized privately by me" Jno. McNally, priest p165

BARTON – Frederick Hawkins, b 9 Nov 1863 lc/o Ignatius D. Barton & Mary Olmire bp 21 Dec 1863 spr Amanda Stein p322

BARTON – Rose Elizabeth, b 15 Jul 1861 lc/o Ignatius P. Barton & Mary Josephine Olmear bp 5 Aug 1861 spr Rose E. Olmear p258

BASIGALUPI – Maria Virginia, b 21 Aug 1858 c/o Vincent Basigalupi & Mary Bora, "his lawful wife" bp 1 Sep 1858 spr John Montaverdi & Maria Montaverde p168

BASKETT – Helen Virginia, b 13 Jan 1869 lc/o John Baskett & Helen Virginia Nierensie bp 18 May 1869 spr Emily Nierensie p471

BASTIN – Eugene Francis, b 12 May 1866 lc/o Emile Bastin & Mary T. Whelan bp 20 Jun 1866 spr Daniel Coakley & Ann J. Coakley p386

BATAILLE – Mary Emily, b 14 May 1856 lc/o Emmanuel Bataille & Marie Bouré bp 10 Jun 1856 spr John F. Hickey & Emily Harper p85

BATCHELOR – Christopher Columbus Lauro, b 12 Mar 1856 lc/o Wallace Batchelor & Mary Beatty bp 3 Aug 1856 spr Christopher & Mary Lauro p92

BAUGHMAN – Ellen Baughman "(born Emberson)", "about 55 years old" bp 28 Sep 1855 spr E. Cahill p59

BAUSKELT – Emily Nerensie, b 21 Oct 1867 lc/o John Bauskelt & Helen V. Nerensie bp 6 Nov 1867 spr Rudolph Nerensie & Susan Ann Clarke p426

BEATTY – Alice Virginia, b 28 Jun 1856 lc/o Joseph Beatty & Mary Higgins bp 3 Aug 1856 spr C & M Lauro p92

BEATTY – George Washington, b 20 Jul 1858 lc/o Joseph Beatty & Mary Higgins bp 26 Sep 1858 spr Maurice Batchelor & Mary Batchelor p169

BEAUCHAMP – Mary Elizabeth, b 23 Mar 1861 c/o Matilda Beauchamp bp 10 Apr 1861 spr Eliza Phipps p248

BECKERSTAFF – James, b 2 Apr 1866 lc/o James Beckerstaff & Mary Leaghey bp 8 Apr 1866 spr Francis Henerman & Bridget O'Donovan p381

BEE – Thomas Henry, b 20 Sep 1854 lc/o Henry Bee & Jane Montgomery "(Harwood)" bp 27 Sep 1854 spr Matilda Sanders p24

BELL – David Ford Romey (c), b 6 Oct 1856 lc/o Hanson Bell & Rosanna Wells (c) bp 12 Nov 1856 spr Anna Givens p101

BELL – Emma, b 4 Sep 1869 lc/o Thomas B. Bell & Emily Brown bp 1 Feb 1870 spr Anna Wolff p492

BELL – George Aughton, b 2 Feb 1865 lc/o Henry Bell & Elizabeth Small bp 22 May 1865 spr G. W. Slater & Mary Ann Sanders p357

BELL – George Beauregard Bell, b 28 Nov 1861 lc/o George M. C. Bell & Mary Maguire bp 20 Feb 1862 spr Amelie Stansbury p275

BELL – Ida Gertrude, b 2 Oct 1865 lc/o John Henry Bell & Catharine Carr bp 11 Oct 1865 spr Mary S. White p366

BELL – Julia Agnes (c), b 16 Jun 1862 c/o Samuel King & Sallie Bell bp 27 Jun 1862 spr Monica Thomas p284

BELL – Mary Anna, b 8 Apr 1865 lc/o G. W. C. Bell & Mary E. Maguire bp 10 Jun 1866 spr Louise Baltzell "I supplied the ceremonies" "This child hand been baptized by her Aunt, Amelia Stansbury, a catholic [*sic*] & competent person" H. B. Coskery, priest p386

BELL – Robert, b 31 Aug 1867 lc/o Henry Bell & Elizabeth Small bp 14 Apr 1868 spr Chas. Grant & Louisa Kelly p439

BELTZHOVER – Sarah, b 5 Feb 1854 lc/o Daniel Beltzhover & Elizabeth Miles bp 1 Mar 1854 spr Robert Miles & Joseph Miekle p6

BELTZHOOVER – William Henry Chase, b 8 May 1855 Daniel N. Beltzhoover & Elizabeth Miles bp 5 Jul 1855 spr Wm. H. Chase & Mary P. Miles p51

BENNETT – Henry Adolphus, b 6 Oct 1855 lc/o Adolphus Bennett & Fanny _____ bp 30 Jan 1856 spr Henry Bennett & Sarah T. Walker p71

BENNETT – Isabella Virginia, b 7 Apr 1865 c/o Virginia Bennett bp 24 Apr 1865 spr Mary Hagan p355

BENNETT – Louise Adele, b 28 Feb 1856 lc/o P. Henry Bennett & Sophie Farnham bp 27 Apr 1856 spr Michl. W. Jenkins & Sarah Walker p81

BENNETT – Mary Eliza, b *ndg* Oct 1855 lc/o _____ Cummings spr Danl. Cummings & Mary ______ bp 2 Dec 1855 [*ed. note: faint record*] p67

BENNETT – William Francis, b 27 Dec 1866 lc/o Patrick Henry Bennett & Sophia Farhan bp 29 Jul 1867 spr Alex. M. Aiken & Julia Spies p418

BENTZ – Edw. Lee, b 9 Nov 1868 lc/o George Bentz & Ellen Clarke bp 15 Nov 1868 spr Edwd. & Ann Clarke p457

BENTZ – Ellen Agnes, b 10 Mar 1870 lc/o George W. F. Benton & Agnes Clark bp 20 Mar 1870 spr George W. Haupt & Mary Clark p497

BENTZ – George Bentz, b *ndg* May 1840 bp 9 Feb 1870 spr Annie Haupt "baptized conditionally" Thos. Foley, priest p493

BENTZ – George Laurence, b 21 Apr 1863 lc/o George Bentz & Ellen Clarke bp 3 May 1863 spr Martin Clarke & Mary Higgins p307

BENTZ – Margaret Ellen, b 15 Jan 1866 lc/o Geo. Bentz & Ellen Clarke bp 18 Jan 1866 spr Margaret Clark p374

BENTZ – Mary Catharine, b 4 Sep 1864 lc/o George Bentz & Ellen Clarke bp 11 Sep 1864 spr Annie Clarke p340

BENTZ – Olivia Rebecca, b 27 Dec 1866 lc/o George Bentz & Ellen Clark bp 5 Jan 1867 spr Mary Clark p403

BENZINGER – Aloysius, b 23 Aug 1869 lc/o Frederick F. Benzinger & Rose Fincknauer bp 2 Sep 1869 spr Thos. Foley & Mary Julia Benzinger p482

BENZINGER – Frederick Joseph, b 3 Oct 1865 lc/o Frederick F. Benzinger & Rose C. Fincknauer bp 15 Oct 1865 spr John Sylvester & Mary E. Benzinger p367

BENZINGER – Josephine Margaret Mary, b 4 Jan 1867 lc/o Frederick F. Benzinger & Rose C. Fincknauer bp 24 Jan 1867 spr Frederick Benzinger & Elizabeth Benzinger p403

BERCKMAN – George Washington, b 20 Aug 1856 lc/o John C. L. Berckman & Ellen Haney bp 15 Sep 1856 spr John & Frances Lewis p95

BERG – Albert Bernard Berg, b 2 Mar 1827 bp 18 Jan 1865 "baptized conditionally" Thos. Foley, priest p348

BERG – Mary Auguste, b 22 Mar 1866 lc/o Albert Berg & Ann Conry bp 29 Mar 1866 spr Thos. Conry & Jane Conry p379

BERGER – <u>Loselto</u> Cornelia Foley, b 19 Mar 1865 lc/o Andrew Berger & Mary Ann Raymond bp 19 Mar 1865 spr S. Foley & Henrietta C. Jackel p353

BERRY – John Berry, "22 years old" lc/o John H. Berry & Louisa West bp 31 Oct 1864 "baptized conditionally" Thos. Foley, priest p343

BERRY – Louisa Berry "(born West)", b *ndg* 1820 lc/o Nathaniel & Mary West bp 4 Nov 1859 "baptized conditionally" Thos. Foley, priest p204

BERRY – Margaret Mary Berry, "age about 32" bp 12 Dec 1855 "baptized conditionally" Jno. McNally, priest p67

BERRY – Mary Ida, b 4 Nov 1863 bp 4 Nov 1863 lc/o Charles Berry & Mary Foley bp 4 Nov 1863 "Rev. Ed. McColgan baptized privately" H. B. Coskery, priest p319

BERRY – Mary Imogene, b 21 Jun 1851 lc/o John H. Berry & Louisa West bp 8 Feb 1862 spr Sarah Modesta Berry "baptized conditionally" H. B. Coskery, priest p273

BERRYER – Mary Catharine Heloise, b 23 Jul 1868 lc/o Jules Berryer & Mary Kreb bp 2 Aug 1868 spr Catharine Mason p449

BERRYMAN – Anne Mary, b 18 Jan 1868 lc/o Edward Berryman & Ellen McCormick bp 15 Mar 1868 spr Eliza Driscoll p436

BETTS – Amanda Adelle, b 31 Mar 1854 lc/o William Betts & Ann Ballentine bp 1 June 1854 spr Margaret Ballentine p13

BEURRIER – Joseph Michael Victor, b 11 Sep 1865 lc/o Jules Beurrier & Mary Kreb bp 1 Oct 1865 spr Ive Paini & Victorina Paini p365

BEURRIER – Victorine, b 29 May 1864 lc/o Jules Beurrier & Mary Kreb bp 30 May 1864 "baptized privately" Thos. Foley, priest p333

BEVANS – Margaret, b *ndg* lc/o William Bevans & Foris, "his wife" bp 8 Jul 1857 "baptized privately" Thos. Foley, priest [twin sister of Sarah Bevans] p126

BEVANS – Sarah, b *ndg* lc/o William Bevans & Foris, "his wife" bp 8 Jul 1857 "baptized privately" Thos. Foley, priest [twin sister of Margaret Bevans] p126

BIAS – Catherine, b 14 Jan 1858 lc/o James Bias & Mary Hughes bp 24 Jan 1858 spr Daniel Connolly & Eliza Wheram p147

BINGHAM – Robert, b 3 Oct 1855 lc/o Robert Bingham & Mary Frances Williams bp 5 Nov 1855 spr John Albert Williams & Mary Fortune p64

BIOUS – William Henry, b *ndg* c/o Jacob Bious "of Baltimore" & Teresa Bantum "of Baltimore" bp 29 Oct 1870 spr Mary Elbert Owens p513

BIRMINGHAM – Charles Dyonisius, b 8 Apr 1855 lc/o Thos. Birmingham & Ellen White bp 29 Apr 1855 spr Mary Burke p44

BIRMINGHAM – Joseph Gibbons, b 16 Apr 1868 lc/o Thomas Birmingham & Ellen McGurk bp 9 Jun 1868 spr Agnes Birmingham p445

BIRMINGHAM – Lorns Terrence, b 16 Jun 1857 lc/o Thomas Birmingham & Ellen McGurk bp 20 Jul 1857 spr Julia Quinn p127

BIRMINGHAM – Mary Cecilia, b 23 Feb 1862 lc/o Thomas Birmingham & Ellen McGrath bp 20 Mar 1862 spr Mary White p276

BIRMINGHAM – Sarah Teresa, b 13 Jun 1865 lc/o Thomas Birmingham & Ellen McGurk bp 9 Jun 1868 spr Mary White "I supplied the ceremonies" Jas. Gibbons, priest p445

BIRMINGHAM – Willie Henry, b 8 Jan 60 lc/o Thomas Birmingham & Ellen McGurke bp 13 Feb 60 spr Ann Donehoe p215

BISHOP – Emma, "8 years old" lc/o Jno. Bishop & Fanny McGrae bp 13 Sep 1870 spr Carrie Meredith "baptized conditionally" Thomas S. Lee, priest p508

BISHOP – Ida, "aged 7" lc/o Jno. Bishop & Fanny McGrae bp 13 Sep 1870 spr Maggie Devine "baptized conditionally" Thomas S. Lee, priest p508

BISHOP – Mary Abi____ (c), b 1 Jul 1863 lc/o Nicholas Bishop & Mary M. Nichols bp 19 Jul 1863 spr Mary Maquette p311

BITTAKER – George Henry, b 8 Aug 1860 lc/o William Bittaker & Mary Kernan bp 16 Sep 1860 spr Margaret Murphy p231

BLACK – Francis Augustus, b 4 Sep 1861 lc/o Henry Black & Maria Gassaway (c) bp 13 Oct 1861 spr Lucinda Smith p263

BLACK – Henry Black (c), "age 20 yrs" bp 26 Feb 1854 p6

BLACK – Mary Elizabeth (c), b 13 Oct 1855 lc/o Henry Black & Maria Gassoway bp 28 Oct 1855 spr Mary _____ (all c) p62

BLACK – Sara Frances (c), b 6 Nov 1858 lc/o Henry Black & Maria Gassoway bp 15 Dec 1858 spr Sarah Howard p176

BLACK – William, b 1 Jan 1854 lc/o Henry Black & Maria Gassonay (c) bp 1 Feb 1854 spr Julianna Briscoe p4

BLACKSON – Charles Francis, b 15 Aug 1864 lc/o John Blackson & Victoria Steffany (c) bp 24 Aug 1864 spr Henry Jackson & Ann Jackson p339

BLACKSTONE – Mary Victoria, b 1 Jun 1869 lc/o John Henry Blackstone & Victoria Stepner (c) bp 18 Jun 1869 spr Mary C. Brown p475

BLAKE – Alfred (c), b 23 Jun 1863 nc/o Charles S. Hollins & Emma Blake bp 6 Sep 1863 spr Mary Ann Dessen p314

BLAKE – John Blake (c), "aged 36 years" bp 3 Nov 1863 p319

BLAKE – John Ishmael Blake (c), "age about 70 years" bp 16 Apr 1854 "conditional baptism" H. B. Coskery, priest p10

BLANCHE – Laura Melinda, b 31 Dec 1857 lc/o Jeremiah Blanche & Amanda Daley bp 12 Mar 1858 spr Elizabeth Knighton p150

BLASSIG – Louis, b 3 Feb 1865 lc/o Louis Gilbert & Magdalen (Baumgaüdner) bp 27 Feb 1865 spr Elena Baumgaüdner p352

BLAY – James Edward, b 22 Jun 1869 lc/o James Henry Blay & Mary Ann Haines (c) bp 4 Aug 1869 spr Deborah Taylor p479

BLINSINGER – William, b 13 Dec 1859 lc/o George F. Blinsinger & Mary A. Daugherty bp 16 Dec 1859 spr Catharine Daugherty p208

BLIZZARD – Chas. Augustus, b 8 Feb 1866 lc/o John A. Blizzard & Caroline Kemp bp 5 Mar 1866 spr J. Gibbons & Josephine Cropper p377

BLONDEL – Ellen, b 12 Jan 1857 lc/o Wm. Blondel & Teresa Gesen bp 25 Jan 1857 spr James Riley & Honora Tully p108

BLONDELL – John Andrew, b 21 Mar 1859 lc/o Anthony Blondell & Margaret Connor bp 2 Apr 1859 spr Lewis Blondell & Margaret Blondell p185

BLONDELL – Mary Blondell, b 12 Sep 1855 lc/o Anthony Blondel & Margaret Rainer bp 30 Sep 1855 spr Mary Martin [*ed. note: faint record*] p60

BLOSS – Rebecca Mary Bloss, "20 years old" bp 25 May 1861 spr Kate Smith p252

BLUNDELL – Anna Cora, b 25 Nov 1854 lc/o Dennis Blundell & Rose Doran bp 7 Mar 1855 spr John E. Toole & Margaret Toole p39

BLUNDELL – Catharine Royal Virginia, b 24 May 1862 lc/o Dennis Blundell & Rose Dolan bp 14 Jul 1862 spr Robert J. Mahan & Sallie Phelan p285

BLUNDELL – Joseph Edward, b 22 Oct 1854 lc/o Malachai Blundell & Ann O'Connor bp 30 Oct 1854 spr Denis Blundell p27

BLUNDELL – Joseph Francis, b 7 Jan 1862 lc/o William Blundell & Honora F. Gleason bp 9 Jan 1862 spr Patrick Tully & Mary Tully p271

BLUNDELL – Rosa Ann Lee, b 9 Feb 1864 lc/o Dennis Blundell & Rose Ann Dolan bp 20 Mar 1864 spr Francis A. Gibbons & Mary C. Brady p329

BLUNDELL – William Walter, b 5 Sep 1858 lc/o William Blundell & Teresa Gleason bp 7 Sep 1858 spr John Burns & Bridget Burns p168

BOGGS – Eliza Virginia, b 1 Apr 1858 lc/o William Boggs & Virginia Croft bp 22 Apr 1858 spr Ann Boggs p154

BOGGS – Mary Ann, b 26 Jan 1856 lc/o William Boggs & Virginia Crawford bp 30 Mar 1855 spr Ann & Eliz. Cassidy p78

BOGGS – Mary Catherine, b 10 Sep 1856 lc/o James Boggs & Lucy Lowey bp 15 Sep 1856 spr Catherine Nayless p95

BOGGS – Virginia Boggs, "aged 18 years" bp 7 April 1854 "baptized conditionally" H. B. Coskery, priest p10

BOHRER – Estelle Mary, b 20 Feb 1861 lc/o Julian S. Bohrer & Lucinda Brown bp 12 Feb 1862 spr Goff [sic] p274

BOLLMAN – Mary Ruby, b 26 Jan 1867 lc/o John N. Bollman & Mary De Mangin bp 27 May 1867 spr Emma De Mangin p413

BOND – John Addison, b 30 Mar 1854 lc/o William Bond & Margaret Addison (all c) bp 4 Jun 1854 spr Emily Byrne p13

BONNEY – Alberta Mary, b 23 Nov 1868 lc/o James Bonney & Mary Phillips bp 29 Apr 1869 spr Henrietta Brighton p470

BONNEY – Mary Philips, "in 20th year" bp 11 May 1868 spr Mary McGurk p441

BONSAL – Charles John, b 15 Aug 1859 lc/o John Bonsal & Caroline Barnes bp 8 Dec 1859 spr Elizabeth Dempsey p207

BONSAL – Henry, b 8 May 1857 lc/o John Bonsal & Caroline Bowers bp 8 Dec 1858 spr Elizabeth Dempsey p176

BOONE – Charles Henry, b 15 May 1870 lc/o William M. Boone & Sallie Kennedy bp 21 May 1870 spr Right Rev. James Gibbons & Helena Jenkins p502

BOONE – Mary Ann Jenkins, b 28 Dec 1866 lc/o William M. Boone & Sallie P. Kennedy bp 5 Jan 1867 spr Thos. Foley & Mary Cromwell p403

BOONE – Wm. Kennedy, b 25 Aug 1868 lc/o Wm. Boone & Sally Kennedy bp 8 Sep 1868 spr Archb. Spalding & Mary Cromwell p453

BOOTH – Francis John, b 22 Dec 1853 lc/o William Booth & Mary Kavanagh bp 9 Jan 1854 spr David John & Ellen O'Brien p2

BORDLEY – Daniel Charles Heath, b 15 May 1856 lc/o Daniel C. H. Bordley & Mary Blake bp 9 May 1856 spr Hannah Bordley p82

BORDLEY – John Wilson, b 2 Oct 1861 lc/o William Bordley & Elizabeth Wilson (c) bp 7 Nov 1861 spr Mary Gallagher p266

BOSHANNON – Florence Catharine, b 2 Oct 1866 c/o Wm. A. Boshannon & Catharine Welch bp 28 Oct 1866 spr Wm. & Anastaisia Shallow p398

BOSIE – Francis, b 3 Oct 1854 lc/o Upton Lee Bosie & Lucy Cole bp 13 Oct 1854 spr Mary Magdalen Johnson (all c) p26

BOSSON – Margaret Frances, b 5 Jan 1867 lc/o James W. Bossan & Mary C. Brady bp 10 Feb 1867 spr James & Mary Brady p405

BOSTON – John, b 23 Jan 1868 c/o Annie Boston bp 24 Mar 1868 spr Mary E. Herbert (c) p437

BOSWELL – Rosanna, b 31 Oct 1866 lc/o Benjamin Boswell & Ellen Brady bp 8 Nov 1866 spr Margaret Keegan p399

BOTTIMER – Lucy Floyd, b 20 Jun 1859 lc/o Thomas Bottimer & Elizabeth Floyd bp 15 Jul 1859 spr Mary C. Bottimer p196

BOTTIMER – Mary Cecilia, b 14 May 1854 lc/o Frederick Bottimer & Susanne Treadway bp 31 May 1854 spr Ann C. Hook p13

BOTTOMER – Francis Joseph, b 30 Jun 1862 lc/o Frederick J. Bottomer & Susan Treadway bp 12 Jul 1862 spr Louis Dieter & Mary Bottomer p284

BOTTOMER – Mary Emma, b 19 Jun 1869 lc/o Frederick Bottomer & Catharine Bottomer bp 15 Jul 1869 spr Joseph O'Neill & Mary Cecilia Bottomer p476

BOUCHET – Victor Emile, b 18 Oct 1859 lc/o William M. Bouchet & Mary O'Brien bp 22 Nov 1859 spr Mary Harbaugh p205

BOULDER– David, "four months old" c/o David Frisby & Eleanor Boulder (c) bp 26 Apr 1861 spr Lizzie Colbert [*ed. note: last name is listed both as Frisby or Boulder in record*] p249

BOURBON – Clotilea Marie Charlotte, b 6 Feb 1867 lc/o Claude Bourbon & Mary Hart bp 17 Feb 1867 spr Claudia Bergier & Jean Bapt. Ciery p406

BOURBON – Gabriel Claude Alfred, b 29 Sep 1863 lc/o Claude Bourbon & Mary Madigan bp 21 Oct 1863 spr Gabriel Geoffrey & Carolin Sautel p318

BOURBON – Mary Virginia, b 11 Mar 1856 lc/o Claude de Bourbon & Mary Manihan bp 6 Apr 1856 spr F. A. & V. Seynarre p79

BOURIE – Edward de la Rue, b 17 Feb 1858 lc/o Edward Bourie & Georgiana Myers bp 29 Jul 1858 spr William & Mary Myers p164

BOURY – Blanche Teresa, b 7 Oct 1855 lc/o Edward M. Boury & Georgiana P. Myers bp 25 Feb 1856 spr P. Tracey & Mary A. Boury p73

BOURY – Louis Joseph, b 18 Jul 1861 lc/o Edward Boury & Georgianna Myers bp 14 Dec 1861 spr Joseph L. Boury & Cora A. Boury p269

BOWDEN – Mary Eliza Susan, "aged 11 weeks" lc/o William Bowden & Mary C. Bentley (c) bp 25 Feb 1863 spr Elizabeth Singleton p302

BOWEN – Amanda Virginia Bowen (c) "aged 13 years" bp 7 Jul 1867 spr Jane Duffy p416

BOWENS – Hannah Ellen, b 27 Dec 1854 lc/o Thomas Bowens & Ellen O'Donnell (c) bp 16 Feb 1859 spr Margaret Wilson p182

BOWIE – Mary Thyrza, b 3 Jun 1840 lc/o Richard C. Bowie & Marsha Magdalen Rappline bp 18 Jun 1860 spr Juliana Scott "baptized conditionally" Thos. Foley, priest p225

BOWLING – Isabel, b *ndg* nc/o R. R. Bowling "of Prince George's County, Maryland" & Frances G. Patterson "of Baltimore" bp 17 Oct 1870 spr [*ed. note: illegible*] p514

BOWYER – Wm. A. Bowyer, "aged 26 years" bp 8 Feb 1870 spr Louis A. Dieter "baptized conditionally" Thomas S. Lee p493

BOYCE – Atedilla Mary, b 1 Jul 1854 lc/o Eduard Boyce & Margaret Pise bp 16 Sep 1855 spr Maria Pise p58

BOYCE – Catherine, b 22 Oct 1856 lc/o James Boyce & Mary Hughes bp 2 Nov 1856 spr Danl. Connelly & Sarah Smith p100

BOYCE – Edward Francis, b *ndg* Mar 1853 lc/o Edw. Boyce & Margaret Pease bp 8 Oct 1854 spr Maria Pease p25

BOYCE – Josephine, b 22 Jan 1860 lc/o Edward Boyce & Margaret Pise bp 27 Jan 1861 spr Maria Pise p241

BOYD – Alice, b 25 Aug 1854 lc/o William Boyd & Alice O'Neal bp 28 Aug 1854 spr James O'Neal & Mary McAvoy p22

BOYD – Ellen Rosa, b 19 Apr 1858 lc/o James Joseph Boyd & Anne Dempsy bp 19 Aug 1858 spr Winifred Caton p167

BOYD – William, b 11 Nov 1855 lc/o William Boyd & Alice O'Neal bp 18 Nov 1855 spr Thomas O'Neal & Margaret Deneed p66

BOYLE – Ann Elizabeth Hooper, b 20 Aug 1865 lc/o James A. Boyle & Julia A. Hooper bp 31 Aug 1865 spr Thos. Foley & Anna Hooper p363

BOYLE – Ellen Frances, b 29 Jun 1863 lc/o James A. Boyle & Julia A. Hooper bp 14 Jul 1863 spr Sam Eccleston Hooper & Annie Boyle p310

BOYLE – Jane Gabriel Boyle, "age about 17 years" bp 6 Jun 1855 spr Brother John Chrys_____ "baptized conditionally" H. B. Coskery, priest p48

BRADAN – Mary Ann, b 9 Apr 1854 lc/o William Bradan & Cecilia Trexler bp 30 Apr 1854 spr Amelia Debow p11

BRADEKAMP – Charles, b 25 Oct 1849 lc/o Harman Bradekamp & and _____, "his wife" bp 4 Jun 1864 spr George Whistler p334

BRADEN – Charles Jerome, b 29 Aug 1860 lc/o William Braden & Catharine C. Trexall bp 30 Sep 1860 spr Cath. Flynn p232

BRADEN – Samuel Wallis, b 7 Oct 1858 lc/o William Braden & Catherine Trexel bp 17 Oct 1858 spr Catherine Carey p171

BRADLEY – Anna Isabel, b 9 Jun 1859 lc/o Robert Bradley & Isabel Ryan bp 22 Jun 1859 spr Hannah McCormick p193

BRADLEY – Catharine, "born about 1860" lc/o James Bradley & Catharine Fox bp 17 Jan 1870 spr Mary Burke "baptized conditionally" Thomas S. Lee, priest p491

BRADLEY – Francis Xavier Stanislaus, b 27 Oct 1854 lc/o Robert Bradley & Isabell Ryson bp 10 Dec 1854 spr Francis & Elizabeth Owings p31

BRADLEY – Robert Stephen, b 26 Dec 1856 lc/o Robert Bradley & Isabella Warnick bp 18 Jan 1857 spr John Irwin & Elizabeth Ryan p108

BRADY – Alexander Pius, b 29 Sep 1867 lc/o John K. Brady & Mary Magdalen Runsel bp 13 Oct 1867 spr Aloysius Spergel & Isabella C. Murphy p423

BRADY – Ann, b 1 Feb 1861 c/o Francis Brady & Ann _____ bp 11 Mar 1861 [*ed. note: text is difficult to decipher*] p245

BRADY – Catharine Bishop, b 9 Sep 1861 lc/o Edward Brady & Catharine Bishop bp 19 Sep 1861 spr Margaret Bishop p261

BRADY – Francis Patrick, b 6 Jun 1863 lc/o Eduard Brady & Catharine Bishop bp 10 Jun 1863 spr Julia Reilly p309

BRADY – Gertrude Celeste, b 30 Jan 1870 lc/o John K. Brady & Mary Magdelen Rimsal bp 6 Feb 1870 spr John Casper Brady & Anna Maria Hassan p493

BRADY – John, b 12 Oct 1856 lc/o Francis Brady & Ann Rey bp 16 Nov 1856 spr And. Martin & Kate Brady p101

BRADY – Joseph Beauregard, b 18 Dec 1862 lc/o John Brady & Mary Rimsal bp 28 Dec 1862 spr Peter Swaggler & Theresa Murphy p298

BRADY – Margaret Isabella, b 23 Jan 1865 lc/o Edward Brady & Cath. (Bishop) Brady bp 26 Jan 1865 spr Joseph & Mary Kelly p349

BRADY – Mary Anne, b 20 May 1867 lc/o John Brady & Isabella Hughes bp 1 Jul 1867 spr Edward Brady & Rose Daley "I supplied the ceremonies" "privately baptized by Dr. Coskery" Jas. Gibbons, priest p415

BRADY – Mary Frances, b 24 Mar 1860 lc/o Edward Brady & Catharine Bishop bp 5 Apr 1860 spr Susan <u>Haguely</u> p218

BRADY – Mary Loretto, b 3 Sep 1870 lc/o Edward Brady & Cath. Bishop bp 8 Sep 1870 spr Mary Morris p508

BRADY – Mary Loretto, b 30 Nov 1868 lc/o Edward Brady & Catharine Bishop bp 15 Dec 1868 spr Mary Morris p460

BRADY – Richard Carr, b 6 Nov 1860 lc/o John Brady & Mary Remsal bp 1 Jan 1861 spr Teresa & John Murphy p238

BRADY – Rosa, "six months old" lc/o John Brady & Isabella Hughes bp 22 Jul 1869 spr Ann Brady p477

BRADY – Viriginia Lee, b 9 Jan 1865 lc/o John Brady & Mary M. Rinsal, bp 5 Feb 1865 spr John L. & Mabel C. Murphy p350

BRAGAZZA – Louis, b 13 Jun 1863 c/o Francis Bragazza & Antony [*sic*] Crovin, "his wife" spr Michael Crovin & Louisa Crovin "baptized condit." "doubtfully baptized by the father" Francis Patrick, Archb. p309

BRAMBLE – George Thomas Crouch, b 11 Jun 1865 lc/o <u>Sora</u> Evans Bramble & Mary Elizabeth Krager bp 22 Feb 1866 spr Lizzie Miller p377

BRAMBLE – Pamelia Mary, b 19 Jan 1868 lc/o <u>Loen</u> Bramble & Mary Elizabeth Creager bp 14 Aug 1868 spr Elizabeth Miller p451

BRANAGAN – James Thomas, b 18 *ndg*1857 lc/o Michael Branagan & Sarah Kallahan bp 3 Jan 1858 spr Charles Fox & Susan Kallahan p146

BRANAGAN – John James, b 23 May 1863 lc/o James Branagan & Ann Welch bp 31 May 1863 spr Sylvester McMahon & Bridget F_____ p308

BRAND – Hellen, b 11 Jan 1859 lc/o Alexander Brand & Margaret Mary H. McGuigan bp 1 Feb 1859 spr Daniel Kirwan & Mary Jane Emory p180

BRANDON – Francis, b 6 Oct 1856 lc/o William Brandon & Catherine ______ bp 23 Nov 1856 spr Bridget M______ & Jno. McNally p102

BRANNIGAN – Joseph Peter, b 7 Feb 1855 lc/o Michael Brannigan & Sarah Callaghan bp 25 Feb 1855 spr Pat. Nugent & Elizabeth McGuire p37

BRANNON – Elizabeth, b 21 Sep 1864 lc/o John Bannon & Catherine Chiskey bp 23 Sep 1864 spr Thomas Burns & Julia McCluskey p341

BRANNON – George Washington, b 4 Jul 1859 lc/o Peter Brannon & Eliza Cunningham bp 17 Jul 1859 spr John Cunningham & Mary Comelan p196

BRAUGHTON – James Braughton, b 14 Jun 1864 lc/o Joseph Braughton & Bridget Carbery bp 24 Oct 1864 spr James Flaherty & Cath Ma_____ p343

BRAUGHTON – Thomas Patrick, b 31 Oct 1859 c/o Joseph Braughton & Bridget Carberg, "his lawful wife" bp 9 Jul 1860 spr Catharine Mary Cliff p226

BRAUNST – Rosa Leona, b 20 Mar 1855 lc/o Charles Braunst & Mary Evarde bp 9 Apr 1855 spr Constant. Braunst & Elizabeth Foudriat p42

BRAY – Ellen (c), b 21 Jul 1857 nc/o James Bray & Lizzy Addison bp 13 Sep 1857 spr Louisa Dorsey (c) p134

BRAYDEN – Mary Elizabeth, b 26 Oct 1865 lc/o George Brayden & Mary E. Boyle bp 1 Nov 1865 spr Amelie Daiger p368

BRAYS – Catharine Margaret, b *ndg* 1840 lc/o Dedrick Brays & Anne, "his wife" bp 22 Apr 1840 spr Mary Gorman p220

BRENAN – Francis _____, b 22 Apr 1865 lc/o _____ X. Brenan & Sarah Chew____ Brenan bp 1 May 1865 spr Michl. E. Brenan & T. P. Chiffin p356

BRENNAN – Charles Henry, b 12 Aug 1855 lc/o Thos. Brennan & Elizabeth Kennedy bp 23 Dec 1855 spr John Eden & Frances Brennan p68

BRENNAN – Frances, b 24 Jan 1858 lc/o Thomas Brennan & Eliza Kennedy bp 2 May 1858 spr Frances Brennan p155

BRENNAN – Francis Patrick, b 5 Jan 1863 lc/o John Brennan & Catharine Closkey bp 7 Jan 1863 spr Thomas Nolan & Catharine Farrell p299

BRENNAN – James [twin], b 4 Oct 1856 lc/o Patrick Brennan & Mary Hookshall bp 6 Oct 1856 spr Sarah E. Martin p98

BRENNAN – John Henry, b 19 Jun 1858 lc/o Peter Brennan & Eliza Cunningham bp 11 Jul 1858 spr Dennis Shannon & Rose McCormick p162

BRENNAN – Joseph, b 30 Oct 1862 lc/o Louis O. Brennan & Harriet Bennett bp 10 Nov 1862 spr Lydia Banks p294

BRENNAN – Samuel [twin], b 4 Oct 1856 lc/o Patrick Brennan & Mary Hookshall bp 6 Oct 1856 spr Bridget Kelly p98

BRENNAN – Thomas, b 13 Dec 1860 lc/o Thomas Brennan & Eliza Kennedy bp 17 Mar 1861 spr Francis Brennan p246

BRENNAN – William Joseph, b 25 Jan 1864 lc/o Peter Brennan & Eliza Cunningham bp 7 Feb 1864 spr Alexander McCabe & Josephine Chambers p325

BRIEN – Anna Isabella, b 8 May 1855 lc/o Luke T. Brien & Mary V. Wilson bp 29 May 1855 spr Ann Williamson p47

BRIEN – Mary Ellen, b 3 Aug 1860 lc/o Garres. Brien "(deceased)" & Margaret Ann Nash bp 12 Aug 1860 spr John Leary & Honora Nash p228

BRISCOE – Mary Jane, b 23 Feb 1860 lc/o Samuel Gabriel Briscoe & Susan Toomey (c) bp 31 May 1860 spr Jane Briscoe p223

BRISCOE – Theresa, b 10 Mar 1866 lc/o Erastus Briscoe & Julia Grosbeck (c) bp 10 Apr 1866 spr Eliza Hall p381

BROADBENT – Felippe Albert, b 16 May 1868 lc/o Stephen Broadbent & M. Alice Murray bp 1 Jul 1868 spr F. S. dos Santos & Martha J. Murphy, "proxy for Mrs. S. S. dos Santos" p448

BRODEKAMP – Harman Gustavus, b 30 Mar 1842 lc/o Harman Brodekamp & Elizabeth, "his wife" bp 12 Jun 1857 spr Winifred Kelly & Br. Le King "baptized conditionally" [brother of John Alexander Brodekamp] Thos. Foley, priest p123

BRODEKAMP – John Alexander, b 31 Mar 1842 lc/o Harman Brodekamp & Elizabeth, "his wife" bp 12 Jun 1857 spr Winifred Kelly & Br. Le King "baptized conditionally" [brother of Harman Gustavus Brodekamp] Thos. Foley, priest p123

BRODERICK – Mary Ann, b 5 Jun 1854 lc/o William Broderick & Ann Broderick bp 18 Jun 1854 spr Frances Daley & Catherine Cooney p14

BRODEKAMP – Mary Ann Clare, b 31 Jul 1858 lc/o Harman Brodekamp & Mary Elizabeth Flaysoller bp 28 Dec 1858 spr Mary G. Lloyd p178

BRODERICK – Thomas, b 28 Mar 1856 lc/o Thomas Broderick & Bridget Diskern bp 30 Mar 1856 spr Andrew Scallan & Margaret Kelly p78

BROGGY – Michael, b 4 Jul 1867 lc/o John Broggy & Ann Long bp 7 Jul 1867 spr Daniel Conroy & Cath. Gray p416

BROOK – Agnes Victoria, b 21 Feb 1854 lc/o John Brook & Agnes Grentfield bp 26 Mar 1854 spr Mary Trueman p9

BROOKE – Laura, b 5 Oct 1868 lc/o Martin Brook & Ann Cunningham bp 29 Nov 1868 spr Patrick Gallagher & Mgt. Gallagher p458

BROOKER – Benjamin C. Brooker, b *ndg* April 1842 bp 17 Oct 1868 p456

BROOKS – Charles Gerard Kelly, b 17 Feb 1869 lc/o Rodney R. Brooks & Mary Ann White bp 3 Mar 1869 spr Mary Concannon p466

BROOKS – Cornelia Roberta Brooks, b *ndg* bp 23 Sep 1859 "baptized condit. … bapt. in infancy in the Methodist sect and received her abduration" Francis Patrick, Archb. p200

BROOKS – Helena Veronica (c), b 6 Jul 1856 lc/o John Brooks & Agnes Grat bp 6 Jul 1856 spr Mary Ann Berry (c) p89

BROOKS – Henry Rodney Aloysius, b 18 Feb 1859 lc/o Rodney Brooks & Mary Ann White bp 9 Mar 1859 spr Catharine Kelly p184

BROOKS – James Edward, b 22 Jun 1854 lc/o Rodney Brooks & Mary Ann White bp 2 Jul 1854 spr Sarah Corcasson p16

BROOKS – James, b 24 Jul 1868 lc/o Richard Brooks & Rose McManus bp 9 Aug 1868 spr Thos. P. Kelly & Rose McKenna p450

BROOKS – Louisa Brooks (c), "about 16 years old" bp 31 May 1859 spr Frances Landigan p191

BROOKS – Mary Florence, b 28 Nov 1864 lc/o Robt. Brooks & Susan Carson bp 23 Aug 1865 spr Emeline Brooks p363

BROWN – Alfred Thomas, b 27 Nov 1860 lc/o Edmore Brown & Henrietta Wallis bp 11 Jan 1861 spr Ann Hammond (all c) p239

BROWN – Anna Jane (c), b 17 Feb 1862 lc/o Charles Brown & Sarah Madden (c) bp 17 Apr 1862 spr Louisa Thomas p279

BROWN – Charles Albert, b 24 Feb 1854 lc/o Charles Brown & Sarah Wheat bp 24 Oct 1854 spr John Doyle p27

BROWN – Charles Carroll, b *ndg* May 1870 lc/o John Brown & Kate Parr bp 23 Jun 1870 spr Thos. Foley & Mary Preston p504

BROWN – Charles Lewis, b 7 Mar 1869 lc/o Charles Brown & Sarah Madden (c) bp 24 Aug 1869 spr Deborah Taylor p481

BROWN – Daniel (c), b 13 Jan 1859 lc/o Edward Brown & Henrietta Wallace bp 27 Feb 1859 spr Ann Constant (c) p182

BROWN – Elizabeth Brown, "21 years of age" lc/o Race & Susan Brown bp 22 Feb 1855 spr James Munday "baptized conditionally" Thos. Foley, priest p37

BROWN – Elizabeth Brown (c), "aged 19 years" bp 26 Jun 1860 "baptized conditionally" H. B. Coskery, priest p225

BROWN – George (c), b 10 Aug 1854 nc/o Elizabeth Young & Lorenzo Brown (both c) bp 8 Mar 1858 spr Celestia Payne (c) "baptized conditionally" H. B. Coskery, priest p150

BROWN – George Isaac Brown (c), "aged about 27 years" c/o John Reynolds bp 5 Nov 1867 p426

BROWN – James Edward, b 15 Jul 1864 lc/o Benjamisn H. Brown & Caroline Virginia Walters bp 24 Nov 1865 spr R. J. Perrine & Georgiana Carr p369

BROWN – James Henry, b 11 Sep 1863 lc/o Edward Brown & Henrietta Wallace (c) bp 18 Oct 1863 spr Maria Frances p318

BROWN – Jesse Brown (c), "aged about 22 years" bp 14 May 1867 "baptized conditionally" Jas. Gibbons, priest p412

BROWN – John B. Brown, "aged 29 years" bp 21 Apr 1869 p469

BROWN – John Reilly, b 29 Jul 1867 lc/o Archibald Brown & Jane Reilly bp 23 Aug 1867 spr Theresa Blundell p419

BROWN – John Richard, b 16 Dec 1865 lc/o Henry Brown & Harriet Goff (c) bp 5 Feb 1866 spr Jane Baxton p376

BROWN – Lucy Ann, b 4 Dec 1867 lc/o Henry Brown & Harriet Gough (c) bp 2 Jan 1868 spr Martha Stone p431

BROWN – Lucy Isabella, b 29 Aug 1863 c/o George Brown & Mary Brown bp 21 Sep 1863 spr Harriet Allston p315

BROWN – Martha Ann Elizabeth, b 19 Jul 1854 lc/o Elmore Brown & Henrietta <u>Wallarel</u> bp 19 Nov 1854 spr Hannah Thames (all c) p29

BROWN – Mary, b 21 Jul 1867 lc/o John Brown & Rachel Kelly bp 30 Jul 1867 spr Michael Kelly & Mary Ellen Green p418

BROWN – Mary Agnes, b 1 Mar 1863 lc/o Jeremiah Brown & Mary Ann Peters bp 9 Apr 1863 spr James Bates & Mary T. Jones p305

BROWN – Mary Henrietta, b 21 Sep 1857 lc/o Edmund Brown & Henrietta Wallace (c) bp 3 Dec 1857 spr Ann Thomas p143

BROWN – Mary Josephine, "20 months old" lc/o George Brown & Sarah Shays bp 31 Mar 1869 "I baptized privately" Thos. Foley, priest p467

BROWN – Mary Virginia, b 15 May 1864 lc/o Charles Brown & Sarah Maddens (c) bp 15 Aug 1864 spr Sarah Hollins p338

BROWN – Mary Virginia, b 16 Mar 1851 lc/o Charles Brown & Sarah Wheat bp 22 Mar 1857 spr Jane Duffy p115

BROWN – Rose Bel, b *ndg* Dec 1869 lc/o Edward Brown & Cecilia Jackson bp 29 Jun 1870 spr Elizabeth Colbert (c) "I baptized (*sub cer*)" John Dougherty, priest p505

BROWN – Susan Jane, b 9 Sep 1856 lc/o John Brown & Catherine Fitzsimmons bp 11 Oct 1856 spr Patrick Preston & Maria Lambkin p98

BROWN – William Emmett, b *ndg* May 1870 lc/o John Brown & Kate Parr bp 23 Jun 1870 spr M. J. Spalding & Mary Preston p504

BROWN – William Henry (c), b 7 Feb 1856 lc/o Edward Brown & Henrietta Wallis bp 12 May 1856 spr Maria Smith (all c) p82

BROWN – William Joseph, b 7 Jul 1855 c/o Mary Teresa Brown bp 29 Aug 1855 spr Anna Tyson (all c) p57

BROWNE – Caroline Mary, b 31 Jul 1869 lc/o Peter Arell Browne & Mary Helen Scott bp 5 Aug 1869 spr Henry C. Scott & Helen M. B_____ p479

BROWNE – Juliana Laura, b 18 Jun 1865 lc/o P. Arrell Browne & Mary Helen Scott bp 19 Jun 1865 spr John White Scott & Carrie A. Scott p358

BROWNE – Mary Helen, b 19 Jan 1867 lc/o P. Arnell Browne & Mary Helen Scott bp 2 Feb 1867 spr C. Oliver O'Donnell & Emily Hayser p404

BROWNE – Peter Arrell, b 11 Apr 1868 lc/o Peter Arrell Browne & Mary Helen Scott bp 22 Apr 1868 spr Wm. Geo. Read & Elise Chatard p440

BROWNE – Thomas Horace Bowyer, b 4 Jun 1862 lc/o Peter Arrell Browne & Mary Helen Scott bp 14 Jun 1862 spr Thomas Park Scott "by his proxy" Wm. P. Scott & Juliana M. Scott p283

BROWNE – Thomas Parkin Scott, b 4 Feb 1864 lc/o Peter Arrell Browne & Mary Helen Scott bp 13 Feb 1864 spr William Parkin Scott & Emily Harper p326

BROWNING – Henry Clay, b 19 Oct 1860 lc/o James Browning & Ann Stewart bp 4 Jul 1861 spr Josephine & Sylvester Keenan p255

BROWNING – Margaret, b 26 Jan 1959 lc/o Edward Browning & Margaret Ring bp 9 Feb 1859 spr Roseann McNulty p181

BROWNLOW – Robert Brownlow, "aged 85 yrs" bp 30 Aug 1857 "I baptized… conditionally" H. B. Coskery, priest p132

BRUGGY – Ann Jane, b 19 Apr 1865 lc/o Martin Bruggy & Ann Cunningham bp 23 Apr 1865 spr James Cunningham & Bridget Cunningham p355

BRUGGY – Catharine, b 16 May 1863 lc/o Martin Bruggy & Ann Cunningham bp 24 May 1863 spr Thos. Conroy & Mary Bruggy p307

BRUGGY – Mary Ann, b 2 Apr 1856 lc/o John Bruggy & Ann Long bp 4 Apr 1856 spr Bridget Conroy p79

BRUGGY – Mary Bridget, b 24 May 1861 lc/o Martin Bruggy & Ann Cunningham bp 2 Jun 1861 spr Patrick Considine & Mary B. Considine p253

BRUGGY – Matthew Sarsfield, b 26 Sep 1862 lc/o John Bruggy & Ann Long bp 11 Oct 1862 spr Michael Long & Bridget Considine p291

BRUGGY – Patrick, b 6 Feb 1855 lc/o John Bruggy & Ann Long bp 17 Feb 1855 spr Martin Bruggy & Mary Bruggy "I supplied the ceremonies to Patrick…baptized by a Catholic layman in danger" Thomas Foley, priest p36

BRUNDIGE – William, "aged 37" bp 24 Apr 1861 "I received abduration… and baptized conditionally on account of doubt concerning baptism in the Methodist Sect" Francis Patrick, Archb. p 249

BRUNS – Mary Jacqueline, b 8 Jan 1860 lc/o Thomas Bruns & Eliza Ward bp 21 May 1861 spr Jane Rutledge p252

BRUNST – Louis Francis Hector, b 18 Jul 1857 lc/o Charles Brunst & Melina Evard bp 6 Dec 1857 spr Francis Fayset & Lucille Fayset p143

BRUNT – Joseph Ward, b 16 Jan 1859 lc/o Thomas Brunt & Eliza Ward bp 1 Dec 1859 spr Frances Rutledge p207

BRUSHMILLER – John, b 7 Nov 1863 lc/o William Brushmiller & Mary Kane bp 8 Nov 1863 spr Theodore Brushmiller & Mary Ann Kearn p320

BRUSHMILLER – Joseph, b 7 Nov 1863 lc/o William Brushmiller & Mary Kane bp 8 Nov 1863 spr Ambrose Higgins & Jane McKenny p320

BRYAN – Catherine, b 18 Dec 1855 lc/o Patrick Bryan & Bridget Batter bp 20 Jan 1856 spr John Brown & Margaret King p70

BRYAN – Josephine, "born about last February" lc/o John Bryan & Louisa Bryan (all c) bp 8 Jun 1868 spr Mary Ferguson (c) p444

BRYAN – Laura, b 11 Mar 1837 lc/o James W. Bryan & Ann M. Washington bp 1 May 1856 spr Thos. Foley p82

BUCCIOGOLUPO – Maria Rosa Dominque, b 8 Jun 1856 lc/o Vincent Bucciogolupo & Mary Dominique Bora bp 16 Jun 1856 spr Giovanni Monteverde & Maria Crova p86

BUCHANAN – James Allen, b 17 Feb 1869 lc/o James M. Buchanan & Susan T. Rogers bp 28 Feb 1870 "baptized conditionally" John Dougherty, priest p494

BUCHANAN – Jane Ellen, b 17 Sep 1869 lc/o James M. Buchanan & Susan Teresa Rogers bp 25 May 1870 spr Susan T. Lea "I supplied the ceremonies" John Dougherty, priest p502

BUCHANAN – Mary Forestina, b 30 Jun 1868 lc/o James M. Buchanan, Jr. & Suzan [sic] Teresa Rogers bp 16 Jun 1868 spr Henry Buchanan "(proxy)" & Helen Turner p445

BUCHER – Francis Hanier Milton, b 25 July 1853 lc/o William Bucher & Mary Agnes O/Brien bp 7 Apr 1854 spr Magdalen O'Brien p10

BUCKINGHAM – Virginia Robertine, b 10 Jun 1868 c/o James Richard Buckingham & Ann Clarke bp 16 Jun 1868 spr Mary A. Brennan p445

BUCKLEY – Mary Cecilia Buckley, "aged 27 years" bp 6 Aug 1866 "baptized conditionally" Thos. Foley, priest p391

BUCKLEY – Mary Sarah Buckley, "aged 8 years" bp 12 Dec 1867 spr Mary Anne Courly & Winifred Conroy p429

BURCH – Mary Parker Burch, b 23 Mar 1843 bp 24 May 1866 spr Anne Rebecca Burch p384

BURCH – Sarah Rebecca Burch, "aged 19 years" bp 26 Oct 1864 "baptized conditionally" Thos. Foley priest p343

BURDEN – Charles Alexander, b 25 Oct 1865 lc/o Richard Burden & Mary Doyle (c) bp 29 May 1866 spr Mary A. Watkins p385

BURK – Annie Laura, b 8 May 1861 lc/o William Burk & Annie Neal bp 21 May 1861 spr Mary Elizabeth Walsh p252

BURKE – Emma Burke, "in her twentieth year" bp 22 Aug 1867 "baptized conditionally" Thos. Foley, priest p419

BURKE – Henry Urban, b 6 Mar 1854 lc/o Henry Burke & Mary McLaughlin bp 14 Jun 1854 spr Rebecca McLaughlin p14

BURKE – Mary, b 15 Mar 1855 lc/o Richard Burke & Elizabeth Welch bp 17 Mar 1855 spr Frank Donnelly & Emily Welsh p39

BURKE – Mary Ann, b 27 Sep 1855 lc/o Michael Burke & Rachel Burke bp 7 Oct 1855 spr John Grant & Margaret Naughty p61

BURKE – Michael, b 27 Jan 1854 lc/o Michael Burke & Bridget Burke bp 9 Feb 1854 spr Michael Kelly & Cath. Ness p4

BURKE – William, b 4 May 1859, lc/o Henry Burke & Ann McLaughlin bp 24 Jul 1860 spr Rebecca McLaughlin p227

BURN – Mary Ann, b 24 Nov 1854 lc/o Charles Burn & Mary Doyle bp 11 Dec 1854 spr William Coscolly & Mary Boot p32

BURNINE – Marian Burnine, "aged about 23 years" bp 4 Nov 1867 "baptized conditionally" James Gibbons, priest p425

BURNS – Catherine Virginia, b 20 Jun 1855 lc/o James Burns & Elizabeth Robinson bp 26 Aug 1855 spr John A. Finton & Elizabeth McDonald p56

BURNS – James, b 22 Mar 1862 lc/o Patrick Burns & Nancy Lavin bp 13 Apr 1862 spr James Gilroy & Mary Burns p278

BURNS – John Thomas, b 27 Nov 1858 lc/o Thomas Burns & Mary Kavanagh bp 26 Dec 1858 spr Frances Roche p177

BURNS – Juliana, b 7 Feb 1854 lc/o John Burns & Bridget Marian bp 13 Feb 1854 spr Dennis Delang & Mary Cley p5

BURNS – Margaret, b 14 Nov 1861 lc/o Pierce Burns & Mary Hughes bp 24 Nov 1861 spr James Lally & Mary Matthews p267

BURNS – Mary, b 8 May 1868 lc/o Joseph Burns & Catharine O'Meara, b 16 May 1868 spr Mary O'Meara p442

BURNS – Matilda H_____, b 5 Dec *ndg* [*ed. note: most likely 1870*] lc/o Walter Burns "of Dublin, Ireland" & Winifred Dyer "of the same place" bp 18 Dec 1870 spr Patrick Carroll & Elizabeth Girty p517

BURNS – Michael Thomas, b 11 Jan 1855 lc/o Michael Francis Burns & Margaret Boylace bp 12 Jan 1855 spr James Boylace & Ann Murray p34

BURNS – Samuel Kennedy Campbell, b 22 Oct 1857 lc/o Edward Burns & Mary Magrath bp 1 Nov 1857 spr David & Ann Crotty p139

BURNS – Sarah Jane Burns, "aged about 26 years" bp 9 Jun 1861 spr Ellen Caton "baptized conditionally" H. B. Coskery, priest p253

BURNS – Susanna Rose, "6 years old" lc/o James Burns & Margaret Burns bp 25 Jun 1866 spr Mary Agnes Mayor p387

BURNS – Wm., b 27 Aug 1865 lc/o Thos. Burns & Kate Farrell bp 3 Sep 1865 spr John Burns & Alice Mack p364

BURR – Francis Burr, b 22 Dec 1842 bp 18 Dec 1865 p372

BURR – Susan Burr (c), "aged 25 years" bp 21 Jul 1868 spr Emily Burr p448

BUSBY – John Milburn, b 15 Jan 186 lc/o Abraham Busby & Jane Russell bp 10 Feb 1861 spr Jenny McGreer & Mary Craugh [*ed. note: twin of William Wilhelm Busby*] p243

BUSBY – Mary Catharine, b 23 Nov 1858 lc/o Abraham Busby & Jane C. Russell bp 19 Dec 1858 spr Ann N. Russell p177

BUSBY – William Wilhelm, b 15 Jan 1861 lc/o Abraham Busby & Jane Russell bp 10 Feb 1861 spr Jenny McGreer & Mary Craugh [*ed. note: twin of John Milburn Busby*] p243

BUSSEY – Anna Maria Bussey, "aged about 58 years" bp 16 Jun 1868 "baptized conditionally" H. B. Coskery, priest p446

BUTLER – Alexius Foley, b 25 Mar 1868 lc/o Thomas C. Butler & Louisa J. Griffiss "(born Tucker)" bp 1 Apr 1868 spr Thomas Foley & Ida Griffis p438

BUTLER – Benjamin Sayre, b 11 Nov 1857 lc/o Samuel E. Butler & Mary Payne bp 4 Feb 1859 spr Edward Ady & Henrietta Ady p181

BUTLER – Cecilia Maria, b 18 Feb 1860 lc/o Peter Butler & Sarah Williams (c) bp 9 Apr 1860 spr Josephine Minor p218

BUTLER – Charles Lewis, b 11 May 1861 ic/o Lewis Pinkney & Ann Butler bp 23 Jun 1861 spr Ann Hammond (all c) [*ed. note: last name is listed both as Pinkney or Butler in record*] p254

BUTLER – Clara Souls, b 20 Sep 1857 lc/o Peter Butler & Sarah Williams (c) bp 12 Oct 1857 spr Clara Clarke p138

BUTLER – Emma b 18 Sep 1861 lc/o Peter Butler & Sarah Williams bp 12 Dec 1861 spr Josephine Minor (all c) p269

BUTLER – John, b 4 Feb 1860 lc/o Samuel Butler & Mary Paine bp 28 Oct 1860 spr Theresa M. Dempsey p234

BUTLER – Joseph, b 8 Sep 1855 lc/o Peter Butler & Sarah Williams (c) bp 7 Oct 1855 spr Sophia Tavet p61

BUTLER – Mary Agnes Joseph, b 27 Oct 1854 lc/o Martin John Butler & Mary Ann Kelly bp 29 Nov 1854 spr Maurice Sheehan & Mary Kelly p30

BUTLER – Mary Butler, "about 28 years old" bp 14 Oct 1861 spr Catharine During p263

BUTLER – Mary Helen, b 24 Aug 1865 lc/o Peter Butler & Mary McDermott Butler bp 27 Aug 1865 spr Thomas & Ellen McDermott p363

BUTLER – Michael, b 1 Apr 1856 lc/o Michael Butler & Margaret Reilly bp 15 Apr 1856 spr Cath. Gorman p80

BUTTON – Clara Virginia, b 18 Jul 1864 lc/o Emory Button & Elizabeth Haupt bp 16 Sep 1864 spr Elizabeth Haupt p340

BYRNE – John Donehue, b 31 Jan 1870 lc/o J. Byrne & Mary Donehue bp 6 Feb 1870 spr Denis & Margaret Byrne p493

BYRNE – Thomas, b 21 May 1867 lc/o Thomas Byrne & Catharine Farrell bp 2 Jun 1867 spr Alice Byrne p414

BYRNE – Vincent, b 7 Jun 1868 lc/o James Byrne & Eliza Montgomery bp 11 Aug 1868 spr Josephus Kuhn & Mary Ellen Frederick "I supplied the ceremonies" "This child had been previously baptized by its mother, an intelligent catholic" H. B. Coskery, priest p450

CADIGAN – William Robert, b 9 Mar 1870 lc/o Matthew Cadigan & Alice Baker bp 20 Mar 1870 spr John Dougherty & Annie Gerrity p497

CAHILL – John Henry, b 30 Jan 1863 lc/o Patk. Cahill & Ann Whalen bp 15 Feb 1863 spr Jas. McNally & Ellen Crain p301

CAHILL – John Winfield Scott, b 2 Nov 1861 lc/o John Cahill & Mary Ann Gallagher bp 16 Mar 1862 spr Sarah O'Donnell p276

CAHILL – Marcella, b 13 Mar 1870 lc/o Patrick Cahill & Ellen Duncan bp 3 Apr 1870 spr John Flemming & Agnes Richter p499

CAHILL – Margaret, b 14 Nov 1861 lc/o Patrick Cahill & Ann Walen bp 24 Nov 1861 spr Thomas McKenna & Elizabeth McCann p267

CAHILL – Mary Ann, b 29 Dec 1859 c/o Patrick Cahill & Ann Quinn, "his wife" bp 1 Jan 1860 spr Hugh Cahill & Mary McCann p209

CAHILL – Thomas Charles, b 28 Aug 1865 lc/o Patrick Cahill & Delia Reynolds bp 17 Sep 1865 spr John Tormay & Catharine Kelly p364

CAIN – Margaret Jane, b 18 Jul 1856 lc/o James Cain & Sarah Bordley bp 27 Jul 1856 spr Rich. Laddam & Marg. Kernan p91

CAIN – Mary Elizabeth, b 10 Jun 1870 lc/o John Cain & Susan Daugherty bp 16 Jun 1870 spr Sarah Daugherty p503

CAIN – Mary, b 2 Sep 1857 lc/o John Cain & Bridget Mitchel bp 5 Sep 1857 spr Nancy Levin p134

CAIN – Thomas, b 25 Dec 1857 lc/o Patrick Cain & Catherine Quinn bp 27 Dec 1857 spr Thomas Murphy & Sarah Dowling p145

CALAHAN – Edward Stephen, b 26 Dec 1867 lc/o John Calahan & Bridget Rielly [sic] bp 31 Dec 1867 spr Mary Reilly p431

CALAHAN – Mary Ann, b 17 May 1857 lc/o John Calahan & Bridget Riley bp 14 Jun 1857 spr Thomas McIntyre & Rosanna Riley p124

CALL – Joseph Henry, b 13 Jun 1856 nc/o Jacob Pfifer & Sarah Call bp 18 Jul 1856 spr Clara O'Connor p90

CALLAGHAN – Mary Ellen, b 13 Dec 1858 lc/o Dennis Callaghan & Mary Dougherty bp 9 Jan 1859 spr John Glenn & Ellen Burke p179

CALLAHAN – Catharine, b 14 Aug 1859 lc/o Henry Callahan & Mary Callahan bp 22 Aug 1859 spr Mary Kenny p198

CALLAHAN – Catharine, b 28 Feb 1861 lc/o Denis Callahan & Mary Dougherty bp 10 Mar 1861spr Michl. Shehan & Kate Nylan p245

CALLAHAN – Charles, b 12 Oct 1863 lc/o John Callahan & Bridget Reilly bp 8 Nov 1863 spr Thomas Moore & Mary Reilly p320

CALLAHAN – Jacob Bernard, b 6 Oct *ndg* [*ed. note: most likely 1870*] lc/o John Callahan "of County Cavan, Ireland" & Bridget Reilly "of County Cavan, Ireland" bp 25 Oct 1870 spr Jane Reilly p513

CALLAHAN – James, b 21 Mar 1861 lc/o John Callahan & Bridget Reilly bp 25 Apr 1861 spr Bridget Reilly p249

CALLAHAN – John Joseph, b 3 Jan 1866 lc/o John Callahan & Bridget Reilly bp 28 Jan 1866 spr Ellen Goodwin p375

CALLAHAN – Margaret Ann, b 19 Feb 1857 lc/o Henry Callahan & Mary Carney bp 6 Mar 1857 spr James Hanley & Mary Galooly p113

CALLAHAN – Rosa, b 5 Aug 1857 lc/o Patrick Callahan & Rosa, "his wife" bp 13 Aug 1857 spr Jane Duffy p130

CALLAN – Theresa Jane, b 28 Apr 1859 lc/o John Callan & Bridget Reilly bp 8 May 1859 spr Patrick Goodwin & Mary Goodwin p189

CAMPBELL – Ann Eliza "(born Hess)", b 27 Aug 1837 lc/o Samuel Hess & Louisa bp 19 Nov 1857 spr Eliza McKern "baptized conditionally" Thos. Foley, priest p141

CAMPBELL – James, b 2 Feb 1856 lc/o Thomas Campbell & Ellen Gallagher bp 10 Feb 1856 spr Patrick Manning & Catherine Winter p72

CAMPBELL – Josephine Campbell, "aged about twenty years" bp 27 May 1860 spr Amelia [*ed. note: [?] given*] "baptized conditionally" H. B. Coskery, priest p223

CAMPBELL – Martha Wilson, b 25 Mar 1835 lc/o George R. & Sarah Campbell bp 27 Aug 1854 spr Eliza McMillan & Eliz. McMillan p21

CAMPBELL – Mary Paulina, b 28 Sep 1867 lc/o Bernard Campbell & Frances Lewis bp 20 Oct 1867 spr John Ryan & Mary Ryan p424

CAMPBELL – Thomas John, b 16 Mar 1857 lc/o Thomas Campbell & Ellen Gallagher bp 5 Apr 1857 spr Patrick Manion & Elizabeth Corley p116

CAMPBELL – William Henry (c), b 3 Jul 1863 c/o Jane Campbell (c), bp 14 Aug 1863 spr Elizabeth Colbert p313

CAMPBELL – Wm. Lewis, b 29 Oct 1869 lc/o Bernard Campbell & Frances Lewis bp 21 Nov 1869 spr Pauline Lewis p488

CANAVAN – Andrew Loring, b 11 Sep 1856 lc/o James Canavan & Mary Whelan bp 21 Sep 1856 spr Edward Dunn & Susanna McCormick p96

CANAVAN – Louisa, b 2 Aug 1859 lc/o James Canavan & Mary Whalen bp 7 Aug 1859 spr Edw. Hughes & Mary Kelly p197

CANAVAN – Philip Jefferson, b 15 May 1863 lc/o James Canavan & Mary Whelan bp 7 Jun 1863 spr Michael Breen & Ann Breen p308

CANOVAN – James, b 12 May 1861 lc/o James Canovan & Mary Whealan bp 26 May 1861 spr James McNally & Hillary McCormick p252

CAPELLINI – Anthony Joseph, b 11 Apr 1861 lc/o John Capellini & Mary Ritagliati bp 11 Apr 1861 spr Anthony Ritagliati & Catharine Ritagliati p248

CAPERON – Ellen Royston, b *ndg* 1864 lc/o Frances Caperson & Olivia Royston bp 1 Jul 1867 "I supplied the ceremonies" "previously baptized by me" Thos. Foley, priest p416

CAPERON – Francis, b 10 Aug 1862 lc/o Francis Caperon & <u>Olivia</u> Royston bp 13 Aug 1862 p287

CAPERON – Lucy Caperon, "aged 29 years" bp 11 Mar 1867 "baptized conditionally" Thos. Foley, priest p408

CAPERON – Mary Olivia, b 24 Oct 1864 lc/o Francis Caperon & Olivia Royston bp 1 Jul 1867 spr Ann M. Foley p416

CAPRON – Ellen, b 10 Nov 1863 lc/o Frances Capron & Olivia Royston bp 16 Nov 1863 p321

CAREY – Alice, b 26 Dec 1855 lc/o Martin Carey & Mary A. Smith bp 24 Oct 1856 spr Geoff. Smith & Frances Smith "I supplied the ceremonies…privately baptized by the Rev. B. J. McMannis" Thos. Foley, priest p100

CAREY – Ann Elizabeth, b 5 Sep 1854 lc/o Charles Carey & Ann Calahan bp 15 Oct 1854 spr Owen Boylan & Mary Ann Smith p26

CAREY – Anna Mary, b 28 Oct 1869 "twin" c/o Jeremiah Carey & Anna Laurence bp 11 Nov 1869 spr Peter & Ellen Ryan, Mike Connolly & Sabrina Mitchell p488

CAREY – Clara, b 30 Apr 1867 lc/o Jeremiah Carey & Ann Lyons bp 9 May 1867 spr Edward Carvan & Mary Lyons p412

CAREY – Francis Xavier b 23 Mar 1862 c/o Jeremiah Carey & Anna Lyons bp 26 Mar 1862 spr John Sullivan [*ed. note: twin of Jeremiah Carey*] p277

CAREY – George, b 30 Apr 1867 lc/o Jeremiah Carey & Ann Lyons bp 9 May 1867 spr Jas. Martin & Mary Monahan p412

CAREY – James Thomas, b 17 Dec 1863 lc/o Jeremiah Carey & Ann Lyons bp 27 Dec 1863 spr Stephen Rorhan & Ann Rorhan p322

CAREY – Jeremiah, b 23 Mar 1862 c/o Jeremiah Carey & Anna Lyons bp 26 Mar 1862 spr John Lyons & Margaret Quirk [*ed. note: twin of Francis Xavier Carey*] p277

CAREY – John Michael, b 20 Jan 1860 lc/o Michael Carey & Anna Warner bp 29 Jan 1860 spr John Mulhare & Ellen Martin p213

CAREY – Joseph, b 28 Oct 1869 "twin" c/o Albert Shriver & Annie Jenkins "of Alfred" bp 10 Nov 1869 spr Peter & Ellen Ryan, Mike Connolly & Sabrina Mitchell p488

CAREY – Julia Anne, b 31 Jan 1866 lc/o Jeremiah Carey & Ann Lyons bp 13 Feb 1866 spr John Tangney & Ellen Mitchell p376

CAREY – Mary, b 2 Apr 1856 lc/o Michael Carey & Mary Cain bp 13 Apr 1856 spr John Carey & Sarah Carey p80

CAREY – Mary Margaret, b 4 Feb 1868 lc/o Martin Carey & Mary Ann Smith bp 25 Mar 1868 spr Emma Hohn p437

CAREY – William Murdoch, b 25 Jun 1870 c/o Thos. Carey & Elizabeth Mulville bp 26 Jun 1870 spr Daniel Gray & Ella Coppafer p504

CARLAND – Elizabeth, b 19 Sep 1855 lc/o Walter Storm & Jane Carland bp 28 Sep 1855 spr Mary Carland p59

CARLIN – Bernard, b 31 Aug 1860 lc/o Matthew Carlin & Ellen O'Brien bp 2 Sep 1860 spr John Carlin & Catherine McCay p230

CARLIN – Henry Alton, b 1 Jan 1869 lc/o James S. Carlin & Mary Staylor bp 13 Jun 1869 spr Henry Stayler & Margaret Roth p474

CARLIN – James Walter, b 19 Jul 1867 lc/o James S. Carlin & Mary Staylor bp 23 Aug 1867 spr Margaret Staylor p419

CARMAN – Anastasia, b 4 April 1860 lc/o James Carman & Catharine Riley bp 24 Feb 1861 spr John Strainor & Margaret Reilly p245

CARMODY – Mary Ann, b 20 Dec 1858 lc/o Patrick Carmody & Honora Agle bp 25 Dec 1858 spr John & Honora Hassen p177

CARMODY – Mary Ann Jane, b 30 Jun 1862 lc/o Patrick Carmody & Honora Hogan bp 6 Jul 1862 spr James McMahon & Kate Hogan p285

CARMODY – William, b 12 Jan 1860 lc/o Patrick Carmody & Honora Hogan bp 15 Jan 1860 spr Michael Donlan & Catharine O'Brien p211

CARNEY – George, b 26 Aug 1868 lc/o Jeremiah Carey & Ann Elizabeth Lyons bp 22 Sep 1868 spr Peter Lyons & Maggie Conan p454

CARNEY – Mary Ann, b 30 Sep 1854 lc/o John Carney & Alice Garrety bp 15 Oct 1854 spr Patrick Loughton & Ann Ward p27

CARR – Edward James, b 1 Nov 1860 lc/o James Carr & Margaret Timmons bp 18 Nov 1860 spr Mary Morris p236

CARR – George William, b 21 Jul 1863 lc/o James Carr & Margaret Timmons bp 23 Aug 1863 spr Ann Eliza Beecham p314

CARR – James, b 21 May 1867 lc/o Jas. Carr & Cath. Moran bp 1 Jul 1867 spr Jane Carr p416

CARR – James Patrick, b 16 Mar 1868 lc/o James Carr & Mary A. Long bp 22 Mar 1868 spr Patrick McMahan & Ann Barrville p436

CARR – John James, b 9 Jun 1854 lc/o James Carr & Catherine Moran bp 9 Jul 1854 spr Alexandra Bradley & Ellen Carr p17

CARR – Josephine Agnes, b 9 Feb 1867 lc/o James Carr & Margaret Simmons bp 9 Mar 1867 spr Mary Morris p407

CARR – Mary Ann, b 23 May 1858 lc/o James Carr & Margaret Simmons bp 30 May 1858 spr Ann Simmons p157

CARR – Mary Catharine, b 18 Jun 1869 lc/o James Carr & Catharine Moran bp 2 Jul 1869 spr Ann Quillan p475

CARR – Nicholas Patrick, b 27 Mar 1866 lc/o Patk. Carr & Rose Branagan bp 28 Mar 1866 spr Ann McCormick p379

CARR – William, b 22 Apr 1855 lc/o Thos. Carr & Eliza McCormick bp 29 Apr 1855 spr Winifred Carey p44

CARRER – Lewis Adolphus, b 4 Oct 1860 c/o Lewis __ Carrer & Mary McDermott bp 28 Oct 1860 spr Mary Kein p233

CARRESE – John Fitzhugh, b 15 Mar 1858 lc/o William Carrese & Marian Calhoun Turner bp 19 Jul 1858 spr Mary Carrese "I supplied the ceremonies—baptized by a pious Catholic nurse" Thos. Foley, priest p163

CARRICK – Henry Jenkins, b 12 Aug 1866 lc/o George M. Carrick & Lucretia Myers bp 27 Sep 1866 p396

CARRICK – Marian Cath., b 10 Dec 1870 lc/o Bernard Carrick "of County Down, Ireland" & Maria Gilsen "of County _____, Ireland" bp 11 Dec 1870 spr Francis Dixon & Delia Gilsen p517

CARRIGAN – John Romullus, b 7 Feb 1865 lc/o John Carrigan & Mary (Byrne) Carrigan bp 12 Feb 1865 spr Dan Cay & Kate Byrne p350

CARROL – James, b 30 Apr 1858 lc/o Anthony Smith & Catherine Leigh bp 7 Jun 1858 spr Thomas Carrol & Margaret Quinn p158

CARROLL – Agnes, b 15 Jan 1863 lc/o Albert Carroll & Cornelia Read bp 20 Feb 1863 spr Robt. Goodloe Harper Carroll & Emily L. Harper "(Emily Read, proxy for R.G.H.C.)" p302

CARROLL – Andrew Patrick, b 12 Mar 1866 lc/o Robert Carroll & Mary Ryan bp 1 Apr 1866 spr Andrew F. Cunningham & Bridget Carroll p380

CARROLL – Anna Edith, b 12 Jul 1864 lc/o Jos. Carroll & Mary Carlan bp 6 Oct 1864 spr Josephine Chatard p341

CARROLL – Benedict, b 6 May 1861 nc/o George Fields & Ellen Carroll bp 13 Apr 1861 spr Caroline Hardey (all c) p248 [*ed note: last name is listed both as Fields or Carroll in record*] p248

CARROLL – Catherine Carroll (c), "aged about 33 yrs." spr Eliza Howard (c) "I baptized privately in danger of death" H. B. Coskery, priest p164

CARROLL – Edw., b 25 Oct 1854 c/o James Carroll & Catherine Harmon bp 5 Nov 1854 spr Arthur Stewart & Ann Breckenbridge p28

CARROLL – Elizabeth, b *ndg* lc/o Thomas G. Carroll & Caroline Judick bp 5 Apr 1865 spr James Carroll & Helen Boyle p354

CARROLL – Ellen, b 22 Mar 1862 lc/o Michael Carroll & Ellen Boland bp 30 Mar 1862 spr John Carroll & Sarah O'Neal p277

CARROLL – Elmira Mary Rawlings, b 10 Nov 1866 lc/o William P. Carroll & Adeline E. Rawlings bp 27 May 1867 spr James P. Carroll & Amelia Rawlings p413

CARROLL – Gertrude Lee, b 2 May 1863 lc/o Stephen John Carroll & Lucy Garrison bp 7 Jun 1863 spr J. R. Carroll & Lucy Blackburn p308

CARROLL – James, b 28 Oct 1860 lc/o John Carroll & Mary Carland bp 5 Feb 1861 spr Eliza Collyer p242

CARROLL – James B. Carroll, b 22 Dec 1850 lc/o Patrick Carroll & Mary Ann Stonebank bp 16 Mar 1854 spr Mary E. Dorsey, James Carroll, John Carroll, & Thomas Carroll p8

CARROLL – John Anthony, b 10 Jan 1854 lc/o Patrick Carroll & Mary Ann Stonebank bp 16 Mar 1854 spr Mary E. Dorsey, James Carroll, John Carroll, & Thomas Carroll p8

CARROLL – John Chapman, b 8 Oct 1854 c/o John Carroll & Lucy Garrison bp 5 Nov 1854 spr Saml. E. & Mary E. Smith p28

CARROLL – John Woods, b 22 Sep 1862 lc/o John Carroll & Mary Carland bp 12 Jan 1863 spr Henry Carroll & Gertrude Stone p299

CARROLL – Josephine, b 7 Dec 1860 lc/o Pierce Carroll & Mary Jane Malcolm bp 24 Nov 1861 spr Rebecca Toner p267

CARROLL – Lucy Frances, b 14 Mar 1859 lc/o Stephen John Carroll & Lucy Garrison bp 10 Apr 1859 spr Anna McDonald p186

CARROLL – Mary Ann, b 19 Oct 1856 lc/o Daniel Carroll & Mary Kirby bp 2 Nov 1856 spr Thomas Kirby & Mary Lynch p100

CARROLL – Mary Catharine, b 18 Sep 1867 lc/o James P. Carroll & Amelie Rawlings bp 20 Oct 1867 spr Andrew Carroll & Anna Carroll p424

CARROLL – Mary Eli_____, b 7 Dec 1860 lc/o Albert Harvey Carroll & Mary Cornelia Read bp 19 Jan 1861 spr Mary & Charles Carroll, Jr. p240

CARROLL – Mary Grace, b 19 Feb 1866 lc/o John Carroll & Ellen Spalding bp 23 Mar 1866 spr Mary Louise Hess p379

CARROLL – Mary Hizea, "age about 4 years" lc/o Robert Carroll & Sally Riordan (all c) bp 31 Oct 1854 spr Alice Quinn p28

CARROLL – Mary Josephine, b 6 May 1859 lc/o John Carroll & Mary Magdalen Carlan bp 23 May 1859 spr Thomas D. Carroll & Jane Stone p191

CARROLL – Mary Sophia, b 6 Feb 1859 lc/o Albert H. Carroll & Mary Cornelia Read bp 4 Mar 1859 spr Wil. Geo. Read & Helen Carroll p183

CARROLL – Rachel Ann, "age about 2 years" lc/o Robert Carroll & Sally Riordan (all c) bp 31 Oct 1854 spr Caroline Reynolds (c) p28

CARROLL – Robert Charles Henry William, b 18 Jul 1860 lc/o Robert William Carroll & Ann Maria Louisa Smith, bp 24 Jun 1861 spr Henrietta <u>Burk</u> (all c) p255

CARROLL – Rosa, "age about 6 [six] years" lc/o Robert Carroll & Sally Sinclair (all c) bp 31 Oct 1854 spr Amelia Wiseman p28

CARROLL – Rosina Veronica, b 30 Apr 1870 lc/o Wm. Henry Carroll & Rosina Smith bp 3 May 1870 spr Mary Ann Smith (all c) p500

CARROLL – Sarah Charles, b 25 Nov 1856 lc/o Stephen John Carroll & Lucy Garrison bp 4 Jan 1857 spr James Carroll & Margaret Conlan p107

CARROLL – Sarah Eliza, b 9 Aug 1845 lc/o Patrick Carroll & Mary Ann Stonebank bp 16 Mar 1854 spr Mary E. Dorsey, James Carroll, John Carroll, & Thomas Carroll p8

CARROLL – Thomas, b 1 Dec 1856 lc/o James Carroll & Catherine Hannon bp 16 Dec 1856 spr Margaret Hannon p104

CARROLL – Thomas Gaither, b 13 Feb 1859 lc/o Thomas W. Carroll & Mary C. Griffith bp 6 Aug 1859 spr John W. Carroll & Mary Carroll p196

CARROLL – Thomas Henry, b 22 July 1848 lc/o Patrick Carroll & Mary Ann Stonebank bp 16 Mar 1854 spr Mary E. Dorsey, James Carroll, John Carroll, & Thomas Carroll p8

CARROLL – Thomas Myer, b 29 Dec 1860 lc/o Stephen John Carroll & Lucy Ann Garrison bp 27 Jan 1861 spr Thomas C. Orendorff & Mary E. Smith p241

CARTER – Charles Dalton, b 15 Jan 1864 lc/o Charles W. Carter & Ellen Dalton bp 24 Jan 1864 spr Richard Purcell p324

CARTER – Florence Virginia, b 6 Sep 1870 lc/o John Carter of Richmond, Virginia" & Maria Horstman "of the same place" bp 7 Nov 1870 spr Margaret Hay p513

CARTER – Vincent Wylie, b 28 Dec 1865 lc/o Charles W. Carter & Ellen Dalton bp 22 Feb 1866 spr Rose McGuinness p376

CARVER – Emma Virginia Carver, "aged about 18 years" bp 7 Apr 1866 spr Julia Baldwin "baptized conditionally" Jas. Gibbons, priest p381

CARVER – Mary Dolphin, b 6 Nov 1864 lc/o William D. Carver & Eliza Dolphin bp 12 Jan 1865 spr Elizabeth Grumby p348

CARVER – William Valentine, b 10 Jun *ndg* [*ed. note: most likely 1870*] lc/o William Valentine Carver "of Havre de Grace, Maryland" & Johanna Dolphin "of Baltimore" bp 26 Sep 1870 spr _____ Gunby p511

CARY – Anna Maria, b 8 Oct 1857 lc/o William Cary & Lucy Ennis bp 18 Oct 1857 spr Christopher Allen & Ann Connolly p138

CASASSA – Giovanni Batista Fappiano, b 12 Jun 1859 lc/o Giovani Casassa & Catarina Laveza bp 25 Jun 1859 spr Gio. Batista Fappiano & Filomena Cella p193

CASASSA – Stephen, b 18 Dec 1860 lc/o John Casassa & Catharine Levezza bp 20 Dec 1860 spr Stephen Mabesta & Catharine Besagna p238

CASEY – Mary Catherine, b 5 Jun 1855 lc/o Peter Casey & Rose McGuinty bp 24 Jun 1855 spr Patrick McDaniel & Bridget Hughes p50

CASEY – Peter, b 19 Aug 1856 lc/o Peter Casey & Rose McK_____ bp 24 Aug 1856 spr John Casey & Rose Riley p93

CASS – George Michael, b 6 Jan 1862 lc/o George Cass & Mary Ann Baker bp 2 Mar 1863 spr Catharine Manning p302

CASSELL – Ann Rebecca, b 12 Feb 1865 lc/o Leonard Cassell & Eliza Ann Woodall bp 8 Jul 1866 spr Mary Heyden p388

CASSEY – John, b 22 Nov 1858 lc/o Michael Cassey & Ellen Mannion bp 28 Nov 1858 spr Martin Mannion & Catharine Mannion p175

CASSEY – Henrietta, b 3 Jul 1855 lc/o Patrick Cassey & Mary Clancy bp 8 Jul 1855 spr John Cassey & Ann Clancy p52

CASSIDY – Elizabeth, b 25 Dec 1853 lc/o Owen Cassidy & Margaret Fillmore bp 29 Jan 1854 spr John P. Foll__ & Margaret McLaughlin p3

CASSIDY – John, b 26 Feb 1855 lc/o John Cassidy & Mary Emiline bp 4 Mar 1855 spr Thomas Cassidy & Teresa Hassen p38

CASSIDY – Rose Ann, b 13 Aug 1859 lc/o Thomas Cassidy & Ann M. Whelan bp 11 Sep 1859 spr Ambrose Whelan & Rose Ann Reilly p200

CASTOR – Ann Maria (c), b *ndg* Sept 1865 lc/o Noel Castor & Jane Johnson bp 1 Jan 1866 spr Fanny Castor p373

CASTOR – Frances Rebecca (c), "about 20 years old" bp 27 Jun 1856 spr John Noel & Margaret Dorseann p87

CASTOR – Mary Alice (c), b 18 Feb 1858 lc/o Noel Castor & Elizabeth Boyer (c) bp 17 Mar 1858 spr Elizabeth Colvert (c) p151

CATON – John, b 27 May 1859 lc/o Parick Caton & Ellen Roach bp 29 May 1859 spr John Reddy & Rose Maguire p191

CATON – Patrick Henry, b 13 Jun 1856 lc/o Michael Caton & Isabella McGlenan bp 19 Jun 1856 spr Henry McGlenan & Maria Fallon p86

CAVANAGH – Julia, b 29 Mar 1859 lc/o Edward Cavanagh & Mary O'Neil bp 3 Apr 1859 spr Michael O'Neil & Ann Burns p185

CAVANAGH – Thomas Alan, b 12 Aug 1868 lc/o Thomas P. Cavanagh & Philomena Kuhn bp 28 Aug 1868 spr Jos. A. Kuhn & Victoria Banon p452

CAVANAUGH – Catherine, b 22 Dec 1856 lc/o Edward Cavanaugh & Mary Neal bp 1 Jan 1857 spr Thos. Brian & Margaret Burns p106

CAVANAUGH – Daniel, b 24 Aug 1854 lc/o Edw.Cavanaugh & Mary O'Neal bp 27 Aug 1854 spr Patk. Thistleburr & Mary Owings p22

CAVANAUGH – George Emory Ellsworth, b 16 Oct 1862 lc/o Lewis Cavanaugh & Ann Broome bp 16 Nov 1862 spr B. Altwood & Maria Whitaker p295

CECIL – Anne Drayton Cecil, b 11 Apr 1845 lc/o W. H. Cecil & J. R. Peters bp 5 Jul 1866 spr Cath. Olivia Turner "baptized conditionally" Jas. Gibbons, priest p387

CECIL – Ernest Thomas Cecil, b 19 Dec 1836 c/o Anthony Cecil & Celia Peters, "his wife" bp 5 Mar 1863 spr Thos. Parkin Scott p303

CECIL – Jas. Cecil, "aged about 36 years" bp 17 Apr 1866 spr M. S. Gosnell "baptized conditionally" Jas. Gibbons, priest 382

CELAHAN – Daniel, b 4 Mar 1870 lc/o Edw. Celahan & Catharine Fahey bp 13 Mar 1870 spr John Clancy & Helen Dunn p496

CELIO – Ellen Caroline, b 13 Sep 1859 lc/o Constantine Celio & Louisa C. Giannini bp 13 Nov 1859 spr John T. Dufou & Caroline White p205

CELICIO – Joshua William, b 20 Oct 1857 lc/o Constantine Celicio & Louisa Clementine Giennini bp 13 Dec 1857 spr Joshua Dagimett & Mary Celicio p144

CELLA – Joseph, b 30 Aug 1857 c/o Andrew Cella & Anne Marie Philomen Gazzola, "natives of Genoa" bp 4 Sep 1857 spr _____ _____ p133

CELLA – Santo Antonio, b 9 Dec 1861 c/o John Andrew Cella & Anna Maria Philomena Gazzolo, "his wife" bp 14 Dec 1861 spr Santo Cella & Elizabeth Cella p269

CENA – Mary Elizabeth, b 20 Dec 1862 lc/o John Cena & Anna Maria F. Gazzolo bp 28 Dec 1862 spr John B. Monteverde & Mary Monteverde p298

CHAIN – Marian May, b 20 Aug *ndg* [*ed. note: most likely 1870*] lc/o William Chain "of County Armagh" (?) & Frances Walker "of the same place" bp 25 Sep 1870 "privately baptized *sine cer*" John Dougherty, priest p510

CHANEY – William Zachariah, "4 years and 6 months old" c/o Zachariah Chaney & Caroline Pierce bp 15 Apr 1862 spr Mary Broderick p279

CHASE – Alfred Henry, "aged about 3½ years" lc/o Henry Chase & Josephine Reese (all c) bp 18 Sep 1863 spr Mary Kilduff p315

CHASTEAU – Sallie A. Chasteau, "aged 24 years" bp 10 May 1864 "baptized conditionally" Thos. Foley, priest p332

CHATAN – Charlotte Mary, b 6 Aug 1854 lc/o Capt. Frederick Chatan, USN & Eliz. McNally bp 4 Sep spr Ann Wilson p23

CHATARD – Ferdinand Henry, b 30 Dec 1856 lc/o Frederick Chatard & Eliza McNally bp 16 Sep 1857 spr Herman Chatard & Catherine Chatard "privately baptized by me" John McNally, priest p135

CHEFFIN – William Charles, b 13 Mar 1866 lc/o Ely C. Cheffin (or Steffin) & Arabella C. Dempsey bp 3 Apr 1866 spr Mary A. Dempsey & John F. Dempsey p380

CHRISTOPHER – Lilly May, b 10 Sep 1868 lc/o Thomas Christopher & Elizabeth Hammer bp 15 Apr 1869 spr Elizabeth Hammer p468

CHRISTY – Catharine Victoria, b 10 Mar 1870 lc/o Joseph Christy & Catharine McCabe bp 27 Mar 1870 spr Matthew McCabe & Elizabeth Metz p498

CHUBB – John Baptist, b 20 June 1850 lc/o Thos. Chubb & Sara Montross "(now Nase)" bp 29 Jan 1854 spr Jonathan Mullan p3

CILIO – Andrew Constantine, b 14 May 1855 lc/o Constantine Cilio & Louisa Clementine Ginini bp 17 Jun 1855 spr Joseph Ginini & Lenora Ginini p49

CILLIA – Rosa Aloysia, b 24 Oct 1859 c/o Andre Cillea & Anna Maria Philomena Gazzola, "his lawful wife" bp 29 Oct 1859 spr Pietro Gazzola & Rosa Cellea p203

CLABAUGH – Joseph, b 5 Mar 1865 lc/o John Clabaugh & Cassandra Clapsaddle bp 12 Mar 1865 spr Eugene Martin & Catharine Wade p353

CLAPSADDLE – Mary Clapsaddle, "aged about 70 years" bp 24 Dec 1859 "baptized conditionally" H. B. Coskery, priest p209

CLARK – Mary Ellen, b 30 Apr 1854 lc/o Timothy C. Clark & Ellen West bp 28 May 1854 spr James Fahey p13

CLARK – Mary Susan, b 28 Mar 1854 lc/o Michael Clark & Margaret McDonnell bp 9 Apr 1854 spr John Murphy & Johann McDonnell "baptized conditionally" Thos. Foley, priest p10

CLARK – Victoria Odin, b 14 Nov 1861 lc/o George N. Clark & Rosa Dunn bp 22 Jun 1864 spr Mary A. Odin p335

CLARKE – Ann Mary, b 22 Jan 1865 lc/o Sylvester Clarke & Mary Cardwell bp 5 Feb 1866 spr Arthur Judge & Ann Clarke p375

CLARKE – Jane, b 16 Jul 1863 lc/o Sylvester Clarke & Mary Cardwell bp 26 Jul 1863 spr Arthur & Elizabeth McCafferty p312

CLARKE – Sylvester, b 9 Jun 1868 lc/o Sylvester Clarke & Mary Cardwell bp 21 Jun 1868 spr Henry Judge & Ellen Clarke p446

CLARKE – Thomas, b 8 Nov 1862 lc/o Oliver Clarke & Kate Smith bp 16 Nov 1862 spr Peter Clarke & Elizabeth Lynch p295

CLEGG – James Clegg, b "age 36" bp 23 Sep 1860 "baptized conditionally" Thos. Foley, priest p231

CLIFTON – Claude Constantine, b 16 Apr 1867 lc/o Theodore Clifton & Rebecca Moore bp 25 May 1867 spr Marcis Clifton p413

CLIFTON – George Granville, b 3 Jul 1864 lc/o Theodore E. Clifton & Mary Rebecca Moore bp 17 Aug 1864 spr Maria Clifton p338

CLIFTON – Mary Theodora, b 14 Apr 1862 lc/o Theodore E. Clifton & Mary Rebecca Moore 22 May 1862 spr James Davis & Mary C. Young p282

CLIFTON – Theodore Arthur Waldmar, b 6 Nov 1859 lc/o Louis Delnol C. Clifton & Louisiana Bodmann bp 27 Dec 1859 spr Theodore Eccleston C. Clifton & Cecilia Young p209

CLINTON – George Glendy, b 12 Oct 1860 lc/o Henry D. Clinton & Mary Court bp 7 Nov 1860 spr Mary A. Dunn p235

CLINTON – Mary Rosalba, b 1 Aug 1862 lc/o DeWitt Clinton & Mary Cortes bp 16 Aug 1862 spr Mary Deal p287

COBB – David Stuart, b 18 Aug 1855 lc/o Edward D. Cobb & Matilda Stuart bp 24 Sep 1855 spr Thos. Foley & Mary Eliz. Stuart p59

COBURN – Mary Loretto (c), b 8 Sep 1855 lc/o Henry Coburn & Ellen Wilson (c) bp 10 Dec 1865 spr Mary Downs p371

COFFAY – Thomas, b 11 Mar 1863 lc/o Thomas Coffey & Catharine Nolan bp 19 Mar 1863 spr Jeremiah Dillon & Margaret Lenaghan p304

COFFEY – Catharine, b 4 Dec 1860 lc/o Thomas Coffey & Catharine Nolan bp 16 Dec 1860 spr Thomas Nolan & Bridget Lenaghan p237

COFFEY – John, b 26 Apr 1858 lc/o Thomas Coffey & Catherine Nolan bp 2 May 1858 spr Peter Smith & Bridget Linahan p155

COLAHAN – Thos. Francis, b 24 Mar 1865 lc/o Edw. Colahan & Catharine Fahey bp 26 Mar 1865 spr Patk. Fahey & Cath. Heenan p353

COLBERT – Andrew Ames, b 13 Jan 1860 lc/o William Colbert & Susan White (c) bp 16 Feb 1860 spr Rachel Jackson p215

COLBERT – Cecilia, b 23 Aug 1857 lc/o William Colbert & Susan White (c) bp 3 Sep 1857 spr Susan Davis p133

COLBERT – Elizabeth Ann, b 27 May 1838 lc/o Nathaniel & Maria Colbert (all c) bp 19 Aug 1854 spr Susan Colbert p20

COLBERT- William August, b 19 Sep 1855 lc/o William Colbert & Susan White (c) bp 5 Oct 1855 spr Elizabeth Colbert p61

COLDTART – John Thomas, b 10 Jun 1859 lc/o John A. Coldtart & Theresa Pollard bp 3 Jul 1859 spr Patrick Daley & Mary A. Loane p194

COLE – Hannah Ann Cole, "about 16 years old" bp 13 May 1859 spr Elizabeth L. Colbert p190

COLE – Mary, b 11 May 1861 c/o Robert Howard & Anne Rebecca Cole (c) bp 19 Jul 1861 spr Minty Lecompte [*ed. note: last name is listed both as Howard or Cole in record*] p256

COLE – Mary Cole, "3 months old" c/o Mary Cole bp 1 Apr 1856 spr Mary Dougherty p78

COLE – Thomas Augustus, b 1 Jul 1859 nc/o Charles Alexander & Hanah [*sic*] Cole (c) bp 11 Jul 1859 spr Maria Smith p195

COLE – Frances Marie Cole, "aged about 19 years" bp 20 Nov 1867 spr Josephine Placide p427

COLLER – Francis Gibney, b 16 Dec 1867 lc/o William Alex. Coller & Mary Ann Stermer bp 26 Mar 1868 spr Mary Gibney p437

COLLIER – Annie Caroline, b 31 Dec 1864 lc/o Charles Collier & Eliza Carland bp 6 Mar 1865 spr Anna Dwyer p353

COLLIER – Charles, b 4 Dec 1869 lc/o Charles Collier & Eliza Carlan bp 2 Feb 1870 spr Mary Dwyer p493

COLLIER – Elizabeth, b 23 Feb 1868 lc/o Charles Collier & Eliza Carland bp 24 Mar 1868 spr Rosina <u>McGinness</u> p437

COLLIER – Henry Marston, b 6 Nov 1857 lc/o Charles Collier & Eliza Carland bp 14 Dec 1857 spr Mary Carland p144

COLLIGAN – Joseph Roby, b 19 Sep 1859 lc/o Charles Collegan & Eliza Carlan bp 28 Feb 60 spr John Dwyer & C _____ [*ed. note: name illegible*] p 215

COLLIGER – Mary, b 19 Dec 1861 lc/o Charles Colliger & Eliza Carlan bp 10 Feb 1862 spr Jane Stone p274

COLLINS – Alice Mary, b 24 Jul 1859 c/o Alfred Davis & Lea Ann Collins bp 11 Jan 1860 spr Mary Gavaghan [*ed. note: see also Davis as priest noted the last name as Davis or Collins*] p211

COLLINS – Ann (c), b 20 Oct 1870 lc/o John Hughes Collins & Silvia Woodland bp 6 Apr 1870 spr Annie Collins (c) & Thomas S. Lee p499

COLLINS – James, b 20 Mar 1856 lc/o Patrick Collins & Mary I. McCrea bp 17 May 1856 spr Jane Holland p82

COLLINS – Lea Ann Collins b 28 Oct 1836 lc/o Elisha Collins & Sophia Horvith bp 7 Jan 1860 "baptized conditionally" Thos. Foley, priest p210

COLLINS – Mary Ann Elizabeth, b 26 Apr 1857 lc/o James Collins & Bridget Irwin bp 10 May 1857 spr Michael Murray & Ann Nolan p120

COLLOBURGH – Mary Ann, b 22 Oct 1854 lc/o James Colloburgh & Elizabeth Riordan bp 29 Oct 1854 spr John O'Brien & Elizabeth Morice p28

COLSTON – Agnes Grover, b 2 Jan 1864 lc/o Joseph H. Colston & Mary Catharine Watson bp 21 Jan 1869 spr Mary Walsh p464

COLSTON – Ann Colston, "aged 57 years" bp 1 Apr 1858 p152

COLTON – Jane Monica, b 17 Nov 1861 lc/o John Colton & Ann Nugent bp 8 Dec 1861 spr Thomas Mulligan & Theresa Monahan p268

COLWILL – Charles Richard, "aged 14 months" bp 19 Aug 1857 "I baptized privately…in danger" Thos. Foley, priest p131

COMERFORD – Stephen Comerford, b *ndg* bp 13 Jun 1859 spr "I baptized under condition Stephen Commerford, infant, privately baptized and apparently dying" Francis Patrick, Archb. p192

<u>COMMODORE</u> – Joseph, b 2 Jun 1868 c/o Isabelle Johnson (c) & William <u>Commodore</u> (c) bp 27 Sep 1868 spr Theresa Queen p454

CONABAUGH – Agnes, b 25 Mar 1868 lc/o Denis Conabaugh & Mary O'Brian bp 5 Apr 1868 spr Julia Fagan p438

CONBAUGH- James Denis, b 18 Dec 1853 lc/o Denis Conbaugh & Mary O'Brien bp 2 Jan 1854 spr James Garrity & Margaret Boyle p1

CONDRY – Mary Catharine, b 26 Jul 1866 lc/o Thomas Condry & Margaret Markham bp 5 Aug 1866 spr Thomas Kenna & Cath. Kenna p391

CONIG – Virginia Jackson, b 14 Aug 1862 lc/o Frederick Conig & Mary Ann Burke bp 24 Aug 1862 spr Mary Ellen Kelly p288

CONKLIN – Alexius Edward, b 17 Jul 1858 lc/o William Conklin & Elizabeth Brown (c) bp 27 Jul 1858 spr Eliza Howard (c) p164

CONKLIN – Laurence, b 17 Aug 1860 lc/o John Conklin & Sarah Bridge (c) bp 23 Jul 1861 spr Eliza Nichols p257

CONKLIN – Sarah Jane (c), b 28 Dec 1854 lc/o John Conklin & Sarah Bridges (c) bp 14 Mar 1855 spr Magdalen Clemens p39

CONKLIN – William Ignatius (c), b 15 Aug 1856 lc/o William Conklin & Elizabeth Brown (c) bp 7 Sep 1856 spr Feliz <u>Durand</u> & Ann E. <u>Durand</u> p95

CONKLING – Mary Isabell (c), b 28 Feb 1861 lc/o Wm. Conkling & Sarah Brown bp 24 Mar 1861 spr Oliver & Mary Conkling p246

CONNABAUGH – Patrick, b 15 Mar 1856 lc/o Dennis Connabaugh & Mary O'Brien bp 31 Mar 1856 spr Mary E. Burns & James Burns p78

CONNELL – Charles Michael, b 20 Sep 1860 lc/o Charles Connell & Mary Maguire bp 14 Oct 1860 spr Peter Kane & Mary Fallon p232

CONNELL – Ellen, b 17 Feb 1859 lc/o Charles Connell & Mary Maguire bp 27 Feb 1859 spr Peter Murray & Catharine McCardle p182

CONNELL – Mary Frances, b 23 Apr 1864 lc/o Francis Connell & Mary Fortune bp 2 May 1864 spr Rev. John Elwick & Emily Roach p332

CONNELLY – George, b 24 Jan 1864 lc/o John Connelly & Ellen Meeney bp 14 Feb 1864 spr John O'Neal & Mary Connelly p326

CONNER – Elizabeth, b 7 Feb 1860 lc/o James Conner & Mary Plunkett bp 12 Feb 1860 spr Michl. Burgen & Ann Hagner p214

CONNER – Francis, b 31 Mar 1854 nc/o Catherine Conner & _____ Anderson bp 7 Apr 1854 spr Elz. Conner p9

CONNERS – Edward Thomas, b 19 Sep 1866 lc/o Edward Connors & Margaret Dermody bp 7 Oct 1866 p397

CONNERTON – John Thomas, b 23 Jun 1859 lc/o James Connerty [sic] & Mary Kelly bp 26 Jun 1859 spr Michl. Conney & Mary Conninghton p193

CONNOBAUGH – Denis, b 9 Nov 1855 lc/o James Connobaugh & Margaret Ann Eliza Riordon bp 18 Nov 1855 spr Denis Connobaugh & Margaret Boyle p65

CONNOBAUGH – Mary, b 20 Dec 1862 lc/o James Connobaugh & Elizabeth Reardon bp 11 Dec 1862 spr Henrietta King p297

CONNOLLY – Charles Ennis, b 7 Jun 1864 lc/o Edward Connolly & Elizabeth Ennis bp 24 Jul 1864 spr Matthew Gorman & Lizzie Dennis p337

CONNOLLY – Charles Henry, b 12 Apr 1868 lc/o John Connolly & Eliza McKenna bp 4 May 1868 spr Sarah Connolly p441

CONNOLLY – George, b 1 Apr 1862 lc/o John Connolly & Ellen Moore bp 27 Apr 1862 spr John Burns & Margaret Burns p280

CONNOLLY – James Patrick, b 1 May 1856 lc/o Patrick Connolly & Mary McGahan bp 31 May 1856 spr Michael Kean & Mary Hanlan p83

CONNOLLY – James, b 2 May 1855 lc/o Adam Connolly & Elizabeth Ennis bp 3 Jun 1855 spr John Connolly & Elizabeth Connolly p48

CONNOLLY – John Thomas, b 16 Sep 1854 lc/o John Connolly & Margaret Greer bp 1 Oct 1854 spr Pat. Moran & Bridget Ryder p24

CONNOLLY – John Thomas, b 9 Nov 1857 lc/o William Connolly & Ann Carley bp 29 Nov 1857 spr Hugh Bannon & Annie Bannon p142

CONNOLLY – John, b 2 May 1862 lc/o Hugh Connolly & Catharine Kirby bp 5 May 1862 spr James Winters & Bridget McManus p281

CONNOLLY – Joseph William, b 14 Mar 1861 lc/o Edward Connolly & Eliza Ennis bp 24 Mar 1861 spr Michael Cassidy & Ida Ennis p246

CONNOLLY – Martin, b 1 Jan 1859 lc/o Patrick Connolly & Mary McGahan bp 12 Apr 1859 spr Neill Carr & Margaret Hanley p186

CONNOLLY – Mary Ellen, b 27 Aug 1866 c/o John Connolly & "his lawful wife" Ellen Neany bp 12 Sep 1866 spr Wm. Burns & Mary Connelly p395

CONNOLLY – Mary Jane, b 4 May 1868 lc/o John Connolly & Elizabeth Welch bp 10 May 1868 spr Matthew John Washington & Mary Flinn p441

CONNOLLY – Mary, b 11 Dec 1863 lc/o J. C. Connolly & Ann Jameston bp 20 Dec 1863 spr Patk. Custy & Sarah Robinson p322

CONNOLLY – Sarah Catharine, b 17 Mar 1859 lc/o Edward Connolly & Eliza Ennis bp 10 Apr 1859 spr Patrick Connolly & Catharine Naughton p186

CONNOLLY – Terence, b 13 Sep 1865 lc/o John Connolly & Ann Quinn bp 24 Sep 1865 spr Thos. Moore & Ellen Corrigan p365

CONNOR – James, b 16 Apr 1857 lc/o John Connor & Rose Colter bp 16 Aug 1857 spr Mary Colter "I supplied the ceremonies of baptism in the case of…" "baptized privately by Rev. Wm. Parson" John McNulty, priest p130

CONNOR – Jane, b 3 Aug 1855 lc/o Jeremiah Connor & Jane Loll bp 2 Sept 1855 spr John Foley & M. Burke p57

CONNOR – John, b 23 Jan 1859 lc/o John Connor & Rose Anne Coulter bp 8 May 1859 spr Elizabeth Coulter p189

CONNOR – Sedonia Louisa, b 23 Feb 1864 c/o Margaret Connor (c) bp 30 Apr 1869 spr Sedonia Chase p470

CONNOUGHTON – Patrick James, b 11 Sep 1856 lc/o James Connoughton & Mary Kelly bp 14 Sep 1856 spr Mich. Kelly & Maria Connoughton p95

CONOBAUGH – Mary Ann, b 1 Aug 1865 lc/o Denis Conobaugh & Mary O'Brien bp 6 Aug 1865 spr Joseph Dunn & Mary Jane Westendorf p361

CONROY – Bridget, b 4 Feb 1858 lc/o Thomas Conroy & Mary Broggy bp 7 Feb 1858 spr Margaret O'Brien p148

CONROY – Johanna, b 25 Jan 1865 lc/o Thomas Conroy & Mary Bruggy bp 5 Feb 1865 spr Bridget Consedine p350

CONROY – John Martin, b 17 Oct 1864 lc/o Stephen Conroy & Margaret Lennan bp 23 Oct 1864 spr Dennis Conroy & Cath. O'Grady p342

CONROY – John, b 15 May 1856 lc/o Decline Conroy & Bridget Whelan bp 22 May 1856 spr Decline Whelan & Mary Foley p83

CONROY – John, b 27 May 1856 lc/o Thomas Conroy & Mary <u>Broapy</u> bp 1 Jun 1850 spr Michael <u>Broapy</u> & Margaret McCann p83

CONROY – Mary Ann, b 23 Oct 1860 lc/o Thomas Conroy & Mary Bruggy bp 26 Oct 1860 spr Joseph M. <u>McLaughlin</u> & Catharine Conroy p233

CONROY – Sarah Agnes, b 28 Sep 1864 lc/o Thos. Conroy & Margaret Markam bp 9 Oct 1864 spr Danl. Markam & Catharine O'Brien p341

CONROY – Thomas Patrick, b 9 Jan 1854 lc/o Thomas Conroy and Mary Bruggy bp 16 Jan 1854 spr Haig Conroy p2

CONROY – Thomas Patrick, b 29 Mar 1863 lc/o Thomas Conroy & Margaret Markum bp 5 Apr 1863 spr Thos. O. Conroy & Cath. Conroy p305

CONROY – Wm. Edw., b 16 Dec 1867 lc/o Thos. Conroy & Mary Bruggy bp 22 Dec 1867 spr Thos. & Kate Conroy p430

CONRY – William, b 19 Jan 1855 lc/o Daglan Conry & Bridget Whelan bp 28 Jan 1855 spr Wm. Burke & Johanna Kane p35

CONSEBINE – Charles, b 7 June 1857 lc/o Michael Consebine & Catherine Brog__ bp 7 June 1857 spr Patrick Consebine & Bridget Conroy p123

CONSIDINE – b 16 Feb 1859 lc/o William Considine & Sarah Wheat bp 18 Jul 1861 spr Elizabeth Griffin p256

CONSIDINE – Henry Theodore, b 27 Aug 1864 lc/o Henry Theodore Considine & Elizabeth McNally bp 28 Aug 1864 spr Jno. McNally & Mary Considine p339

CONSIDINE – Mahala "(Mary)", "aged about 27 years" bp 6 Apr 1868 spr Harriet Spalding p438

CONSIDINE – Mary Ann, b 28 Oct 1859 lc/o Michael Considine & Catharine Bruggy bp 30 Oct 1859 spr Pat. Considine & Cath. Connolly p204

CONSTANTINE – Catherine Constantine, b 10 Dec 1856 lc/o Samuel Constantine & Ellen Corbitt bp 18 Dec 1856 spr Michael Lyons & Mary Gallagher p105

CONSTANTINE – Michael, b 4 Sep 1855 lc/o Michael Constantine & Kate Brennan bp 12 Sep 1855 spr Katherine _____ & Nancy Loray p57

COOK – Anne Elizabeth, b 28 Dec 1867 lc/o William T. Cook & Anne Eliz. Martin bp 19 Jan 1868 spr Eliz. Martin p432

COOK – Catherine Elizabeth, b 10 Jul 1855 lc/o Jno. Cook & Margaret Burke bp 19 Aug 1855 spr Michl. & Cath Burke p56

COOK – Charles Edward, b 19 Mar 1867 lc/o William Cook & Caroline Fritz "(born Whittington)" bp 18 Sep 1867 spr Margaret Cook p421

COOK – Dorothea Ann Cook, "aged 45 years" bp 18 Oct 1869 "baptized conditionally" Thos. Foley, priest p486

COOK – Ella Manfred, b 5 Sep 1865 lc/o William Cook & Alice Hopkins bp 19 Nov 1865 spr John Gallagher & Martha Gallagher p369

COOK – John Wilson, b 14 Jul 1866 lc/o William Cook & Ellen Dillon bp 19 Aug 1866 spr David Dillon & Bridget Hughes p392

COOK – John, b 4 Dec 1859 lc/o Alexander Cooke & Catharine Kehne bp 14 Dec 1859 spr Elizabeth Ellet p208

COOK – Mary Catharine Cook, b 28 Dec 1867 William T. Cook & Anne Eliz. Martin bp 19 Jan 1868 spr C. Ellen Marks p432

COOK – Mary Elizabeth, b *ndg* 1859 lc/o _____ Cook & _____ _____ bp 20 May 1866 p384

COOK – Mary Jane, b 9 Sep 1861 lc/o William Cooke & Ellen Dillon bp 6 Oct 1861 spr Cecilia Daley p262

COOK – Rebecca, b 12 Sep 1857 lc/o James & Clara Cook (c) by 27 Apr 1865 spr Abby Nicholls p355

COOK – Thomas, b 11 Jul 1869 lc/o Edward Cook & Eleanora Williams (c) bp 12 Sep 1869 spr Theresa Queen p482

COOK – Viriginia, b 4 Jul 1855 lc/o James & Clara Cook (c) bp 27 Apr 1865 spr Abby Nicholls p355

COOK – William Francis, b 2 Mar 1864 lc/o William Cook & Ellen Dillon bp 27 Mar 1864 spr Terry McCann & Mary McCarthy p329

COOKSEY – Catharine Cooksey, "aged 15 years" bp 20 Dec 1864 spr John F. Hunter & "lady" "baptized conditionally" H. B. Coskery, priest p347

COOLAHAN – Catharine, b 27 Oct 1862 lc/o Edward Coolahan & Catharine Fahey bp 9 Nov 1862 spr Patrick Grady & Anne Clancy p293

COOLAHAN – Julia, b 12 Sep 1860 lc/o Edward Coolahan & Catharine Fahey bp 23 Sep 1860 spr Thos. Flannigan & Ann Hardman p231

COOLAHAN – Mary Ann, b 30 Oct 1858 lc/o Edward Coolahan & Catharine Fahey bp 7 Nov 1858 spr Martin Nolan & Winneford Hardiman p173

COOLIHAN – Edward, b 24 Aug 1867 lc/o Edward Coolihan & Catharine Fahey bp 1 Sep 1867 spr Patrick Coolihan & Catharine Coolihan p420

COOLOGAN – Mary Ann, b 9 Oct 1859 lc/o Daniel Cooligan ("died 6 months ago") & Margaret Breen bp 11 Oct 1859 spr John Keefe & Ann Cooligan p202

COONAN – John Francis, b 28 Dec 1863 lc/o Michael Ignatius Coonan & Mary Adele Brenan bp 3 Jan 1864 spr John P. A. & Josephine Brenan p323

COONAN – Rosa Dell, b 31 Jan 1865 lc/o Daniel Coonan & Adele Brennan bp 10 Jan 1866 spr J. Coonan & E. Brennan p374

COONEY – William, b 31 Jan 1860 lc/o Michael Cooney & Catharine Kennedy bp 6 Feb 1860 spr Michael Jordan & Ellen Kennedy p214

COONIS – Mary Margaret, b 29 Aug 1854 lc/o Charles Coonis & Rose Calahan bp 15 Oct 1854 spr Mary Calahan p26

COOPER – Andrew Thomas, b 29 Jul 1862 lc/o Andrew Cooper "(deceased)" & Joanna Kantz bp 6 Oct 1863 spr Mary Hughes p317

COOPER – Ann Barbara, b 22 Oct 1857 lc/o Nicholas Cooper & Mary Buckley bp 5 Sep 1860 spr Bridget Clarke p230

COOPER – Anne Amelia, b 28 Aug 1856 lc/o Andrew Cooper "(deceased)" & Ann Kince bp 12 Feb 1864 spr Sarah Hardesty p326

COOPER – Mary Elizabeth, b 12 May 1860 lc/o Andrew Cooper "(deceased)" & Ann Kince bp 12 Feb 1864 spr Elizabeth Root p326

COOPER – Michael Henry, b 28 Aug 1859 lc/o Nicholas Cooper & _____ _____ bp 26 Mar 1860 spr [*ed. note:text faded*] p217

CORMELL – Bridget, b 20 Jan 1857 lc/o Charles Cormell & Mary McGuire bp 22 Feb 1857 spr Ambrose Hughes & Ann Curran "privately baptized by Rev. John McNally" H. B. Coskery, priest p112

CORNELL – Francis John, b 9 Feb 1870 lc/o Edwin F. Cornell & Martha A. Gallagher bp 8 Mar 1870 spr Charles J. McAllser & Emma Thompson p495

CORRIE – James Thompson, b 7 Mar 1862 lc/o James W. Corrie & Elizabeth Thompson bp 5 Jun 1862 spr Margaret Conlan p282

CORRIE – John Walter, b 6 Oct 1863 lc/o James Corrie & Elizabeth Thompson bp 10 Feb 1864 spr Mary <u>Mettee</u> p326

CORRIE – Peter, b 30 Nov. 1833 bp 1 Mar 1859 spr Mary Berry p183

COSGROVE – John T. Ford, b 18 Aug 1867 lc/o James Cosgrove & Martha Eliza Murphy bp 11 Jun 1868 spr Bridget Connolly p445

COSKERY – Elizabeth, b 3 Mar 1870 lc/o Henry J. Coskery & Betty Sitler bp 20 Apr spr Julia Reynolds & Henry Coskery Butler p500

COSKERY – Henry Morris, b 1 Aug 1866 c/o Henry J. Coskery & "his lawful wife" Betty Sitler bp 20 Sep 1866 spr Virginia Dorsey p396

COSKERY – Oscar M., b 14 Jul 1868 lc/o Henry J. Coskery & Betty Sitler bp 14 Aug 1868 spr Oscar J. Coskery & Caroline Tubman p451

COSKERY – Rebecca Coskery, "55 years old" c/o Lawrence _____ of Boston & Sarah Griffin "of Baltimore County" bp 17 Oct 1870 spr Martha Coskery "baptized conditionally" H. B. Coskery, priest p514

COUGHLAHAN – Michael, b 8 Sep 1856 lc/o Edward Coughlahan & Catherine Fahey bp 21 Sep 1856 spr Michael Fahey & Mary Coughlahan p96

COULAHAN – John, b 1 Feb 1855 lc/o Edward Coulahan & Catherine Fahey bp 11 Feb 1855 spr Jn. Coulahan & Bridget Fahey p36

COULSON – Eugenie Coulson, b 25 Dec 1844 lc/o Charles Coulson & Marguérité [sic] de D_____ bp 22 Nov 1868 spr Kate Hutchinson p457

COULTER – William Thomas, "6 years old" lc/o Andrew Coulter & Sarah McDonald bp 17 Feb 1870 spr Rebecca Coulter p494

COUNABAUGH – Ellen, b 13 Aug 1870 lc/o James Counabaugh & Elizabeth Reardon bp 14 Aug 1870 spr Lizzie Counabaugh p506

COURCELLE – Cecile Blanche, b 1 Feb 1867 lc/o Adrien Van S. Courcelle & Marie Josephine Courcelle bp 13 Apr 1867 spr Chas. Momonier & Theresa Van S. Courcelle p410

COURCEY – Stephen Henry Courcey (c), "aged 23 years" bp 1 May 1856 "baptized conditionally" H. B. Coskery, priest p82

COURLAENDER – Maria Cecilia Frances, b 28 Nov 1856 lc/o Bernard Courlaender & Eliza Colonne bp 18 Feb 1857 spr Amanda Courlaender & Cecilia Courlaender p111

COURLANDER – Julia Matilda Henrietta Marie Courlander, b 15 Apr 1855 lc/o Bernard Courlander & Eliza Caltiner bp 28 Jun 1855 spr Frederick Berrata & Mathilda Berrata p50

COURLANDEZ – Gustave Thomas, b 13 May 1858 lc/o Bernard Courlandez & Eliza Calonne bp 19 Jul 1858 spr J. T. Stoddard & Ann E. Stoddard p163

COURTNEY – Mary, b 4 Sep 1857 lc/o Stephen Courtney & Jane Carr bp 1 Jan 1858 spr George Courtney & Sally McLaughlin p145

COURTNEY – William George, b 30 Jan 1866 lc/o Stephen Courtenay & Jane Carr bp 29 Apr 1866 spr Catharine Conroy p383

COURTOIS – Clementine, "25 years old" lc/o Armand Courtois & Sophia Posey bp 30 Aug 1865 spr Mary C. Burk p363

COURY – Elizabeth, b 29 Oct 1862 lc/o Thomas Coury & Mary Bruggy bp 2 Nov 1862 spr Bridget Bates p293

COUSINS – Joseph, b 25 Mar 1866 lc/o Thomas Cousins & Honora Tully bp 19 Apr 1866 spr Mark Tully & Maria Flood p382

COWELL – George Patrick, b 20 Nov 1869 lc/o Wm. Patrick Cowell & Ada Rawlins bp 4 Jan 1870 spr Mary Carroll p491

COX – John Thomas, b 28 Dec 1850 c/o Thomas Cox & Mary Mooney, "his wife" bp 1 Jan 1860 spr Michael Roddy & Ann Cahill [*ed. note: birth year looks like 1850, but it could have been 1859*] p210

COYLE – William Edward, "six weeks old" lc/o Terence Coyle & Catherine Callaghan bp 25 Feb 1855 spr Philip Denmead & Mary Denmead p37

COYNE – Eleanor, b 17 May 1854 lc/o Jeremiah Coyne & Mary Aroy bp 4 Jun 1854 spr Frances Lusby p13

CRAIG – Charles, b 25 Mar 1857 lc/o Charles B. Craig & Ellen Torney bp 8 Jul 1857 spr Ellen Smith p126

CRAIN – Charles Joseph, b 16 Mar 1866 lc/o Adolphus P. Crain & Eva Ann Rockefeller bp 15 Apr 1866 spr Rose Daley p382

CRANE – George Francis, b 19 Aug 1870 lc/o Adolphus Crane & Eva Rockfort bp 5 Sep 1870 spr James Cornbaugh & Mary Lizzy Henry p508

CRAWFORD – Frances, b 29 Jun 1858 lc/o William R. Crawford & Ann Masterson bp 9 Feb 1859 spr Ellen Merritt p181

CRAWFORD – George Dalton, b 29 Jan 1857 lc/o William Crawford & Elizabeth Hardey bp 24 Aug 1863 spr Caroline G. Coskery p314

CRAWFORD – Henry, b 9 Jan 1861 lc/o William R. Crawford & Ann Masterson bp 23 May 1861 spr Eliza Donelan p252

CREAMER – Ellen, b 6 Aug 1865 lc/o Nicholas Creamer & Sarah Connolly bp 8 Aug 1865 spr Maggie Johnson p361

CREAMER – Mary Frances, b 3 Apr 1864 lc/o Joseph Creamer & Maria Butler bp 10 Jan 1869 spr Henry Westfall, Catharine Cain, John Cain & Rosa Anderson p463

CREAMER – Virginia, b 21 Aug 1856 c/o William Creamer & Caroline Robinson bp 27 May 1857 spr Nellie Tyler p121

CREAMER – William Wen_____, b 20 Oct 1864 lc/o Henry Westfall & Maria Buller bp 10 Jan 1869 spr Henry Westfall, Catharine Cain, John Cain & Rosa Anderson p463

CREEVAN – Mary Ann, b 28 Sep 1856 lc/o Thomas Creevan & Bridget McCann bp 28 Sep 1856 spr James Flannigan & Mary R______ p 97

CREIGHTON – Mary Adeline, b 24 Sep 1861 lc/o Francis Creighton & Julia Camerson bp 14 Nov 1861 spr Mary Polley p266

CRIMMINS – Jeremiah, b 25 Feb 1859 lc/o Patk. Crimmins & Ellen Toomey bp 18 Mar 1860 spr Thos. Madden & Ellen Barry p217

CRIMMINS – Mary Ann, b 28 Jul 1858 lc/o Patrick Crimmins & Ellen Tooney bp 8 Aug 1858 spr Bernard Hughes & Mary Lynch p166

CROCKER – George B., b 29 Jul 1864 lc/o Theodore Crocker & Catharine Smith bp 7 Aug 1864 spr John McGilley & Bridget Reynolds p338

CROCKER – Mary Ann, b 3 May 1861 lc/o Theodore Crocker & Catharine Smith bp 12 May 1861 spr Margaret Smith p251

CROCKER – Theodore Crocker, "aged about 32 years" bp 31 Mar 1861 spr Peter Smith p247

CROCKETT – Margaret, b 3 Feb 1867 lc/o Theodore Crockett & Kate Smith bp 10 Feb 1867 spr Michael Ward & Catharine Whelan p405

CROCKETT – Mary Ellen, b 3 Jul 1859 lc/o Theodore Crockett & Kate Smith bp 17 Jul 1859 spr Michl. Cain & Ellen Naughton p196

CROCKETT – Virginia, b 2 Jun 1869 lc/o Theodore Crockett & Catharine Smith bp 13 Jun 1869 spr Martin Leahy & Bridget O'Shea p474

CROMWELL – Charles Hammond, b 18 Apr 1868 lc/o Richard Cromwell & Mary Kennedy bp 27 Apr 1868 spr Wm. Boone & Sally Boone, "proxy for C. C. Lancaster" p440

CROMWELL – John (c), b 10 Jun 1857 lc/o John Cromwell & Catherine Scott bp 16 Aug 1857 spr Elizabeth Gaines p130

CROMWELL – Mary Ann, b 11 May 1866 lc/o Richd. Cromwell & Mary Kennedy bp 20 May 1866 spr Sally Boon p384

CROMWELL – Richard, b 15 Mar 1864 lc/o Richard Cromwell & Mary Kennedy bp 19 Mar 1864 spr Joseph & Mary Loretto Hunter p328

CROMWELL – William Kennedy, b 18 Apr 1862 lc/o Richard Cromwell & Mary Kennedy bp 26 Apr 1862 spr H. B. Coskery & Sallie Kennedy p280

CRONIN – Catharine, b 25 Oct 1867 lc/o Philip Cronin & Catharine Wilson bp 17 Nov 1867 spr Jas. Cunningham & Cath. Cunningham p427

CROSS – David Henry, b 24 Jan 1865 lc/o David Henry Cross & Margaret Hughes bp 22 Feb 1865 spr Mary Keenan p351

CROSS – George Washington, b 29 Jun 1859 lc/o David Cross & Margaret Hughes bp 11 Jul 1859 spr Rose Hughes p195

CROSS – Margaret Ann Virginia, b 27 Mar 1867 lc/o David Cross & Margaret Hughes bp 3 Apr 1867 spr Joanna Hughes p409

CROSS – William Henry, b 15 Jan 1861 lc/o David Cross & Margaret Hughes bp 11 Feb 1861 spr Mary Orr p243

CROTTY – Ann Nora, b 1 Dec 1861 lc/o David Crotty & Eleanor Welsh bp 8 Dec 1861 spr David J. Welsh & Ellen Lone p269

CROW – Charles Lewis, b 15 Sep 1857 lc/o Joseph Francis Crow & Cecilia Hutchins bp 1 Jan 1858 spr Mary Grady p145

CUGAN – Edward Francis, bp 17 Mar 1854 lc/o Patrick Cugan & Rosa Flannigan bp 26 Mar 1854 spr Sarah Williams p9

CULLEN – Catharine, b 15 Dec 1860 lc/o Patrick Cullen & Mary Mullaney bp 6 Jan 1861 spr Catharine Cullen p239

CULLEN – John, b 27 Mar 1861 lc/o Patrick Cullen & Ellen Quinn bp 7 Apr 1861 spr Lizzie Nunan p248

CULLIMORE – Georgina Harrison, b 12 Sep 1839 lc/o John Cullimore & "Ellen, "his wife" bp 5 Apr 1861 spr Julia Harper p248

CULLIMORE – John Edward Hooper, b 7 Oct 1853 lc/o John Cullimore & Harriet Hooper bp 20 Jun 1861 spr Georgina Cullimore p254

CULP – Constantine Florentine, b 5 Oct 1854 c/o Henry Emory Culp & Barina F. Coupain bp 28 Feb 1855 spr Lewis Clifton & Kate Little p38

CUMMINGS – John Cummings, "aged 33 years" bp 5 May 1860 "baptized conditionally" Thos. Foley, priest p220

CUMMINGS – John, b 4 Jul 1854 lc/o Francis Cummings & Jane Kelly bp 9 Jul 1854 spr James Egan & Mary Twellan "I supplied the ceremonies" H. B. Coskery, priest p17

CUMMINGS – Mary Cecilia Cummings, "aged 16 years" lc/o Augustus & Julia Cummings bp 25 Feb 1868 spr Ann Brady "baptized conditionally" H. B. Coskery, priest p435

CUMMINGS – Mary, b 26 Feb 1856 lc/o Francis Cummings & Jane Kelly bp 2 Mar 1856 spr Peter Gill & Mary Cummings p74

CUNABAUGH – Catharine Ellen, b 12 Jul 1866 lc/o James Cunabaugh & Bessie Reardon bp 18 Jul 1866 spr John Coolahan & Mary Hinehan p389

CUNEBAUGH – Margaret, b 9 Nov 1868 lc/o James Cunebaugh & Elizabeth Riordan bp 23 Nov 1868 spr Matthew Noonan & Mary Noonan p457

CUNEO – Andrew, b 7 Jan 1858 c/o Stephen Cuneo & Maria Peretta bp 19 Jan 1858 spr Charles Cuneo & Henrietta Sacco p147

CUNIO – Martin Rose, b 27 Nov 1856 lc/o Stephen Cunio & Mary Feretta "of Genoa" bp 6 Dec 1856 spr Antonio Gruo & Maria Fontana Rosa p103

CUNIS – Giovani Fortunato, b 15 Jun 1859 lc/o Antonio Cunis & Catasina Ruggio bp 3 Jul 1859 spr Giovani Sturla & Rosa Sturla p193

CUNNABAUGH – Mary Helen, b *ndg* lc/o James Cunnabaugh & Elizabeth Reardon bp 4 Jan 1857 spr Thos. Murphy & Kate Karney p107

CUNNIBAL – Elizabeth, b 22 Jan 1858 lc/o James Cunnibal & Elizabeth Reardon bp 7 Feb 1858 spr Edw. Roach & Sarah Conway p148

CUNNIGAN – Mary Jane, b 5 Jun 1856 lc/o Nicholas Cunnigan & Elizabeth Isabelle Boaldson bp 9 Jun 1856 spr Patrick Martin & Teresa Boaldson p84

CUNNIGAN – Michael, b 15 Nov 1854 c/o Michael Cunnigan & Isabella Booner bp 26 Nov 1854 spr Patrick McCaul & Mary Booner p30

CUNNINGHAM – Agnes Virginia, b 26 Nov 1865 lc/o Nicholas Cunningham & Isabel Boner bp 30 Nov 1865 spr Cornelius Malony & Mary Jane Tuillan p370

CUNNINGHAM – Ann, b 1 Aug 1863 lc/o Nicholas Cunningham & Belle Boner bp 4 Aug 1863 spr Thos. Cane & Ann McQuillan p312

CUNNINGHAM – Edward Carroll, b 18 Dec 1861 c/o Elizabeth Ann Cunningham bp 27 Dec 1861 spr Fanny Broderick p270

CUNNINGHAM – Henry Thomas, b 9 Oct 1856 lc/o James Cunningham & Mary Eaton bp 12 Oct 1856 spr Owen Quillan & Ann Eaton p98

CUNNINGHAM – James Thomas, b 17 Mar 1861 lc/o Nicholas Cunningham & Isabella Boner bp 28 Apr 1861 spr Teresa Boner p250

CUNNINGHAM – Mary Isabel, b 6 Mar 1858 lc/o Nicholas Cunningham & Isabel Boner bp 15 Mar 1858 spr Mary Boner p151

CUNNINGHAM – Patrick, b 5 Mar 1857 lc/o Patrick Cunningham & Bridget Coyne bp 8 Mar 1857 spr William Bryan & Margaret Cunningham p114

CURLEY – Mary Ellen, b 18 May 1859 lc/o Daniel Curley & Mary Kirby bp 29 May 1859 spr Charles Arthur & Bridget Egan p191

CURTIN – Joanna, b 26 Jan 1869 lc/o Patrick Curtin & Annie Sarny bp 31 Jan 1869 spr William Curtin & Joanna Sullivan p464

CURTIS – Daniel Suc_____ (c), b 7 Nov 1864 lc/o Daniel Curtis & Mary Hill (c) spr Alfred Landers & Henrietta Coates p346

CURTIS – James Henry, b 11 Jul 1869 lc/o Daniel Curtis & Mary Curtis (c) bp 20 Aug 1869 spr Harriet Fenell p481

CUSHING – Joseph Richard, b 25 Aug 1863 lc/o Richard Cushing & Catharine Broderick bp 15 Sep 1863 spr Fanny Broderick p315

DAIGER – Charles Vincent, b 29 Jul 1866 lc/o Edward Daiger & Susan Meeks bp 20 Aug 1866 spr Susan Daiger p393

DAIGER – Mary Gertrude, b 9 Jun 1868 lc/o Edward Daiger & Susan Meeks bp 20 Aug 1868 spr Martha Fillinger p451

DAIGER – William Henry, b 9 Jun 1860 lc/o Edward Daiger & Susan Meeks bp 15 Jun 1860 spr Mary Sloan p224

DAIGNON – James, b 20 Nov 1865 lc/o Patk. Daignon & Mary Conroy bp 26 Nov 1865 spr Michl. & Bridget Daignon p370

DALEY – Albert Joseph, b 10 Jun 1856 lc/o Michael Daley & Julia Elizabetta Treivan bp 24 Mar 1856 spr Maria Redveleske p77

DALEY – Anna, b 21 Feb 1863 lc/o Martin Daley & Ellen Hallon bp 4 Mar 1863 spr Kate Daley p303

DALEY – Augustine, b 19 Nov 1870 c/o Timothy Daley "of County Cork, Ireland" & Maria Infant Mayo "of County Cork, Ireland" bp 4 Dec 1870 spr Cornelius Daley & Ann Flattly p516

DALEY – Catharine, b 1 Feb 1864 lc/o Timothy Daley & Mary Infant bp 7 Feb 1864 spr William McCarron & Honora Fitzpatrick p325

DALEY – Charles Emile, b 28 Jan 1868 lc/o Eugene Daley & Ellen Carney bp 23 Feb 1868 spr Michael Henry & Mary J. Bastien p434

DALEY – Clara Virginia, b 1 Mar 1867 lc/o James Daley & Mary Ellen Bollman bp 6 Sep 1867 spr Kate McLaughlin p420

DALEY – Emily, b 19 Jun 1865 lc/o James Daley & Mary Osmond bp 9 Nov 1865 spr Chas. McLaughlin & Rebecca McLaughlin p368

DALEY – Emily Eliza, "19 months old" nc/o Henry Harwood & Margaret Daley bp 17 Jul 1854 spr Cecilia Daley p18

DALEY – Eugene Morgan, b 15 Feb 1863 lc/o Eugene Daley & Ellen Carney bp 1 Mar 1863 spr James Daley & Kate Carney p302

DALEY – Frederick Francis, b 21 May 1858 lc/o John Daley & Mary Daley bp 29 Aug 1858 spr Bridget Mitchell p168

DALEY – James, b 24 Jun 1854 lc/o Maurice Daley & Mary McConnell bp 2 Jul 1854 spr Pat. McGlone & Mary M. Givan p16

DALEY – James Henry, b 8 Oct 1866 lc/o Eugene Daley & Ellen Carney bp 18 Oct 1866 spr James Carney & Kate Daley p397

DALEY – James William, b 22 Nov 1868 lc/o James Daley & Mary Infant bp 6 Dec 1868 spr Patk. Infant & Mary McClellan p459

DALEY – John Owen, b 13 Jun 1857 lc/o Mark Daley & Mary McConnell bp 14 Jun 1857 spr John Gorman & Elizabeth Cahill p124

DALEY – John William, b 22 Jan 1865 lc/o Eugene Daley & Ellen Carney bp 10 Jan 1865 spr John Carey & Kate Noonan [*ed. note: baptism date is recorded as Jan, but it is listed between two Feb baptisms, thus this probably should have been recorded as Feb. As birth month is "ult", it most likely was Jan and not Dec if Feb is baptism month*] p350

DALEY – Joseph Francis, b 13 Apr 1869 lc/o Eugene Daley & Ellen M. Carney bp 21 Apr 1869 spr John Carney & Bridget Carney p469

DALEY – Marietta, b 15 Oct 1857 lc/o Thomas Daley & Josephine Satterfield bp 4 Nov 1857 spr Harriet McMahon "baptized privately in case of sickness" H. B. Coskery, priest p139

DALEY – Mark, b 6 Apr 1866 lc/o Mark Daley & Mary McConnell bp 8 Apr 1866 spr Matthew Gorman & Teresa Flinn p381

DALEY – Martin, b 8 Dec 1861 lc/o Martin Daley & Ellen Hanlan bp 29 Dec 1861 spr Ann Sheahan p271

DALEY – Mary, b 15 Oct 1855 lc/o Patrick Daley & Catherine Carberry bp 18 Jul 1856 spr Fr. & Mary Daly p91

DALEY – Sarah Ann, b 1 Apr 1860 lc/o Martin Daley & Bridget Kelly bp 25 Apr 1860 spr Michael McNeal & Catharine Daley p220

DALEY – Susanna Agnes, b 10 Feb 1856 lc/o James Daley & Mary E. Allman bp 22 Sep 1856 spr Susanna A. Daley p96

DALEY – Thomas, b 22 Aug 1866 c/o Timothy Daley & "his wife" Mary Infant bp 9 Sep 1866 spr Patk. Nestor & Bridget Infant p395

DALEY – William Thomas, b 21 Nov 1856 lc/o Henry Daily [sic] & Mary Trainor bp 18 Dec 1856 spr Rosa Trainor p105

DALLAM – Mary Elizabeth, b 8 Dec 1864 lc/o Edward B. Dallam & Cecilia Plowden Jenkins bp 19 Dec 1864 spr Robert & Rebecca Jenkins p347

DALTON – Charles Edward, b 12 Jun 1858 lc/o Edward Dalton & Mary Dougherty bp 27 Jun 1858 spr John Hunt & Martha Ann Wilson p161

DALTON – Jane Elizabeth, b 29 Mar 1857 lc/o James Dalton & Ellen Devereux bp 25 Jun 1857 spr Mary Rafferty p124

DALTON – Mary Catherine, b 8 Sep 1857 lc/o Patrick Cloak & Elizabeth Dalton bp 15 Sep 1857 spr James Dalton & Ellen Foley p134

DANDELET – John Charles, b 13 Apr 1863 lc/o Francis Dandelet & Pauline Goulié bp 24 May 1863 spr John Fenillan & Lucille Fayset p307

DANDELET – Jules François, b 2 Sep 1858 lc/o Henry DeWitt Clinton & Mary Coarts bp 10 Oct 1858 spr Mary Dean p171

DANDELET – Juliette Charlotte Adeline Marie, b 21 Nov 1859 lc/o Francis Dandelet & Lucille Eugenia Constance Mignot bp 18 Dec 1859 spr Jules Legrand & Charlotte M. Etoffe p208

DANDELET – Pauline Josephine Charlotte, b 19 Jun 1865 lc/o François Dandelet & Pauline Guillon bp 23 Jul 1865 spr Joe Paini & Charlotte Eloffe p360

DANDELET – Victorine, b 25 May 1855 lc/o Francis Dandelet & Pauline Gollott bp 19 Aug 1855 spr John P. Cohne & V. Guernande p55

DANDRIGE – Antonias M_____ (c), b 13 Mar 1870 lc/o Emick Dandrige & Delia Larkin bp 27 Mar 1870 spr Joseph Karch p498

DANSKIN – Washington Aloysius, b 14 Jan 1858 lc/o Washington Danskin & Rose Cahill bp 9 Jan 1859 spr Flora Norris p179

DAUGHERTY – Andrew, b 20 Jun 1856 lc/o James Daugherty & Anna Lynch bp 20 Jul 1856 spr James Kavanaugh & Mary Lynch p91

DAUGHERTY – George Anthony, b 21 May 1861 lc/o Michael Dougherty & Margaret Mooney bp 2 Jun 1861 spr Martin Clarke & Kate Daugherty p253

DAUGHERTY – Margaret, b 8 Jan 1858 lc/o Stephen Daugherty & Bridget Wulby bp 9 Feb 1858 spr Jonathan Mullan & Catherine Burton p149

DAUGHERTY – Mary Agnes, b 28 Apr 1869 lc/o John F. Daugherty & Sarah C. Platson bp 14 May 1869 spr Edward S. Daugherty & Elizabeth McClellan p471

DAUGHERTY – Mary Elizabeth, b 21 Apr 1864 lc/o James Daugherty & Anne Donnelly bp 28 May 1864 spr Bridget McCann p333

DAUGHTY – Mary Marion Clarke, "about 13 months old" "foundling accepted by John C. Daughty & Mary Stresser, his wife" bp 13 Dec 1863 p322

DAVID – Palmyse Marie, "15 years old" "native of Havre, France and supposed to be of Jewish descent" bp 1 Feb 1859 Thos. Foley, priest p180

DAVIDSON – Charles Francis, b 19 Jan 1857 lc/o Samuel Davidson & Anna Mullan bp 23 Apr 1857 spr Caroline Addison p117

DAVIDSON – Eugene Singleton, b Dec. 1853 lc/o Dr. Samuel Davidson & Martha Palmer bp 26 May 1854 spr Henrietta Plater p13

DAVIDSON – Francis Walter Granville, b 9 May 1856 lc/o Dr. Saml. Davidson & Martha Palmer bp 26 Sept 1856 spr Virginia Warner p97

DAVIDSON – Joseph Clark Y. Davidson, "age about 20 years" bp 7 Dec 1854 spr Annette Bartlett (c) "baptized conditionally" H. B. Coskery, priest p30

DAVIS – Alice Mary, b 24 Jul 1859 c/o Alfred Davis & Lea Ann Collins bp 11 Jan 1860 spr Mary Gavaghan [*ed. note: see also Collins as priest noted the last name as Davis or Collins*] p211

DAVIS – Ann Davis (c), "aged about 25 years" bp 7 Sep 1859 spr Emily Roach "baptized conditionally" H. B. Coskery, priest p199

DAVIS – Catharine Mary Davis, "adult", b *ndg* bp 22 Jan 1870 spr Elizab. Ann Jenkins p492

DAVIS – Clara Ellen, b 5 Nov 1858 lc/o John Davis & Susan Galloway (c) bp 6 Mary 1859 spr Clara Colbert p188

DAVIS – John Henry, b 6 Feb 1866 c/o John Davis & Anna Martin bp 12 Mar 1866 spr Margaret Mannion p377

DAVIS – Mary Virginia Davis, "aged 21 years" bp 20 Feb 1867 "baptized conditionally" Thos. Foley, priest p406

DAVIS – Sophia Davis (c), "aged about 24 years" bp 17 Nov 1859 p205

DAVIS – Stephen Smith (c), b 14 Oct 1866 lc/o Alexander Griffin Davis & Ann Elizabeth Carver bp 3 Dec 1867 spr Lizzie Greatfield p428

DAVIS – Thomas Davis, b *ndg* bp 23 Dec 1855 "adult Episcopalian in danger" "baptized conditionally" Francis Patrick, Archb. Balt. p69

DAVIS – William James Galloway, b 14 Jun 1863 lc/o Alexander Davis & Ann Maria Gavin (c) bp 21 Jul 1867 spr Minty Lecompte p311

DAVIS – William Thomas, "16 months old" lc/o Thomas P. Davis & Elizabeth Knight bp 4 Dec 1868 "baptized privately" Thos. Foley, priest p459

DAVISON – Mary Cora Estell, b 20 Feb 1860 lc/o Dr. Saml. Davison & Mary Palmer bp 13 Jun 1860 spr Louisa Billups p224

DAYS – Emily, b 2 Dec 1854 lc/o James Days & Mary Swann bp 4 Mar 1855 spr John Jordan p38

DEAN – Margaret Dean (c), "14 years old" bp 9 Jun 1860 spr Sophie Robinson p224

DEAVER – Catharine Carrie, b 24 Aug 1866 lc/o James Deaver & Emma Oliver (c) bp 25 Oct 1867 spr Ellen Taylor p424

DEAVER – James Nelson, b 21 Sep 1866 lc/o George Deaver & Mary Maquette (c) bp 5 Dec 1866 spr Josepine Maquette p400

DEAVER – Lewis Smith, b 26 Mar 1855 lc/o Smith Deaver & Ann Victoria Gratefield (all c) bp 9 Apr 1855 spr Mary E. White p42

DEAVER – Mary Louisa, b 11 Nov 1863 lc/o James Deaver & Emma Oliver (c) bp 25 Oct 1867 spr Caroline Addison p424

DEEVEN – Mary Frances Anastasia, b 19 Aug 1868 lc/o George Deven & Mary Mongnette bp 30 Sep 1868 spr Mary Kelly p455

DEGOEY – Charles Mary Caspani, b 27 Jun 1864 lc/o William DeGoey & June E. Finger bp 10 Jul 1864 spr Rebecca Dryden p336

DELANEY – Catherine, b 17 Aug 1854 lc/o James Delaney & Catherine Kelly bp 18 Sep 1854 spr Fanny Delaney p24

DELANEY – Francis Michael, b 16 Sep 1865 lc/o Patk. Delany & Ann Smith bp 15 Oct 1856 spr Mary Ryan p367

DELANEY – John, b 10 May 1863 lc/o Patrick Delaney & Ann Smith bp 12 Jul 1863 spr Mary Ellen Green p310

DELANEY – Margaret, b 6 Feb 1861 lc/o Patrick Delaney & Ann Smith bp 8 May 1861 spr Annie Foley p251

DELANEY – Mary Ann, b 28 Dec 1858 lc/o Patrick Delaney & Ann Smith bp 16 Jan 1859 spr Barney Flately & Winifred Dunn p179

DELANEY – Mary Grace, b 1 Jan 1864 lc/o John Delaney & Elizabeth King bp 7 Feb 1864 spr Margaret McCabe p326

DELANEY – Sarah Catharine, b 30 Dec 1867 lc/o Patrick Delaney & Ann Smith bp 1 Jun 1868 spr Ann McCa_____ p444

DEMANGIN – Teresa Hortense, b 12 Dec 1859 c/o Charles H. T. Demangis & Rebecca Ann Moor, "his lawful wife" 25 Aug 1862 g - Teresa V. A. Demangin p288

DENMEAD – Ann Virginia, b 13 May 1857 lc/o Edward Denmead & Henrietta Sanders bp 29 May 1857 spr Eduard J. Sanders & Ann R. Sanders p122

DENNEY – George Beauregard Lee, b 5 Feb 1865 lc/o John Denney & Susan McGivans bp 26 Feb 1865 spr George M. Givens & Bridget Green p352

DENNEY – James Emm____, b 12 Dec 1863 lc/o John Denney & Susan McGowan bp 27 Dec 1863 spr Henry Maylan & Ann McLaughlin p322

DENNING – John H. Denning, b 9 Sep 1836 lc/o John Denning & Maria Maxwell bp 16 Jan 1858 "I received a profession of faith. Baptized in Methodist sect and conditionally baptized him." Francis Patrick Archb. p147

DENNISON – Emma Dennison, b 25 May 1844 lc/o William W. Dennison & Ellen Martin bp 15 May 1865 "baptized conditionally" Thos. Foley, priest p357

DENNY – Dennis Boone (c), "aged 40" bp 1 May 1867 p411

DENSMORE – Mary, b *ndg* Jul 1846 lc/o Robert Densmore & Ellen Roche bp 27 Nov 1868 spr Margaret Welch p458

DENSON – Elizabeth "(born Pittman)" Denson, "52 years old" bp 19 Feb 1865 spr Rebecca Bloss & Elizabeth Stuart p351

DENSON – Sophronia Mary Denson, "age 10 years" bp 19 Feb 1865 c/o John Denson & Elizabeth (Pittman) Denson p351

DESERY – Mary Elizabeth, b 1 Mar 1855 lc/o John Shark Desery & Anna Fell (c) bp 6 Nov 1860 spr Virginia Castor p235

<u>DESEY</u> – Elizabeth Ann, p 26 Jan 1857 lc/o John <u>Desey</u> & Victoria Crocket bp 10 Jun 1857 spr Margaret Hubert p123

DEVER – Francis Nichols (c), b 22 Jan 1857 lc/o Smith Dever & Ann Gratefield bp 15 Mar 1857 spr Julia Gratefield (all c) p114

DEVILIN – Jane Mary, b "about 3 weeks ago" lc/o Bernard Devilin & Catharine Patterson bp 9 Jul 1859 spr Ellen Mallaghan p194

DEVINE – John Thomas, b 10 Aug 1869 lc/o John Devine & Catharine Garing bp 29 Aug 1869 spr Patrick Curtin & Margaret Dunn p481

DEVORGE – Alphonse, b 13 Dec *ndg* [*ed. note: most likely 1870*] lc/o Alphonse Devorge "of Baltimore" & Teresa O'Farrell "of the same place" bp 18 Dec 1870 spr Patrick Fran_____ & Pauline ______ p517

DEVRIS – Elizabeth Jane, b 16 Jul 1853 lc/o Charles Devris & Elizabeth Taylor bp 14 Feb 1857 spr Amanda Hodges p110

DIEHL – John Louis Pierre, b 7 Aug 1867 lc/o John Diehl & Marie Louis Fermen bp 15 Sep 1867 spr Louis Fermen & Ernestine Diehl p421

DIETRICH – Alice Augusta, b 15 Jun 1870 lc/o Charles Wm. Dietrich & Rosalind Oranger bp 20 Jun 1870 spr George W. Jenkins & Caroline Dietrich p503

DIGNAN – John, b 7 Mar 1863 lc/o Peter Dignan & Julia Walsh bp 15 Mar 1863 spr James Ryan & Winifred Spelman p304

DILLOWAY – Ann Catherine, b 10 Dec 1856 lc/o Dofrity Dilloway & Ann M. Watson bp 22 Feb 1857 spr Mary Jane Quinan p111

DINGLE – Eliza Jane, b 14 Dec 1859 lc/o Jacob R. Dingle & Rosaina Herbert bp 5 Sep 1860 spr Julian Herbert p230

DINGLE – Julia, b 18 May 1858 lc/o Jacob Dingle & Rose Ann Herbst bp 9 Jun 1858 spr Julia Ann Herbert p159

DINSMORE – Marion Mary, b 29 Jan 1854 lc/o Daniel Dinsmore & Margaret Moran bp 17 Aug 1854 spr Mary Suple p20

DIX – Grace Mary Dix (c), "in 75th year of age" bp 2 Mar 1855 spr Mary Perry p38

DIXON – Margaret Jane, b 18 Oct 1863 lc/o Patrick Dixon & Rosanna Mitchel bp 28 Oct 1863 spr Patk. Fogarty & Ann Dixon p319

DIXON- Emily, "about 40 years" bp 20 May 1868 spr Mary Tubman "baptized conditionally" H. B. Coskery, priest p442

DOBBINS – Cecilia Elizabeth, b 10 Nov 1852 lc/o Amelia Audibert & James Dobbins bp 1 May 1857 spr Harriet Lowe p118

DOBBINS – Joseph, [*ed. note: surname is recorded both as Dobbins and Hardy*] b 24 Apr 1869 c/o Henry Dobbins & Mary Elizabeth Hardy bp 15 May 1869 spr Caroline Hardy (all c) p471

DOLAN – Joseph, b 27 Aug 1856 lc/o Patrick Dolan & Eliz. Fisher bp 7 Sep 1856 spr Margaret Carr p95

DOLAN – Louis, b 5 Jul 1856 lc/o James Dolan & Mary J. Martin bp 13 Jul 1856 spr Samuel Martin & Jennie Whelan p89

DOLAN – Thomas, b 13 Jul 1857 lc/o Maurice Dolan & Ellen Vaughn bp 19 Jul 1857 spr Stephen Murphy & Cath. Farrell p127

DONALD – Margaret, b 22 Jun 1870 lc/o James Donald & Margaret _____ bp 10 Jul 1870 spr Andrew Breid & Elizabeth Bannon p505

DONAVAN – Mary Agnes, b 4 Jul 1855 lc/o John Donavan & Catherine Flynn bp 12 Aug 1855 spr Henry _____ & Catherine Hurley p55

DONEHOE – Thomas, b 19 Dec 1857 lc/o Maurice Donehoe & Barrett bp 2 May 1858 spr Nicholas James & Sarah Gibbon p154

DONNELLY – Alice Ann, b 19 Nov 1856 lc/o Francis Donnelly & Margaret Donnelly bp 30 Nov 1856 spr Mich. Ryan & Ann Gordon p103

DONNELLY – Arthur, b 2 Sep 1854 lc/o John Donnelly & Rose Murphy b 12 Sep 1854 spr Wm. Broderick & Ann Murphy p23

DONNELLY – Catherine, b 14 Oct 1855 lc/o James Donnelly & Bridget Ford bp 21 Oct 1855 spr James McGovern & Catherine McGovern p62

DONNELLY – Joseph Francis, b 6 Jan 1865 c/o Ellen Smith & Joseph Donnelly bp 19 Jan 1866 spr Mary Conlin p374

DONNELLY – Mary Ann, b 13 Oct 1863 nc/o Joseph Donnelly & Ellen Smith bp 3 Nov 1863 spr Mary Ann Conlan p319

DONNELLY – William Thomas, b 18 Dec 1860 lc/o Thomas Donnelly & Hannah Garey bp 20 Feb 1861 spr Ellen Garey p244

DONOVAN – John Daniel, b 1 Oct 1856 lc/o John Donovan & Catherine Flynn bp 19 Oct 1856 spr Wm. McElwen & Julia Flynn p99

DONOVAN – Julia, b 6 Sep 1855 lc/o Dennis Donovan & Honora Cobsley bp 12 Sep 1855 spr Dennis Daley & Cath. Starke p58

DONOVAN – Mary Elizabeth, b 8 Jul 1863 lc/o Denis Donovan & Eliza Miskelly bp 19 Jul 1863 spr Thos. Finn & Ann Flinn p311

DOOLEY – Mary, b 31 Jul 1858 lc/o John Dooley & Catharine Brick bp 1 Aug 1858 spr Mary Dooley p165

DORAN – Mary Alexander, b 29 Nov 1864 lc/o Peter J. Doran & Mary A. Cullan bp 8 Dec 1864 spr Harriet Lavinia Leonard p346

DORMAN – Samuel Dorman, "aged 37 years" bp 6 Jan 1868 p431

DORSEY – Anna Vernon, b 10 Jan 1865 lc/o Vernon Dorsey & Kate Costigan bp 19 Feb 1865 spr Cornelia Carroll p350

DORSEY – Arthur Pue, "10 years old" lc/o James Dorsey & Hannah Welsh bp 18 Nov 1860 spr Mary Jamison p236

DORSEY – Blanche, b 17 Feb 1857 lc/o Joseph Dorsey & Amanda Mitchell bp 31 Aug 1857 spr Rachel Riley p133

DORSEY – John Baptist, b 26 Jun 1855 lc/o Washington Dorsey & Catharine, "his wife" bp 15 Jul 1855 spr Thomas Creamer & Sarah Cullen p52

DORSEY – John Martin, b 6 Jan 1866 lc/o Denis Dorsey & Mary Carr "(both of Springfield, Carroll County)" bp 6 Apr 1866 spr Patrick Gill & Mary Loftis p381

DORSEY – John Tolley Washington, b 6 Mar 1866 lc/o Samuel Dorsey & Viriginia Thompson bp 27 Sep 1866 spr Henry Riardon p397

DORSEY – Margaret Matilda, b 4 Oct 1863 lc/o Ignatius B. & Annie R. Dorsey bp 5 Feb 1864 spr Sarah J. Agnew p325

DORSEY – Mary Catharine, b 1 Jan 1860 lc/o James Dorsey & Margaret Maxwell bp 28 Mar 1860 spr Annie Morgan p218

DORSEY – Mary Catherine Dorsey (c), b 1 May 1785 bp 6 Jan 1856 spr Mary Harrington p70

DORSEY – Mary Elizabeth (c), b 29 May 1857 lc/o Thomas Dorsey & Julia Cafrel bp 28 Jun 1857 spr Caroline Hardy (c) p125

DORSEY – Virginia (c), b 5 Nov 1868 lc/o Alfred Dorsey & Theresa Banlon (c) bp 19 Nov 1868 spr Mary Z. Elvert p457

DORSEY – William Dorsey, "aged 29 years" bp 24 Mar 1867 "baptized conditionally" Thos. Foley, priest p408

DOS SANTOS – Josephine Amalia, b 6 Nov 1858 lc/o Fillip Simors dos Santos & Mary Murray bp 8 Dec 1858 spr Carlos Nitze & Hellen [sic] Turner p175

DOU – Joseph Hico Dou, "age 18 yrs." "Japanese" bp 30 Oct 1854 p27

DOUGHERTY – Francis, b 10 Jan 1869 lc/o Michel Dougherty & Margaret Mooney bp 17 Jan 1869 spr Francis Daley & Mary McNeale p463

DOUGHERTY – Geo. W. Dougherty, "aged about 22 years bp 28 Jul 1866 spr Josephine McIntosh p390

DOUGHERTY – Gilbert, b 19 Jan 1863 lc/o Michael Dougherty & Mary Mooney bp 25 Jan 1863 spr Michl. Mooney & Catharine Daley p300

DOUGHERTY – James, b 13 Aug 1860 lc/o James Dougherty & Hannah Lynch bp 26 Aug 1860 spr Ann Welsh & Michael Lynch p229

DOUGHERTY – James, b 8 Jul 1866 lc/o Michl. Dougherty & Margaret Mooney bp 15 Jul 1866 spr _____ Daley & Mary Mooney p389

DOUGHERTY – Margaret Agnes, b 21 Nov 1869 lc/o Michael Daugherty & Mary Ann Gilson bp 28 Dec 1869 spr Sarah Jane Dougherty p490

DOUGHERTY – Michael, b 8 Jan 1865 lc/o Michael Dougherty & Margaret Mooney bp 19 Jan 1865 spr Patk. & Ann Gormley p349

DOUGLASS – James Buchanan, b 30 Nov 1856 lc/o Peter Douglass & Clara C. L. White bp 24 May 1857 spr Joseph Bookman & Sarah Bookman p121

DOUGLASS- Joseph Roberts, b 2 Dec 1853 lc/o Lewis Douglass & Ann R. Hatter bp 1 Jan 1854 spr Joseph & Sarah Bookman p1

DOWLING – Ann Elizabeth Turner, b 14 Dec 1858 lc/o Edward Dowling & Ann Eliza Turner, "since deceased" bp 21 Mar 1859 spr Mary Dowling p184

DOWLING – Joseph Dominic, b 16 Apr 1854 lc/o James Dowling & Mary Jane Martin bp 23 Apr 1854 spr John Clark & Ann Dowling p10

DOWNS – James Downs, b 3 Jan 1859 lc/o David Downs & Honora Foley bp 5 Jan 1859 spr Patrick Lane & Catharine McDonald p178

DOWNS – Joseph, b 8 Jan 1855 lc/o John Downs & Mary Corryhan bp 14 Jan 1855 apr James Downs & Margaret Keilly p34

DOWNS – Mary, "2 years & 2 weeks old" "child of a woman named Downs" bp 2 Nov 1861 spr Mary McQuaid p265

DOYLE – _____ Pat, b 31 May 1865 lc/o William Doyle & Mary Ann (Monahan) Doyle bp 15 Jun 1865 spr Wm. J. Doyle & Mary E. Doyle p358

DOYLE – Augustine Aloysius Thomas, b 23 Jun [*ed. note: year not written, probably 1868*] lc/o William Doyle & Mary Monahan bp 11 Jul 1868 spr Andrew Doyle & Agnes Gallager [sic] "I supplied the ceremonies" "This child was previously baptized by Dr. Chatard" James Gibbons, priest p448

DOYLE – Bridget Mary, b 7 Oct 1855 lc/o Matthew Doyle & Catherine Kavanaugh bp 30 Oct 1855 spr Isabel Kelly & J. Kavanaugh p62

DOYLE – Charles, b 10 Aug 1869 lc/o James Doyle & Margaret Simmons bp 18 Aug 1869 spr Charles Polley & Kate Doyle p480

DOYLE – Ferdinand Eager Chatard, b 25 Apr 1859 lc/o William Doyle & Margaret Monaghan bp 28 Apr 1859 spr William Doyle & Mary I. Gallagher p188

DOYLE – John, b 2 Oct 1859 lc/o Matthew Doyle & Catharine Cavanaugh bp 2 Dec 1859 spr John Murphy & Bridget Murphy p207

DOYLE – Mary Ann Elizabeth b 13 Jul 1862 lc/o William Doyle & Margaret Monahan bp 17 Jul 1862 spr Helen Gallagher p285

DOYLE – Mary Elizabeth, b 20 Apr 1854 lc/o Thomas Doyle & Ann Burns bp 30 Apr 1854 spr Michael Gallagher & Cath. Burns p11

DOYLE – Mary Jane, b 11 May 1868 lc/o Owen Doyle & Margaret Brady bp 17 May 1868 spr Francis Maguire & Margaret O'Meara p442

DOYLE – Matthew Laurence, b 24 Sep 1857 lc/o Matthew Doyle & Catherine Cavanaugh bp 1 Nov 1857 spr Annie Doyle p139

DOYLE – Sarah Ann, b 29 Jun 1856 lc/o Thomas Doyle & Ann Burris bp 6 Jul 1856 spr Laurence Kennedy & Julia O'Neal p89

DOYLE – William Francis Michael, b 27 Nov 1856 lc/o William Doyle & Margaret Monahan bp 30 Nov 1856 spr James Doyle & Catherine McCann p103

DRANE – James Francis, b 9 Jun 1868 lc/o John Drane & Pauline Davide bp 21 Jun 1868 spr Jas. Drane & Mary A. McGorvan p446

DRANE – Mary Salina, b 7 Oct 1858 lc/o James Drane & Margaret Rice bp 7 Nov 1858 spr William Dixon & Mary Rice p173

DREXELL – Edwin Celestine, b 11 May 1867 lc/o Herman C. Drexel & Theresa Mansted bp 30 May 1867 spr Mary Ann Reiler p414

DRISCOL – Fanny Barbara, b 9 Jun 1863 lc/o Richard Joseph Driscol & Elmira Youse bp 2 Aug 1863 spr Barbara Beltz p312

DRISCOLL – Cecilia, b 21 Sep 1857 lc/o Richard Joseph Driscoll & Ann Maria Yeonay bp 1 Nov 1857 spr Patrick Lynch & Mary McWilliam p139

DRISCOLL – Frances, b 14 Aug 1869 lc/o Richard Joseph Driscoll & E. Gonse bp 12 Sep 1869 spr Sarah Driscoll p483

DRISCOLL – Mark Vincent, b 20 Apr 1861 lc/o Richard J. Driscoll & May M. Yonse bp 13 May 1861 spr Barbara Belts p251

DRISCOLL – Richard Joseph, b 25 Jun 1859 c/o Richard Joseph Driscoll & Elmira M. Gouse J., "his lawful wife" bp 28 Nov 1859 spr Mary Beltz p206

DRISCOLL – Robert Emmet, b 2 Apr 1866 lc/o Richard Driscoll & Elmira Youse bp 24 Jun 1866 spr Barbara Beltz p386

DROHAN – Ann Maria, b 2 Oct 1863 lc/o David Drohan & Mary Roche bp 15 Nov 1863 spr Bernard McQuaid & Celeste Drohan p320

DROHAN – Charles Henry, b 6 Dec 1860 lc/o David Drohan & Mary A. Roche bp 6 Jan 1861 spr Mary Welsh p239

DROHAN – Florence Amelia, b 16 Sep 1859 lc/o David Drohan & Mary Roche bp 31 Oct 1859 spr Celestia Rohan p204

DROHAN – John Myers Beauregard, b 11 Apr 1862 lc/o David Drohan & Mary Roche bp 4 May 1862 spr Delia O'Brien p280

DROHAN – Mary Ann, b 18 Aug 1854 lc/o Thomas Drohan & Mary Mornet bp 18 Aug 1854 spr Mary Grier p20

DROHAN – Mary Ellen, b 2 Oct 1863 lc/o David Drohan & Mary Roche bp 15 Nov 1863 spr Thos. Drohan & Mary Welsh p320

DRONEY – Francis Patrick, b 8 Mar 1870 lc/o Martin Droney & Mary Dorsey bp 20 Mar 1870 spr Mary Ann Dorsey & John Francis Slane p497

DRUMMER – Mary Josephine, b 21 Mar 1833 lc/o Eran Drummer & Ann Deshield bp 10 Dec 1855 spr Martha Berry p67

DRUMMOND – John (c), "age about nineteen years" bp 14 Nov 1857 "baptized conditionally" H. B. Coskery, priest p140

DRURY – Mary Ann, b 3 Dec 1854 lc/o Saml. Drury & Catherine Kelly bp 24 Dec 1854 spr Jno. Kelly & Ellen Ginnity p32

DRYDEN – Blanch Edmonia, b 20 Mar 1865 lc/o Saml. J. Dryden & Rebecca Costello bp 30 Apr 1865 spr Julia Clancy p356

DRYDEN – Mary Ann Dryden, "age 15 years" bp 24 Jan 1870 spr Mary Ninny p492

DUANE – William Theodore, b 27 Jan 1867 lc/o John Duane & Cathrine Garvey bp 3 Feb 1867 spr Mich. S. Sullivan & Ann Garvey p405

DUBARRY – Clara Mary, b 21 Dec 1869 lc/o Ernest Dubarry & Kate Mullan bp 2 Jan 1870 spr Robert McCafferty & May A. Mullan p490

DUBOUR – Ellen Marie Emma, b 23 Dec 1869 lc/o John Dubour & Catharine Leach bp 16 Mar 1870 spr Marie Etoffe & Thos. Foley p496

DUCCEPHRIL – Mary Julia, b 23 Dec 1856 lc/o Patrick Joseph Duccephril & Sophia Moran bp 1 Feb 1857 spr Margaret L______ p109

DUDLEY – Alfonse (c), "about 18 months old" c/o Elizabeth Dudley (c) "of Washington City" bp 28 Jan 1855 spr Minty Williamson p35

DUERING – Eleanore, b 14 Mar 1858 lc/o George S. Duering & Catherine E. Richter bp 30 May 1858 spr Mary A. Richter p157

DUERING – Mary, b 3 Feb 1863 lc/o George S. Duering & Catharine E. Reiter "who died 15th inst." bp 23 Feb 1863 spr Theresa Drexel p302

DUFFY – Ann Elizabeth, b 5 Jun 1855 lc/o Hugh Duffy & Elizabeth _____ bp 10 Jun 1855 spr Hugh _____ & Margaret McElvey p49

DUFFY – Bernard, b 11 Jun 1855 lc/o James Duffy & Catherine Burrow bp 24 Jun 1855 spr Owen McAvey & Catherine Smith p50

DUFFY – Catherine, b 12 Apr 1856 lc/o Michael Duffy & Mary Farren bp 20 Apr 1856 spr James Duffy & Bridget Farren p80

DUFFY – George Francis, b 20 Dec 1861 lc/o James Duffy & Mary Clarken bp 29 Dec 1861 spr Bernard McGurk & Anne Smith p271

DUFFY – Herbert James, b 22 Dec 1854 lc/o James Duffy & Teresa Welch bp 2 Jan 1855 spr Francis Brorick & Mary Elroy p33

DUFFY – James, b 23 Mar 1860 lc/o James Duffy & Mary Clark bp 1 Apr 1860 spr Owen Finnigan & Margaret Farley p218

DUFFY – James Buchanan, b 10 Jan 1857 lc/o Michael Duffy & Elizabeth Marsh bp 17 Mar 1857 spr Maria Carr p114

DUFFY – John Thomas, b 10 Jul 1858 lc/o Bernard Duffy & Catherine O'Neal bp 18 Jul 1858 spr James Rial & Catherine Hardy p163

DUFFY – Margaret, b 10 May 1865 lc/o James Duffy & Mary Clarke bp 14 May 1865 spr John Clarke & Mary McMahon p356

DUFFY – Margaret Ann, b 28 Oct 1860 lc/o John Duffy & Mary O'Brien bp 4 Nov 1860 spr John McKay & Ann Haley p234

DUFFY – Mary Ann, b 15 Oct 1856 lc/o James Duffy & Catherine Berry bp 20 Oct 1856 spr Peter McCabe & Catherine McMahon p100

DUFFY – Mary Catherine, b 13 Feb 1856 lc/o Bernard Duffy & Catherine O'Neill bp 24 Feb 1856 spr John O'Neal & Cath. Duffy p73

DUFFY – William Edward, b 23 Oct 1856 lc/o Patrick Duffy & Teresa Welch bp 28 Oct 1856 spr Luke Quinn & Catherine Brovigan p100

DUGAN – Anna Maria, b 19 Aug 1866 lc/o Cumberland Dugan & Harriet Buchanan bp 8 Sep 1866 spr Thomas B. Dugan & Emily Dugan p395

DUGAN – Emma Chatard, b 22 Jun 1857 lc/o Cumberland Dugan & Harriet Buchanan bp 27 Jun 1857 spr Emily Josephine Warde p125

DUGAN – Ferdinand Chatard, b 18 Sep 1861 lc/o Cumberland F. Dugan & Harriet Buchanan bp 7 Oct 1861 spr Thomas "(proxy for) Ferdinand Chatard" & Mary Chatard p262

DUGAN – Francis Cumberland, b 8 Sep 1859 lc/o Cumberland F. Dugan & Harriet Buchanan bp 23 Sep 1859 spr John P. Van Bibber & Emily I. Dugan p200

DUGAN – Hammond Jones, b 17 Jun 1867 lc/o Hammond James Dugan & Lelia Mary Irvine bp 8 Jul 1867 spr Dr. James B. Read & Jane Mary Read p417

DUGAN – Harriet, b 6 Jun 1865 lc/o Cumberland Dugan & Harriet Buchanan bp 22 Jun 1865 spr Hammond Dugan & Sallie Kennedy p358

DUGAN – James Hammond, b 30 Mar 1864 lc/o Cumberland Dugan & Harriet Buchanan bp 11 Apr 1864 spr Pierre VanBibber "proxy for Laurence McCluskey" & Mary McCluskey p330

DUGAN – John Thomas, b 6 Nov 1867 lc/o Pierre Dugan & Agnes Matthias bp 19 Nov 1867 spr Thomas Foley & Emily Dugan p427

DUGAN – Louisa Shorb, b 3 Jan 1870 lc/o Pierre C. Dugan & Agnes Mathias bp 11 Jan 1870 spr Cumberland Dugan & Josie Mathias p491

DUGAN – Mary Agnes, b 21 Nov 1868 lc/o Pierre Dugan & Agnes Mathias bp 3 Dec 1868 spr Charles Roberts & Agnes Reppolier p459

DUGAN – Mary Coale, b 1 Nov 1862 lc/o Cumberland Dugan & Harriet Buchanan bp 17 Nov 1862 spr Kate Chatard & Pierre VanBibber p295

DUGAN – Mary Margaret, b 21 Aug 1856 lc/o John Dugan & Bridget Taylor bp 24 Aug 1856 spr Pat Kennedy & Mary Kennedy p93

DUGAN – Thomas Buchanan, b 22 Jul 1858 lc/o Cumberland F. Dugan & Harriet Buchanan bp 6 Aug 1858 spr Pierce Dugan & Josephine Van Bibber p165

DUGAN – William Kennedy, b 2 Aug 1860 lc/o Cumberland Dugan & Harriet Buchanan bp 16 Aug 1860 "baptized privately" "This child died on 20th Aug." Thos. Foley, priest p229

DUGGAN – Anna, b 22 Sep 1862 lc/o John Duggan & Bridget Taylor bp 24 Sep 1862 spr Bridget Duggan p290

DUGGAN – Edmund D., b 18 Aug 1857 lc/o William Duggan & Catherine Markham bp 21 Aug 1857 spr John McMahon & Mary McMahon p131

DUGGAN – Edward William, b 21 Jul 1858 lc/o John Duggan & Bridget Taylor bp 21 Jul 1858 spr Thos Kranan & Bridget Kranan p163

DUGGAN – Marcella, b 15 Jun 1860 lc/o John Duggan & Bridget Taylor bp 24 Jun 1860 spr Thos. McMahon & Catharine Whalan p225

DUGGAN – Margaret, b 5 Nov 1855 lc/o William Duggan & Catherine _____ bp 23 Dec 1855 spr Cath. _____ [*ed. note: faint record*] p69

DUKE – Ann Catharine, b 29 Oct 1861 lc/o Thomas Duke & Louisa Wolf bp 7 Feb 1867 spr Mary Wilkinson p405

DUKE – Catharine Sepple, b 5 Dec 1864 lc/o John Boone Duke & Maria Louisa Griffith bp 24 Apr 1865 spr Josephine Griffith p355

DUKE – Ella, b 14 Mar 1858 lc/o James Duke & Margaret Tracy bp 28 Mar 1858 spr Annie McDonald p152

DULANY – Frances Margaret Catharine, b 11 Dec 1859 c/o John Dulany & Eliza King, his wife bp 1 Jan 1860 spr John O'Brien & Mary Wade p210

DUNAN – Lewis Adolphus, b 10 Jul 1854 lc/o Lewis Dunan & Mary Jane Watson bp 27 Jul 1854 spr Ann Watson p18

DUNIGAN – James Aloysius, b 26 Jul 1858 lc/o James Dunigan & Mary Kin____ bp 17 Oct 1858 spr Obetha Colston p171

DUNN – Alice, b 14 Jul 1870 lc/o Michael Dunn & Alice Garvey bp 17 Jul 1870 spr James Garvey & Catharine MgGee p505

DUNN – Alice Jane, b 11 Jul 1858 lc/o Bernard Dunn & Mary Clark bp 21 Aug 1858 spr Mary A. McDermott p167

DUNN – Ellen, b 5 Oct 1854 c/o Patrick Dunn & Sophia Moreland bp 5 Nov 1854 spr Edw. Kernan & Mary Ann Barrow p28

DUNN – John, b 4 Jul 1870 lc/o Patk. Dunn & Bridget, "his wife" bp 17 Jul 1870 spr John Joseph Dunn & Mary Ann Dunn "I supplied the ceremonies." "This child had been baptized by Dr. Brewer, a Catholic." H. B. Coskery, priest p505

DUNN – John Henry, p 26 May 1856 lc/o Bernard Dunn & Mary C. Clark bp 22 Jun 1856 spr Thomas McDermot & Johanna Broderick p87

DUNN – John Nicholas, b 8 May 1858 lc/o Joseph Dunn & Mary Ann McMahon bp 21 May 1858 spr Bridget Hughes p156

DUNN – Margaret, b 10 Dec 1864 lc/o Michael Dunn & Alice Garvey bp 18 Dec 1864 spr Thomas Luby & Mary C. Garvey p347

DUNN – Mary Cath., b 9 Oct 1868 lc/o Michael Dunn & Alice Garvey bp 11 Oct 1868 spr Mary McShane & J_____ Epley p455

DUNN – Peter, b 14 Jan 1857 lc/o Peter Dunn & Ann Rooney bp 18 Jan 1857 spr Teresa Dunn & Mary <u>Butter</u> p108

DUNNE – Peter, b 9 Jul 1867 lc/o Patrick Dunne & Ellen Murray bp 21 Jul 1867 spr Joseph Dunne & Jane Preston p417

DUNNIGAN – Catharine Ellen, b 4 Oct 1860 lc/o Edward J. Dunnigan & Susan Fitzpatrick bp 2 Nov 1860 spr Anna Betts p234

DUNNING – Henrietta Dunning (c), "about 16 years of age" bp 16 Jul 1856 spr Susan Butler p90

DUNSON – Ann Elizabeth, b 1 Aug 1863 c/o Ann Dunson (c) bp 13 May 1864 spr Kate Lambert p332

DUNSON – Ann Miranda, b 17 Feb 1855 lc/o Bernard Dunson & Cornelia Richfield (all c) bp 28 Jul 1855 spr Mary Richfield p53

DUNSON – Ann Rebecca, "5 years old" lc/o Henry Dunson & Ann Maria Wilson (c) bp 22 Feb 1861 spr Minty Lecompte (c) p244

DUNSON – Bernard Forde, b 7 Jan 1854 lc/o Bernard Dunson & Cornelia Richfield (all c) bp 15 Aug 1854 spr Louisa Forde p20

DUNSON – Emma Mary, b 23 Nov 1859 lc/o Henry Dunson & Ann Wilson (c) bp 20 Jul 1860 spr Elizabeth Colbert p227

DUNSON – James Thomas, b 17 Apr 1856 lc/o Bernard Dunson & Cornelia Richfield (c) bp 22 Jul 1856 spr Mary Matthews "I supplied the ceremonies" "baptized by a priest" Thos. Foley, priest p91

DWYER – Caroline Catharine, b 12 Oct 1869 lc/o John Dwyer & Frederica, "his wife" bp 25 Nov 1869 spr Andrew & Catharine <u>Memoni</u> p488

DWYER – Giles, b 6 Sep 1868 lc/o Baker Dwyer & Rose Boleyn bp 23 Sep 1868 spr Joseph H. Boleyn & Rose Boleyn p454

DWYER – John Frederick, b 23 Jan 1866 lc/o John Dwyer & Frederica Wilt bp 17 Mar 1866 spr John Saurenwald & Ann Dwyer p378

DWYER – Leo Flavian, b 4 Jul 1867 lc/o John Dwyer & Frederica Wilt bp 1 Aug 1867 spr P. L. Dwyer & Mary A. Dwyer p418

DWYER – Mary Ann, b 22 Feb 1854 lc/o William Dwyer & Winfrid Connolly bp 5 Mar 1854 spr Patrick & Bridget Burns p7

DYER – Joseph, b 11 Nov 1868 lc/o Jermiah Dyer & Mary C. Mudd bp 24 Nov 1868 spr Joseph Blanford & Cecilia Blanford p458

DYER – Mark, b 27 Nov 1862 lc/o John Dyer & Margaret McDermott bp 8 Dec 1862 spr Mary A. Kilduff p297

EARHART – George Walter, b 22 Dec 1869 lc/o George Washington Earhart & Lucy Lepper bp 2 Feb 1870 spr Virginia Tolson p493

EARHART – Jenry Lee Sturms, b 2 Nov 1860 lc/o George Earhart & Elizabeth Leech bp 2 Jan 1861 spr Celestia Lepper p238

EARHART – Oliver Perry, b 23 Dec 1867 lc/o George Earhart & Lucy Lipper bp 13 Feb 1867 spr Appolonia Dobbin p434

EARLY – Ella Early "(born Morrell)", "aged 24" bp 2 Jul 1860 spr Emily Mactavish p225

EASTON – Charles Francis, b 18 Jan 1865 lc/o Jas. R. Easton & Catharine (Ryan) Easton bp 12 Feb 1865 spr Valentine Travers & Cath. McIntyre p350

ECKART – Mary Elizabeth, "aged 16 months" lc/o Wm. Eckert & Elizabeth Turner "non catholics" bp 4 Sep 1860 spr Susanna Jones p230

ECKERT – John Jefferson Davis, b 1 May 1861 lc/o William Peter Eckert & Elizabeth R. Turner bp 15 Aug 1861 spr William Jordan & Mary Delaney p258

EDMONDSTON – Mary Clare Frances Edmonston, "aged 16 years on Saturday" bp 28 Jul 1868 spr Mary Banon p449

EDWARDS – Amelia Edwards "(born Jones)", "age 24 years" bp 27 Nov 1854 "baptized conditionally" H. B. Coskery, priest p30

EDWARDS – Henrietta May, b 20 May 1870 lc/o John Richardson "of Philadelphia" & Frances Emma Dolphin "of Baltimore" bp 26 Sep 1870 spr Elizabeth J. Carver p511

EGAN – Daniel, b 18 Apr 1859 lc/o Patrick Egan & Bridget Gorick bp 7 Mary 1859 spr John Gorrick & Cath. McDermott p189

EGAN – Mary Ellen, b 4 Feb <u>1865</u> lc/o William J. Egan & Anna M. Walter bp 2 Jun 1867 spr Mary J. Egan p414

<u>EHRDMAN</u> – Mary Ann, b 2 Nov 1856 lc/o John <u>Ehrdman</u> & Sarah E. Bamberger bp 17 Dec 1856 spr Jane Staylor p105

EICHELBERGER – Laura, "six weeks old" lc/o William Eichelberger & Maria L. Burdick bp 10 Dec 1866 p401

EICHELBERGER – Virginia Burdick, "14 months old" lc/o William Eichelberger & Maria L. Burdick bp 17 Apr 1861 "baptized privately" Thos. Foley, priest p249

EICHELBERGER – William, b 17 May 1858 lc/o William Eichelberger & Maria L. Burdick bp 17 Apr 1861 "baptized privately" Thos. Foley, priest p249

EICKEAR – Catharine Theresa, b 2 Dec 1868 lc/o Henry M. Eickear & Mary A. Mansted bp 10 Dec 1868 spr Charles Drexel & Mary Drexel p460

ELBERT – Mary Elizabeth, b 8 Jan 1869 lc/o Frisby Elbert & Mary Bantrum (c) bp 14 Jan 1869 spr Theresa Bantrum p463

ELDER – Francis William, b 4 Mar 1867 lc/o Francis M. Elder & Matilda M. Wincherster bp 14 Mar 1867 p408

ELDER – Henry Stewart, b 11 Nov 1855 lc/o <u>Bart.</u> _____ Elder & Josephine M. Mitchell bp 22 Nov 1855 spr H. S. Coskery & Margaretta Elder [*ed. note: faint record*] p66

ELDER – Mary Carmelite, b 20 Apr 1859 lc/o Francis W. Elder & Matilda Deurig "(born Winchester)" bp 2 May 1859 spr Philip Laurenson Elder & Margeretta Elder, "the latter being proxy for Julia Winchester" "Basil S. Elder and lady, grandparents of the child wish to be noted that they were present in this baptism" p188

ELDRICH – Mary Alberta Claudinia Eldrich, b 7 Mar 1867 c/o Isabella Young bp 16 May 1867 spr Sophia Wilson p412

ELEAGH – Francis William, b 16 Jun 1856 lc/o John Eleagh & Catherine Bogue bp 3 Jul 1856 spr Ellen Smith "I supplied the ceremonies of baptism" – Jonth. McNally, priest p88

ELEECHE – John, b 9 Aug 1858 lc/o John Eleeche & Catharine Bogue bp 5 Sep 1858 spr John Moran & Ann Bogue p168

ELLECHE – Margaret, b 18 Sep 1854 lc/o John Elleche & Catherine Bogue bp 8 Oct 1854 spr John Moran & Ann Bogue p25

ELLERY – Martha, b 12 Nov 1854 lc/o Augustus Ellery & Mary Ellen McLaughlin bp 8 Nov 1857 spr Sylvester Kuhn, E. Louisa Kuhn & Philip McLaughlin p140

ELLERY – William, b 15 May 1855 lc/o Augustus Ellery & Mary Ellen McLaughlin bp 8 Nov 1857 spr Sylvester Kuhn, E. Louisa Kuhn & Philip McLaughlin p140

EMERICK – Caroline Elizabeth, b 1 Oct 1860 lc/o William Emerick & Catharine Lambden bp 23 Apr 1861 spr Caroline Lambden p249

EMORY – Alice, b 11 Jan 1867 lc/o Wm. Emory & Agnes Leonard bp 14 Feb 1867 spr Ann Casey p406

EMORY – Alice Vernon, b 25 Feb 1864 lc/o Ambrose Marechal Emory & Mary Jane Tilyard bp 10 Mar 1864 spr John B. Piet & Mary Piet p328

EMORY – Ambrose Marechal, b 4 Mar 1867 lc/o Ambrose M. Emory & Mary Jane Tilyard bp 2 Apr 1867 spr Jerome Walter & Anne Jamison p409

EMORY – Cecilia Florence, b 17 Oct 1864 lc/o William Emory & Agnes Leonard bp 24 Nov 1864 spr John Leonard & Ellie Leonard p345

EMORY – Georginna (c), b 22 Sep 1855 c/o Frances Emory (c) bp 24 Mar 1856 spr Ann Sougande p77

EMORY – Mary Gertrude Elizabeth, b 23 Feb 1862 lc/o Ambrose Marechal Emory & Mary Jane Tilyaid bp 12 Mar 1862 spr Thos. Foley & Anna M. Emory p276

ENEY – Joseph R. Eney, "aged 22 years" bp 14 Mar 1867 "baptized conditionally" Thos. Foley, priest p408

ENNIS – Ellen Rebecca, b 12 Dec 1860 lc/o Michael Ennis & Ellen McManus bp 20 Jan 1861 spr Peter Callahan & Honora Rudge p240

ENNIS – Harriet Ennis, "aged 50 years" bp 11 Sep 1863 "baptized conditionally" Thos. Foley, priest p314

ENNIS – Ida Matilda, b 12 Apr 1839 lc/o James Ennis & Matilda Turner bp 20 Jan 1860 "baptized conditionally" Thos. Foley, priest p211

ENNIS – James Thomas, b 27 Aug 1857 lc/o Thomas Ennis & Harriet Hart bp 31 Mar 1858 spr Elizabeth O'Brien p152

ENNIS – Sarah Catharine Ennis, "aged 22 years" bp 30 Sep 1864 "baptized conditionally" Thos. Foley, priest p341

ENNIS – Thomas, "aged 53" bp 26 Mar 1865 registry date: 20 Mar 1865 "received his profession of faith" "baptized previously by a preacher" Thos. Foley, priest p354

ENNIS – Thomas Henry, b 11 Jul 1870 lc/o Thomas H. Ennis & Virginia Nevitt bp 12 Aug 1870 spr Lydia A. Ennis p506

EPLEY – George Alpher, b 5 Sep 1869 lc/o John A. Epley & Margaret Holland bp 21 Nov 1869 spr Geo. W. Quinn & Mary McGowan p488

EPPLEY – John A. Eppley, "aged 26 years" bp 30 Jan 1867 "baptized conditionally" Thos. Foley, priest p404

ESCHBACH – Ida Virginia, b 16 Aug 1866 lc/o Louis A. Eschbach & Clementine Courtois bp 28 Aug 1866 spr Margaret Eschbach p393

ESCHBACH – Lee Buchanan, b 2 Mar 1857 lc/o Frederick Eschbach & Rebecca Lipton bp 25 Mar 1857 spr Francis Eschbach & Margaret Eschbach p116

ESTEP – Mary Estep, "aged about 18 years" bp 3 Jul 1867 spr Mary Behan & Mrs. Middleton "baptized conditionally" Jas. Gibbons, priest p416

EVANS – William Augustine, b 13 Feb 1863 lc/o John Evans & Mary Jane Joy bp 8 Mar 1863 spr John T. & Mary Ann Darling p303

EVATTS – George Columbus, b 13 Apr 1868 lc/o Geo. Evatts & Elizabeth McCoffee bp 10 May 1868 spr Catharine Gleason p441

EVERSON – Mary Ann, b 6 May 1858 lc/o John Everson & Ann Lennish bp 22 Jul 1858 spr James Hagan & Bridget Everson p164

EYANSON – Caroline, b 25 Sep 1861 lc/o John E. Eyanson & Annie Knipse bp 20 Dec 1861 spr Rosalie Knipse p270

EYANSON – John Edward, b 16 May 1864 lc/o John E. Eyanson & Anna C. Knipse bp 13 Jun 1864 spr Mary Dunnigan p334

EYCKELBERGER – Anna Mary, b 13 May 1855 lc/o _____ B. Night & Maria Louisa Eyckelberger bp 13 May 1855 spr Jno. McNally & Laura Eyckelberger p46

EYENSON – Elizabeth, b 16 Sep 1866 lc/o John E. Eyenson & Anne C. Kniepe bp 8 Oct 1866 spr Obetha Colston p397

FAGAN – Ann, b 23 Aug 1854 lc/o Patk. Fagan & Jane Campbell bp 27 Aug 1854 spr Matthew & Ann Fagan p22

FAHEY – John, b 20 Mar 1857 lc/o Patrick Fahey & Mary Fitzpatrick bp 29 Mar 1857 spr Peter Fitzpatrick & Winifred Hardwin p116

FAHEY – Mary Catharine, b 24 Apr 1861 lc/o Patrick Fahey & Susan Murphy bp 4 May 1861 spr Catharine Barrowitz p250

FAHEY – Patrick, b 21 Oct 1856 lc/o Thomas Fahey & Winifred Cartey bp 26 Oct 1856 spr Patk. Liam & Ellen Cartey p100

FAHEY – William, b 14 Aug 1855 lc/o James Fahey & Catherine Burch bp 26 Aug 1855 spr Timothy Fahey & Catherine Mullan p56

FALLON – Charles Edward, b 8 Mar 1870 lc/o John Fallon & Josephine Lillenthal bp 16 May 1870 spr Martha McNally p501

FALLON – Daniel, b 15 Aug 1861 lc/o John Fallon & Bridget Gavagan bp 25 Aug 1861 spr Dennis Donvan & Mary Clark p259

FALLOW – John William, b 17 Nov 1867 lc/o John C. Fallon & Josephine Lilienthal bp 4 Dec 1867 spr Ann Fallon p428

FARLEY – Edward, b 28 Jul 1856 lc/o Patrick Farley & Catherine Donovan bp 15 Aug 1856 spr James & Jane Farley p92

FARLEY – Ida Elizabeth, b 3 Jul 1859 lc/o Matthew Farley & Ida Harman bp 14 Aug 1859 spr John Smith & Cath. Ann Riley p197

FARLEY – James, b 9 Mar 1855 lc/o Patrick Farley & Catherine Dunnace bp 5 Apr 1855 spr John McKahace & Bridge Dunnace p42

FARLEY – James Edward, b 4 Sep 1859 lc/o Edward Farley & Catharine Ward bp 12 Sep 1859 spr Martha Williams p200

FARLEY – Jane, b 1 Jan 1854 lc/o Patrick Farley & Catherine Donovan bp 8 Jan 1854 spr Edw. Farley & A____ Danaho p2

FARLEY – John, b 16 May 1858 lc/o Patrick Farley & Catherine Donovan bp 31 May 1858 spr Bernard Donoghue & Margaret Donelley p157

FARMER – Catherine, b 8 Oct 1844 lc/o Frances Farmer & Rosarina Keelgar bp 20 Jun 1854 spr Eliz Ryan "I supplied the ceremonies of baptism. Privately baptized." Thos. Foley, priest p15

FARMER – George Edward, b 2 Feb 1854 lc/o John Farmer & Ellen Newman bp 2 Apr 1854 spr Ann Harman p9

FARREL – William, b 29 Oct 1855 lc/o John Farrel & Ellen Noan bp 18 Nov 1855 spr Michael Welsh & Ellen Homes p65

FARRELL – James, b 17 Aug 1857 lc/o Patk. Farrell & Mary Aitken bp 20 Sep 1857 spr Patk. Hacket & Ellen Murray p135

FARRELL – John Thomas, b 20 Mar 1858 lc/o Jeremiah Farrell & Mary McDermott bp 4 Apr 1858 spr John McDermott & Mary Castell p153

FARRELL – Matthew, b 28 Mar 1867 lc/o Thomas Farrell & Anna Crosby bp 7 Apr 1867 spr Thomas Callan & Christina Crosby p410

FARRELL – Michael, b 4 Jul 1856 lc/o Bartol Farrell & Margaret Larner bp 6 Jul 1856 spr John McLaughlin & Bridget Larner p89

FARRELL – Michael, b 24 Dec 1857 lc/o John Farrell & Sarah Ellen Gibbons bp 21 Feb 1858 spr Michael Kelly & Ellen Kelly p149

FAYSET – Marie Anise, b 9 Nov 1856 lc/o Francis Fayset & Lucille Goulland bp 6 Dec 1857 spr Francis Lagsane & Anise Fayset "baptized privately by Rev. Irvin McNally, Thos. Foley, priest p143

FAYSET – Marie Victorine Lucy, b 16 Feb 1859 lc/o Francis Fayset & Lucy Gouliard bp 17 Apr 1859 spr Victor Devouyes & Victorine Beufils p187

FEENAN – Catherine, b 10 Sep 1854 lc/o Patk. Feenan & Margaret Kelley bp 13 Sep 1854 spr John Flaherty & Cath. Kelly "proxy for Bridget Kelley" p23

FEINOUR –Georgiana Ombla "(alias)", b *ndg* "(Episcop.)" bp 3 Dec 1857 "after abjuration in presence of Mary Doherty" Francis Patrick Kennote Archb. p143

FENNELLY – George Washington, b 13 Apr 1860 lc/o Simon Fennelly & Mary Ann Hackett bp 25 Jun 1860 spr Richard Fenelly & Catharine Fennelly p225

FENTON – Mary Catharine, b 8 Aug 1861 lc/o Thomas I. E. Fenton & Mary McFarland bp 18 Aug 1861 spr Dan. A. Fenton & Rosanne Mulligan p258

FERCIOT – Emily Pauline, "aged 23 years" lc/o Pierre Ferciot & Sophie Schaeffer bp 19 Mar 1866 spr Joseph Paini & Charlotte Etoffe p378

FERGUSON – Adolph Mallory, b 25 Oct 1851 lc/o Thomas Jefferson Ferguson & Rosalinda Corcoran bp 16 Sep 1866 p396

FERRARI – Emily Ferrari, "aged about 13 years" "a slave of Dr. Robert Tubman" bp 8 Aug 1859 spr Mary Tubman p197

FERRETTI – Anthony Andrew, b 17 Jan 1860 c/o John Ferretti & Giacinta Rattagliate, "his lawful wife" bp 17 Jan 1860 spr Anthony Rattagliate & Margaret Capellini p 211

FERRON – Joseph, b 4 Jun 1854 lc/o Michael Ferron & Bridget Ward bp 18 Jun 1854 spr Michl. Hendley & Mary Ward p14

FETHERALL – James, b 11 May 1854 lc/o David Fetherall & Sarah Bradley bp 21 May 1854 spr James Cain & Cath. Cain p12

FIELDS – Benedict, b 6 May 1861 nc/o George Fields & Ellen Carroll bp 13 Apr 1861 spr Caroline Hardey (all c) p248 [*ed note: last name is either Fields or Carroll in record*] p248

FIELDS – Edward, b 27 Apr 1870 lc/o John Fields & Mary Joice bp 1 May 1870 spr James McGerney & Cath. Joice p500

FIELDS – Martha Fields, "aged about 21 years" bp 28 Feb 1859 spr Wm. Ginnity "baptized conditionally" H. B. Coskery, priest p183

FIELDS – Peter, b 24 Apr 1870 lc/o John Fields & Mary Joice bp 1 May 1870 spr Patrick McGerney p500

FINDER – Laura Jane, b 6 Jan 1856 lc/o Frederick Finder & Jane Roach bp 30 Apr 1850 spr Thomas Walsh & Elizabeth C. Romis p81

FINK – Charles Aloysius, b 8 Aug 1861 lc/o Henry S. Fink & Rosanna McSherry bp 15 Aug 1861 spr Charles Henisler & Elizabeth Henisler p258

FINK – Clotildis Catharine, b 9 May 1859 lc/o Henry Sylvester Fink & Rosanna McSherry bp 22 May 1859 spr John A. McSherry & Clementine McSherry p190

FINK – Helen Virginia, b 21 Sep 1863 lc/o Henry S. Fink & Rosie A. McSherry bp 1 Oct 1863 spr Wm. A. McSherry & Mary V. McSherry p316

FINK – Lewis Joseph, b 13 Feb 1870 lc/o Henry S. Fink & Rose A. McSherry bp 16 Feb 1870 spr Lewis Sneeringer & Mary Sneeringer p494

FINK – Rosa Eugenia, b 3 Jan 1868 lc/o Henry Sylvester Fink & Rosa McSherry bp 16 Jan 1868 spr William Bartlett & Mary Fink p432

FINK – Thomas Sylvester, b 13 Dec 1865 lc/o Henry Sylvester Fink & Rose A. McSherry bp 27 Dec 1865 spr Thos. Foley & Julia Spies p372

FINKE – James Keyser, b 20 Feb 1857 lc/o Martin Finke & Elizabeth Keyser bp 25 Apr 1857 spr Wm. Robertson & Mary White p118

FINLEY – Agnes, b 15 Jan 1865 lc/o John Finley & Mary McDonough bp 2 Feb 1865 spr Mark Tully & Catharine Lawn p349

FINLEY – Catherine Gsegoia, b 28 Nov 1856 lc/o John Finley & Catherine Simmons bp 14 Dec 1856 spr Michael Mackin & Mary A. Simmons p104

FINLEY – James Joseph, b 12 Apr 1858 lc/o James J. Finley & Mary Quigley bp 4 May 1858 spr John Starkey & Catherine Finley p155

FINLEY – Julia, b 23 Jan 1867 lc/o John Finley & Mary "(McDonough)" Blundell bp 7 Feb 1867 spr Malachi Blundell & Ellen Lachesi p405

FINLEY – Sarah Augusta, b 16 Oct 1856 lc/o James I. Finley & Mary Ellen Quigley bp 20 Nov 1856 spr Thomas McCann & Rose Dolan p101

FINLEY – Thomas Francis, b 24 Dec 1858 lc/o John Finley & Catharine Simmons bp 9 Jan 1859 spr Charles N. Simmons & Catharine Harnay p178

FINLEY – Virginia Black, b 11 Dec 1868 lc/o James Finley & Mary Blundell bp 30 Dec 1868 spr John F. McNarrie & Mary Finley p461

FINN – Alexander, b 18 Nov 1856 lc/o John Finn & Catherine Cecilia Finn bp 7 Dec 1856 spr Alexander Bradley & Rose Cummings p103

FINN – Catherine Cecilia, b 29 Jan 1855 lc/o John Finn & Catherine C. Bradley bp 18 Mar 1855 spr Henry McGowan & Jane Cain p40

FINN – Hugh Bartholomew, b 13 Jan 1858 lc/o John Finn & Catherine Bradley bp 7 Feb 1858 spr George McGowan & Margaret Ann Martin p148

FINN – Maurice, b 18 Sep 1858 lc/o Thomas Finn & Margaret Stack bp 26 Sep 1858 spr John Stack & Mary Feeley p169

FINN – Thomas, b 27 Jul 1860 lc/o Thos. Finn & Margaret Stack bp 5 Aug 1860 spr Michl. McEnright & Mary Lynch p228

FINNALL – James Henry Finnall (c), "born in 1851 in Vicksburg, Miss" lc/o William Finnall, "name of mother unknown" bp 24 Feb 1857 spr Emily Goldsburg p112

FINNEGAN – Catharine, b 29 May 1861 lc/o William Finnegan & Ellen, "his wife" bp 9 Jun 1861 spr Wm. Keenan & Ann McGee p253

FINNELLY – Ellen Ross, b 27 Jan 1864 lc/o William Finnelly & Anne McSweeney bp 31 Jan 1864 spr John & Jane McSweeney p325

<u>FINNERAN</u> – Edward, b 5 Jul 1855 lc/o Patrick <u>Finneran</u> & Mary O'Neal bp 15 Jul 1855 spr Jas. Burns & Ann Guirk p52

<u>FINNIAN</u> – John Michael, b 27 Jul 1857 lc/o Patrick <u>Finnian</u> & Mary O'Neal bp 15 Aug 1857 spr John Farrell & Margaret Gallagher p130

FINNIAN – Mary Alice, b 31 Mar 1857 lc/o Bernard Finnian & Margaret McNichol bp 12 Apr 1857 spr Wm. H. Maguire & Bridget McNichol p117

FINNIGAN – James Emory, b 8 Feb 1869 lc/o Arthur Finnigan & Ann Triplett bp 18 Jun 1869 spr John Finnigan & Mary Finnigan p474

FIRMIN – Mary Ann, b 11 Dec 1859 lc/o William Firmin & Mary Ann Kelly bp 14 Dec 1860 spr Elizabeth Colbert p237

FISHER – Ann, b 5 Jul 1857 lc/o Molineux Fisher & Bessie Carney bp 11 Aug 1857 spr Julia Quinn p130

FISHER – John, b 18 Oct 1859 lc/o Mollineux Fisher & Elizabeth Kearny bp 24 Dec 1859 spr Mary Mooney p209

FISHER – Mary Jane, b 1 May 1840 lc/o John Fisher & Agnes Kelly bp 6 May 1860 "baptized conditionally" Thos. Foley, priest p221

FISHER – Walter Adam Forney, b 8 Feb 1846 lc/o Adam Fisher & Mary Jane Rollins bp 26 Dec 1856 spr Mary A. <u>Gain</u> p105

FISHER – William, b 31 Jan 1862 lc/o Molinix Fisher & Lizzie Carney bp 12 Apr 1862 spr Jane McConnell p278

FITZER – Rose Mary, b 21 Aug 1855 lc/o Edw. Fitzer & Ellen McNorton bp 1 Sep 1856 spr Nich. Quirk & Mary J. Rudolph p94

FITZGERALD – Margaret, b 25 Aug 1858 lc/o David Fitzgerald & Annie Cotter bp 19 Sep 1858 spr Nicholas Cotter & Ellen Broderick p169

FITZMAURICE – Francis Patrick, b 29 Aug 1859 lc/o William Fitzmaurice & Anne Bell bp 3 Sep 1859 spr Wm. Coghlan & Alice Coghlan p199

FITZMYER – John Henry, b 2 Apr 1859 lc/o John Fitzmyer & Catharine Murphy bp 25 Apr 1859 spr John McNally & Ellen Miller p188

FITZPATRICK – Eliza, b 10 Jun 1855 lc/o Thomas Fitzpatrick & Bridget Connolly bp 5 Jul 1855 spr Thomas Ford & Maria Sheets p51

FITZPATRICK – Ellen, b 12 Jun 1868 lc/o Philip Fitzpatrick & Catharine Divine bp 30 Jun 1868 spr Charles Divin & Mary Ann McCarnbley p447

FITZPATRICK – James, b 3 Oct 1856 lc/o Owen Fitzpatrick & Mary Ryan bp 21 Jan 1860 spr Cecilia Barry "I supplied the ceremonies…and baptized privately by me" Thos. Foley, priest p212

FITZPATRICK – Michael Edward, b 7 Aug 1864 lc/o Michael Edw. Fitzpatrick & Mary Murphy bp 21 Aug 1864 spr Michael Cooney & Mary Barman p338

FITZPATRICK – Rose, b 12 Feb 1860 lc/o Owen Fitzpatrick "since killed in Cuba" & Mary Ryan bp 2 Mar 1860 spr Bridget McPoland p216

FITZPATRICK – Terence Edward, b 10 Jul 1859 lc/o Hugh Fitzpatrick & Bridget Riley bp 24 Jul 1859 spr John Hutheria Fitzpatrick p196

FLAHERTY – Mary, b 21 Jan 1855 lc/o Patrick Flaherty & Bridget Burn bp 22 Jan 1855 spr Valentine Mannion & Theresa Mahony p35

FLAMM – Elizabeth Stella, "six weeks old" lc/o George Flamm & Mary A. Carroll bp 25 Mar 1866 spr Jos. A. Prevost & Mary Carroll p379

FLANAGAN – Denis, b 27 Mar 1868 lc/o James Flanagan & Esther Flanagan bp 5 Apr 1868 spr Frank Flanigan & Mary J. Flanigan p438

FLANAGAN – Ellen Jane, b 6 Oct 1865 lc/o James Flanagan & Esther Flanagan bp 15 Oct 1865 spr Denis Flanagan & Rose Boyd p367

FLANNIGAN – Catharine, b 14 Dec 1862 lc/o James Flannigan & Esther Flannigan bp 21 Dec 1862 spr Patk. Flannigan & Mary Gillooly p298

FLANNIGAN – Cecilia, b 30 Sep 1857 lc/o James Flannigan & Esther Flannigan bp 11 Oct 1857 spr Thomas Gilchrist & Ann Gilluly p137

FLANNIGAN – Francis, b 22 May 1860 lc/o James Flannigan & Esther Flannigan bp 3 Jun 1860 spr James Gilchrist & Bridget Closkey p223

FLANNIGAN – James, b 28 Jul 1854 lc/o James Flannigan & Esther Flannigan bp 20 Jul 1854 spr Pat. Gallonay & Ann Gilenist p18

FLANNIGAN – Mary Ann, b 7 Dec 1855 lc/o James Flannigan & Esther Flannigan bp 9 Dec 1855 spr Pat. Flannigan Genily p67

FLANNIGAN – Thomas, b 19 Sep 1856 lc/o James Flannigan & Sarah Reap bp 28 Sep 1856 spr Hugh Riley & Mary Riley p97

FLEDDERMAN – Charles Lewis, b 28 Jul 1864 lc/o Henry J. Fledderman & Catharine Stoltz bp 22 Aug 1864 spr Wilhelmina Fledderman p339

FLEDDERMAN – James Henry, b 20 Jan 1861 lc/o Henry G. Fledderman & Catharine Stolpp bp 3 Feb 1861 spr John H. Fredderman & Elizabeth Fledderman p242

FLEDDERMAN – Joseph Alan, b 22 Mar 1868 lc/o H. G. Fledderman & C. S. Stalpp bp 12 May 1868 spr Joseph A. Kuhn & Mary B. Maker p442

FLEDDERMANN – Catharine Augusta Fleddermann, "aged about 26 years" bp 30 Mar 1867 spr Mary Grady p409

FLEDDERMANN – John Bernhardt, b 23 Jun 1862 lc/o Henry Gerhardt Fleddermann & Catharine Stalp bp 7 Jul 1862 spr John Gerhardt & Elizabeth Fleddermann p285

FLEETWOOD – Robert Francis Assisiam, b 8 May 1860 lc/o Avenick Fleetwood & Zachariah Jefferson (c) bp 6 Jan 1869 spr Wm. A. Wylliams & Bridget Callahan p462

FLETTERMAN – Gerhard Eugene, b 29 Jan 1870 lc/o Gerhard Fletterman & Kate Starr bp 15 Mar 1870 spr Gerhard Rheinig & Maggie Fletterman p496

FLYNN – Bernard, b 9 Dec 1855 lc/o David Flynn & Catharine McDonald bp 16 Dec 1855 spr John Goarman & Ann M. Connell p68

FLYNN – Eleanora, b 8 Nov 1864 lc/o Michael Flynn & Mary Clarke bp 13 Nov 1864 spr Martin & Ellen Clarke p345

FLYNN – James, b 24 Apr 1857 lc/o James Flynn & Catherine Flannigan bp 10 May 1857 spr Peter Reilly & Susan Plega______ p119

FLYNN – Mary, b 19 May 1860 lc/o Maurice Flynn & Margaret Dillon bp 27 May 1860 spr Mary Dunford [*ed. note: this person was not listed in the Register index of baptisms*] p222

FLYNN – William Francis, b 28 May 1860 lc/o Thomas Flynn & Catharine Flannigan bp 1 Jun 1860 spr Margaret Flynn p223

FOLEY – Ann, b 5 Jan 1859 lc/o Michael Foley & Mary Donohue bp 9 Jan 1859 spr Patrick Ward & Catharine Moore p179

FOLEY – Annie Marie, b 29 Sep 1855 lc/o Daniel J. Foley & Annie M. Sanders bp 9 Oct 1855 spr Thomas Foley & Maria Sanders p61

FOLEY – Bernard Foley, b 8 Dec 1858 lc/o John Foley & Mary Dunn bp 30 Jan 1859 spr Bernard Dunn & Ann Foley p180

FOLEY – Catharine, b 29 Mar 1870 lc/o Michael Foley & Mary Flaherty bp 3 Apr 1870 spr Dennis Flannigan & Mary Jane Gallagher p498

FOLEY – Henry, b 24 Jul 1868 lc/o Michael Foley & Mary Donehoe bp 28 Jul 1868 spr Rose Gallagher p449

FOLEY – John Thomas, b 14 Sep 1864 lc/o Matthew J. Foley & Mary W. A. Roper bp 17 Sep 1864 spr Ruth S. Foley "proxy for Francis Merceret" & Mary Foley p340

FOLEY – Julia, b 2 Jan 1861 lc/o Matthew I. Foley & Mary W. A. Roper bp 7 Jan 1861 spr Daniel I. Foley & Annie M. Foley p239

FOLEY – Louis Roper, b 25 Aug 1862 lc/o Matthew I. Foley & Mary N. A. Roper bp 28 Aug 1862 spr Rev. John S. Foley & Jeanette Roper p288

FOLEY – Mary, b 21 Nov 1856 lc/o Keon Foley & Margaret Falin bp 28 Nov 1856 spr Michael McAvey & Mary Ann Hogan p102

FOLEY – Mary, b 13 Dec 1857 lc/o Michael Foley & Mary Donehoe bp 20 Dec 1857 spr Arthur Kilduff & Ann Donet p144

FOLEY – Mary Dolores b 22 Sep 1867 lc/o Matthew J. Foley & Mary Rosser bp 24 Sep 1867 spr Ambrose A. White & Mary Hazzard p422

FOLEY – Mary Elizabeth, b 27 Mar 1859 lc/o Matthew Foley & Mary __ Roper bp 31 Mar 1859 spr Thomas Foley & Mary White p185

FOLEY – Mary Isabella, b 18 Jun 1869 lc/o Matthew J. Foley & Mary M. J. Roper bp 21 Jun 1869 spr Thomas Foley & Bessie Foley p475

FOLEY – Rebecca, b *ndg* Jul 1850 lc/o Jacob Foley "of Baltimore" & Maria "of the same place" bp 29 Oct 1870 spr Margaret O'Brien "baptized *sub cer*" John Dougherty, priest p513

FOLEY – Thomas, b 20 May 1857 lc/o Daniel I. Foley & Anne M. Sanders bp 28 May 1857 spr Matthew I. Foley & Josephine Sanders p121

FOPIANO – Mary Elizabeth, b 21 Mar 1858 c/o Francis Fopiano & Mary Cielo, "his wife" bp 27 Mar 1858 spr Vincent Araldo & Marion Elizabeth Cielo p152

FORD – Eliza Jane, b 12 Nov 1866 lc/o John Ford & Mary Connolly bp 25 Nov 1866 spr Patrick Byrne & Emily A. Farmer p399

FORD – John Francis, b 26 *nmg* 1854 lc/o Robert Ford & Mary Donnelly bp 13 Aug 1854 spr _____ Donnelly p20

FORD – John Henry, b 27 Oct 1870 "of County Roscommon, Ireland" & Mary Connolly "of County Louth, Ireland" bp 27 Oct 1870 spr Patrick J. Connolly & Emma Rotte p515

FORD – Mary Catharine, b 23 Nov 1866 lc/o John Ford & Rose Miles bp 30 Nov 1866 spr Elizabeth Miles p400

FORD – William Thomas, b 20 Jun 1869 lc/o John Ford & Mary Connolly bp 18 Jul 1869 spr Tho. Burns & Ellen Carroll p477

FORRESTER – Mary, b 3 Jul 1863 lc/o Robert Forrester & Margaret McCoy bp 12 Jul 1863 spr K. J. Kerwick & Elizabeth Aiking p310

FOSTER – Mary Ella Foster, b *ndg* c/o William Foster & Amellia Keller "not his wife" bp 6 Jan 1869 spr Cecilia Miller p462

FOUNTAIN – Florence, b 11 Jul 1867 lc/o Mercer Fountain & Ann bp 10 Jan 1869 spr Patrick Consedine & Delia Kelly p463

FOUSSÉ – Geneviève Marie Rose, b 20 Sep 1867 lc/o Fréderic Foussé & Céline Geneviève Marie de Sacy "both parents natives of Paris, France" bp 22 Sep 1867 spr Louis Ernest Lacoulare, "proxy for Ustuzade Samuel Silvestre de Sacy" & Honorie Rose Foussé p422

FOWLER – Fanny Fowler, "age about 19 years" bp 8 Dec 1856 spr H. B. Coskery "baptized conditionally" H. B. Coskery, priest p104

FOWLER – Francis Martin Fowler, b 30 Sep 1849 lc/o Francis P. & Matilda C. Fowler bp 14 Feb 1865 "baptized conditionally" Thos. Foley, priest p350

FOX – Ann, b 11 Aug 1869 lc/o Thomas Fox & Catharine Murray bp 15 Aug 1869 spr Lutte Carney & Josephine Trainor p480

FOX – Elizabeth, b 12 Nov 1867 c/o Elizabeth S. Fox bp 2 Dec 1867 p428

FOX – Isabel, b 17 Jul 1861 lc/o Thomas Fox & Catharine Murray bp 21 Jul 1861 spr James & Mary Fox p257

FOX – John Aloysius, b 6 Apr 1860 lc/o Peter Fox & Ellen Roche bp 15 Jul 1860 spr Mary Fleishell p226

FOX- Mary Ann, b 23 Dec 1853 lc/o Patrick Fox & Ann Smith bp 1 Jan 1854 spr Hugh & Mary Fox p1

FOX – Mary Catharine, b 16 Dec 1863 lc/o Thomas Fox & Catharine Morris bp 20 Dec 1863 spr Wm. Doyle & Mary E. Wallis p322

FOX – Mary Cornelia Carr, b 22 Mar 1870 lc/o Wm. T. Fox & Ella Carr bp 19 May 1870 spr Christopher Columbus Shriver p501

FOX – Thomas James, b 29 Aug 1866 lc/o Thomas Fox & Catharine Murray bp 2 Sep 1866 spr John Murray & Jane Myers p394

FOY – Ellen Euphemia Mulvey, b 16 Sep 1859 lc/o Philip Charles Foy & Sarah Jane Aburn bp 24 Sep 1859 spr Elizabeth Gurnby p201

FOY – Laura, b 2 Apr 1854 lc/o Philip C. H. Foy & Sarah J. L. Aburn bp 28 Mary 1854 spr Eleanor Foy p13

FOY – Margaret, b 18 Feb 1858 lc/o P. Charles H. Foy & Sarah Jane F. Aburn bp 24 Feb 1858 spr Eleanora Foy p149

FOY – Philip Charles Henry, b 25 Dec 1855 lc/o Philip C. H. Foy & Sarah J. Aburn bp 31 Dec 1855 spr Eleanor Foy p69

FOY – Susanna Theresa, b 16 Oct 1860 lc/o Philip Charles H. Foy & Sarah I. Abarn bp 29 Oct 1860 spr Eleanora Foy p234

FRANKLIN – Elizabeth Franklin, "about five months old" "a foundling left on the steps of the Maryland Club House. She was taken to St. Vincent's Infant Asylum by Policeman Eckert" bp 19 Jul 1860 spr Ann McNally, Thos. Foley, priest p227

FRANKLIN – John Franklin, "aged 60 years" bp 28 Apr 1867 "baptized conditionally" Thos. Foley, priest p411

FREEBURGER – Mary Elizabeth, b 20 Sep 1857 lc/o Francis Freeburger & Julia Spriggs bp 7 Oct 1857 spr Eliza Dunn p 137

FREELAND – Ruth Ann Freeland (c), "aged 19 years" bp 27 Jun 1864 spr Mary Ellen Herbert (c) "baptized conditionally" H. B. Coskery, priest p335

FREGE – Margaret Jane Renno, b 8 Feb 1862 lc/o Frederick Frege & Mary Ann Roden bp 4 Jul 1862 spr James Garby & Jane McCann p284

FRENCH – Mary Louisa French, "aged 23 years" bp 22 Sep 1868 spr Elizabeth Butler p454

FRISBY – David, "four months old" c/o David Frisby & Eleanor Boulder (c) bp 26 Apr 1861 spr Lizzie Colbert [*ed. note: last name is listed both as Frisby or Boulder in record*] p249

FUCHS – Marie Maurice Pierre Guido Robert, b 18 Jan 1868 lc/o Guido Fuchs & Marie Terise Blanche Verdier bp 3 May 1868 spr Charles Hilgenberg & Joanna Hilgenberg p440

FULLINGER – Anton Gunter, b 16 May 1869 lc/o John M. Fullinger & Cath. A. Smith bp 7 Jun 1869 spr Elizabeth Boden & Wm. Fullinger p473

FULTON – John William, "about 28 years old" lc/o John Fulton & Margaret Griffin bp 28 Nov 1858 spr Jno. Mullan p175

FULTON – Mary Ann, b 20 Dec 1859 c/o John Fulton & Susan McKeever, "his wife" bp 1 Jan 1860 spr Bernard Green & Isabella McMullan p209

FULTON – Robert, b 23 Jan 1861 lc/o John Fulton & Susan McKeever bp 24 Feb 1861 spr Robert Fulton & Rose Maguire p245

FURLONG – James, b 23 Jul 1859 lc/o William Furlong & Cath. Doyle bp 18 Jul 1859 spr Elleanora Ahern p196

GAFFNEY – Patrick, b 24 Apr 1857 lc/o James Gaffney & Elizabeth Reynolds bp 25 Apr 1857 spr Mary Reynolds p117

GAHAN – Florence Agnes, b 3 Oct 1870 lc/o Patrick Gahan "of Baltimore" & Mary Niven "of the same place" bp 20 Oct 1870 spr Daniel Carty & Mary J. Hogan p514

GAHAN – Marian, b 10 Jul 1832 lc/o William Powers "of Ireland" & Mary Pettifer "of Ireland" bp 25 Oct 1870 spr Bridget Fryer "baptized conditionally" John Dougherty, priest p513

GAHAN – Marie Victorine, b 27 May 1868 lc/o Peter Gahan & Mary Poirier bp 28 Jun 1868 spr Thomas Gahagan & Marie Etoffe p447

GAHAN – Sarah, b 1 Jun 1866 lc/o Patrick Gahan & Susan Bride bp 27 Jun 1866 spr Pat. Gahan & Jane Moran p387

GAINES – Charles Lewis, "2 years old" lc/o Joseph Gaines & Letitia Mathews (c) bp 12 Apr 1857 spr Ellen Polls p117

GAINES – Margaret Gaines, "aged 40 years" bp 18 Aug 1869 "baptized conditionally" Thos. Foley, priest p480

GAINES – Mary, b 10 Apr 1860 lc/o Henry Gaines & Margaretta Baum bp 17 Dec 1869 spr Amelia Boyd p489

GAINES – Violetta, b 13 Feb 1857 lc/o Henry Gaines & Margaretta Baum bp 17 Dec 1869 spr Amelia Boyd p489

GALE – Tenez Elizabeth Gale, "aged ten years" lc/o Joseph Gale & Rachel Ann Christmas (all c) spr Emily Road "baptized privately in danger of death" H. B. Coskery, priest p139

GALL – Mary, b 19 Aug 1862 lc/o Stephen Gall & Catharine Griffin bp 31 Aug 1862 spr William Good & Johanna Griffin p289

GALL – Thomas, b 14 Dec 1858 lc/o Stephan Gall & Catharine Griffin bp 19 Dec 1858 spr Edward Barrens & Margaret Farrell p177

GALLAGER – Catharine, b 31 Aug 1863 lc/o Charles Gallagher & Rose Kirby bp 13 Sep 1863 spr Pat. Kirby & Ann Kearney p314

GALLAGHER – Arthur, b 3 Jul 1864 lc/o Arthur Gallagher & Susan Griffith bp 10 Jul 1864 spr Frances Gallagher & Susanne Colton p336

GALLAGHER – Emma Regina Elizabeth, b 23 Feb 1856 lc/o Michael Gallagher & Mary Monahan bp 16 Mar 1856 spr William Doyle & Margaret Doyle p75

GALLAGHER – James Bernard, b 3 May 1862 lc/o James Gallagher & Rose Kirby bp 18 May 1862 spr John Kirby & Mary A. White p281

GALLAGHER – John Andrew, b 14 Jul 1863 lc/o Patrick Gallagher & Elizabeth Bian bp 16 Aug 1863 spr John Bian & Margaret McNeal p313

GALLAGHER – John Henry, b 27 Feb 1860 lc/o John Gallagher & Rosa Lauro bp 11 Mar 1860 spr Hugh La___ & Eliza McFaul p217

GALLAGHER – John William, b 24 Feb 1862 lc/o Arthur Gallagher & Bridget Colton bp 9 Mar 1862 spr Hugh Gallagher & Mary Devine p275

GALLAGHER – Joseph, b 2 Mar 1866 lc/o Joseph Gallagher & Ellen Mullin bp 11 Mar 1866 spr John Mullin & Elizabeth Mullan p377

GALLAGHER – Margaret Elizabeth, b 20 Mar 1858 lc/o Patrick Gallagher & Elizabeth Barnes bp 30 May 1858 spr William Butler & Mary Barnes p157

GALLAGHER – Martin, b 1 Jan 1857 lc/o Martin Gallagher & Catherine Stoffel bp 11 Jan 1857 spr Thomas Magnan & Mary Joyce p107

GALLAGHER – Martin Buchanan, b 9 Apr 1856 lc/o Patrick Gallagher & Elizabeth Burns bp 15 Jun 1856 spr Martin Burns & Margaret Hogan p85

GALLAGHER – Michael Martin, b *ndg* lc/o Martin Gallagher & Catherine Stoll bp 26 Aug 1855 spr Martin Gallagher & Maria Gavin p56

GALLAGHER – Rose, b 10 Apr 1865 lc/o James Gallagher & Rose Kirby bp 23 Apr 1865 spr Frank Duffy & Rose McAdam p355

GALLAGHER – Thomas John, b 21 May 1868 lc/o Jos. Gallagher & Ellen Mullan bp 31 May 1868 spr Wm. Mullin & Eliz. Mullin p443

GALLAGHER – Thomas John, b 30 Oct 1869 lc/o Joseph Gallagher & Ellen Mullan bp 2 Dec 1869 spr S. Mullan p489

GALLAGHER – William, b 2 Apr 1864 lc/o Joseph Gallagher & Ellen Mullan bp 10 Apr 1864 spr Frank Duffy & Catharine Winter p330

GALLAGHER – William, b 7 Jul 1867 lc/o James Gallagher & Rose Kirby bp 21 Jul 1867 spr John Kirby & Lizzie Kirby p417

GANLY – Mary, b 12 Feb 1859 lc/o Andrew Ganly & Honora <u>Fludd</u> bp 20 Feb 1859 spr Andrew Pheely & Margaret Flinn p182

GANTT – Frederick Renatus, b 5 Mar 1854 lc/o Caesar A. Gantt & Rosa Q. P_____ bp 22 Mar 1854 spr Frederica Renata Lambertz p8

GANTY – Frances Catharine, b 11 Jul 1870 lc/o William Ganty & Ann Manning bp 1 Sep 1870 spr Arthur Delivingere & Fannie Perkins p508

GANTZ – James Edmond, "about 3 months old" lc/o John T. Gantz & Catherine Sullivan bp 7 Jun 1855 spr Eugene Sullivan & Mary A. Sullivan p48

GANTZ – Thomas Sullivan, b 15 Apr 1859 lc/o John T. Gantz & Catharine Sullivan bp 8 May 1859 spr Eugene Sullivan & Mary A. Sullivan p189

GARDINER – Clara Mary Gardiner, "aged about 30 years" bp 25 Mar 1865 p353

GARDINER – Georgianna, b 4 Jul 1867 lc/o David Gardiner & Mary Kearns bp 20 Oct 1867 spr Isaac McAdams & Bridget Kearns p424

GARDINER – Mary Carroll, b 14 Sep 1865 lc/o David Gardiner & Mary Kieran bp 17 Dec 1865 spr Mary Hughes p371

GARDINER – Mary Ida, "aged 11 years" lc/o Robert Gardiner & Mary Straper bp 20 Dec 1864 spr A. McCoffney & "lady" p347

GARDNER – Margaret, b 25 Feb 1864 lc/o David S. Gardner & Mary Kearns bp 6 Mar 1864 spr Owen McEnarry & Bridget Higgins p328

GARDNER – William, "26 months old" lc/o James Gardner & Mary E. Curtis bp 14 Nov 1864 spr Jos. Ploude p345

GARMENDIA – Annita Theresa, b 2 Jun 1861 lc/o Carlos de Garmendia and Nannie Spalding bp 12 Jun 1861 spr George Jenkins & Rosa S. Ford p254

GARMENDIA – Basil Spalding, b 28 Feb 1860 lc/o Carlos de Garmendia & Nannie Spalding bp 10 Mar 1860 spr Edward F. Jenkins & Sarah Jenkins "I supplied the ceremonies of baptism" "was baptized privately by Rt. Rev. Martin Spalding, Bishop of Louisville, KY" Thos. Foley, priest p217

GARMENDIA – Carlos Maria Guillermo, b 7 Feb 1863 lc/o Carlos de Garmendia & Nannie Spalding bp 14 Feb 1863 spr John G. Welsh & Annie Jenkins "of Alfred" p301

GARMENDIA – Maria de le Caridad, b 7 Mar 1869 lc/o Carlos de Garmendia & Nannie Spalding bp 18 Mar 1869 spr Rev. John Patrick Dunn & _____ Garnett p467

GARMENDIA – Maria Josefa, b 17 Oct 1864 lc/o Carlos De Garmendia & Nannie Spalding bp 25 Oct 1864 spr Maria Josefa Garmendia de Lage "by Mrs. C. A. Spalding" & The Archbishop of Baltimore, The Most Rev. M. J. Spalding p343

GARMENDIA – Martin John, b 28 Jun 1866 lc/o Carlos de Garmendia & Nannie Spalding bp 7 Jul 1866 spr Prospero de Garmendia, Charles Gola & Clotilda Gola p388

GARMENDIA – Prospero Thomas, b 1 Aug 1867 lc/o Carlos de Garmendia & Nannie Spalding bp 9 Aug 1867 spr Thomas Foley & Larni Hunter p419

GARMENDIA – Thomas Meredith, b 8 Jul 1870 lc/o Carlos de Garmendia & Ann Spalding bp 16 Jul 1870 spr M. L. Lafe & Roberta Shriver p505

GARNETT – Julian De Courcy, b 14 Jun 1869 lc/o John J. Garnett & Julia De Courcy bp 26 Jul 1869 spr Charles A. Williamson & Rosa May p478

GARNETT – Mary Theresa, b 24 Aug 1869 lc/o Thomas Garnett & Ann Jackson (c) bp 19 Sep 1869 spr Mary Ann Williams p484

GARRETT – Mary Jane Garrett, "aged 20 years" bp 8 Feb 1862 spr Justine Smith p273

GARRISON – Mary Catherine, b 21 Nov 1842 lc/o Jacob Garrison & Mary Jane, "his wife" bp 13 Jun 1857 spr Maggie A. Conlan "baptized conditionally" Thos. Foley, priest p124

GARRITY – Francis Joseph, b 31 Oct 1863 lc/o John Garrity & Susannah Welsh bp 8 Nov 1863 spr Francis Creighton & Martha Donnelly p319

GARRITY – John Henry, b 9 Aug 1857 lc/o John Garrity & Susan Welch bp 20 Sep 1857 spr Jno. Flarity & Catherine Lemon p135

GARRITY – Susan, b 20 Oct 1859 lc/o John Garrity & Susanna Welsh bp 30 Oct 1859 spr John Irvin & Elizabeth McNally p203

GARRITZ – Francis Edward, b 5 Oct 1861 lc/o John Garritz & Susanna Welsh bp 13 Oct 1861 spr John Gorman & Cath. Lewis, p263

GARRY – Francis, b 7 Feb 1856 lc/o James Garry & Catherine O'Rook bp 17 Jan 1856 spr Rose More "I supplied the ceremonies…baptized in danger of death by a layman" Jnoth. McNally, priest p72

GARVEY – Hugh, b 10 Mar 1859 lc/o Michael Garvey & Bridget Cunningham bp 19 Mar 1859 spr Ann Garvey p184

GARVEY – James Garvey, b 28 Jul 1866 lc/o James Garvey, Jr. & Jane McCann bp 19 Aug 1866 spr Charles Lewis & Pauline Lewis p392

GARVEY – Peter James, b 17 Jul 1868 lc/o Peter Garvey & Mary Hogan bp 9 Aug 1868 spr Patk. & Mary Carmody p450

GARY – Alberta Georgietta, b 20 Sep 1858 c/o James Albert Gary & Lavinia G. _____, "lawful wife" bp 19 Apr 1859 g - Margaret Nettee p187

GARY – Edward Stanley, b 26 Jul 1862 lc/o James A. Gary & Lavinia Corrie bp 25 Dec 1862 spr Mary I. Nettee p298

GARY – James Sullivan, b 17 Nov 1860 lc/o James A. Gary & Lavinia Corrie bp 13 Jan 1862 spr Margaret Mettee p272

GARY – Lilian Mary, b 27 Nov 1865 lc/o James A. Gary & Lavinia Corries bp 12 Sep 1866 spr Aveline Mette p395

GATCH – Augustine, b 4 May 1857 lc/o Joseph Gatch & Maria Hopkins bp 21 May 1869 spr Mrs. Mary Kries "baptized conditionally" Thomas S. Lee, priest p471

GATELY – John, b 26 Sep 1857 lc/o Thomas Gately & Delia Fitzpatrick bp 3 Oct 1857 spr John Fizpatrick & Mara Sheets p136

GATELY – Mary Ellen, b 26 Oct 1855 lc/o Thomas Gately & Bridget Fitzpatrick bp 4 Nov 1855 spr Patrick Burke & Mary A. Boner p64

GAULE – Alice, b 22 Aug 1866 lc/o Michael Gaul & Bridget Clarke bp 2 Sep 1866 spr Thomas Gaul & Kate Gaule p395

GAULE – Catharine Gaule, b 16 Sep 1855 lc/o Stephen Gaule & Catherine Griffin bp 30 Sep 1855 spr Thomas Griffin & Antonia Gaule [*ed. note: faint record*] p60

GAULE – Margaret May, b 18 May 1857 lc/o Stephen Gaule & Catherine Griffin bp 31 May 1857 spr Paul Griffin & Mary Gaule p122

GAULE – Mary, b 27 Feb 1862 lc/o Michael Gaule & Bridget Clark bp 16 Mar 1862 spr Frances Margaret Gaule p276

GAULE – Michael John, b 3 Aug 1868 lc/o Stephen S. Gaule & Catharine Griffin bp 6 Aug 1868 spr Matt. P. O'Brien & Cecilia De Roncerie p450

GAULE – Stephen, b 16 Jun 1861 lc/o Stephen Gaule & Catharine Griffin bp 23 Jun 1861 spr Thomas Tracy & Kate O'Neal p254

GAULE – Thomas, b 26 Jun 1854 lc/o Stephen Gaule & Catherine Griffin bp 6 Jul 1854 spr Bridget Farrell p17

GAULL – Michael, b 30 Apr 1860 lc/o Stephen S. Gaull & Catharine Griffin bp 13 May 1860 spr Thomas Broadus & Ann O'Neal p221

GAZZOLA – Aloysius, b 1 Oct 1859 c/o Peter Gazzola & Julia Brennan, "his lawful wife" bp 8 Oct 1859 spr John Andrew Cella & Rosina Merritt p202

GEAGAN – Joseph O'Reilly, b 24 Oct 1858 lc/o Michael Geagan & Sarah Kennedy bp 17 Nov 1858 p173

GEE – James Nicholas, b 7 Apr 1865 lc/o Henry Gee & Kate Baggs bp 11 Apr 1865 spr Richard M. Landers & Anna Landers p354

GEGAN – Emily, b 16 Jan 1854 lc/o Joseph Gegan & Catherine A. Whelan bp 25 Jan 1854 spr H. B. Coakley & Emily Hillery p3

GEHRING – Elizabeth, b 17 Apr 1870 lc/o Charles Gehring & Cath. Foster bp 15 May 1870 spr James J. Kennedy & _____ Fields p501

GEHRING – Mary Magdalen, b 19 Oct 1868 lc/o Charles Gehring & Kate Foster bp 20 Dec 1868 spr Sarah Fells p461

GERAHTY – Mary Frances, b *ndg* 1819 lc/o Gerahty, Peter & Ann Dessau bp 19 Oct 1858 spr Eleanor Foy p171

GERRITY – Julia, b 3 Dec 1868 lc/o Patrick Gerrity & Julia Matthews bp 13 Dec 1868 spr Francis Mullan & Ann Downey p460

GESTLER – John Joseph, b 8 Jan 1857 lc/o John Gestler & Catherine Donse bp 6 May 1857 spr Elizabeth Power p119

GETTIER – John C. Gettier, b 21 Feb 1824 bp 4 Sep 1859 p199

GETTY – James Fields, b 12 Feb 1856 lc/o David A. Getty & Catharine Fields bp 13 May 1856 spr Louisa Quinlan p82

GETTY – James Getty, "aged about 70 years" bp 23 Aug 1859 p198

GHEE – Joseph Henry, b 5 Dec 1859 lc/o Henry Ghee & Kate Bagge bp 14 Dec 1859 spr H. Foley & Mary Cady p208

GHEE – William Thomas, b 25 Apr 1862 lc/o Henry Ghee & Kate Bugye bp 1 May 1862 spr Thomas Casey & Mary Landers p280

GIBBIE – Maria Elizabeth, b 21 Feb 1869 lc/o Geo. Gibbie & Mary E. Fitzgerald bp 28 Apr 1869 spr Annie E. G. Berg & Delbert E. Berg p470

GIBBNEY – Mary Ann, b 23 Jun 1858 lc/o Christopher Gibbney & Sarah Austin bp 27 Jun 1858 spr Michael Gibbney & Mary Gibbney p161

GIBBON – Aloysius Luhrman Gibbon, "aged about 12 years" bp 24 May 1866 spr Mrs. Gibbon p384

GIBBON – John, b 5 Jul 1861 lc/o Capt. John Gibbon, USA & Fanny Moale bp 1 Nov 1861 spr Henry Moale & Anna Smith "ceremonies supplied July 7th, 1862" H. B. Coskery, priest p265

GIBBON – John, b 16 Jul 1864 lc/o Major Genl. John Gibbon, USA & Fanny Moale bp 20 Jul 1864 spr V. Rev. H. B. Coskery & Augusta Moale p337

GIBNEY – Christopher Michael, b 8 Dec 1859 lc/o Patrick Gibney & Mary Burns bp 20 Dec 1859 spr James Doyle & Margaret Gill p 209

GIBNEY – Ellen, b 17 Dec 1861 lc/o Patrick Gibney & Mary Burns bp 18 Dec 1861 spr Mary Gibney p270

GIBNEY – Francis Patrick, b 13 Dec 1863 lc/o Patrick Gibney & Mary Burns bp 15 Dec 1863 spr Mary Gibney p322

GIBNEY – Henry John, b 26 Dec 1863 lc/o Henry Gibney & Ellen Larkins bp 6 Dec 1863 spr Thos. Young & Mary Lyons p321

GIBNEY – James, b 21 Oct 1854 lc/o Pat Gibney & Mary Burns bp 12 Nov 1854 spr Michael Gibney & Mary Gibney p29

GIBNEY – James, b 25 Sep 1862 lc/o Henry Gibney & Ellen Larkin bp 30 Sep 1862 spr John Cooney & Cath. Larkin "baptized privately" H. B. Coskery, priest p291

GIBNEY – John Thomas, b 24 Jun 1866 lc/o Henry Gibney & Ellen Larkin bp 30 Jun 1866 spr John M. Mahan & Alise Clarken p387

GIBNEY – Josep Laurence, b 16 Apr 1860 lc/o Henry Gibney & Ellen Larkin bp 28 Apr 1860 spr John Daley & Catharine Larkin p220

GIBNEY – Joseph, b 15 Feb 1858 lc/o Patrick Gibney & Mary Burns bp 3 Mar 1858 spr George McGann & Kate Hutchinson p149

GIBNEY – Rosanna, b 2 Jun 1856 lc/o Patrick Gibney & Mary Burns bp 12 Jun 1856 spr Martin Ganton & Ellen Connor p 85

GIBSON – James, b 7 Jan 1854 lc/o Michael Gibson bp 29 Jan 1854 spr James Kelly, Thomas & Jane Gibson p4

GIBSON – Mary Ellen, b 23 Nov 1855 lc/o Michael Gibson & Ellen Kelly bp 16 Dec 1855 spr John Garrity & Sarah Nicholson p68

GIERTY – Anna, b 5 Feb 1867 lc/o Patrick Gierty & Julia Matthews bp 10 Feb 1867 spr Bernard Reilly & Julia Reilly p406

GILBERT – Charles Baumgardner, b 3 May 1862 lc/o Lewis Gilbert & Magdalen Baumgardner bp 1 Nov 1862 spr Jane Hutton p292

GILBERT – Edward, b *ndg* lc/o Edward Gilbert & _____ McCoy bp 4 Oct 1858 spr Daniel McCoy & Mary McCoy p170

GILBERT – John Richard, b 19 Jan 1868 lc/o Louis Gilbert & Magdalen Baumgardiner bp 5 Mar 1868 spr Louise Clementine Connolly & Jerome W. Overman "(proxy)" p435

GILBERT – Julia Viroque, b 26 Feb 1860 lc/o Edward Gilbert & Georgiana M. Howell bp 6 Apr 1860 "baptized privately" H. B. Coskery, priest p218

GILCRIST – John, b 24 Jun 1861 lc/o John Gilcrist & Mary McDermott bp 30 Jun 1861 spr Thomas Gilcrist & Cecilia Gilcrist p255

GILDEA – George Alfonsus, b 9 Jul 1859 lc/o Francis Gildea & Susan Gable bp 7 Aug 1859 spr Michl. Sloan & Mary Gildea p197

GILDEA – John, b 30 Jun 1868 lc/o Martin Gildea & Mary Bogan bp 4 Jul 1868 spr Michael Gildea & Sarah Bogan p448

GILDEA – Laura Pauline, b 15 May 1865 lc/o Francis Gildea & Susan Gable bp 25 May 1865 spr Mary Josephine Connolly p357

GILDEA – Mary Ann Eliza, b 30 Nov 1861 lc/o Francis Gildea & Susan Gable bp 17 Dec 1861 spr Susan Daiger p270

GILDEA – Susanna Gildea "(born Gable)", "about 84 years old" bp 28 Oct 1859 spr Cecilia Barry "I made their abduration of Prot. before baptism" Thos. Foley, priest [*ed. note: 'their' references all four individuals the priest baptized that day*] p202

GILDENFENNAY – Charles, b 25 Aug 1867 lc/o Charles Gildenfennay & Maria Ware bp 3 May 1868 spr Ann Smith p441

GILDER – William Howard, b 9 Aug 1857 "in Baltimore" lc/o William Gilder & Mary E. Howard "of New York" bp 31 Aug 1857 spr Thos. Foley & Ann Howard p133

GILL – Theresa May Jer____, b *ndg* lc/o Samuel Gill & Helen [sic] bp 24 Jul 1862 spr Wm. A. Griffith & M. Griffith p286

GILLAHAN – Thomas Jefferson, b 25 Sep 1862 lc/o William Gillahan & Sarah Smith bp 5 Dec 1862 spr Mary O'Keefe p297

GILLAN – Edward Henry, b 18 May 1861 lc/o Patrick Gillan & Ellen Ryan bp 11 Jun 1861 spr John McGlennan & Mary McGlennan p253

GILLAN – James, b 20 May 1856 lc/o James Gillan & Rosa McGaraghan bp 25 May 1856 spr Pat. McGaraghan & Mary Flaherty p83

GILLAN – John, b 27 Jun 1858 lc/o Patrick Gillan & Sarah Connolly bp 11 Jul 1858 spr James Gillan & Margaret McGinty p162

GILLAN – John Patrick, b 19 Jul 1863 lc/o Patrick Gillan & Ellen Ryan bp 16 Aug 1863 spr John Davis & Mary Ryan p313

GILLAN – Mary Ellen, b 24 Oct 1858 lc/o James Gillan & Rose McGargle bp 24 Oct 1858 spr Patrick McGargle p172

GILLANS – Anna, b 3 Jan 1867 c/o Patrick Gillans & Marsha [sic] bp 6 Aug 1867 spr Kate Lambert p419

GILLEN – Ellen Regina, b 12 Aug 1866 lc/o Patrick Gillen & Ellen Ryan bp 30 Aug 1866 spr Geo. Morgan & Mary Morgan p394

GILLEN – Mary Elizabeth, b 8 Sep 1859 lc/o Patrick Gillen & Ellen Rie bp 25 Sep 1859 spr Edward Road & Margaret Grimes p201

GILLEN – Robert Joseph, b 16 Apr 1869 lc/o Patrick Gillen & Ellen Ryan bp 27 May 1869 spr James B. Trainor & Mary A. Bowen p473

GILLESPIE – Isabella Gillespie, "18 years old" bp 30 Oct 1859 "baptized conditionally" Thos. Foley, priest p204

GILLIARD – Juliana, b 17 May 1869 lc/o Nicholas Gilliard & Mary A______ bp 12 Oct 1869 spr Elizabeth Roberts (all c) p485

GILLIGAN – Francis Patrick, b 9 Oct 1857 lc/o Patrick Gilligan & Ann McMahon bp 9 Oct 1857 spr Julia McGowan p137

GILLIGAN – Louisa, b 14 Apr 1861 lc/o John Gillagan & Catharine Lynch bp 7 May 1861 spr Isabell Boussifer p250

GILLIOTTI – Mary Annetina, b 7 Mar 1860 lc/o James Gilliotti & Julia Poggi bp 10 Mar 1860 spr Antony Ritagliati & Mary Ritagliati p216

GILLIS – Mary, b 31 May 1869 lc/o Levi Gillis & Eleanora Thomas (c) bp 2 Sep 1869 spr Bridget McCarron p481

GILPIN – Mary Montieth Gilpin, b *ndg* April 1842 lc/o John Gilpin & Mary Montieth bp 16 Oct 1868 p456

GILROY – William, b 19 Jan 1854 lc/o William Gilroy & Julia Riley bp 5 Mar, 1854 spr Edward A. Veil & Ann Cope p7

GITEHULL – Mary Austin, b 15 Mar 1857 c/o John Gitehull & Mary Connor bp 22 Mar 1857 spr Thomas Connor & Mary McGraw p115

GIVNEY – Catherine, b 26 Apr 1855 lc/o Christopher Givney & Sarah Austin bp 29 Apr 1855 spr Wm. & Eliz. Givney "I supplied the ceremonies in the case…previously baptized" H. B. Coskery, priest p44

GLEASON – Emily, b 13 May 1853 lc/o Michael Gleason & Elizabeth Hardesty bp 29 Jun 1854 spr Julia Ferris p16

GLENN – Catherine, b 5 Oct 1857 lc/o John Glenn & Sarah Fahey bp 12 Oct 1857 spr Patrick Gilligan & Margret Glenn p138

GLENN – Edward, b 16 Nov 1854 lc/o Terence Glenn & Mary Denison bp 26 Nov 1854 spr James Kelly & Ellen Caitelnaugh p29

GLENN – John Edward, b 16 Feb 1857 lc/o Patrick Glenn & Cecilia Ward bp 22 Feb 1857 spr Laurence Glenn & Margaret Rourk "privately baptized by Dr. O'Donnell" "I supplied the ceremonies" H. B. Coskery, priest p112

GLENN – John, b 1 Jan 1855 c/o John Glenn & Cecilia Haley bp 7 Jan 1855 spr Patk. Connaughton & Winfred Perse p33

GLENN – Julia Glenn, b 21 Nov 1861 lc/o Laurence Glenn & Mary Denash bp 28 Nov 1861 spr Patk. & Bridget Glenn p268

GLENN – Margaret, b 11 Nov 1857 lc/o Peter Glenn & Mary Mannion bp 12 Nov 1857 spr Patk. Dunn & Margaret Riley p140

GLENN – Mary Agnes, b 11 Jun 1858 lc/o Laurence Glenn & Mary Nash bp 20 Jun 1858 spr Michl. Kelly & Bridget McDown p160

GLENN – Patrick, b 29 Mar 1856 lc/o John Glenn & Celia Fahey bp 3 Apr 1856 spr Thomas Fahey & Bridget Glenn p79

GLENN – Rose Glenn, b 13 Oct 1853 c/o John Glenn & Mary Grady bp 22 Jan 1854 spr John Grady & Cath. Manion p3

GLONINGER – James Ledlie, b 30 Apr 1862 lc/o John R. Gloninger & Mary Ledlie bp 22 May 1862 spr Anabella N. Betzhoosier p282

GLONINGER – John Henry, b 8 May 1860 lc/o John Regis Gloninger & Mary Ledlie bp 26 May 1860 spr Alex. Baugher & Auguste Gloninger p222

GLYNN – Patrick, b 26 Nov 1855 lc/o Patrick Glynn & Cecilia Ward bp 27 Nov 1855 spr Owen Jourdon & Mary Connofit "I supplied the ceremonies of baptism" Jno. McNally, priest p66

GODMAN – Isabella, b 28 Sep 1868 lc/o John E. Godman & Elizabeth Renner bp 28 Oct 1868 spr Elizabeth Renner p456

GODMAN – John Thomas, b 5 Apr 1866 lc/o John Godman & Elizabeth Renner bp 8 Jun 1866 spr Elizabeth Renner p386

GOLBERT – Mary Ellen (c), "6 months old" lc/o William Colbert & Susan Dorsey bp 4 Oct 1868 spr Jane E. Hendrichs p455

GOLDBURN – William Edward, b 21 Nov 1857 lc/o James William Goldburn & Mary McGrace bp 27 Nov 1857 spr Margaret Fitzpatrick p142

GOLDEN – George Andrew, b 30 Aug 1855 lc/o Charles Golden & Martha Young (c) bp 31 Aug 1857 spr Bridget Connelly p133

GOLDEN – John, "11 months old" lc/o William Golden and "his wife" Susan (c) bp 23 Aug 1855 spr Rebecca Rayburn p56

GOLDSBORO – Alice Goldsboro, "aged 14 years" bp 21 Jun 1862 "an orphan in St. Mary's Asylum" p283

GOLDSBOROUGH – Robert John, b 29 Apr 1856 lc/o Henry Goldsborough & Emily Addison bp 2 Jun 1856 spr Catherine Addison p84

GOLDSMITH – Ann Cecilia Goldsmith, b 6 Apr 1834 bp 19 Oct 1865 witness: Julia Baldwin "baptized *sub conditione*" Martin J. Spaulding, Archb. Balt. p367

GONCE – William Henry, b 28 Jan 1857 lc/o John J. Gonce & Catherine Sullivan bp 15 Feb 1857 spr Owen & Mary Daley p110

GONCE – Benjamin Meade, b 8 Nov 1863 lc/o John Gonce & Catharine Sullivan bp 22 Nov 1863 spr Patrick McCann & Sarah Sullivan p321

GOODMAN – Sarah Stanislaus Goodman, "aged 21 years" bp 24 Sep 1866 spr Kate Barron "baptized conditionally" Thos. Foley, priest p396

GORDON – Ellen, b 3 Jan 1867 lc/o James Gordon & Elizabeth Lawler bp 21 Feb 1867 spr James & Ellen Lawler p406

GORDON – James Gordon, "aged 23 years" bp 5 Nov 1865 p368

GORMAN - Owen, b 1 Jun 1854 lc/o Brien Gorman & Christina Gorman bp 2 Jul 1854 spr John Smith & Julia Harety p16

GORMAN – Ann, b 26 Apr 1855 lc/o Owen Gorman & Margaret Brady bp 12 May 1855 spr Mich. Burns & Margaret King p46

GORMAN – James, b 10 Jan 1861 lc/o Bernard Gorman & Christine McDonnell bp 11 Jan 1861 spr Jonathan Mullan & Mary Gaitland p239

GORMAN – John, "about 3 years old" lc/o Owen Gorman & Hannah Moran bp 6 Aug 1854 spr Wm. Gorman & Betty Donnelly "I supplied the ceremonies to John previously baptized by The Rev. H. B. Coskery" Thos. Foley, priest p19

GORMAN – John, b 23 Jun 1856 lc/o Henry Gorman & Margaret Hopkins bp 24 Jun 1856 spr A_____ Rice & Bridget Hopkins p87

GORMAN – Mary Ann Elizabeth, b 20 Mar 1854 lc/o John Gorman & Bridget McCarthy bp 25 Mar 1854 spr Dennis McCarthy & Catherine Callain p9

GORMAN – Theresa, b 22 Sep 1858 lc/o Bryan Gorman & Christina McConnell bp 23 Sep 1858 spr Ann Nolan p169

GORMLEY – Henry Vincent, b 28 Jan 1861 lc/o Thomas Gormley & Margaret Hargmon bp 5 Mar 1861 spr Geo. M. Guffey S. Connelly p245

GORMLEY – Thomas Jefferson Gormley, "aged 32 years" bp 5 Jul 1861 p255

GORSUCH – John Craggs, b 10 Apr 1870 "born in Kent Co., Md" lc/o John Craggs Gorsuch & Hillary Coleman bp 7 Sep 1870 spr James & Jane Road p508

GOSNEL – Ann, b 20 Jan 1854 c/o Maurie Gosnel & Ellen Brannon bp 26 Apr 1856 spr M. Killduff p81

GOSS – John Jackson, b 6 Jun 1858 lc/o John Goss & Mary Austin bp 7 Jun 1858 spr Catherine Smith p158

GOSS – Lilan Austin, b 30 Mar 1858 lc/o John Goss & Mary Austin bp 7 Jun 1858 spr John Doyle p158

GOTTSHALK – Joseph Bernard Gottshalk, b 9 Jun 1864 c/o Jacob Gottshalk & Jane Oliver (c) bp 21 Jun 1864 spr Kate Lambert p335

GOUDY – Mary Esther Goudy, "aged 23 years" bp 13 Sep 1865 spr Sally Perine p364

GOULDING – John Emory, b 9 Jun 1858 lc/o Charles Goulding & Martha Young (c) bp 16 Jun 1858 spr Bridget O'Connor p159

GOVER – Emily Gover, "aged about 17 years" bp 27 May 1865 spr Marie S. J. L. Aubry p357

GOWAN – Rosa, b 17 Jul 1870 lc/o Michl. Gowan & Ann Carr bp 17 Jul 1870 spr John Gowan & Catharine McNally p505

GRACY – Eliza Jane Gracy, "aged 22" bp 26 Mar 1865 "baptized conditionally" Thos. Foley, priest p354

GRADY – John Lewis, b 26 Sep 1863 lc/o John Grady & Mary Grady bp 9 Jun 1864 spr John Lewis & Maggie Lewis p336

GRAHAM – Emma Elizabeth, b 13 Mar 1857 lc/o William Graham & Sarah Jane Haney bp 1 May 1857 spr Mary Gorman p118

GRANDALL – Albert James Grandall, "aged about 25 years" bp 20 Apr 1867 spr Jas. Gibbons "baptized conditionally" James Gibbons, priest p411

GRANGER – Ambrose Walter, b 31 Aug [*ed. note: year not written, probably 1868*] lc/o W. H. Granger & Juliana F. Smith bp 7 Sep 1868 spr _____ Foy p452

GRANGER – Eugene Isadore, b 3 May 1855 c/o William Granger & Frances Smith bp 20 May 1855 spr Elizabeth V. Lambert p47

GRANGER – Florence Mary, b 12 Mar 1865 lc/o William H. Granger & Juliana F. Smith bp 20 Mar 1865 spr Elizabeth Grumby p353

GRANGER – Frances Marion, b 16 Nov 1862 lc/o William Granger & Juliana Frances Smith "Edwin" [sic] bp 24 Nov 1862 spr Mary J. Seim p295

GRANGER – Ida Estelle, b 22 Jul 1860 lc/o Wm. Henry Granger & Anne Frances Smith bp 10 Aug 1860 g – Victorina Meriga p228

GRANGER – Thomas Foley, b 1 May 1858 lc/o William Granger & Frances Smith bp 9 May 1858 spr Thos. Foley & Margaret McCullough p155

GRANGER – Walter, b 26 Mar 1867 lc/o William Granger & Frances Smith bp 1 Apr 1867 spr Mary Garretty p409

GRANT – Adeline Marie, b 15 Feb 1856 lc/o Edward B. Grant & Cornelia Duval bp 16 Mar 1856 spr James Grant & Josephine Grant p75

GRASON – Mary Catharine Caroline, b 8 Jul 1866 c/o Thomas Francis Grason & Louise Hoburg, "his wife" bp 1 Aug 1866 spr Catharine Grason p391

GRATEFIELD – Mary Elizabeth, b 21 Aug 1868 lc/o John Gratefield & Sarah Dashiels bp 28 Dec 1868 spr Julia Gratefield (all c) p461

GRATEFIELD – Sarah Ellen, b 3 Aug 1862 lc/o John Gratefield & Sarah Dashiels bp 20 Oct 1862 spr Virginia Matthews p292

GRAVIER – Marie Helen, b 1 Jan 1856 lc/o Leon Gravier & Marie Pauline Desjardins bp 9 Oct 1863 spr John McDevitt & Helen Restin p317

GRAY – Charles Henry, b 9 Jul 1855 lc/o James Gray & Frances Smith (c) bp 10 Aug 1858 spr Maria Smith p166

GRAY – Ezechial Gray, b 23 Apr 1833 bp 12 May 1861 spr Thos. Foley p251

GRAY – Mary Frances, b 9 Nov 1857 lc/o William Gray & Isabel Lewis (c) bp 16 Aug 1858 spr Mary F. Brown p167

GRAY – Richard, b 13 Mar 1855 nc/o Mary Gray (c) bp 26 Mar 1855 spr Eliza Cole p41

GRAY – Sarah Ann, b 18 Sep 1863 lc/o Thomas Gray & Mary O'Brien bp 6 Oct 1863 spr Kate Lambert p317

GRAY – Thomas Joseph, b 21 Mar 1870 lc/o Thomas Gray & Mary Brian bp 14 Apr 1870 spr Mary C. Daly p500

GRAY – William Spence, b 18 Jun 1868 lc/o Thomas Gray & Mary O'Brien bp 30 Jun 1868 spr Lizzie Miller p447

GRAY – William Thomas, b 29 Jul 1865 lc/o Thomas Gray & Mary O'Brien bp 8 Aug 1865 spr Mary Hughes p361

GREAR – John, b 21 Feb 1858 lc/o Matthew Greer & Letitia Griffin bp 21 Mar 1858 spr Bridget Carroll p151

GREELEY – Agnes, b 1 Jan 1860 lc/o Patrick Greeley & Mary Hogan bp 15 Jan 1860 spr John Clarkin & Rosa Henry p211

GREELY – Catharine, b 8 Dec 1862 lc/o Patrick Greely & Mary Quinn bp 14 Dec 1862 spr Arthur Stewart & Ann Carthy p297

GREEN – Anna Miller, b 10 Mar 1862 lc/o William Green & Catharine Lightheiser bp 5 Aug 1862 spr Mary E. Green p286

GREEN – Catharine Marie, b 16 Sep 1860 lc/o William Green & Catharine Lightiser bp 25 Mar 1861 spr Mary E. Green p247

GREEN – Elizabeth, b 16 Sep 1847 lc/o George & Sophy Green bp 5 Nov 1867 spr Mary Clare Ross p426

GREEN – George Andrew, b 2 Oct 1855 lc/o Henry Green & _____ _____ bp 2 Dec 1855 [*ed. note: faint record*] p67

GREEN – George Haig, b 9 Dec 1858 c/o William Green & Catharine Lifeheiser bp 3 Apr 1859 spr Mary Ellen Green p185

GREEN – Henry Eugene bp 23 Dec 1865 lc/o William Green & Catharine Lighthuser bp 1 Feb 1867 spr Mary McGurgan p404

GREEN – Hugh Thomas, b 20 Sep 1861 lc/o Henry Green & Amanda Ray bp 14 Oct 1861 spr Margaret Smith p263

GREEN – John Henry, b 6 Nov 1859 lc/o Henry Green & Alexandra Ray bp 28 Nov 1859 spr Mary Green p206

GREEN – Joseph, b 6 Jul 1854 lc/o William Green & Catherine Lighthouse bp 4 Oct 1855 spr Mary E. Green p60

GREEN – Lucy Ann Green, "aged 62 years" bp 17 Apr 1868 p439

GREEN – Mary Green "(born Glass)", b 12 Oct 1837 lc/o David M. & Sarah A. Glass bp 28 Oct 1859 spr Eliza Donelan "I made their abjuration of Prot. before baptism" Thos. Foley, priest [*ed. note: 'their' references all four individuals the priest baptized that day*] p203

GREEN – Robert Emmett, b 10 Mar 1864 lc/o William P. Green & Cath. (Breithaüser) Green bp 29 Jan 1865 spr Mary Ellen Green p349

GREEN – Sarah Jane, b 31 May 1859 lc/o Hugh Thomas Green & Mary Louisa Glass bp 28 Sep 1859 spr Ann S. Smith p201

GREEN – William Matthew, b 9 Jan 1864 lc/o Henry Green & Amanda Ray bp 25 Jan 1864 spr Margaret Smith p324

GREEN – William, b 19 Dec 1869 lc/o John Green "of Baltimore" & Mary "of Baltimore" bp 20 Oct 1870 spr Anna Miller p512

GREENWELL – Elizabeth, b 23 Jul 1860 lc/o James Greenwell & Mary Slater bp 9 Aug 1860 spr Elizabeth Root p228

GREENWELL – William George, b 27 Sep 1861 lc/o James C. Greenwell & Mary Ann Slater bp 5 Oct 1861 spr Wm. Slater "(proxy for) Andrew Jackson Spalding" & Margart Ann Spalding p262

GREER – Henrietta Greer "(born Irwin)", "age 43 years" bp 1 Oct 1867 p423

GREGG – John, b 26 Jan 1856 lc/o John Gregg & Ann Smith bp 27 Jan 1856 spr Winifred Burke p71

GREGORY – John, b 14 Apr 1856 lc/o Peter Gregory & Mary Connolly bp 2 Jun 1856 spr Ann Ackheart & Jno. McNally p84

GREY – John, b 8 Apr 1867 lc/o Thomas Grey & Mary O'Brien bp 22 Apr 1867 spr Alice McCarney p411

GRIFFIN – George, b 7 Jul 1866 lc/o Paul Griffin & Bridget Gillooly bp 8 Jul 1866 spr Stephen Gall & Catharine Gall p388

GRIFFIN – Gerald, b 26 Aug 1867 lc/o Thomas Griffin & Mary Anne Quigley bp 29 Sep 1867 spr Luke Cassidy & Julia Whelan p422

GRIFFIN – Mary Elizabeth, b 6 May 1870 lc/o Thomas B. Griffin & Mary Ann Quigley bp 26 Jun 1870 spr John Quigley & Mary Regnant p504

GRIFFIN – Mary, b 13 May 1858 lc/o Anthony Griffin & Mary Hogan bp 29 May 1858 spr Catherine McGlennan p157

GRIFFIN – Mary, b 26 Jul 1861 lc/o Paul Griffin & Bridget Galooley bp 28 Jul 1861 spr Michael Griffin & Esther Flanigan p257

GRIFFITH – John J., "11 years old" lc/o John J. Griffith & Louisa J. Tucker bp 15 Aug 1867 spr Fanny Griffith p419

GRIFFITH – Mary Jane, b 5 May 1867 lc/o Wm. Thos. Griffith & Margaret Carr bp 6 May 1867 spr John Carr "(by proxy)" & Anne Greely p411

GRIFFITHS – Daniel (c), b 4 Jul 1862 lc/o John Griffiths & Martha Brown bp 3 Sep 1863 spr Mary E. Lambert p314

GRINNELL – John Wilfred, b 16 Jun 1869 lc/o Randolph Grinnell & Susan Wilson (all c) bp 31 Jan 1870 spr Jane Blackson p492

GRINNELL – James Alexander, b 14 Jul 1869 c/o James Grinnell & Mary Bennett bp 1 Aug 1869 spr Teresa Queen (all c) p478

GRINNELL – James Alexander, b 31 Dec 1868 lc/o Alexander Grinnell & Maria Dorsey (c) bp 19 Mar 1869 spr Nathan Smith & Sarah Ford p467

GROOMES – Amelia Frances, b 2 Aug 1856 lc/o Nathaniel Groomes & Elizabeth Mays (c) bp 25 Aug 1856 spr Laura Groomes p94

GROOMES – James (c), b 16 Sep 1854 lc/o Nat G. Groomes & Elizabeth May bp 15 Oct 1854 spr Emily Sullivan p27

GROOMS – Ellen Gertrude, b 4 Oct 1867 lc/o Joseph N. Grooms & Cornelia Kemp (c) bp 25 Oct 1867 spr Theodore Grooms & Mary R. Grooms p425

GROOMS – Germaine Priscilla, b 21 Oct 1858 lc/o Nathaniel Grooms & Elizabeth Mays (c) bp 17 Nov 1858 spr Caroline Bullen p174

GROOMS – Mary Ann Eliza (c), b 4 Feb 1854 lc/o Robert Proctor & Mary A. Grooms (c) bp 12 Mar 1854 spr Hester Bullen p7

GROOMS – Sarah Jane, b 30 Jul 1863 lc/o Nathaniel & Elizabeth Grooms (c) bp 3 Aug 1863 spr Sylvester Grooms & Antoinette Jordon p312

GROSS – Josias Gross (c), "aged about 26 years" bp 26 Jul 1863 spr Catharine Coolahan "baptized conditionally without ceremonies" H. B. Coskery, priest p312

GROSS – Mary Adeline, b 3 May 1866 lc/o _____ Gross & Annie Williams (c) bp 17 Sep 1866 spr Mrs. Goldsmith p396

GRUB – Anna Adelaide Aurelia, b 4 Feb 1855 lc/o George Grub & Anna Eliza Grub bp 28 Aug 1857 spr Mary Christina Adelaide Booth p132

GRUBB – Mary Joseph Grubb, "aged about 9 years" lc/o Geo Grubb & Ann Eliz. McGinnis bp 18 Jun 1868 spr Mary Clarke p446

GUEST – John, b 13 Apr 1856 lc/o George Guest & Honora Bankhead bp 13 Apr 1856 spr John McNally p80

GUILLIGAN – William, b 17 Nov 1855 lc/o Patrick Guilligan & Anna McMahon bp 18 Nov 1855 spr William McMahon & Elizabeth McMahon p65

GUISE – Robert Gilmore, b 8 Dec 1867 lc/o Andre J. Guise & Isabella N. Menniss bp 15 Mar 1868 spr Wm. J. Senninger & Louisa Hargins p436

GURGIN – Thomas Nathaniel, b 26 Jun 1857 lc/o Thomas Gurgin & Elizabeth Tilghman (c) bp 27 Jul 1857 spr Fanny Castor p129

GUYNON – Effy Augustine Mary, b 20 Feb 1869 lc/o Andrew J. Guyon & Louise Keene bp 1 Mar 1869 spr Mrs. Hilary p466

GUYTON – Mary Frances Guyton "(born Perdue)", "about 30 yrs old" bp 21 Feb 1854 spr Emma Small p5

GWYNN – Andrew Keene, b 12 Jun 1870 lc/o Andrew J. Gwynn & Louise Keene bp 24 Jul 1870 spr Ellen Keene p 506

GWYNN – Mary Louisa, b 23 Nov 1868 lc/o Owen Gwynn & Ann Holland (c) bp 3 May 1869 spr Mary S. Elliott p470

GWYNN – Richard Lawrence, b 30 May 1867 lc/o Richard Gwynn & Elizabeth Burns bp 21 Jul 1867 spr Jane Crandall & Elizabeth Crandall p417

HACKETT – Henry Joseph, "born 3 weeks ago" lc/o John Hackett & Mary Bear bp 3 Apr 1870 spr Patrick Hanley & Mary <u>Kippy</u> p498

HACKETT – Mary Ann, b 5 Nov 1858 lc/o Patrick Hackett & Ann Fannell bp 7 Nov 1858 spr Thomas McKuhn & Mary Dolan p173

HADLEY – Helen, b 14 Aug 1860 lc/o Wm. Hadley & Harriet Doolittle bp 28 Feb 1869 spr Mary McCormick p466

HAGAN – John, b 10 Jul 1855 lc/o Terrence Hagan & Esther Dunn bp 12 Jul 1855 spr John Dunn & Mary Conroy p52

HAGAN – Lewis Anthony, b 15 Jul 1866 lc/o John Hagan & Catharine Keife bp 29 Jul 1866 spr Lewis Devaux & Ella Keife p390

HAIG – Angelina Margaret, b 17 Feb 1856 lc/o Goerge H. Haig & Kate Proudfoot bp 17 Apr 1856 spr James M. Haig & Josephine _____ p80

HAIG – Catharine, b 5 Jul 1859 lc/o George M. Haig & Kate Proudfoot, "who died immediately after the birth of her child" bp 6 Jul 1859 p194

HAIG – Catharine, b 5 Jul 1859 lc/o George <u>M</u>. Haig & Kate Proudfoot bp 13 Dec 1859 spr James M. Haig "I supplied the ceremonies" "baptized privately by me" Thos. Foley, priest p208

HAIG – George Haig, b 19 Jun 1827 bp 11 Feb 1861 "baptized conditionally" Thos. Foley, pries p243

HAIG – James Morris, b 12 Jul 1854 lc/o George H. Haig & Kate Proudfoot bp 10 Oct 1854 spr James U. Haig & Anabella DeVille p26

HALE – Aloysius Frank Fuller Hale, b 30 Oct 1850 c/o William H. Hale & Anna M. Hale, "his lawful wife" bp 27 Jan 1861 spr Charles Du Pont Bird p241

HALE – John Harry Winfield Scott Hale b 19 April 1848 c/o William H. Hale & Anna M. Hale, "his lawful wife" bp 27 Jan 1861 spr Charles Du Pont Bird p241

HALE – Mrs. Ann Margaret Hale "(alias Knapp)", b *ndg* bp 12 Sep 1859 "bapt. in infancy in Lutheran sect, and in adult age by Baptists" Francis Patrick, Archb. p200

HALL – Cecilia, "six weeks old" lc/o Jacob E. Hall & Frances Jones (all c) bp 1 Feb 1863 spr Terinda Jenkins p301

HALL – Frances Elizabeth, b 19 Jul 1855 lc/o William Hall & Jane Brennan bp 19 Aug 1855 spr Francis Brennan p55

HALL – John Thomas, b 10 Dec 1858 lc/o William Hall & Jane Brennan bp 2 Jan 1859 spr Frances Brennan "I supplied the ceremonies in sickness; previously baptized by its [*sic*] Aunt, an intelligent Catholic woman" H. B. Coskery, priest p178

HALL – Joseph Andrew, b 16 Dec 1856 lc/o John Hall & Louisa Hines bp 22 Mar 1857 spr Henrietta Platts p115

HALL – Joseph Hollison, b 3 May 1857 lc/o William Henry Hall & Susan Day bp 31 May 1857 spr Ellen Welsh p122

HALL – Mary Elizabeth Hall (c), "17 years old" bp 1 Oct 1865 spr Anna Green p365

HALL – Mary Hall, "aged 30 years" bp 6 Nov 1867 spr Walter McCann [*ed. note: word after "Hall" in record not discernible*] p426

HALL – Robert Thomas (c), b 5 Nov 1862 lc/o Basil Hall & Margaret Quinn bp 11 Nov 1862 spr Mary Harrison p294

HAMILTON – Lavinia Hamilton, b 6 Aug 1865 lc/o William Hamilton & Angeline Skipper bp 18 Sep 1865 spr Rose Reilly p365

HAMILTON – Mary Di, b *ndg* lc/o _____ Hamilton & Lyons [sic] p278

HAMMER – Ida Elizabeth, b 6 Nov 1866 lc/o John Hammer & Philomena Fleddermann bp 19 Nov 1866 spr Elizabeth Heinekamp p399

HAMMER – Philomena Josephine, b 25 Feb 1868 lc/o John Hammer & Philomena Fledderman bp 10 Mar 1868 spr Henry & Elizabeth Fledderman p435

HAMMETT – Jesse Clifton, b 5 Sep 1856 lc/o Jesse Hammett & Eliza Murray bp 13 Nov 1856 spr Elizabeth Cash p101

HAMMILL – Mary Ann, b 7 Nov 1865 lc/o Patk. Hammill & Mary Maher bp 16 Nov 1865 spr Edwd. & Mary Hughes p369

HANDRISHAW – Edward James, b 19 Aug 1856 lc/o Bryan Handrishaw & Catherine Griffin pb 22 Aug 1856 spr Elizabeth Griffin p93

HANEY – Cecilia, b 21 Sep 1865 lc/o James Haney & Mary Falcony bp 15 Oct 1865 spr Francis Bourget & Mary Hult p367

HANEY – Mary Frances, b 9 Mar 1868 lc/o Jane Haney & Mary Fulemet bp 17 Apr 1868 spr Martin Hutois & Mary Hutois p439

HANEY – William, b 21 Oct 1863 lc/o James Haney & Mary Stalconet bp 7 Dec 1863 spr Patk. Haney & Cecilia Heweth p321

HANLAN – Catharine, b 13 Jan 1862 lc/o Bernard Hanlan & Rose Hanlan bp 25 Jan 1862 spr Kate Hanlan p272

HANLAN – Ella Martina, b 30 Jan 1869 lc/o Bernard Hanlan & Rose Hanlan bp 13 Feb 1869 spr Ella Cavanagh p465

HANLAN – Emily, b 3 May 1866 lc/o Bernard Hanlan & Rose Hanlan bp 19 May 1866 spr Kate Garvey p383

HANLAN – Margaret Emily, b 3 Oct 1864 lc/o Bernard Hanlan & Rose Hanlan bp 15 Oct 1864 spr Bridget Hanlan p342

HANLAN – Mary Elizabeth, b 19 Jun 1859 lc/o Bernard Hanlan & Rose Hanlan bp 3 Jul 1859 spr Hugh Kelly & Ellen Grimes p194

HANLY – Catharine, b 22 Jul 1865 c/o Michael Hanly & Catharine Ward Hanly bp 30 Jul 1865 spr Jno. Ward & Cath. Rooney p361

HANSEN – Catharine Amelia Hansen, "aged 21 years" bp 3 Jul 1869 spr Barbara Smith "baptized conditionally" H. B. Coskery, priest p475

HANSY – John Henry, b 5 Dec 1870 lc/o John Hansy "of Baltimore" & Catharine Debring "of the same place in Maryland" bp 8 Dec 1870 spr Henry Henkins & Elizabeth Minnick p516

HARDEN – Daniel, b 17 Jan 1857 lc/o Daniel Harden & Sebar Smith bp 5 May 1857 spr Mary Ann Bogue p119

HARDEN – James, b 17 Jan 1857 lc/o Daniel Harden & Sebar Smith bp 5 May 1857 spr Mary Hagan p119

HARDESTY – Anna Hardesty, "age about 18 years" bp 16 Mar 1856 spr Caroline Coskery p76

HARDEY – Edward, b 23 Oct 1862 lc/o John Hardey & Caroline Cassell bp 4 Dec 1862 spr Ann Mitchell (all c) p297

HARDEY – Thomas, b 23 Oct 1862 lc/o John Hardey & Caroline Cassell bp 4 Dec 1862 spr Caroline Thomas (all c) p297

HARDING – John Lackland, b 5 Sep 1863 William Harding & Harriet ______ bp 21 Sep 1863 spr Louisa Quinlan p315

HARDY - Joseph, [*ed. note: surname is recorded both as Dobbins and Hardy*] b 24 Apr 1869 c/o Henry Dobbins & Mary Elizabeth Hardy bp 15 May 1869 spr Caroline Hardy (all c) p471

HARDY – Agnes, b 17 May 1855 lc/o John Hardy & Caroline Cassin (c) bp 31 Jul 1855 spr Caroline Carrolton p54

HARDY – Frances, b 13 Dec 1857 lc/o John Hardy & Caroline Cassel (all c) bp 16 Jan 1858 spr Henrietta Plater p147

HARDY – Joseph, b 2 Sep 1859 lc/o John Hardy & Caroline Hardy (c), bp 27 Sep 1859 spr Agnes Boyd p201

HARE – Ann Cora, b 25 Aug 1856 lc/o Edward Hare & Rosina Foy bp 3 Oct 1856 spr Eleanor Foy p98

HARE – Margaret Catharine, b 18 Jan 1861 lc/o Edward Hare & Rosina A. Foy bp 27 Jan 1861 spr Elizabeth Gumby p241

HARE – Mary Rosalia, b 4 Sep 1866 lc/o Edward Hare & Rosina Foy bp 12 Sep 1866 spr Loretta Smith p395

HARE – Peter Foy, b 25 Jan 1864 lc/o Edward Hare and Rose Foy bp 2 Feb 1864 spr Henry Sundig & Mary E. Nonan p325

HARGAN – David Patrick, b 14 Mar 1856 lc/o John Hargan & Ann Powers bp 23 Mar 1856 spr Mark Hargan & Mary Buckley p76

HARKER – Mary Louisa Harker, b 6 Oct 1844 lc/o William & Eugenia Carmichael bp 21 Sep 1864 spr Julia Spies "baptized conditionally" Thos. Foley, priest p340

HARRIG – Julia Gertrude, b 20 Jun 1869 lc/o Joseph Harrig & Julia Spies bp 23 Jul 1869 spr Mary Theresa Harrig p477

HARRIGAN – Ellen Mildred, b 17 Jan 1869 lc/o Bryan Harrigan & Jennie Horan bp 23 Feb 1869 spr John Gillen & Sophy Horan p465

HARRINGTON – Edward, b 3 Jan 1864 lc/o Abraham Harrington & Maria Boland bp 10 Jan 1864 spr Michael Boland & Riddy Millechise p323

HARRINGTON – Francis Harrington, "aged 18 years" bp 22 May 1869 "baptized conditionally" Thos. Foley, priest p471

HARRINGTON – John Joseph, b 4 Jan 1866 lc/o Abraham Harrington & Maria Boland bp 7 Jan 1866 spr John Noonan & Mary Cashen p373

HARRINGTON – John Samuel, b 30 Jul 1866 lc/o John Harrington & Bridget Silk bp 15 Aug 1866 spr Rebecca Drugan p392

HARRINGTON – Julia, b 27 Jul 1859 lc/o Abraham Harrington & Maria Boland bp 31 Jul 1859 spr Thomas Quark & Margaret Quinn p196

HARRINGTON – Mary, b 9 Feb 1862 lc/o Abraham Harrington & Mary Boland bp 16 Feb 1862 spr Geo. Nunan & Mary Boland p274

HARRIS – Agnes Alberta, b 25 Sep 1869 c/o George Harris & Mary Brown bp 7 Oct 1869 spr Georgiana Waltkins (all c) p485

HARRIS – Benjamin Francis, b 10 Nov 1859 lc/o Benjamin G. Harris & Elinor Ann Neale bp 13 Nov 1859 spr Dr. Francis Neale & Rose Neale "baptized privately" "ceremonies supplied May 4th 1860" H. B. Coskery, priest p205

HARRIS – Clarence Edmond, b 4 Feb 1862 lc/o Benjamin G. Harrris & Eleanor A. Neale bp 20 Feb 1862 spr Wilfred Neale "proxy for Clarence Edmon Neale" & Abbie Neale p275

HARRIS – Eliz. Conkling, b 6 Feb 1851 lc/o Thomas Harris & Isabel Barnes bp 9 Feb 1854 spr Ann Foley p5

HARRIS – Elizabeth A. Harris, "about 16 years old" "servant of _____ Dowling" bp 4 Jun 1859 p192

HARRIS – Elizabeth, b 5 Mar 1861 nc/o James Sewel & Rose Harris bp 29 Apr 1861 spr Ann Phipps [*ed. note: last name is listed both as Sewel or Harris in record*] p250

HARRIS – Ellen Mira, b 14 Jul 1863 [*ed. note: birth month must be recorded incorrectly*] lc/o Benjamin G. Harris & Ellen Ann Neale bp 2 Jul 1863 spr Francis & Ellen Neale p310

HARRIS – Emma Jane (c), b 23 Jan 1868 lc/o Thomas Harris & Mary Orvilla Queen bp 19 Mar 1868 p436

HARRIS – Frances Elizabeth, b 2 Jul 1861 lc/o George Harris & Julia Johnson (c) bp 14 Jul 1861 spr Francis Burgess p256

HARRIS – John Emanuel, b 16 May 1862 lc/o Thomas Harris & Mary Evidella Queen bp 20 May 1862 spr Margaret Hall (all c) p281

HARRIS – Joseph Conkling, b 25 Feb 1849 l c/o Thomas Harris & Isabel Barnes bp 28 Jan 1854 spr Thos. Foley & E. Blenkins p3

HARRIS – Mary A. Harris (c), "aged 25" bp 25 Aug 1864 "baptized conditionally" Thos. Foley, priest p339

HARRIS – Mary Frances, "aged about 9 weeks" lc/o Leroy Harris & Ginny Bell bp 3 Nov 1863 spr Sarah Ridgely (all c) p319

HARRIS – Mary Ida, b 26 Jul 1865 lc/o Lawr. Harris & Mary McKenna bp 17 Jun 1869 spr Mary Carroll p474

HARRIS – Mary Regis, b 20 May 1865 lc/o Benjamin G. Harris & Ellen Neale bp 30 May 1865 spr Wilfred & Mary Catharine Neale p357

HARRIS – Mary, "2 yrs 4 months old" lc/o John Harris & Amelia Lewis (c) bp 14 May 1854 spr Arnette Bartlett p12

HARRIS – Matilda, b 25 Oct 1846 lc/o Thomas Harris & Isabel Barnes bp 9 Feb 1854 spr Ann Foley p5

HARRIS – Thomas C. Harris, "aged 52 years" bp 21 Mar 1870 spr Sophia C. Reed p498

HARRIS – William Barney, b 27 Nov 1860 lc/o Thomas C. Harris & Isabella Barney bp 13 Dec 1860 spr Thomas Foley & Mary M. Lane p237

HARRIS – William Harris (c), "aged 45 years" bp 22 Jul 1863 p311

HARRISON – Ann Elizabeth, "6 months old" nc/o Charles U. Harrison & Margaret L. Catherine bp 19 Jun 1854 spr Margaret E. Glenn p15

HARRISON – Eleonora Harrison, "aged 18 years" bp 11 Nov 1861 "baptized…conditionally" H. B. Coskery, priest p266

HARRISON – Elizabeth Annette, b 25 Nov 1857 lc/o Loyd [sic] Harrison & Rebecca Colston bp 21 Oct 1857 spr Elizabeth Colston p138

HARRISON – Jane Harrison, "aged 26 years" bp 12 Oct 1860 "baptized conditionally" Thos. Foley, priest p232

HARRISON – John Mortimer, b 13 Aug 1862 lc/o John Harrison & Eleanora Treul bp 19 Aug 1862 spr Fanny Jenkins p287

HARRISON – Mary Elizabeth (c), b 18 Dec 1865 lc/o Elias Harrison & Ann Boston spr Harriet Laurence p381

HARRISON – Sarah Obetha, "6 years old" lc/o Loyd Harrison & Rebecca A. Colston bp 28 Dec 1855 spr Obetha Colston p69

HARRISS – Thomas, b 11 Oct 1854 lc/o Thomas Harriss & Isabella Barney bp 1 Nov 1854 spr Emily Jones p28

HART – Anne Hart (c), "aged about 32 years" bp 24 May 1868 "baptized privately" J. Gibbons, priest p442

HART – John, b 23 Jun 1859 lc/o Edward Hart & Mary Callahan bp 28 Jun 1859 spr Susan Kelly p193

HART – Lewis, b 3 Dec 1866 lc/o William Hart & Appolonia Addison (c) bp 13 Jan 1867 spr Elizabeth Bantz & Henry Hart p403

HART – Margaret, b 25 Fb 1865 lc/o Edward Hart & Mary Gallagher, bp 27 Feb1865 spr Mary Carroll p352

HART – Mary, b 2 Apr 1862 lc/o Edward Hart & Mary Callahan bp 26 Apr 1862 spr Susan Callahan p279

HART – William, b 9 Feb 1857 lc/o Eduard Hart & Mary Kallahan bp 10 Feb 1857 spr Margaret Harlekin p110

HARTY – Margaret, b 24 Oct 1861 lc/o John Harty & Honora Hogan bp 27 Oct 1861 spr Tim. Collins & Bridget Ryan p265

HARTY – Sarah, b 29 Mar 1863 lc/o John Harty & Honora Hogan bp 5 Apr 1863 spr James Hand & Bridget Hand p305

HARVEY – Lucille Mary Harvey, "aged 24 years" bp 30 Sep 1869 p484

HARWOOD – Louis Francis, b 17 Jan 1861 lc/o Louis Harwood & Ann Matilda Petit bp 26 Mar 1861 spr Mrs. Kilduff p247

HASE – Edward, b 16 Oct 1858 lc/o Edward Hase & Rosina A. Foy bp 9 Dec 1858 spr Mary E. Morrow p176

HASLERN – Samuel, b 30 Nov 1858 lc/o Samuel Haslern & Catharine Daley bp 5 Dec 1858 spr Bridget Mitchell p175

HASSAN – Ellen, b 19 Dec 1856 lc/o Charles Hassan & Sarah Taylor bp 11 Jan 1857 spr Joseph Hassan & Mary E. Cole p108

HASSEN – Elijah, b 19 Feb 1861 lc/o Charles Hassen & Sarah Taylor bp 3 Mar 1861 spr Michael Furlough & Sarah Halloway p245

HASSEN – Thomas Jackson, b 27 Sep 1862 lc/o Malcom Hassen & Ellen Nynce bp 27 Nov 1862 spr Julia Leahy p296

HASSEN – William, b 13 Sep 1858 lc/o Malcolm Hassen & Ellen Muntz bp 7 Oct 1858 spr Mary E. Welsh p170

HATCH – Sarah H., b 19 Nov 1857 lc/o Charles Hatch & Winifred Collins bp 13 Dec 1857 spr James Collins & Bridget Irwin p143

HAUPT – Elizabeth Ann Haupt "(born Myers)", b 11 Oct 1842 lc/o Robert & Eliza Myers bp 5 Mar 1860 spr Eleanor Haupt "baptized conditionally" Thos. Foley, priest p216

HAUPT – Elizabeth Ann, "about 2 months" lc/o John Haupt & Eliz. Abett Favorite bp 9 Jul 1854 spr Jon. & Mary Farrell p17

HAUPT – Mary Frances, b 24 May 1860 c/o Mary Jane Haupt & John Wright bp 10 Jun 1860 spr Elizabeth Haupt p224

HAUPT – Mary Josephine, b 1 Sep 1859 lc/o Charles M. Haupt & Elizabeth A. Miles bp 11 Sep 1859 spr Isabella Haupt p199

HAUPT – William Thomas, b 18 Aug 1862 lc/o Charles Haupt & Elizabeth A. Miles bp 7 Oct 1862 spr Eleanora Haupt p291

<u>HAVEREN</u> – Mary, b *ndg* lc/o Peter <u>Haveren</u> & Cath. <u> C   </u> bp 13 Aug 1854 spr Thos. Dagam & Mary <u>Haveran</u> p20

HAWK – John Henry, b 23 May 1855 lc/o Thomas Hawk & Elizabeth <u>Buttzell</u> bp 7 Aug 1855 spr Margaret Carroll p54

HAWKINS – William Francis, b 8 Nov 1868 lc/o Francis Hawkins & Anna Turner (c) bp 31 Jan 1869 spr Caroline Boury p464

<u>HAYARD</u> – George <u>Hayard</u>, Capt. USA, b *ndg* bp 13 Aug 1862 "baptized conditionally (died next day)" H. B. Coskery, priest p287

HAYS – John Antony, b 16 Mar 1857 lc/o John Hays & Ann Dorsey bp 12 Apr 1857 spr Felix Feenan & Mary McR_____ p117

HAYS – Laurence, b 19 Nov 1854 lc/o John Hays & Ann Dorsey bp 26 Nov 1854 spr Patrick McDonald & Mary McDonald p30

HAYS – Mary Ellen, b 22 May 1855 lc/o Patrick Hays & Ellen Madigan bp 11 Jun 1855 spr Patk. Kelly & Mary A. Budd p49

HAYS – William, b 15 Jan 1863 lc/o William Hays & Bridget Goonan bp 31 Jan 1863 spr Daniel Sheehan & Nora Tuorney p300

HAYSER – Clara Bertha, b 10 Nov 1864 lc/o Alexander Hayser & Mary Boscke bp 1 Jan 1865 spr Adolph Heyben & Agnes Freyholler p347

HEADLEY – Charles John, b 28 Aug 1822 lc/o John Headley & Charity Burrow bp 21 May 1857 spr John McNally p121

HEALEY – Francis Stephen Patrick, b 14 Mar 1854 lc/o Francis Healey & Mary Sarsfield bp 9 Apr 1854 spr Stephen Sarsfield & Catherine Dorsey p10

HEALEY – Joanna, b 8 Apr 1865 lc/o James Healey & Joanna Starkey bp 16 Apr 1865 spr James Ryan & Alice Ryan p355

HEALY – Ellen Alice, b 26 Sep 1867 lc/o James Healy & Joanna Stack bp 4 Oct 1867 spr Daniel Sweeney & Ellen Sweeney p423

HEALY – John, b 12 Aug 1869 lc/o James Healy & Joanne Stack bp 15 Aug 1869 spr James Healy & Mary Healy p480

HEALY – Margaret, b 5 Dec 1866 lc/o John Healy & Margaret Curtin bp 9 Dec 1866 spr Edward Healy & Alice Ryan p401

HEALY – Mary Rosa, b 10 May 1857 lc/o Francis John Healy & Mary Ann Sarsafield bp 4 Jul 1857 spr Mary Jane Ferguson p125

HEDGES – Charles Hedges, "aged about 55 years" bp 17 Feb 1870 spr H. B. Coskery p494

HEDWIG – Fredericka Elizabeth Hedwig, b 5 Jun 1860 nc/o Frederick William Rauch & Fredericka E. Hedwig bp 3 Dec 1860 spr Ann Brachland p237

HEFERMAN – Peter James, b 28 Jan 1859 lc/o Peter Heferman & Catharine Crane bp 3 Feb 1859 spr Michael Miskell & Mary Dolan p180

HEFFERNAN – John Flynn, b 18 Jun 1857 lc/o Peter Heffernan & Catherine Creighton bp 28 Jun 1857 spr Joseph Flynn & Bridget Cos_____ p125

HEINNEMAN – Mary Heinneman, b 18 May 1837 bp 15 Dec 1861 spr Germaine Garcia p269

HEMMICK – Sarah Maria, b 20 Oct 1855 lc/o William Hemmick & Caroline Totsipaw bp 7 Apr 1856 spr Agnes Connelly p79

HENDERSON – John Walter, b 10 Oct 1870 lc/o Samuel Henderson "of Baltimore" & Maria Considine "of Baltimore" bp 26 Oct 1870 spr Bridget Du_____ p515

HENDERSON – Mary Clare Virginia, b 7 Jan 1864 lc/o William Henderson, M.D. & Frances Lydia Thomas bp 25 Jan 1864 spr Mary Clare Thomas p324

HENDESSON – Eliza Minerva, b 6 Jul 1868 lc/o Samuel Hendesson & Mary Considine bp 7 Aug 1868 spr Michael Henchy & Lizzie Henchy p450

HENDIX (Simmons) – Anne, b 12 Jun 1864 nc/o John Simmons "white" & Jane Hendix (c) bp 18 Jun 1864 spr Maria Lowry (c) p335

HENNIGAN – Jane Elizabeth, b 27 Dec 1863 lc/o Charles Hennigan & Ann Conlan bp 3 Jan 1864 spr Saml. & Jane Baker p323

HENNING – David Henning, "aged 23 years" bp 14 Aug 1866 "baptized conditionally" Thos. Foley, priest p392

HENRY – Agnes Martina, b 24 Jan 1869 lc/o Patrick Henry & Rebecca Smith bp 3 Feb 1869 spr Eva Crain p464

HENRY – Ann Rebecca, b 30 Aug 1857 lc/o Patrick Henry & Ann Rebecca Smith bp 7 Sep 1857 spr James & Mary Carr p134

HENRY – Maria Catharine, b 8 Nov 1863 lc/o Patrick Henry & Rebecca Smith bp 6 Mar 1864 spr John Bannon & Maria Bannon p328

HENRY – Mary Elizabeth, b 29 Oct 1855 lc/o Patrick Henry & Ann R. Smith bp 4 Nov 1855 spr John Dugan & Catherine Henry p63

HENRY – Rosa Eva, b 5 Sep 1866 lc/o Patrick Henry & Rebecca Smith bp 9 Dec 1866 spr A. B. Crane & Margaret Cummings p401

HENSHAW – Mary Blanche, b 12 Sep 1855 lc/o John Henshaw & Eliza Jane Clark bp 29 Jan 1856 spr Elizabeth Clark p71

HEPBURN – Mary Rebecca, b 7 May 1855 lc/o Francis Hepburn & Rebecca Wilson bp 12 Aug 1855 spr Peter J. Fitzpatrick & Ann Marie _____ p55

HERBERT – Ann, b 15 Sep 1854 lc/o Michael Herbert & Ann Hays bp 18 Sep 1854 spr Mary Ryan p24

HESS – Delia Hess, b 14 Sep 1840 lc/o Samuel & Louisa Hess bp 27 May 1861 spr Mary Grady p252

HESS – Mary Louisa, b *ndg* April 1854 lc/o Samuel & Louisa Hess bp 8 Dec 1858 spr Ellen Reilly p176

HESS – Samuel, b 16 Jul 1829 lc/o Samuel & Louisa Hess bp 3 Feb 1858 p148

HEWITT – Lucinda, "aged 30 years" "wife of Edwin Bailey" bp 16 Aug 1857 spr Mary A. Ryan "I supplied the ceremonies to Lucinda Hewitt" Thos. Foley, priest p130

HICKEY – Mary Ann, b 13 Feb 1854 lc/o James Hickey & Ann Fahey bp 19 Feb 1854 spr James O'Brien & Bride Gillan "I supplied the ceremonies in case of Mary Ann previously baptized by her father in danger of death." H. B. Coskery, priest p5

HICKLEY – Mary Agnes Hickley, b 20 Jul 1854 lc/o James Hickley & Mary Whitaker bp 3 Jan 1855 spr Ann <u>Hare</u> p33

HICKS – Susan Lucinda Gertrude, b 27 Nov 1863 lc/o John Hicks & Georgia Uncles (all c) bp 14 Feb 1864 spr Andrew Kelly & Melvina Gibbs (c) p326

HIGGINS – Catharine, b 1 Jan 1863 lc/o James Higgins & Bridget Crane bp 26 Jan 1863 spr Ann McDevitt p300

HIGGINS – Eugenia Antoinette, b 17 Sep 1868 lc/o James Higgins & Amelia Larimore bp 19 Oct 1868 spr Helen Gaitley p456

HIGGINS – Mary, b 17 Mar 1858 lc/o James Higgins & Bridget _____ bp 7 Mar 1858 spr John Murray & Margaret Murray p150

HIGGINS – Mary Ann, b 4 Feb 1866 lc/o Jas. Higgins & Catharine Murray bp 18 Feb 1866 spr Patrick Ward & Cath. Ward p376

HIGGINS – Michael, b 11 Jun 1861 lc/o James Higgins & Catharine Murray bp 16 Jun 1861 spr John Kelly & Anna Gleeson p254

HIGGINS – Timothy James, b 21 Aug 1860 lc/o James Higgins & Bridget Crane bp 26 Aug 1860 spr John Brady & Mary Orr p229

HIGHLAND – Anastasia, b 27 Sep 1856 lc/o William Highland & Mary Jean bp 28 Sept 1856 spr John ______ & Anastasia Jeen p97

HIGHLAND – Daniel, b 27 Sep 1856 lc/o William Highland & Mary Jean bp 28 Sept 1856 spr Richard Spencer & Margaret Power p97

HILARY – Edward, b 12 Jan 1855 lc/o Felix Hilary & Judith Kelly bp 14 Jan 1855 spr Mary Colligan p34

HILL – Josephine, b 11 Dec 1847 lc/o Reuben & Catharine Hill bp 7 May 1865 p356

HILL – Julia, b 14 Sep 1865 lc/o Nicholas S. Hill & Mary M. Johnson (born Cooke) bp 7 Oct 1865 spr M. J. Spaulding, Archb. Balto. & Charity Ann Spaulding p366

HILL – Mary Catharine, b 7 Sep 1844 lc/o Reuben & Catharine Hill bp 7 May 1865 p356

HILL – Mary Ellen, b 8 Feb 1849 bp 29 Apr 1870 spr Catharine Boylan bp 29 Apr 1870 "baptized (*sub cer*)" John Dougherty, priest p500

HILLEN – Elenora, b 29 Jan 1854 lc/o Solomon Hillen & Emily O'Donnell bp 1 Feb 1854 spr Ellen Lee p4

HILLEN – Emily Mary, b 15 Apr 1855 lc/o Solomon Hillen & Emily O'Donnell bp 15 Apr 1855 spr Oliver & Luizhina O'Donnell p43

HILLEN – Solomon, b 7 Dec 1858 lc/o Solomon Hillen & Emily O'Donnelly bp 7 Dec 1858 "I baptized privately" Thos. Foley, priest p175

HILLENGEIST – Ida Mary, b 1 Sep 1869 lc/o Arnold Hillengeist & Alice Gray bp 17 Sep 1869 spr Louisa R_____ p483

HILLIARD – Otis K. Hilliard, "aged 33 years" bp 10 Sep 1865 p364

HINDER – Frederick Joseph, b 12 May 1857 lc/o Frederick Hinder & Jane O'Rourke bp 15 Jun 1857 spr Ann M. Kelly & James L. Derand p124

HINDER – Thomas Jackson, b 17 Aug 1862 lc/o Frederick Hinder & Jane Rourke bp 24 Nov 1862 spr Edwin Bailey & Mary A. Cassidy p295

HINDER – William Charles, b 19 Jun 1859 lc/o Frederick Hinder & Jane Rourke bp 13 Jul 1859 spr Joseph Cassiday & Elizabeth A. Harrman p195

HINES – Catharine, b 22 Feb 1868 lc/o John Hines & Mary Weld bp 1 Mar 1868 spr Patk. Man & Honora Haugh p435

HINES – Thomas, b 14 Nov 1854 lc/o Patrick Hines & Catherine Gallagan bp 26 Nov 1854 spr Michael Haily & Catherine McCullam p29

HISS – Mary Virginia, b 17 Aug 1855 lc/o Samuel Hiss & Harriet Owings bp 4 Sep 1857 spr Caroline Hanly p133

HISS – Sarah Louisa, "four years old" lc/o Samuel Hiss & Harriet Owings bp 4 Sep 1857 spr Caroline Hanly p133

HITCHCOCK – Laura Jane, b 17 Dec 1862 lc/o William H. Hitchcock & Mary Ann Nelson bp 9 Feb 1863 spr John P. Clarke & Sarah J. Clarke p301

HITCHCOCK – Robert Laurence, b 28 Jul 1868 lc/o William Henry Hitchock & Mary Ann Nelson bp 23 Sep 1868 spr Sarah Carr p454

HITSELBERGER – Edward, b 2 Mar 1862 lc/o John Hitselberger & Laura V. Morgan bp 7 Mar 1862 spr Theophilus I. Kelly & Mary A. Kelly p275

HITSELBERGER – Mary, b 18 Sep 1856 lc/o John Hitselberger & Laura Morgan bp 25 Sep 1856 spr Lewis Morgan & Jane Hitselberger p96

HITSELBERGER – Thomas Foley, b 9 Aug 1859 lc/o John H. Hitselberger & Laura V. Morgan bp 15 Aug 1859 spr Thos. Foley & Ann Hitselberger p197

HITSELBERGER – William Henry, b 28 Nov 1852 lc/o William Hitselberger & Eliz. Farman bp 10 Oct 1854 spr Caroline Elizab. Retrace p26

HOAR – Mary Elizabeth, b 27 Dec 1860 lc/o Patrick Hoar & Mary Devereux bp 6 Jan 1861 spr Dennis Conroy & Mary Nolan p239

HOBAN – Mary Ann, b 20 Jul 1860 lc/o Thomas Hoban & Mary Connor bp 15 Aug 1860 spr Joseph Baker & Mary Baker p228

HOBBS – Celia Alexena, b 10 Nov 1868 lc/o John Hobbs & Frances E. Fillinger bp 8 Aug 1869 spr Josephine Berry p479

HOBLEIN – Mary Loretta Josephine, b 20 Jun 1857 lc/o John Alexander Hoblein & Julia Elizabeth Corbet bp 30 Aug 1857 spr James Reil & Loretta Dunace p132

HOFFMAN – Barbara Hoffman, b 4 Jul 1843 "in Germany" bp 31 May 1859 spr Emily E. Long p191

HOFFMAN – Mary Frances, b 3 May 1865 lc/o Charles Hoffman & Mary Daugherty bp 4 Jun 1865 spr Patk. Henry & Kate Daugherty p357

HOFFMAN – Matilda Mary, b 2 June 1837 lc/o Henry & Elizabeth Hoffman bp 7 Mar 1856 spr Emily Jones p74

HOGARTY – Bernard, b 3 Apr 1858 lc/o Edward Hogarty & Mary Quail bp 11 Apr 1858 spr John Reardon & Catherine Ryan p153

HOGARTY – William Henry, b 22 Jan 1861 lc/o Edward Hogarty & Mary McQuaide bp 3 Feb 1861 spr Jane Boylan & Mary McMahon p242

HOGGSON – Hamilton Samuel, b 24 Sep 1861 lc/o Hamilton Hoggson & Mary Ann Cunningham bp 3 Oct 1861 g – Mary Finigan p261

HOHN – Mary Catharine, b 6 Jul 1865 lc/o Edward Hohn & Emma Smith bp 13 Aug 1865 spr Charles Davis & Cath. Roche p362

HOLBEIN – Annie Cecilia, b 1 May 1863 lc/o John Holbein & Julia Corbitt bp 1 Jul 1863 spr Jane E. Holbein p310

HOLBROOK – Edward Winfield, b 15 May 1859 nc/o Edmund Salmon & Mary Eliza Holbrook bp 6 Oct 1859 spr Ann E. Holbrook p201

HOLDEN – Margaret, b 13 Nov 1868 lc/o Richard Holden & Mary Maloy bp 15 Nov 1868 spr Tho. Giloy & Joanna Malon p457

HOLDEN – Margaret, b 19 Sep *ndg* [*ed. note: most likely 1870*] lc/o Richard Holden "of County Wexford, Ireland" & Mary Malloy "of the same place" bp 25 Sep 1870 spr Mary J. Delaney p510

HOLLAND – Mary, b 8 Apr 1859 lc/o Bernard Holland & Catharine M. McTague bp 29 Apr 1859 spr Timothy Rogan & Mary McTague p188

HOLLINGSWORTH – Cyrus, b 20 Sep 1816 "in Virginia" c/o Isaac Hollingsworth & Hannah Parkins bp 19 Dec 1859 "I confirmed him at the same time" Francis Patrick Archb. p 209

HOLLOHAN – Mary Ann, b 4 Sep 1856 lc/o Peter Hollohan & Hannah Finigan bp 4 Sep 1856 spr James Kelly & Ann Cockland p94

HOLLORAN – Mary Ellen, b 10 Feb 1856 lc/o Timothy Holloran & Alice Hughes bp 16 Mar 1856 spr Jas. Hays & Honora Shehey p76

HOLMES – Alexander Holmes, "aged 27 years" bp 27 Jun 1867 p415

HOLMES – Charles Alexander, b 1 Mar 1870 lc/o Alex Holmes & Lucy Griffith bp 13 Mar 1870 spr Mrs. Dulles "baptized (priv)" Thomas S. Lee, priest p495

HOLMES – Mary Vincent, b 10 Feb 1851 "an orphan in St. Joseph's Home of Industry" bp 21 Nov 1865 spr Rebecca Thompson p369

HOLZER – Adolphus Holzer, b 8 Mar 1870 lc/o Adolphus F. Holzer & Margaret O'Grady bp 9 Mar 1870 spr Thomas O'Grady & Annie O'Brien p495

HOME – Anna, b 11 Apr 1868 lc/o John Home & Sarah Hughes bp 22 Apr 1868 spr Mary Hughes p440

HOME – Mary Cecilia, b 25 Dec 1862 lc/o John Home & Sarah Hughes bp 30 Dec 1862 spr Mary Hughes p298

HONEYWELL – Caroline Clarke, b 9 Oct 1858 lc/o John Honeywell & Frances Smith bp 9 Jul 1859 spr Margaret Cassin p194

HONEYWELL – Cecilia Frances, b 20 Jul 1865 lc/o John Honeywell & Frances Smith bp 17 Jul 1866 spr Fanny Elder p388

HONEYWELL – Eugenia Stenson, b 9 Mar 1861 lc/o John Honeywell & Frances Smith bp 11 Feb 1863 spr Mary Honeywell & Mary E. Baldwin p301

HONEYWELL – Frances Dallam Honeywell, b *ndg* spr Mary E. Baldwin bp 12 Apr 1867 "baptized conditionally" Jas. Gibbons, priest p410

HONEYWELL – Francis Levi, b 24 Mar 1857 lc/o John Honeywell & Frances D. Smith bp 26 Aug 1857 spr Mary Cassin [brother of Ann Matilda Hunter Honeywell] p131

HONEYWELL – George Gover, b 8 Jul 1854 lc/o John Honeywell & Frances Smith bp 23 Jul 1855 p53

HONEYWELL – James McGraw, b 4 Jul 1862 lc/o John Honeywell & Frances Smith bp 11 Feb 1863 spr Mary Honeywell & Mary E. Baldwin p301

HONEYWELL – Marion Grant Agnes, 1 May 1864 lc/o John Honeywell & Frances Smith bp 14 Dec 1864 spr Mary E. Smith p346

HONEYWELL – Mary, b 30 Aug 1849 lc/o John Honeywell & Frances Smith bp 12 Jul 1859 "Wm. Robt. Jenkins had baptized this child when in danger of death. I administered the ceremonies." H. B. Coskery, priest p195

HONEYWELL –Ann Matilda Hunter, b 24 Dec 1855 lc/o John Honeywell & Frances D. Smith bp 26 Aug 1857 spr Mary Cassin [sister of Francis Levi Honeywell] p131

HOOK – Henry Matthew, b 26 Oct 1853 lc/o J. Hook & Maria King bp *ndg* May 1855 spr Maria Sophia Kelly [*ed. note: baptism day omitted in record; record was entered in baptismal record between 18 & 19 May 1855*] p47

HOOK – Margaret Ann, b 25 Feb 1866 lc/o Rudolph Hook & Marg. McCoy bp 21 Apr 1866 spr Ann McCoy p382

HOOPER – Ann Hooper, "37 years old" bp 12 Feb 1869 p465

HOOPER – Anna Hooper, "aged about 20 years" bp 29 May 1868 spr Rosa Hooper p443

HOOPER – Arthur Jerome Hooper, b 15 Jan 1860 lc/o James Hooper & Mary Vernet__ bp 3 Mar 1860 spr Mary Ward p216

HOOPER – Charles Leander, b 15 Dec 1868 lc/o George W. Hooper & Mary Ginniss bp 3 Jan 1869 spr Mary Ann Hooper p462

HOOPER – James Martin, b 9 Aug 1858 lc/o James Hooper & Mary E. Vernetson bp 17 Apr 1859 spr James Boyle & Annie Hooper p187

HOOPER – John Philip, b 13 Mar 1860 lc/o James Benjamin Hooper & Marietta Greenwall bp 25 Mar 1860 spr Arabella Jordan p217

HOOPER – Joseph, b 9 Aug _____ lc/o George Hooper & Mary Ginniss bp 19 Aug 1866 [*ed. note: year of birth is not written, however, it most likely was 1866*] p392

HOOPER – Maria, b 3 Sep 1849 lc/o William Henry Hooper & Martha Ann Hodges bp 8 Aug 1859 spr Rose Hooper "baptized conditionally" H. B. Coskery, priest p197

HOOPER – Martha Rosalia, b *ndg* May 1844 lc/o William Henry Hooper & Ann Hodges bp 20 Jun 1857 spr Virginia Hooper "baptized conditionally" H. B. Coskery, priest p124

HOOPER – Virginia, bp 20 May 1857 spr Ann Hooper "baptized conditionally" H. B. Coskery, priest p121

HOPKINS – Laura Augusta Hopkins, b *ndg* bp 22 Jun 1863 spr J. M. Hopkins p309

HOPKINSON – Benjamin Merrill Rhoades, b 18 Sep 1857 lc/o Dr. Moses A.A. _____ Hopkinson & Elizabeth Ann Frailey bp 17 Oct 1857 spr Betty Slater p138

HOPKINSON – Emily Jones, b 22 Jul 1855 lc/o Moses A. _____ F. Hopkinson & Elizabeth Ann Failey bp 22 Aug 1855 spr Dr. Felix Jenkins & Julia Pittman p56

HORAN – Eliza, b 28 Jul 1865 lc/o Francis Horan & Margaret Geoghan bp 16 Aug 1865 spr Rudy Grady & Eliza Murphy p362

HORAN – Margaret, b 24 May 1856 lc/o Francis Horan & Margaret Gahagan bp 12 Jul 1856 spr William Gahagan & Maria Farrell p89

HORE – Joanna, b 5 Aug 1858 lc/o Patrick Hore & Mary Devereux bp 8 Aug 1858 spr Thos. Devereux & Bridget Doyle p166

HORNE – Ellen, b 17 Aug 1866 lc/o John Horne & Sarah Hughes bp 22 Aug 1866 spr Kate Hughes p393

HORNE – Francis Edward, b 2 Apr 1870 lc/o John Horne & Sarah Hughes bp 8 Apr 1870 spr Mary Hughes p499

HORNE – John Thomas, b 16 Jul 1861 lc/o John Horne & Sarah Hughes bp 23 Jul 1861 spr Mary Kearns p257

HORNER – William Francis, b 20 Oct 1864 lc/o Robert Horner & Anastasia O'Loughlin bp 26 Feb 1865 spr Francis O'Loughlin & Margaret Butler p352

HORREST – Mary Maud, b 29 Nov 1863 lc/o Patrick A. Horrest & Abie Mary Wilderman bp 28 Feb 1864 spr Mary Hook p327

HORRIE – Sarah Elizabeth, b 31 Jul 1864 lc/o John Horrie & Sarah Hughes bp 2 Aug 1864 spr Elizabeth Miller p337

HORRIGAN – John Thomas, b 20 Sep *ndg* [*ed. note: most likely 1870*] lc/o Michael Horrigan "of County Tipperary, Ireland" & Elizabeth McCormick "of County Galway, Ireland" bp 25 Sep 1870 spr Owen Boylan & Winifred McCormick p510

HOSHAL – Joseph Carroll, b 22 Jan 1860 lc/o Caleb Hoshak & Maria Creaney bp 17 Apr 1860 spr Thomas Creaney & Philippina Henislee "I supplied the ceremonies" "baptized privately by a Catholic woman" Thos. Foley, priest p219

HOSHALL – Abretta Mary, b 18 Aug 1862 lc/o Caleb Hoshall & Maria Greaney bp 26 Oct 1862 spr Terrence Coyle & Ann Coyle p292

HOSHALL – Jane Belle, b 27 Nov 1854 c/o Caleb Hoshall & Maria Craney bp 7 Jan 1855 spr Thos. & Mary Jane Crainey p33

HOSHAR – Helen Spence, b 11 Nov 1856 lc/o Caleb Hoshar & Maria Creaney bp 23 Dec 1856 spr Mary E. Bottimer p105

HOSSEFROS – Sarah Ellen, b 22 Nov 1856 lc/o Lewis Hossefros & Sarah Farrell bp 30 Nov 1856 spr Jas. C______ & Mary Farrell p103

HOWARD – Florence Emilia, b 22 Nov 1866 lc/o Matthias Howard & Anne Lyons bp 11 Dec 1866 spr Catharine Nolan p401

HOWARD – Leon Sanders, b 4 Jun 1854 lc/o James Gibson & Susan Winder (all c) bp 19 Jan 1855 spr Jane Cromwell (c) p34

HOWARD – Mary Elizabeth, b 9 Jan 1864 lc/o William Howard & Anne Lyon bp 12 Jan 1864 spr Mary Hoey p324

HOWARD – Mary, b 11 May 1861 c/o Robert Howard & Anne Rebecca Cole (c) bp 19 Jul 1861 spr Minty Lecompte [*ed. note: last name is listed both as Howard or Cole in record*] p256

HOWARD – William, b 20 Oct 1861 lc/o Matthias Howard & Ann Lyons bp 24 Oct 1861 spr Mary Kelly p264

HOWER – John Joseph, b 30 Jun 1861 lc/o Joseph Hower & Amanda Horn bp 18 Aug 1861 spr Mary E. Quigley p258

HOWER – John William, b 21 Sep 1869 lc/o Joseph Hower & Amanda Horn bp 24 Oct 1869 spr John Quigley & Rosa Seeger p487

HOWSER – George, b 26 Oct 1860 lc/o George Howzer & Ellen Kelly bp 13 Dec 1860 spr Mary Cox p237

HUDGEN – Mary Catharine, b 30 Jun 1865 lc/o Joseph Hudgen & Catharine Davey bp 23 Jul 1865 spr Patrick McCarron & Mary McCarron p360

HUDGIN – Willam John, b 21 Mar 1858 lc/o Joseph Hudgin & Catherine A. Dolan bp 11 Apr 1858 spr James Clement & Margaret Kernan p153

HUGHES – Catharine, b 1 Jan 1859 lc/o Martin Hughes & Catharine Flynn bp 9 Jan 1859 spr Michael Daugherty & Catharine Daugherty p178

HUGHES – Catherine, b 9 Mar 1856 lc/o William Hughes & Catherine _____ bp 16 Mar 1856 spr Thomas Gahagan & Margaret Hughes p75

HUGHES – Ellen, b 26 Sep 1855 lc/o John Hughes & Mary Maughlar bp 2 Oct 1855 spr Susan Murphy "I supplied the ceremonies of baptism" Jonathan McNally, priest p60

HUGHES – Joseph James, b 26 Jan 1858 lc/o Patk. Hughes & Mary Brannon bp 7 Feb 1858 spr Patk. McCain & Mary O'Brien p148

HUGHES – Mary Ann, b 22 Sep 1854 lc/o Patk. Hughes & Gaughan bp 19 Nov 1854 spr Thos. Gavin & Bridget Whalen p29

HUGHES – Mary, b 22 Feb 1855 lc/o James Hughes & Susan McKeon bp 11 Mar 1855 spr Pat. Hughes & Bridget Tracey p39

HUGHES – Michael, b 22 Dec 1856 lc/o Martin Hughes & Catherine Flynn bp 28 Dec 1856 spr Michael Dogherty & Bridget French p106

HUGHES- Mary Agnes, b 6 Dec 1861 lc/o John Hughes & Margaret Dougherty bp 13 Dec 1861 spr Margaret Dougherty p269

HUISTER – Mary Jane, b 24 Aug 1862 lc/o William Huister & Martha Baker bp 14 Dec 1862 spr Joanna Wright p298

HULIHON – Catharine, b 23 Jun 1859 lc/o Peter Hulihon & Ann Finigan bp 26 Jun 1859 spr Joseph & Bridget McNamara p193

HUMPHREY – Mary Elizabeth, b 10 Aug 1856 lc/o Edw. Humphrey & Mary Ann Gillen bp 7 Sep 1856 spr Margaret Carr p95

HUMPHRIES – Margaret Ann, b 6 Oct 1859 lc/o Edward Humphries & Mary A. Gillan bp 30 Oct 1859 spr Thomas Malloy & Margaret Reilly p203

HUNT – Catherine Ann, b 19 Aug 1854 lc/o Philip Hunt & Catherine Magee bp 20 Aug 1854 spr Richard Spenser & Ellen McGee p21

HUNT – John Francis, b 25 Sep 1856 lc/o Patrick Hunt & Mary Murray bp 19 Oct 1856 spr John Maguire & Ann Murray p99

HUNT – Michael, b 21 "inst" 1858 lc/o Patrick Hunt & Mary Murray bp 16 Jan 1859 spr Michael & Julia Fenton [*ed. note: entry birth date is "21 inst.", which would be 21 Jan 1859; this is obviously an error*] p179

HUNTER – Aherta Virginia, b 28 Nov 1853 lc/o Robert Hunter & Susan Starr bp 15 Jan 1854 spr Emily Diffendall p2

HUNTER – Daniel, b 28 Aug 1855 lc/o Robert Hunter & Susannah Starr bp 15 Mar 1858 spr Ann Doyle & Mary Hogan p151

HUNTER – George Henry, b 26 Sep 1864 lc/o George Henry Hunter & Mary Barbara Hoffman bp 31 Oct 1864 spr Geo. W. Simmons & Mary Lesch p343

HUNTER – Martha, b 12 Aug 1857 lc/o lc/o Robert Hunter & Susannah Starr bp 15 Mar 1858 spr Ann Doyle & Mary Hogan p151

HUNTER – Mary Eliza, b 14 Jul 1865 lc/o Israel Hunter & Rachel Norris bp 7 Oct 1865 spr Louisa Hepburn (all c) p366

HUSTER – Mary Isabel b 27 Apr 1861 lc/o Wm. Huster & Martha Bacon bp 23 Jun 1861 spr Sarah Jane Bacon p254

HUTCHINSON – Clara, b 16 May 1869 lc/o James Hutchinson & Ann Reisinger bp 24 Oct 1869 spr Kate Hutchinson p487

HUTCHINSON – George Leander, b 28 Aug 1868 lc/o George Hutchinson & Esther Phillips bp 12 Sep 1869 spr Catharine Hutchinson p483

HYDE – William Daniel Hyde, "aged about ten years" bp 29 May 1867 spr Margaret Nolan "baptized conditionally" Jas. Gibbons, priest p413

HYSON – Mary Laura, b 23 Feb 1864 lc/o Joseph Hyson & Josephine Dinkel bp 12 Mar 1865 spr James McCann & Louisa Dinkel p353

IGO – Charles Ambrose, b 24 Apr 1857 lc/o Michael Igo & Mary Ellen Cross bp 8 May 1857 spr Rose Campbell p119

INEMER – Louis Charles, b 6 Apr 1858 lc/o Lewis P. Inemer & Mary A. McCann bp 26 Dec 1858 spr Patrick I. Costolay & Mary McMananus p177

INGLE – Henry Ingle, "aged 24" bp 15 Nov 1863 "baptized conditionally" Thos. Foley, priest p320

INGLES – Ann Elizabeth, b 31 Dec 1861 lc/o William Ingles & Margaret Grainger bp 2 May 1862 spr Ann Reilly p280

IRVIN – Ann Grace, b 5 Feb 1866 lc/o John Irvin & Emily Clantice bp 21 Feb 1866 spr Peter & Agatha Clantice p376

IRVIN – Catharine Helen, b 25 Oct 1863 lc/o John Irvin & Emily Clantice bp 23 Nov 1863 spr Kate Clantice p321

IRVIN – Emily Victoria, b 2 Sep 1860 lc/o John A. Irvin & Emily Clantice bp 7 Sep 1860 spr Wm. Francis & Victoria Clantice p231

IRVIN – George William, b 7 May 1862 lc/o John Irvin & Emily Clantice bp 14 Jun 1862 spr Peter & Elizabeth Clantice p283

IRVIN – Henry Howard, b 7 Jul 1857 lc/o James Henry Irvin & Catherine Schimp bp 20 Jul 1857 spr Willie Wiley & Emily Road p128

IRVIN – James Henry, b 26 Nov 1858 lc/o John Andrew Irvin & Emily Clantice bp 1 Dec 1858 spr George Clantice & Emily Roach p175

IRVIN – John Henry Leo, b 18 Jan 1857 lc/o James Irvin & Ann Maria Sullivan bp 12 Oct 1857 spr Catherine C. Braden p138

IRVIN – Mary Elizabeth, b 31 May 1857 lc/o John Andre Irvin & Emily Clantice bp 3 June 1857 spr Wm. Wiley & Alexine Donnelly p122

IRVIN – Mary Gertrude, b 7 Jul 1869 lc/o John S. Irvin & Emily Clantice bp 15 Jul 1869 spr Wm. F. Clantice & Lucy M. Gildea p477

IRVIN – Nina, b 19 Apr 1863 lc/o James Irvin & Kate Schimp bp 17 Jul 1862 spr Ann Heffner p286

IRVINE – Mary Irvine, b *ndg* "received Mary Irvine in church" "baptized in infancy" bp 28 Sep 1864 Thos. Foley, priest p341

IRWIN – John Andrew, b 2 Sep 1854 lc/o James Irwin & Catherine Schirmp bp 18 Sep 1854 spr Ann Heffern p24

ISELAN – Harriet Iselan (c), "about 74 yrs old" bp 20 Sep 1855 spr U. Berry p58

ISOLA – Maria Teresa, b 26 Jun 1860 lc/o John Isola & Catharine Ferretti bp 29 Jun 1860 spr Anthony Rattagliati & Giacinta Farretti p225

ISRAEL – John, "aged 6 years last month" c/o Edward Israel & Catharine Adams "who being divorced married said Israel, her husband still living" H. B. Coskery, priest p448

IYAMS – Catharine, b 20 Jun 1851 lc/o William Howard Ijams & Ann Maria, "his wife" bp 19 Nov 1867 spr Emilie H. Falls p427

JACKSON – Anna Jackson (c), "20 years old" bp 19 Nov 1865 spr Anna Green p369

JACKSON – Emeline Amelia Jackson (c), b 14 Oct 1841 bp 23 Aug 1863 p314

JACKSON – Harriet Augusta, b 18 May 1852 lc/o James Jackson & Ann Maria Johnson (all c) bp 16 Jan 1855 spr Ann Hammond p34

JACKSON – Jane Frances, "born on or about 25 Nov 1857" lc/o William Jackson & Anne Eliza Carr (c) bp 30 Mar 1866 spr Mrs. Hanna Reynolds p380

JACKSON – Martha Ann, "5 yrs old" lc/o William L. Jackson & Lia Chalk bp 6 Jan 1854 spr Helena Jenkins, Caroline Jenkins, & C. A. Spaulding p1

JACKSON – Martha Jane, b 9 Nov 1855 lc/o Valette Jackson & Mary Ellen Bryan (c) bp 19 Dec 1855 spr Teresa Ward p68

JACKSON – Mary Aher, "7 mos old" lc/o William L. Jackson & Lia Chalk bp 6 Jan 1854 spr Helena Jenkins, Caroline Jenkins, & C. A. Spaulding p1

JACKSON – Mary Gertrude, b 23 Oct 1835 lc/o Abraham Jackson & Margaret Robinson (c) bp 27 Sep 1861 spr John Noel & Mary E. Green p261

JACKSON – William Hutchinson Jackson, "aged 27 years" bp 8 Dec 1868 "baptized conditionally" Thos. Foley, priest p459

JACKSON- Josephine, "7 yrs old" lc/o William L. Jackson & Lia Chalk bp 6 Jan 1854 spr Helena Jenkins, Caroline Jenkins, & C. A. Spaulding p1

JAKES – Anna Josephine, b 11 Jan 1855 lc/o Henry Jakes & Mary Ann Brooks (c) bp 18 Feb 1855 spr Susanna Hicks p37

JAKES – Philip, b 6 Nov 1857 lc/o Henry Jakes & Mary Brooks (c) bp 29 Nov 1857 spr Ann Brooks p142

JAKES – Rosina, b 10 May 1860 lc/o Henry Jakes & Mary Ann Brooks (c) bp 31 May 1860 spr Mary T. Brown p223

JAMES – Francis (c), b 10 Oct 1858 lc/o Henry James & Mary Richardson bp 2 Jan 1859 spr Joannah Carroll (c) p178

JAMES – Mary Ann (c), b 16 Dec 1855 lc/o Lewis James & Susan Mason bp 6 Jan 1856 spr Amelia Murphy & Henrietta Platter p69

JAMES – Mary Ann, b 26 Sept 1862 lc/o Lewis James & Susan Mason bp 6 Oct 1862 spr Mary Catharine Brown (all c) p291

JAMES – Mary Frances (c), b 16 Dec 1855 lc/o Lewis James & Susan Mason bp 6 Jan 1856 spr Amelia Murphy & Henrietta Platter p69

JAMES – Mary Jane James (c), "aged 17 years" bp 20 Nov 1860 spr Mary McGowan p236

JAMES – Richard Lewis (c), b 26 Jul 1857 lc/o Lewis James & Susan Mason bp 11 Oct 1857 spr Henrietta Plater (c) p137

JAMISON – Douglass C. Jamison, "aged 49 years" bp 17 Feb 1868 "baptized conditionally by Rev. James Gibbons" Thos. Foley, priest p434

JAMISON – William Douglass, b 24 Jan 1867 lc/o Dr. William D. Jamison & Eleanor A. Croxall bp 1 Feb 1867 spr Thos. Foley & Annie Emory p404

JANTY – Eugenia Pauline, b 15 Nov. 1858 "parents unknown, adopted by William & Ann Janty" bp 1 Nov 1859 spr Barbara M. Laughlin p204

JANTY – Mary Virginia, b 7 Jul 1859 lc/o William Janty & Ann Manning bp 10 Oct 1859 spr Catharine Hartegan p202

JARBOE – Richard Fuller, b 26 Jun 1867 lc/o John W. Jarboe & Annie Maria McMullan bp 2 Oct 1867 spr Obethe Colston "I supplied the ceremonies" "(baptized privately by me)" Jas. Gibbons, priest p423

JARRETT – John Edward, b 30 Oct 1865 lc/o Christopher Jarrett & Anna Mary Barry bp 22 Feb 1866 spr Ann Alderson p376

JEAN – Cecilia Elizabeth, b 27 Jun 1868 lc/o William F. D. Jean & Cecilia Elizabeth Phelps bp 28 Jul 1868 spr Mary Phelps p449

JEFFERSON – Peter, "aged 8 months" c/o Jane Jefferson bp 19 Jun 1861 spr Ann Harriman (all c) p254

JENKINS – Albin, b 11 May 1859 lc/o John M. Jenkins & Alice I. Shaw bp 22 May 1859 spr Mark M. Jenkins & Ann Jenkins p190

JENKINS – Alfred, b 13 Oct 1869 lc/o Alfred Jenkins, Jr. & Jeanette H. Roper bp 24 Oct 1869 spr Alfred Jenkins & Elizabeth Jenkins p486

JENKINS – Arthur, b 1 Feb 1866 lc/o John Jenkins & Alice Shaw bp 9 Feb 1866 spr Edw. Jenkins "of James" & Sally Bussey p376

JENKINS – Austin, b 2 Aug 1868 lc/o Austin Jenkins, Jr. & Adelaide Lowe bp 20 Aug 1868 spr Michael Jenkins & Isabelle Jenkins p452

JENKINS – Catharine, b 13 Aug 1857 lc/o Edward Jenkins & Ellen M. Rufner bp 21 Sep 1857 spr Wm. Kennedy Jenkins & Helena Jenkins "baptized privately dangerously ill" "ceremonies supplied 7 Oct. 1857" H. B. Coskery, priest p135

JENKINS – Edward Jerome, b 27 Nov1861 lc/o Edward Jenkins & Ellen Mary Hüffner bp 4 Dec 1861 spr Geo. Jenkins "proxy for Courtney Jenkins" & Ellen Jenkins p268

JENKINS – Elizabeth, b 1 Jun 1867 lc/o John W. Jenkins & Alice Julia Shaw bp 16 Jun 1867 spr Jas. G. Jenkins & Lilla Bryan p415

JENKINS – Emily May, b 14 May 1869 lc/o Felix Jenkins & Nancy Jenkins "of William" bp 23 May 1869 spr Robert Jenkins & Lizzie Jenkins p472

JENKINS – Eugene, b 18 Sep 1857 lc/o John Wilcox Jenkins & Alice Julia Shaw bp 2 Oct 1857 spr Wm. Jenkins & Aveline Webb p136

JENKINS – Felix Samuel, b 13 Feb 1862 lc/o Dr. Felix Jenkins & Annie Jenkins "of William" bp 24 Feb 1862 spr Austin Jenkins & Annie Jenkins "of Alfred" p275

JENKINS – Francis, b 18 Feb 1857 c/o Austin Jenkins & Margaret Ann Jenkins bp 6 Mar 1857 spr Harriet Jenkins, "proxy for Isabel Jenkins" p113

JENKINS – Franny Helen, b 23 Jan 1865 lc/o Felix Jenkins & Nanny Jenkins bp 1 Feb 1866 spr Michael Jenkins & Sally Jenkins p375

JENKINS – James Carrell, b 6 Jun 1862 lc/o John Jenkins & Alice Shaw bp 18 Jun 1862 spr Edw. F. & Sarah Jenkins p283

JENKINS – John, b 2 Sep 1855 lc/o John W. Jenkins & Alice Julia Shaw bp 8 Sep 1855 spr Adam _____, Jno. King & Rebecca Hillen Jenkins p57

JENKINS – Joseph Rogers, b 3 Oct *ndg* [*ed. note: most likely 1870*] lc/o Joseph W. Jenkins "of Baltimore" & Mary E. Rogers "of Baltimore" bp 12 Oct 1870 spr Rt. Rev. Dr. Foley & Eleanor M. Jenkins p512

JENKINS – Lewis Lowe, b 5 Jul 870 c/o Edw. Dustin Jenkins & Adelaide Lowe bp 30 Aug 1870 spr Meredith & Haddie Jenkins "I supplied the ceremonies" "baptized by an intelligent Catholic physician, Felix Jenkins" H. B. Coskery, priest p507

JENKINS – Mark Wilcox, b 4 Jan 1861 lc/o John W. Jenkins & Alice Shaw bp 13 Jan 1861 spr Sarah Jenkins & Sarah George p239

JENKINS – Mary Loretta Josephus, b 11 Oct 1863 lc/o T. Robert Jenkins & Rebecca Hunter bp 17 Oct 1863 spr Francis X. Jenkins & Mary Loretta Hunter p318

JENKINS – Mary Rebecca Hillen, b 8 May 1857 lc/o S. Robert Jenkins & Rebecca Ann Hunter bp 22 Aug 1857 spr Rebecca Hillen p131

JENKINS – Michael Courteney, b 28 Nov 1862 lc/o Thomas C. Jenkins & Caroline C. Piet bp 10 Dec 1862 spr Caroline O'Donnell p297

JENKINS – Robert Oliver, b 16 Jul 1860 lc/o Robert Jenkins & Rebecca Ann Hunter bp 19 Jul 1860 spr James & Ellen Hunter p227

JENKINS – Sarah Lilly, b 12 Oct 1863 lc/o Felix Jenkins & Nannie Jenkins bp 19 Oct 1863 spr Edgar L. & Hannah Jenkins p318

JENKINS – Thomas Courtney, b 7 Sep 1869 lc/o George Jenkins & Kate Key bp 19 Sep 1869 spr William S. Key & Eliza Jenkins p484

JENKINS – Thomas Meredith, b 18 Jul 1855 lc/o Austin Jenkins & Margaret Ann Jenkins bp 30 Jul 1855 spr H. B. Coskery & Maria Meredith p54

JENNINGS – Ellen, b 10 Mar 1869 lc/o Peter Jennings & Bridget Clancy bp 17 Mar 1869 spr Michl. Coolahan & Kate Clancy p466

JOHNS – Henry Franklin, b 1 Aug 1866 lc/o William Johns & Eliza Franklin bp 5 Sep 1866 spr Ann Marie Doheny p395

JOHNS – James Franklin, b 8 Apr 1860 lc/o William Johns & Eliz. Franklin bp 17 May 1860 spr Catharine Kuhn p222

JOHNS – Joseph, b 21 Sep 1863 lc/o William Johns & Eliza Franklin bp 30 Sep 1863 spr Eliz. Magauran p316

JOHNSON – Ann Ellen Cornelia Johnson (c) bp 25 Nov 1862 "baptized privately…in danger of dying" Thos. Foley, priest p296

JOHNSON – Charles, b 5 Jun 1857 lc/o William Johnson & Nancy William (c) bp 9 Jul 1857 spr Margaret Wilson p126

JOHNSON – Clara Hellen, b 7 Jun 1856 lc/o Clement Johnson & Hellen McFaul bp 15 Jul 1856 spr John McFaul & Jane Richard p90

JOHNSON – Clement Johnson, "aged 38 years" bp 19 Jan 1866 "baptized conditionally" Thos. Foley, priest p386

JOHNSON – Edward Joseph, b 24 May 1865 lc/o Edward Johnson & Mary Limbourg bp 22 Jan 1866 spr Rebecca Ploss p375

JOHNSON – Elizabeth, b 10 Sep 1860 lc/o Michael Johnson & Mary Blacklock bp 16 Sep 1860 spr Patrick Kane & Ann Johnson p231

JOHNSON – Ethel Mary, b 8 Jan 1867 lc/o Simeon M. Johnson & Nellie Theresa Reilly bp 27 Feb 1867 spr Jas. L. Brent & Mary Rebecca Young p407

JOHNSON – Francis, b 29 Sep 1861 nc/o Elliot Johnson & Johanna O'Connor bp 9 Oct 1861 spr Mary O'Connor [*ed. note: last name is listed both as either Johnson or O'Connor in record*] p262

JOHNSON – Francis Patrick, b 9 Aug 1868 lc/o Patrick Johnson & Mary McElroy bp 23 Aug 1868 spr Francis Trainor & Ellen Trainor p452

JOHNSON – James Andrew, b 1 Dec 1856 lc/o James Johnson & Catherine Rice bp 19 Dec 1856 spr Mary Ann Handley p104

JOHNSON – James Johnson (c), *ndg* "belonging to Wm. John Randall of Annapolis" bp 16 Jul 1855 spr Eliza Randall - H. B. Coskery, priest p53

JOHNSON – Jas. Henry (c), b 12 Apr 1867 c/o Mary H. Johnson bp 31 Jul 1867 spr Mary Louise Keene p418

JOHNSON – John Alexander b 20 Oct 1867 lc/o Clement Johnson & Ellen McFaul bp 27 Oct 1867 spr John McFaul & Marybelle Meeks p425

JOHNSON – Joseph (c), b 26 Oct 1855 lc/o Wilson Johnson & Ann M. Breenan (c) bp 19 Dec 1855 spr Mary A. Lewis p68

JOHNSON – Joseph Edward (c), b *ndg* Feb 1858 lc/o Joseph Johnson & Elizabeth Boggs bp 29 Dec 1865 spr Adele Augustus "baptized by a Catholic woman" "I supplied the ceremonies of baptism" Thos. Foley, priest p372

JOHNSON – Joseph Watermore, b 7 Jul 1867 lc/o Joseph E. Johnson & Anna C. Maxwell bp 15 Aug 1867 spr Matilda <u>Hiskey</u> p419

JOHNSON – Laurence, b 7 Oct 1868 c/o Mary Johnson (c) bp 11 Oct 1868 p455

JOHNSON – Lily Elizabeth May, b 15 Jun 1865 c/o Frances Johnson (c) bp 27 Aug 1865 spr Sarah _____ Lavette (c) p363

JOHNSON – <u>Magmina</u> <u>Vannertrand</u>, b 13 Aug 1870 lc/o Abraham Johnson & Cath. C. White bp 30 Aug 1870 spr James Brooks & Mary <u>Concrannan</u> p507

JOHNSON – Mary Ann Johnson (c) "17 years old" bp 26 May 1866 spr Blake _____ p384

JOHNSON – Mary Celia, b 9 May 1864 lc/o Col. Simon M. Johnson & Nellie Roche bp 16 Jun 1864 spr William Riley & Eliza Lee Mitchell "by Gessie Morre" p334

JOHNSON – Mary Elizabeth, b 22 Jan 1861 c/o William Oshier & Mary Johnson bp 4 Aug 1862 spr Caroline Smith p286

JOHNSON – Mary Elizabeth, b 23 Jul 1854 lc/o Clement Johnson & Ellen C. McFaul bp 23 Aug 1854 spr Ellen McFaul p21

JOHNSON – Mary Ellen (c), b 26 May 1854 lc/o Joseph Johnson & _____ Burgess bp 4 Jul 1854 spr Eliza. Brooks (all c) p17

JOHNSON – Mary Joseph, b 4 May 1857 lc/o Jacob Johnson & Ann M. Hurdy (c) bp 19 Aug 1857 spr Joseph M. Jordan p131

JOHNSON – Mary Stanislaus, "14 years old" lc/o Thomas & Mary Elizabeth Johnson bp 30 Aug 1866 p394

JOHNSON – Mary Virginia, b 2 Feb 1860 c/o Cornelius Smith & Jane Johnson (c) bp 7 May 1861 spr John Castor & Fanny Castor [*ed. note: last name is listed both as Smith or Johnson in record*] p251

JOHNSON – Sarah, "aged about 15 months" lc/o Jacob Johnson & Ann Maria Hardy (c) bp 3 Sep 1860 spr Anne Johnson (c) "I baptized …in danger of death and not catholic" H. B. Coskery, priest p230

JOHNSON – Thomas Charles, "born six weeks ago" lc/o Thomas Johnson & Margaret Whelan bp 4 Nov 1855 spr Martin Whelan & Rose Kelly "baptized by a Catholic layman." "I supplied the ceremonies of baptism" Thomas Foley, priest p63

JOHNSON – Thomas Legnos, b 14 June 1856 lc/o Joseph Johnson & Elizabeth F. Bayses (c) bp 7 Apr 1857 spr Amelia Coal p117

JOHNSON – William Johnson (c), "about 54 years" bp 1 Apr 1864 "baptized privately" H. B. Coskery, priest p330

JOHNSON – William, b 17 Oct 1856 lc/o Robert Johnson & Elizabeth Teresa Rice bp 2 Nov 1856 spr Wm. G. Girvan & Ann Handley p100

JOHNSTON – Edward, b 12 Dec 1859 lc/o James Johnston & Catharine Rice bp 16 Dec 1859 spr Maria Quinn p208

JOHNSTON – John Thomas, b 29 Jun 1866 lc/o Patrick Johnston & Mary McElroy bp 8 Jul 1866 spr James McGarrity & Kate McElroy p388

JOHNSTON – Maria Louisa, b 5 Feb 1861 lc/o Clement Johnston & Ellen McFaul bp 6 Feb 1861 spr John McFaul & Ellen McElroy p243

JOHNSTON – Mary Ann, b 5 Jun 1864 lc/o Patrick Johnston & Mary McElroy bp 19 Jun 1864 spr Thomas Cassidy & Ann McGarrity p335

JONES – Alfred Alexander (c) b 23 Nov 1867 c/o Wm. Jones & Rebecca Scott bp 30 May 1868 spr Susan Clarke (all c) p443

JONES – Charles, b 1 Oct 1853 lc/o Basil Jones & Ann Burgess (c) bp 19 Jun 1854 spr Minty LeCompte & ______ ______ p15

JONES – Joseph Levet, b 5 Apr 1863 lc/o John Jones & Margaret Foreman bp 2 Jun 1863 spr Laura Jones (all c) p308

JONES – Josephine, b 14 Oct 1851 lc/o Ashbury Jones & Ann Burgess bp 17 Aug 1856 spr Henrietta Plater (all c) p93

JONES – Mary Matilda Jones (c), "aged about 19 years" bp 28 Feb 1866 spr Helena Chalat, "baptized conditionally" James Gibbons, priest p377

JONES – Rebecca Jane Jones, "aged 24 years" bp 26 Dec 1861 spr Maria Lyons "baptized conditionally" Thos. Foley, priest p270

JONES – Sarah Jane Jones "(born Baker)", b 13 Jan 1842 lc/o William Baker & Mary Potee bp 2 Feb 1860 spr Susan Jones p213

JONES – William Franklin, b 20 Dec 1867 c/o Mary Jones bp 23 Dec 1867 spr Olivia Turner p430

JONES – William Raymond, b 30 Dec 1860 lc/o John R. Jones & Mary Keenan bp 7 Feb 1861 spr Francis Gallagher & Ellen Clarke p243

JORDAN – Frederick, b 17 Sep 1865 lc/o John C. Jordan & Mary F. Wood (c) bp 6 May 1867 spr Ann Cummins p411

JORDAN – Joseph G. N. Jordan, b 20 Jul 1827 bp 12 Sep 1870 spr Francis Kelly p509

JORDAN – Margaret Ann, b *ndg* lc/o Henry T. Jordan & Margaret _ Jordan bp 10 Feb 1870 spr Charles Jordan & Mary Hipsley p493

JORDAN – Margaret Maria, b 1 Dec 1854 lc/o Owen Jordan & Ellen Kanes bp 11 De 1854 spr Jno. Ryan & Hillary Clarke p31

JORDAN – Martha A. Jordan, b *ndg* bp 11 Nov 1864 "I received in the Church Martha A. Jordan – previously baptized by immersion" Thos. Foley, priest p345

JORDAN – Mary Ellen Teresa b 25 Dec 1867 lc/o Henry Jordan & Ellen Wright bp 5 Feb 1868 spr Thomas Murphy & Catharine Murphy p433

JORDEN – Mary, b 7 Jul 1867 lc/o Henry F. Jorden & Mary Ann Hipsley bp 28 Jul 1867 spr Rev. Wm. J. Jorden & Mary E. Jorden p418

JOYCE – Florence Mary, b 4 Mar 1869 lc/o Edward J. Joyce & Marella Jean bp 10 Aug 1869 spr Gassoway Watkins & Anna Watkins p479

JUDGE – Agnes, b 13 Feb 1855 lc/o Henry Judge & Anna McNulty bp 4 Mar 1855 spr Mary Jane Fitzgerald & Henry Judge p38

JUDGE – Anna Mary, b 26 Oct 1861 lc/o Arthur Judge & Catharine Clarke bp 1 Nov 1861 spr Henry Judge & Ann Clarke p265

JUDGE – Arthur, b 18 Dec 1864 lc/o Arthur Judge & Catharine Clarke bp 1 Jan 1865 spr Stephen B. Spellan & Mary Clarke p348

JUDGE – Kate Helena, b 18 Jun 1863 lc/o Arthur Judge & Catharine Clarke bp 5 Jul 1863 spr Henry Judge & Ellen Clarke p310

JUDGE – Sylvester Clark, b 27 Dec 1866 lc/o Arthur Judge & Catharine Clark bp 1 Jan 1867 spr Sylvester Clark & Ellen Judge p403

KAMMER – Gerhard William, b 16 Mar 1855 lc/o Gerhard Kammer & Eliza _____ bp 25 Apr 1855 spr Albert Sontiron & Emiy Sontiron p44

KANE – Francis, b 28 Dec 1855 lc/o Michael Kane & Bridget Corcoran bp 27 Jan 1856 spr Thomas Madden & Bridget Drogars p71

KANE – James Edward, b 23 Dec 1855 lc/o Patrick Kane & Margaret O'Brien bp 25 Dec 1855 spr Edw. O'Connor & Joanna Powell p69

KANE – James Joseph, b 25 May 1868 lc/o Martin Kane & Joanna Griffin bp 7 Jun 1868 spr Theo. Griffin & Sarah Ferguson p444

KANE – Johanna, b 21 Feb 1859 lc/o Patrick Kane & Margaret Bryan bp 21 Feb 1859 spr James Kane & Mary Noylan p182

KANE – John William, b 24 Nov 1857 lc/o Patrick Kane & Margaret O'Brien bp 26 Nov 1857 spr Thomas Kane & Mary Martin p141

KANE – John, b 10 Jun 1956 lc/o John Kane & Bridget Mitchell bp 15 Jun 1856 spr James Flannigan & Esther Flannigan p85

KANE – John, b 26 Oct 1855 lc/o Patrick Kane & Catherine Quinn bp 2 Nov 1855 spr James Quinn & Mary Quinn p63

KANE – Margaret Ann, b 27 Jan 1863 lc/o Patrick Kane & Margaret Quinn bp 2 Feb 1863 "baptized privately" Thos. Foley, priest p301

KANE – Mary Elizabeth, b 23 May 1860 lc/o Patrick Kane & Margaret O'Brien bp 27 May 1860 spr William Quinn & Catharine Smith p222

KAVANAGH – Mary Lilian, b 26 Mar 1870 lc/o Thomas P. Kavanagh & Minnie Kuhn bp 6 Apr 1870 spr Joseph S. Kuhn & Maggie Kavanagh p499

KAYSER – Charles August, b 2 Oct 1857 lc/o Alexander Kayser & Mary Boschke bp 29 Nov 1857 spr Albert Aug. Boscheke & Anna Mary Linden p142

KAYSER – Edward Lewis, b 21 Aug 1861 lc/o Alexander Kayser & Mary Boschker bp 27 Oct 1861 spr Mary L. Boschker p264

KAYSER – Ida Mary, b 4 Aug 1863 lc/o Alexander Kayser & Mary Boschke bp 13 Sep 1863 spr Gustav Gusl & Ida Boschke p315

KEANARD – William Jacob, b 10 Nov 1857 lc/o George Keanard & Margaret Mills bp 15 Dec 1857 p144

KEANE – John, b 8 May 1860 lc/o James Keane & Mary O'Connor bp 13 May 1860 spr John McSweeney & Jane McSweeney p222

KEARNS – Ann, b 2 Mar 1856 lc/o Alexander Keans & Elizabeth McDonald bp 4 Mar 1856 spr Jane Rollette p74

KEARNS – Mary Vincent, b 19 Jul 1857 lc/o Alexander Kearns & Elizabeth McDonald bp 23 Jul 1857 spr Sarah Conlan p128

KEATING – Margaret Ann, b 24 Aug 1856 lc/o Patrick Keating & Susan Roche bp 24 Aug 1856 spr Henry Sherly & Margaret Sherly p94

KEATING – Sarah, b 15 Feb 1862 lc/o Patrick Keating & Ellen Roche bp 15 Feb 1862 spr Pat. Dunn & Cath. Whelan p274

KEEDY – Dr. James Keedy, "26 years old" register date: 14 Dec 1864 "baptized at 14 years of age by a Lutheran" "received the profession of faith" Thos. Foley, priest p346

KEEDY – <u>Gabril</u> Daley, b 15 Feb 1869 lc/o Dr. Samuel H. Keedy & Julia A. Darley bp 24 Apr 1869 spr Eliza Jenkins p469

KEEFE – Martin John, b 1 Feb 1859 lc/o John Keefe & Mary Leary bp 6 Feb 1859 spr Michael Keefe & Ann Leary p181

KEEFER – Clarence George, b 28 Sep 1867 lc/o Dennis Keefer & Sophie Dorf bp 5 Dec 1868 spr Helen Dixon p459

KEEGAN – Ella Pumphrey, b 1 Jul 1866 lc/o John Keegan & Rachel R. Pumphrey bp 19 Jul 1866 spr Martha <u>Ninsett</u> p389

KEELLY – Mary Ellen, b 7 Mar 1855 lc/o Patrick Keelly & Mary Green bp 9 Apr 1855 spr Thomas Green & Bridget Morace p42

KEENAN – James Henry, b 5 Jan 1864 lc/o Daniel Keenan & Mary Jane Derry bp 12 Jan 1864 spr Ann Derry p323

KEENAN – John Thomas, b 23 Dec 1856 c/o John Keenan & Catherine Keenan bp 19 Mar 1857 spr Janet Barry p115

KEENAN – Joseph Franklin, b 18 Jan 1860 lc/o Joseph Daniel Keenan & Mary Jane Derry bp 27 Apr 1860 p220

KEENAN – Terence, b 3 Mar 1859 lc/o Thomas Keenan & Bridget Conroy bp 3 Apr 1859 spr Patk. Lennan & Mary Bilan p185

KEENAN – Thomas Vincent, b *ndg* Jan 1862 lc/o Daniel Keenan & Mary Jane Derry bp 2 Feb 1862 spr Catharine Finn p273

KEENAN – Thomas, b 15 Jul 1857 lc/o Thomas Keenan & Bridget Conry bp 19 Jul 1857 spr Patk. Larkin & Ann Mahan p127

KEENE – Elizabeth Keene, "aged about 22 years" bp 7 Dec 1865 spr Susan Tubman p371

KEENE – Ella Agnes, b 20 Jul 1850 lc/o Benjamin G. Keene & Susan McMullan bp 13 Jun 1863 spr Susan Tubman p309

KEENE – Emily Keene, "aged about 40 years" bp 9 Apr 1864 spr Susan Tubman p330

KEENE – Helen August Keene, "aged about 19 years" bp 5 Aug 1868 "I baptized conditionally" H. B. Coskery, priest p228

KEENE – Joseph Mallone, b 1 Nov 1847 lc/o Benjamin G. Keene & Susan McMullan bp 13 Jun 1863 spr Augusta Keene p309

KEENE – Louise Keene, "aged about 25 years" bp 23 Mar 1866 spr Mrs. Austin Jenkins p379

KEENE – Mary Adelaide, b 1 Jan 1855 lc/o Benjamin G. Keene & Susan McMullan bp 13 Jun 1863 spr Augusta Keene p309

KEENE – Samuel, b 10 May 1862 lc/o Benjamin Robert Kenne & Virginia Water Ricketts bp 14 Jun 1862 spr Susan Tubman p283

KEENER – Joseph Morse, b 10 May 1868 lc/o Henry Keener & Mattie Jane Morse bp 1 Oct 1868 spr Sarah Ann Morse p455

KEEVES – James, b 23 Sep 1856 lc/o Andrew Keeves & Joanna Tool bp 28 Sep 1856 spr Clarence Leonard & Ellen Leonard p97

KEEZY – Mary Catherine, b 19 Feb 1856 lc/o William Keezy & Margaret Keirnan b 23 Mar 1856 spr Bridget Irwin p76

KEILHOLTZ – Jacob Keilholtz, "aged 51 years" bp 8 Oct 1865 p366

KEILY – Joseph Turner, b 26 Jul 1869 lc/o John D. Keily & H. Helen Turner bp 4 Aug 1869 spr Joseph J. Turner & Catharine B. Turner p479

KELLER – William Tell, b 5 Jan 1857 lc/o Williams S. Keller & Rosa Donnelly bp 17 May 1857 spr Rebecca Jane Eschbach p120

KELLY – Agnes Grace, b 17 Jan 1867 lc/o Joseph Kelly & Mary Ann Bishop bp 22 Jan 1867 spr Mary Jos. Butler & Michael Hallahan p403

KELLY – Andrew Jackson, b 25 Jul 1864 lc/o Andrew J. Kelly & Amelia J. Miller bp 6 Nov 1864 spr Rosanna Zell p344

KELLY – Bridget, b 27 Apr 1868 lc/o Patrick Kelly & Marg. Nicholson bp 25 May 1868 spr John Dorsey & Mary Dorsey p443

KELLY – Cecilia Helen, b 15 Nov 1854 lc/o Michael J. Kelly & Cecilia H. Hitselberger bp 22 Nov 1854 spr Timothy Kelly & Jane R. Hitselberger p31

KELLY – Denna Russell, *ndg* Jul 1857 lc/o Peter A. Kelly & Mary Jane Russell bp 28 Jul 1857 spr Timothy Kelly & Hannah Russell p129

KELLY – Eliza, b 29 Jan 1854 nc/o Mary Kelly bp 10 Feb 1854 spr Elizabeth Palmer p4

KELLY – Elizabeth Eleanor, b 10 Jan 1861 lc/o Thomas Kelly & Julia Welsh bp 12 Nov 1861 spr Sarah Bostick p266

KELLY – Emma _____ Regina, b 24 Apr 1859 lc/o Patrick Henry Kelly & Elizabeth Tierney bp 19 May 1859 spr Mary Jane Kelly p190

KELLY – Esther Ann, b 18 Dec 1860 lc/o Thomas Kelly "(deceased)" & Sarah Best bp 5 Feb 1861 spr Mary Douglass p242

KELLY – Harriet, b 24 Jul 1867 lc/o Thomas Kelly & Hannah Clark bp 1 Sep 1867 spr James Rooney & Mary Finnigan p420

KELLY – Ida Catharine, b 3 Dec 1866 lc/o John Kelly & Frances Logan bp 23 Dec 1866 spr George McGowan & Ann Cooney p402

KELLY – James, b 28 Jul 1854 lc/o James Kelly & Eliza Fox bp 13 Aug 1854 spr Wm. Woods & Mary Fox p20

KELLY – James, b 13 Aug 1862 lc/o James Kelly & Catharine Broderick bp 7 Sep 1862 spr John Neal & Mary J. Higgins p289

KELLY – James, b 22 Feb 1863 lc/o Michael Kelly & Catharine Kelly bp 1 Mar 1863 spr Michl. Egan & Dora Flanagan p302

KELLY – James Abraham, b 21 Sep 1865 lc/o George Michael Kelly & Caroline Chambers bp 8 Oct 1865 spr John Noel & Virginia Benjamin (all c) p366

KELLY – James Henry, b 21 Nov 1869 lc/o Henry Kellay & Ann Williams (c) bp 26 Jan 1870 p492

KELLY – James Patrick, b 17 Apr 1867 lc/o James Kelly & Rose Riley bp 10 May 1868 spr James & Susan Reilly p441

KELLY – Jane, b 25 Oct 1856 [sic] [*ed. note the birth year is incorrect as the bapitism month is May of 1856*] lc/o Michl. Kelly & Mary Gamon bp 3 May 1856 spr Wm. Duffy p82

KELLY – John, b 23 Dec 1853 nc/o Martin Nolan & Eliza. Kelly bp 189 Jan 1854 spr Mary Naughton p3

KELLY – John, b 15 Feb 1858 lc/o Michael Kelly & Catherine Kelly bp 17 Feb 1858 spr Martin Flannigan & Elizabeth Flannigan p149

KELLY – John, b 12 Aug 1859 lc/o Thomas Kelly & Margaret Reagan bp 15 Aug 1859 spr Thomas Reynolds & Ann Reagan p197

KELLY – John, b 12 Apr 1861 lc/o James Kelly & Catherine Broderick bp 21 Apr 1861 spr James Riley & Catharine Daley p249

KELLY – John Frances, b 3 Nov 1865 lc/o Thos. Kelly & Ellen McCabe bp 12 Nov 1865 spr Michael Murray & Kate McCabe p368

KELLY – John Henry, p 18 Jun 1856 lc/o Patrick Henry Kelly & Elizabeth Tierney Kelly bp 15 Jul 1856 spr Michael Tierney & Georginna Kelly p90

KELLY – John Michael, b 6 Nov 1856 lc/o Michael & Mary B______ bp 16 Nov 1856 spr John Kelly & Ann Gegan p101

KELLY – Joseph Alphonsus (c), b 1 Oct 1860 lc/o George Michael Kelly & Caroline Chambers bp 8 Nov 1860 spr John Noll & Mary Teresa Dubois p235

KELLY – Julia, b 11 Nov 1859 lc/o Thomas Kelly & Julia Welch bp 9 Feb 1860 spr Caroline Acum p214

KELLY – Julia Anna Kelly, "aged 35 years" bp 17 Jul 1866 spr Julia Greatfield p389

KELLY – Lucy, b 22 Jan 1856 lc/o Wm. Kelly & Ann McDonald bp 3 Feb 1856 spr Chas. Sellay & Sarah Tracy p71

KELLY – Margaret Lydia, b 30 Aug 1866 lc/o Henry Kelly & Lydia Gaines (c) bp 1 Oct 1866 spr Elizabeth Gaines p397

KELLY – Maria Ambrose, b 16 Aug 1855 lc/o Jeremiah Kelly & Mary Watson bp 7 Sep 1855 spr Anna Moore p57

KELLY – Maria Helen, b 5 Oct 1864 lc/o Joseph Kelly & Maria Anna (Bishop) Kelly bp 19 Oct 1864 spr James Sullivan & Ellen Sullivan p342

KELLY – Martha Ann, b 27 Mar 1863 lc/o George M. Kelly & Caroline Chambers (c) bp 13 Apr 1863 spr John Noel & Mary T. Dubois p306

KELLY – Martin, "age about two weeks" lc/o Martin Kelly & Julia Marrow bp 23 Oct spr Eliza Lavers p27

KELLY – Mary, b 6 Nov 1854 lc/o Peter A. Kelly & Mary Jane Russell bp 12 Nov 1854 spr Francis X. & Agnes Kelly p29

KELLY – Mary, b 19 Nov 1859 lc/o Martin Kelly & Julia Morran bp 24 Nov 1859 spr James Bickenstaff & Bridget Kelly p206

KELLY – Mary, b 7 Nov 1862 lc/o Michael Kelly & Mary Bradigan bp 16 Nov 1862 spr Michael Hogan & Mary Landigan p295

KELLY – Mary Ann, b 8 Jul 1860 lc/o Thaddeus Kelly & Mary Ann Carney bp 22 Jul 1860 spr Thomas McDermott & Mary McDermott p227

KELLY – Mary Anne, b 8 Mar 1868 lc/o Patrick Kelly & Rose Finnigan bp 15 Mar 1868 spr Thomas Nolan & Mary Bradley p436

KELLY – Mary Catharine, b 5 Aug 1866 lc/o James Kelly & Rose Reilly bp 22 Aug 1866 spr Mary Reilly p393

KELLY – Mary Catharine, b 5 Aug 1866 lc/o James Kelly & Rose Reilly bp 26 Aug 1866 spr Charles Reilly & Catharine Kelly "I supplied the ceremonies" "previously baptized by Rev. Dr. Foley" Jas. Gibbons, priest p393

KELLY – Mary Emma, b 26 May 1858 lc/o John Kelly & Bridget Fahey bp 30 May 1858 spr Jonathan Brown & Susan Fahey p157

KELLY – Michael Henry, b 4 Mar 1858 lc/o Michael Kelly & Mary Gannon bp 15 May 1858 spr Mary Barrett p156

KELLY – Michael Joseph, b 15 Sep 1867 lc/o Thomas Kelly & Ellen McCabe bp 29 Sep 1867 spr Daniel O'Rourke & Catharine Garry p422

KELLY – Michl., b 2 Jan 1857 lc/o Wm. Kelly & Margaret Troy bp 25 Jan 1857 spr Michl. Long & Catherine Kelly p108

KELLY – Rebecca, b 24 Oct 1855 lc/o Patrick Kelly & Mary Gilling bp 18 Nov 1855 spr Mary Ann Kelly p65

KELLY – Sarah, b 6 Sep 1859 lc/o Michael Kelly & Mary Brodigan bp 18 Sep 1859 spr Wm. Hickey & Mary Kelly p200

KELLY – Sarah Georgiana, b 20 Jan 1854 lc/o Dennis Kelly & Sarah Scarlet bp 23 Apr 1854 spr Ellen Kelly [*ed. note: entry for Sarah Georgiana Armstrong is listed as being baptized on the same date-baptized name of one child could have been incorrectly entered*] p11

KELLY – Sarah Jane, b 29 Dec 1863 lc/o Thomas Kelly & Ellen McCabe bp 10 Jan 1863 spr Timothy Loftus & Kate Glennan p323

KELLY – Thaddeus Alexr., b 18 Mar 1865 lc/o Thaddeus Kelly & Mary Ann Carney bp 26 Mar 1865 spr Susan Murray p353

KELLY – Thomas Henry, b 14 Jan 1870 lc/o Thomas Kelly & Ellen McCabe bp 23 Jan 1870 spr Patk. Killely & Ellen Kelly p492

KELLY – William, b 21 Feb 1854 lc/o Wiliam Kelly & Mary Kavanaugh bp 15 Mar 1854 spr Mary Burns p8

KELLY – William Thomas, b 4 Apr 1858 lc/o John Kelly & Solina Wrenn bp 24 May 1858 spr Margaret Carroll p156

KELLY – Winefred, b 13 May 1870 lc/o John Kelly & Mary Stofer bp 26 Jun 1870 spr John Henry Bell & Winefred Kelly p504

KELTY – Ann, b 11 Apr 1864, lc/o Martin & Sarah Kelty bp 29 Apr 1864 spr Peter Finnan & Alice Kilduff, p332

KEMP – Charles William, b 3 Nov 1869 lc/o Charles Milton Kemp & Matilda O'Keefe bp 21 Nov 1869 spr Patrick Rulty & Mary Ward p488

KEMP – Francis Kenwick Kemp b 8 Apr 1862 c/o Wm. A. Kemp & Caroline Holmes, "his lawful wife" bp 27 Aug 1862 g – Josephine Cropper p288

KEMP – Henrietta Kemp (c), "aged 55 years" bp 24 May 1804 "baptized conditionally" Thos. Foley, priest p333

KEMP – John Thomas, "6 months & 5 days old" lc/o Andrew Kemp & Anna Jackson bp 27 Sep 1866 spr Sophia Robinson p397

KEMP – Mary Virginia Kemp (c), "aged 8 years" bp 24 May 1864 "grand-daughter" of Henrietta Kemp p333

KEMP – Willian Henry (c), "aged 18 years" bp 10 Nov 1862 "baptized privately" Thos. Foley priest p294

KENDALL – Emily, *ndg* lc/o John Kendall & Elizabeth McEnespy bp 22 Jul 1867 spr Isabella Wilson p417

KENDALL – Walter John, b 7 Sep 1868 lc/o John Kendall & Elizabeth Wilson bp 21 Dec 1868 spr Malachi & Julia Bondell p461

KENDELL – Mary Kendell "(adult)", b *ndg* bp 13 Feb 1860 "baptized condit." "lawfully bapt. in the Methodist sect and received her abduration in presence of Eliza Doherty" Francis Patrick, Archb. p215

KENNA – Edward Kenna, b 10 Jan 1855 lc/o Edward Kenna & Ann Donavan bp 26 Mar 1855 spr Mary Quinn p41

KENNA – Mary Estelle, b 30 Sep 1869 lc/o William Kenna & Isabella Lowden bp 27 May 1870 spr Teresa Queen (all c) p502

KENNARD – Martha Lucinda (c), b 13 Jul 1867 lc/o Isaac Kennard & Mary Holly bp 28 Aug 1867 spr Jane Blackstone p420

KENNEDY – Charlotte, b 10 Jul 1869 lc/o Patk. Kennedy & Margaret McKew bp 15 Aug 1869 spr Louis & Mary Kolbing p479

KENNELL – Matthew, b 18 Mar 1870 lc/o John Kennell & Elizabeth McNasby bp 7 Apr 1870 spr Isabella Wilson p499

KENNY – Emma Jane, b 10 Sep 1858 lc/o Jeremiah Kenny & Mary Voxen bp 10 Oct 1858 spr Helen Lueekesi p170

KENNY – Mary, b 9 May 1857 lc/o Matthias Kenny & Catherine Conroy bp 10 May 1857 spr Thos. Conroy & Bridget Caton p119

KENNY – William Steward, b 26 Jan 1855 lc/o Dr. John Kenny & Emily Parrott bp 24 Feb 1855 spr Ann Howard p37

KERCHNER – Francis William, b 4 Dec 1857 lc/o Frederick August Kerchner & Ann Catherine Berger bp 16 Dec 1857 spr Frederick Wm. Kerchner & Mary Pratt "baptized privately in sickness. Ceremonies supplied Jan 6 1858." H. B. Coskery, priest p144

KERNAN – Margaret Ann, b 12 Sep 1855 lc/o Daniel Kernan & Margaret Kirby bp 23 Sep 1855 spr Michael McMahon & Mary A. Dean p59

KERR – Ellen, b 21 Dec 1866 lc/o Thos. Kerr & Anne Duffy bp 30 Dec 1866 spr Jas. Kerr & Annie M. Crogan p402

KEY – Martha Ann (c), b 29 Sep 1856 c/o Comfort Key (c) bp 7 May 1857 spr Emma Wharton p119

KEYS – Anna Newman Stewart, b 18 Nov 1855 lc/o Richard Keys & Mary Baker bp 2 May 1857 spr Sarah Mullan p118

KEYS – Cary Peysano William, "10 weeks old" lc/o Richard B. Keys & Rachel Barker bp 13 Apr 1867 spr Harriet _____ p410

KEYS – Mary Josephine, b 8 Jan 1859 lc/o Richard B. Keys & Mary Barker bp 8 Sep 1869 spr Thos. Foley p482

KEYS – Mary Keys "(born Barker)", "aged 36 years" bp 16 Jul 1869 "baptized conditionally" Thos. Foley, priest p477

KILDARY – John Thomas, b 24 Jul 1858 lc/o John Kildary & Emily Batchel bp 10 Oct 1858 spr Mary Ann Kildary p170

KILDUFF – Charles William, b 9 Jan 1857 lc/o Arthur Kilduff & Jane Gershafan bp 25 Jan 1857 spr Michl. Foley & Ann Long p108

KILDUFF – Ellen, b 6 Feb 1855 lc/o Stephen Kilduff & Ellen Carey bp 18 Feb 1855 spr Pat. Kilduff & Mary Carey p37

KILDUFF – John, b 14 Sep 1865 lc/o John Kilduff & Emma Batchelor bp 1 Oct 1865 spr Mary A. Kilduff p365

KILDUFF – Joseph Edward, b 21 Nov 1859 lc/o John Kilduff & Emma Batchelor bp 22 Nov 1859 spr Mary A. Kilduff p205

KILPATRICK – Mary Adela, bp 27 May 1857 c/o Martha Kilpatrick bp 16 Jul 1857 spr Catherine Welsh p127

KING – Ellen King, "aged 38 years" bp 30 Jun 1865 "baptized conditionally" Thos. Foley, priest p359

KING – John, b 30 Dec 1859 lc/o John King & Catharine Ferguson bp 22 Jan 1860 spr Hugh Barmore & Louisa Ferguson p212

KING – Mary Adelle, (c), b 26 Dec 1854 lc/o Richard King & Louisa Barnes bp 25 Feb 1854 spr Adelle Brennan p6

KING – Mary Henrietta King, "aged about 55 years" bp 9 Jul 1855 "baptized conditionally" H. B. Coskery, priest p52

KING – Susan Emily, b 8 Jun 1856 lc/o Laurence King & Mary Clingher bp 29 Jun 1856 spr Frances Wagner p88

KINNINGHAM – Mary Dolores, "in her 9th year" "an orphan of St. Mary's Asylum" lc/o ______ Kinningham & Mary Ann, "his wife" bp 2 Apr 1857 spr Mary Kelly p116

KINSELLA – Sarah, 28 Oct 1855 lc/o Wm. Kinsella & Sarah Doyle, bp 11 Nov 1855 spr Edw. _____ & Ann Boyce [*ed. note: faint record*] p64

KINSELLA – William, b 2 Oct 1863 lc/o John Kinsella & Kate Boland bp 4 Oct 1863 spr Edw. Boland & Winifred Quirk p316

KIPPEY – Margaret Ann, b 22 Dec 1860 lc/o William Kippey & Margaret Kernan bp 20 Jan 1861 spr Ann Scully p240

KIPPY – Agnes, b 19 Dec 1865 lc/o William Kippy & Mary Coonan bp 7 Jan 1866 spr Patrick Connolly & Mary Teresa Oates p373

KIRBY – Ann Theresa, b 30 Apr 1861 lc/o Dennis Kirby & Ann Travers bp 14 May 1861 spr John Travers & Mary Kirby p251

KIRBY – Charles Henry, b 18 Nov 1858 lc/o Dennis Kirby & Ann Travers bp 19 Dec 1858 spr John Henry & Mary Travers p176

KIRBY – Henry Kirby, b 5 Dec 1866 lc/o Dennis Kirby & Ann Travers bp 23 Dec 1866 spr Daniel Kerney & Mary Kearney p402

KIRBY – John Joseph, b 18 Mar 1857 lc/o Dennis Kirby & Ann Travers bp 12 Apr 1857 spr Charles Dunn & Kate Travers p117

KIRBY – Mary Catherine, b 13 Sep 1855 lc/o Dennis Kirby & Ann Travers bp 1 Oct 1855 spr John M. Tavers & Mary A. Travers p60

KIRBY – Sarah, b 6 Apr 1865 legit. c/o Dennis & Anna (Travers) Kirby bp __ Apr 1865 spr Joseph & _____ Kirby [*ed. note: baptism day illegible, but entry was between 11 & 16 April*] p354

KIRCHNER – Mary Catherine Dorothy, b 9 Apr 1855 lc/o Frederick Kirchner & Ann Catherine Berger bp 25 Apr 1855 spr Margaret Kirchner p44

KLINGLE – Susan Gay Julia Beatrice, b 18 Jul 1867 "in Washington D.C." lc/o Joshua Pierce Klingle & Laura Cecilia Tiernan bp 26 Sep 1867 spr Henry A. Fenwick & Anna D. Tiernan p422

KNIGHT – Andrew Johnson Knight, "aged 10 months" bp 16 Oct 1865 p367

KNIGHT – Ann Elizabeth Knight, "in her third year" bp 9 Aug 1866 "baptized privately" Thos. Foley, priest p391

KNIGHT – Anne Augusta, b 12 Apr 1866 lc/o Perry Knight & Mary Dove bp 21 May 1868 spr Catharine Braden p443

KNIGHT – Elizabeth Knight, "about 21 years old" bp 25 Mar 1856 spr Mary Carron p77

KNIGHT – George Washington Horice King, "aged 2 years and 10 months" bp 18 Dec 1865 "baptized privately" Thos. Foley, priest p372

KNIGHT – Gertrude Knight, b 25 Jul 1846 bp 20 May 1870 spr Mrs. Josephine Duke p501

KNIGHT – Mary Elizabeth, b 8 Jun 1864 lc/o Perry Knight & Mary Duff bp 7 Jul 1864 spr Barbara Bragdon p336

KNIGHT – Susan Gertrude, b 11 Oct 1870 lc/o Perry Knight "of Baltimore" & Mary Duff "of Baltimore" bp 11 Nov 1870 spr Mary Brodan p513

KNIGHT – Thomas Foley, b 20 Sep 1870 lc/o Isaac Henry Knight "of Baltimore County, Maryland" & Mary Miller "of Baltimore City" bp 7 Oct 1870 spr Elizabeth Anna Miller p511

KNIGHT – William Henry, b 27 May 1869 lc/o Isaac Henry Knight & Mary Miller bp 13 Jun 1869 spr Lizzie Miller p474

KNOWLES – Charles Meredith, b 8 May 1856 lc/o Henry Murray Knowles & Catherine Knowles bp 15 Jun 1856 spr John O'Neal & Bridget O'Neal p85

KNOWLES – Ellen Theresa, b 13 Feb 1854 lc/o Henry Knowles & Catherine Cuthbert bp 26 Mar 1854 spr Michael Hoar & Mary Knowes p9

KOENIG – Mary Catherine, "born about 8 months ago" lc/o Frederick Koenig & Mary Burke bp 22 Feb 1858 spr Mary A. Derry p149

KONIG – Alexander, b 30 Nov 1864 lc/o Frederich Konig & Mary Burke bp 1 Jan 1865 spr Mary A. Nooney p347

KONIG – Henry, b 21 Oct 1855 lc/o Frederick Konig & Mary Burke bp 2 Dec 1866 spr J. Gibbons & Annie Murray Gibbons "baptized conditionally" Jas. Gibbons, priest p400

KONIG – Jas. Thomas, b 11 Nov 1866 "(died on same)" lc/o Frederick Konig & Mary Burke bp 2 Dec 1866 spr J. Gibbons & Scervilia Nelson p400

KONIG – John Frederich, b 7 Jan 1860 lc/o John F. Konig & Mary A. Burke bp 9 Feb 1860 spr Ann Doyle p214

KONIG – Mary Ellen, b 25 Dec 1869 lc/o Frederick Konig & Mary Burke bp 4 Jan 1870 spr Eliza Ann Welsh p490

KOONS – Henry August, b 15 Aug 1868 l/co Thomas Koons & Alice Rooney bp 24 May 1869 spr Augustus Hepler & Mary Lusby p472

KREBS – Mary Elizabeth, "aged about 40 years" bp 8 Nov. 1864 "in a dying condition" "clinical baptism" Thomas Becker, priest p344

KREBS – Mary Ellen, b 20 Nov 1865 lc/o William Krebs & Catharine Whitaker bp 14 Jan 1866 spr Augustine Whitaker & Margaret Whitaker p374

KREMELBERG – John Dietrick, b 24 Sep 1863 lc/o John D. Kremelberg & Gertrude Jenkins "daughter of Jos. N. Jenkins" bp 5 Nov 1863 spr Josh. N. Jenkins & Gertrude S. Jenkins p319

KREMILBERG – Mary Augusta, b 22 Feb 1870 lc/o John D. Kremilberg & Gertrude Jenkins bp 12 Mar 1870 spr Thomas C. Jenkins & Louisa Jenkins p495

KRONER – Caroline Adams Kroner, "aged 17 years" lc/o John Kroner "(dec)" & Mary _____, "his wife" bp 4 Nov 1867 spr Lorie Hunter p425

KUHN – John Lewis, b 5 May 1865 lc/o James Sylvester Kuhn & Mary Staylor bp 18 Jun 1865 spr Margaret Staylor p358

KUHN – Mary Estelle, b 10 Jan 1860 lc/o Sylvester Kuhn & _____ Lippo bp 5 Feb 1860 spr Philip McLaughlin & Agnes C. McLaughlin p213

KUHN – Sylvester Joseph, b 13 Jun 1862 lc/o Sylvester J. Kuhn & Louisa Lipp bp 26 Jun 1862 spr A. Leo Knott & Fanny McLaughlin p284

KURNS – Mary, b 24 Aug 1854 lc/o Alexander Kurns & Elizabeth McDonald bp 27 Aug 1854 spr. Jno. Sebykec Easavius & Mary Smith p22

KYSER – Martin Fink, b 18 Sep 1855 lc/o James Keyser & Ellen McNulty bp 25 Aug 1856 spr Catherine White p94

LA REINTRIE – Julia Blanca, b 18 Nov 1869 lc/o Henry Roy de la Reintrie & Candelanie Cecilia de la Reintrie bp 28 Nov 1869 spr Louis Vincent Schmidt & Juliette _____ p489

LACEY – Vintie Ann Lacey, b *ndg* bp 24 Jul 1866 spr Sophia Gardiner "baptized conditionally" Thos. Foley, priest p390

LACY – Mary Louisa, b 2 Oct 1864 lc/o Maurice Lacy & Emily "(Smyth)" Lacy bp 16 Oct 1864 spr Daniel Lacy & Catharine Sullivan p342

LAFFERTY – Francis, b 5 Jan 1856 lc/o James Lafferty & Bridget McLaughlin bp 24 Feb 1856 spr James Gillan & Margaret McGinnity p72

LAFFERTY – Mary Lafferty, "22 years old" bp 16 Dec 1869 spr S. Mullan p489

LALLEY – Joseph Augustine, b 19 Mar 1869 lc/o Malachi Lalley & Jane McCann bp 28 Mar 1869 spr Ellen Sheck p467

LALLEY – Joseph Malachy, b 31 Mar 1855 lc/o Malachy Lalley & Jane McCann bp 15 Apr 1855 spr Peter Lalley & Ann S. McCarthy p43

LALLY – John Francis, b 6 Jun 1856 lc/o Malachi Lally & Jane McCann bp 22 Jun 1856 spr Francis Gallagher & Ellen Leman p87

LALLY – Joseph Maria, b 28 May 1858 lc/o Malachy Lally & June McCana bp 13 Jun 1858 spr Frances Elmira Fillinger p159

LALLY – Martin, b 26 Nov 1859 lc/o Martin Lally & Ann Hanley bp 4 Dec 1859 spr Michael Fallon & Margaret Connor p207

LALLY – Stephen Malachy, b 29 Dec 1864 lc/o Malachy Lally & Jane McCann bp 6 Jan 1865 spr Charles Lally & Mary Lally p348

LALLY – Thomas Henry, b 12 Aug 1862 lc/o Malachai Lally & Jane McGann bp 24 Aug 1862 spr Mary Lynch & James Lally p288

LAMPIUS – William Edward James, b 8 Jan 1870 lc/o Isaias Lampius & Margaret Ann Dorsey (all c) bp 17 Mar 1870 spr Mary Ellen Green p496

LANAHAN – John Alphonsus, b 25 Oct 1855 lc/o John Lanahan & Catharine Britt bp 20 Nov 1855 spr Maria Carr p66

LANCE – Joseph, b *ndg* Jul 1864 lc/o Joseph Lance & Emma Bunion bp 22 Jul 1866 spr Josephine Lance p390

LANCE – Josephine, "aged about 7 weeks" lc/o Joseph Lance & Emma Bunion bp 22 Jul 1866 spr Josephine Lance p390

LANE – Florence Ann, b 5 Dec 1863 lc/o Philip L. Lane & Harriet Brown (c) bp 1 Jan 1864 spr Georgianna H. London p323

LANE – Margaret Ann, b 16 Jul 1855 lc/o Timothy Lane & Margaret Connor bp 21 Oct 1855 spr James Hagerty & Joanna Hagerty p61

LANG – John Sinclair, b 22 Oct 1857 c/o John Land & Clara Turner bp 20 Dec 1857 spr Elizabeth Cassard "Said Land having married said Turner after having obtained through civil law a divorce from his lawful wife, who is still living." H. B. Coskery, priest p145

LANGDON – Charles Edw., b 17 May 1868 lc/o James Langdon & Mary Garrity bp 28 Jun 1868 spr Charles Kaler & Anna Barrenger "I supplied the ceremonies" "This child had been baptized by its mother, an intelligent catholic" H. B. Coskery, priest p447

LARKINS – Phebe Larkins (c) "aged 35 years" bp 21 Apr 1866 p382

LAROQUE – Pauline Virginia Laroque, "about 20 years old" lc/o William S. & Angeline A. Bladen bp 28 Apr 1868 spr Mary Alice Williams p440

LARY – John, b 20 May 1858 lc/o John Lary & Abbey Casry bp 23 May 1858 spr Jeremiah Murphy & Mary Lyons p156

LAUER – Michael John, b 22 Mar 1863 lc/o Michael J. Lauer & Mary E. O'Connor bp 1 Apr 1863 spr Theresa O'Neill p304

LAURENCE – Mary Ann, b 4 Oct 1858 lc/o John Laurence & Bridget Collins bp 10 Oct 1858 spr Mary Elizabeth Smith p170

LAURENSON – Frances, b 1 Jul 1858 lc/o Michael Laurenson & Bridget Conry bp 4 Jul 1858 spr James Laurenson & Catherine O'Brien p162

LAURO – John, b 5 Jun 1854 lc/o Richard Lauro & Isabelle Wilson bp 2 Jul 1854 spr Hugh Lauro & Ann McSherry p16

LAVALTE – Sarah Frances, b 8 Mar 1846 lc/o Washington & Maria Lavalte (c) bp 3 Mar 1864 spr Mary Feeney "baptized conditionally" Thos. Foley, priest p327

LAWLESS – Martin, b 27 Mar 1857 lc/o Patrick Lawless & Bridget Broady bp 29 Mar 1857 spr Mary Lyon p116

LAWSON – Mary Nellie Norris, b 5 Jan 1868 lc/o Thomas Lawson & Eveline Cobb bp 28 Jan 1868 spr Nellie Norris p433

LAWSON – Rose Cobb, b 24 Feb 1866 lc/o Thomas Lawson & Eveline Cobb bp 15 Mar 1865 spr Mary Hughes p378

LE GOURDE – Mary Agatha, b 21 Dec 1860 lc/o Laurence Le Gourde & Sarah Small bp 1 Feb 1861 spr Thos. Foley & Sarah Dorsey p242

LE GOURDE – Sarah Cathareine Le Gourde "(born Small)", "20 years of age" bp 30 Oct 1860 "baptized conditionally" Thos. Foley, priest p234

LEAHY – Nora Alice, b 22 Nov 1855 lc/o William Leahy & Julia Fitzpatrick bp 25 Nov 1855 spr Bernard Holton & Alice Fitzpatrick p66

LEDOYEN – Ellen Philomena, b 21 Mar 1866 lc/o John B. Ledoyen & Frances Slaine bp 15 Apr 1866 spr Thos. Foley & Mary Ellen Green p381

LEDWICK – Thomas, b 27 Jun 1856 lc/o Michl. Ledwick & Eliza Norton bp 6 Jul 1856 spr John Larkin & Sabina Norton p89

LEE – Benjamin, b 1 Aug 1856 lc/o Daniel Lee & Elizabeth Thompson bp 7 Sep 1856 spr Daniel Thompson & Rosanna B______ p95

LEE – Edward Grant Francis Anthony Lee, b 17 Mar 1861 lc/o Chas. Carroll Lee & Ella Grant bp 24 Mar 1861 spr Ed. Grant & Josephine Swartz p246

LEE – Francis, b 12 Sep 1967 lc/o Wm. Lee & Sarah Atwell bp 23 Mar 1868 spr Hannah Atwell "ceremonies omitted" H. B. Coskery, priest p437

LEE – Joseph Jenkins, b 9 Oct 1870 lc/o Carol O'Donnell Lee "of Frederick County, Maryland" & Matilda Dale Jenkins "of Baltimore" bp 18 Oct 1870 spr Joseph Jenkns & Mary P. Gouverneur p512

LEE – Lucy Ann, b 25 Oct 1869 lc/o Joseph Lee & Lucy Williams (c) bp 20 Dec 1869 spr Jane Thompson p489

LEE – Margaret Ann, b 14 Apr 1864 lc/o Farrell Lee & Margaret Carroll bp 19 Apr 1864 spr Rachel Bitman p331

LEE – Robert Clary Harry, b 21 Oct 1866 lc/o Geo. J. Lee & Martha Josephine Cross bp 16 Aug 1868 spr Henry Rogers & Susan Teresa Buchanan p451

LEE – William Duncan Keene, b 27 Feb 1861 lc/o William D. Lee & Isabella V. Keene bp 4 Oct 1861 spr Benj. Keene & Maria Tubman p262

LEECH – Mary Elizabeth, b 23 Mary 1860 lc/o George Leech & Margaret Carney bp 6 May 1860 spr Joseph Hyson & Mary Dinkle "I supplied the ceremonies. This child had been previously baptized by a Wm. Mullan, an intelligent Catholic" H. B. Coskery, priest p221

LEECH – William Henry, b 22 Jun 1858 lc/o George Leech & Margaret Connolly bp 1 Aug 1858 spr Thomas McIntyre & Mary Burke p165

LEFFLER – Charles Leffler, "aged 27 years" bp 23 Jan 1868 p432

LEFFLER – Mary Georgiana Leffler, "aged about 17 years" bp 5 Apr 1859 spr H. B. Coskery & Margaret Owens p185

LEGOURDE – Francis [sic] Alice, b 6 Dec 1866 lc/o Laurence LeGourde & Sara Small bp 24 Jan 1867 spr Alice B. Bell p404

LEGOURDE – Lawrence Lee, b 17 Oct 1862 lc/o Lawrence LeGourde & Sarah Small bp 16 Nov 1862 spr Susanna DeLoughrey p295

LEGOURDE – Mary Helen, b 15 Sep 1864 lc/o Laurence LeGourde & Sarah Small bp 16 Oct 1864 spr Alice Bell p342

LEGOURDE – Rose Estelle, b 24 Dec 1868 lc/o Laurence LeGourde & Sarah Small bp 25 Jan 1869 spr Charles Grant & Emma Bell p464

LEHR – Charles Bonninger, b 1 Jul 1861 lc/o Robert Lehr & Mary H. Moore bp 24 Jul 1861 spr Sophia C. Read p257

LEHR – Fanny, b 18 Nov 1859 lc/o Robert Lehr & Mary Frances Moore bp 28 Nov 1859 spr C. Olivia O'Donnell & _____ "baptized privately" "ceremonies supplied Dec 22, 1859" H. P. Coskery, priest p206

LEHR – Henry, b 1 Dec 1857 lc/o Robert Lehr & Mary Frances Moore bp 3 Dec 1857 spr M. Russell & Margaret Moore p142

LEIBENSTORN – Alexander, b 30 July 1854 lc/o Alex. Leibenstorn & Mary Hace "(born Carr)" bp 27 Mar 1855 spr Ellen Slade "baptized conditionally" H. B. Coskery, priest [*ed. note: faint record*] p41

LEINARD – William Francis, b 14 Jan 1870 c/o William Leinard & Mary Brogan bp 15 Mar 1870 spr Mrs. Bottomer "I supplied the ceremonies of baptism" John Dougherty, priest p496

LEITCH – Mary Emilie, b 6 Apr 1857 lc/o Leonard Leitch & Mary Leitch, "his lawful wife" bp 9 Jul 1857 g Anne J. Cropper p126

LENEHAN – Catharine, b 19 Jan 1860 lc/o Patrick Lenehan & Bridget Welch bp 22 Jan 1860 spr Patrick Ford & Winifred Monihan p212

LENOX – Sarah Lenox (c), "about 110 years" bp 29 Mar 1856 spr Mary Augusta p77

LEONARD – Anna, b 23 Dec 1855 lc/o Richard Leonard & Sarah Kenna bp 27 Jan 1856 spr Patrick Leonard & Bridget Ford p70

LEONARD – Francis Edwin, b 5 Aug 1869 lc/o Alexander Leonard & Elizabeth Coleman bp 6 Sep 1869 spr Bridget Coleman p482

LEONARD – Michael, b 18 Mar 1856 lc/o Patrick Leonard & Bridget Ford bp 23 Mar 1856 spr Tho. Leonard & Bridget Coles p76

LEONARD – William Francis, b 5 Jan 1870 lc/o William Leonard & Mary Brogan bp 8 Jan 1870 spr M. Bottomer p491

LEONGINOTTI – Carlo Antonio, b 8 Nov 1862 lc/o Carlo Leonginotti & Maria Botti bp 30 Nov 1862 spr Antonio Passano & Terese Passano p296

LEPPER – Agnes, b 23 Jun 1870 lc/o Chas. V. Lepper & Margaret A. Grady bp 13 Jul 1870 spr Wm. E. S. Starr & Mary E. Gallagher "supplied the ceremonies" Wm. E. Starr, priest p505

LEPPER – Mary Grace, b 8 Jul 1868 lc/o Charles Lepper & Margaret Grady bp 27 Jul 1868 spr William Starr & Mary E. Powell p449

LEPPER – Mary Teresa, b 23 Jun 1870 lc/o Chas. V. Lepper & Margaret A. Grady bp 13 Jul 1870 spr Wm. E. Starr & Nattie A. Cornell p505

LEVERING – Francis, b 5 Jul 1861 c/o Samuel Levering & J. McCall bp 12 Jul 1861 spr Isabella McCall [*ed. note: last name is listed both as Levering or McCall in record*] p256

<u>LEVILY</u> – Alice <u>Levily</u>, "aged 32 years" bp 16 Jun 1869 p474

LEVY – Henry Ehlen, b 7 Sep 1862 lc/o Alexander Levy & Emily F. Mackenheimer bp 8 Apr 1863 spr Margaret Doyle p305

LEWIS – <u>Albey</u>, b 16 Sep 1867 lc/o Francis & Margaret Lewis bp 13 Oct 1867 spr <u>Palmyri</u> David p423

LEWIS – Charles Borromeo, b 14 Jan 1855 lc/o John Lewis & Frances Stewart bp 18 Feb 1855 spr John Kennedy & Ellen McKenna p37

LEWIS – Edward (c), "aged about 10 years" lc/o Francis Lewis & Laura Cupid bp 16 Jul 1855 spr John McNally p52

LEWIS – Francis Coleman Lewis, b 17 Feb 1867 lc/o Eugene Lewis & Ella Connolly bp 3 Mar 1867 spr Mary Connolly & John McAbee p407

LEWIS – George Lewis, "slave" b 5 May 1840 ic/o George & Julianna Lewis bp 26 Oct 1854 (all c) p27

LEWIS – Julianda Lewis (c), "about 45 years old" bp 5 Aug 1855 spr Catherine Jenkins p54

LEWIS – Loretta Elizabeth, b 31 May 1856 lc/o Francis Lewis & Loretta Cupid (c) bp 24 Jun 1856 spr Elizabeth <u>Colvers</u> p87

LEWIS – Mary Agnes Lewis "(born <u>Cupidl</u>)" (c), "about 35 years old" bp 15 Aug 1855 spr Mary E. Williams "baptized conditionally" Thos. Foley, priest p55

LEWIS – Mary Lewis, "aged 15 years" bp 16 Mar 1861 "baptized conditionally" Thos. Foley, priest p246

LEWIS – Philip Augustus Morgan, b 28 Jun 1863 lc/o John Lewis & Julia Ann Taylor (c) bp 18 Aug 1863 spr Caroline LePratt p313

LEWIS – Sarah, b 14 Dec 1865 lc/o Joseph Lewis & Margaret McKewen bp 17 Dec 1865 spr Margaret Ann Spence p371

LEYBURN – Mary Thomas, b 4 Jun 1853 lc/o William & Mary Leyburn bp 30 Aug 1866 p394

LEYBURN – Thomas Leyburn, "aged about 30 years" bp 5 Jan 1859 "baptized conditionally in imminent danger of death" H. B. Coskery, priest p178

LEYDEN – Agnes Leyden, "aged 20 years" bp 3 Jan 1866 spr Mary Clarke p373

LIDDONS – Henrietta Irene Waverly, b 12 Oct 1866 lc/o Laurence L. Liddons & Felicité Nivers bp 14 Sep 1868 spr Saml. & Clara Gandolfo p453

LINAS – Mary Alice (c), b 15 Jan 1855 nc/o Henrietta Linas (c) "father unknown" bp 1 Apr 1855 spr Mary Ann Linas p41

LINN – Charles Valentine, b 13 Feb 1864 lc/o Charles Linn & Mary Flynn bp 21 Feb 1864 spr Bernice Linn & Margaret Linn p326

LINN – Peter Joseph, b 17 Apr 1866 lc/o Terence Linn & Mary McCall bp 22 Apr 1866 spr Margaret Linn p382

LINTNER – Mary, b 14 Jul 1866 lc/o John A. Lintner & Mary Iven bp 29 Jul 1866 spr John Manley & Anne McCall p390

LINTON – Henry S., b 19 Jun 1862 lc/o Saml. Linton & Matilda Balloof bp 31 Jan 1863 spr Mary Agnes Winhaltz p300

LIPP – Catharine Gertrude, b 16 Oct 1861 lc/o Francis X. Lipp & Laura Cecilia Getty bp 1 Nov 1861 spr Bolivar D. Dunels & Virginia Getty p265

LITSINGER – Sophia Litsinger, "aged 24 years" lc/o Richard & Maria Litsinger bp 4 Feb 1857 spr A. E. Taylor "baptized conditionally" Thos. Foley, priest p109

LITTLE – Elizabeth Little "(born Guy)", "aged 30 years" bp 27 Nov 1861 "baptized conditionally" Thos. Foley, priest p267

LITTLE – William Guy, b 17 Apr 1861 lc/o Samuel Little & Elizabeth Guy bp 27 Nov 1861 spr Thos. Foley & Mary Kennedy p267

LIVINGSTON – Louisa, b 10 Sep 1869 lc/o Levigens Livingston & Eliza Young bp 16 Sep 1869 spr Archb. Spalding & Jane Walbach p483

LLOYD – Elizabeth Lloyd, "aged 24 years" bp 21 Apr 1866 spr Margaret Anne Gallagher "baptized conditionally" Thos. Foley, priest p382

LODDEN – Mary Frances (c), b 1 Dec 1854 c/o Mary Lodden (c) bp 10 Jul 1855 spr Frances M. Watson p52

LOFTIS – Laura Virginia, b 8 Mar 1863 lc/o James Loftis & Susan Lanehart bp 13 Jul 1865 spr Mary Loftis p359

LOGUE – James Harrison, b 29 Nov 1853 lc/o John Logue & Elizabeth Pillsington bp 19 May 1854 spr Mary Peacock p12

LOGUE – John Clinton, b 24 May 1858 lc/o Peter Logue & Catherine Miller bp 27 Jun 1858 spr Augustus Struck & Anna Struck p161

LOGUE – William Henry, b 21 Jan 1864 lc/o Peter Logue & Catharine Miller bp 20 Mar 1864 spr Charles A. Masterman & Mary E. Masterman p329

LONEY – John, "born 3 or 4 months ago" lc/o Robert Loney & Rose Ann O'Brien bp 25 Jun 1865 spr Anna Ballard p359

LONEY – Mary Ann, b 25 Oct 1862 lc/o Robert Loney & Rosanna O'Brien bp 3 Jan 1864 spr Ann O'Brien p323

LONG – James Patrick, b 15 Feb 1862 lc/o Michael Long & Bridget Conroy bp 18 Feb 1862 spr James Vaughn & Johanna Long p274

LONG – Johanna, b 5 Mar 1863 lc/o Michael Long & Bridget Conroy bp 8 Mar 1863 spr Stephen Conroy & Catharine Grady p303

LONG – Mary, b 18 Jan 1860 lc/o Michael Long & Bridget Connolly bp 27 Apr 1860 spr Catharine Carney p220

LORIGAN – Eliza, b 23 Mar 1866 lc/o John Lorigan & Hannah Tuhy bp 25 Mar 1866 spr Michl. McMahan & Mary Tuhy p379

LORIGAN – Ellen, b 23 Mar 1866 lc/o John Lorigan & Hannah Tuhy bp 25 Mar 1866spr Michael Ford & Anna Malory "this child had been previously baptized by Dr. Chatard" H. B. Coskery, priest p379

LORNE – Henry, "aged 7 years" bp 22 May 1862 "baptized privately" Thos. Foley, priest p281

LOUDEN – Laura Virginia (c), b 6 Jun 1865 lc/o Isaac Louden & Letitia Nicholson bp 7 Sep 1865 spr Ann Hollins p364

LOUDON – Mary Priscilla, b 4 Jul 1862 lc/o Isaac Loudon & Letitia Ann Nicholson bp 7 Sep 1862 spr Mary Thomas (all c) p289

LOVE – Almira Virginia Love, b 11 Oct 1843 bp 2 Feb 1861 "baptized *sub conditione sine ceremoniis*" Archb. Spalding, priest p375

LOVEDAY – Charles Anna, b 11 Feb 1835 lc/o Charles Loveday & Eliza Stranberg bp 20 Aug 1856 spr Mary S. Proby "baptized conditionally" Thos. Foley, priest p93

LOVEDAY – Ida Mary, b 12 Mar 1844 lc/o Charles T. Loveday & Eliza Stanley bp 4 Apr 1861 spr Charles Anna Loveday p248

LOW – Mary Agnes, b 9 Dec 1862 lc/o John Low & Catharine Kelly bp 22 Dec 1862 spr Thomas Flannagan & Margaret Murray p298

LOWDNES – Charles Henry Tilghman, b 7 Jul 1866 lc/o Dr. Charles Lowndes & Catharine Mary Tilghman bp 10 Jun 1867 spr Louisa Tilghman p415

LOWE – George Francis, b 14 Jan 1866 lc/o John Lowe & Catharine Kelly bp 5 Feb 1866 spr Pat. Tury & Bridget Mullany p375

LOWNDES – Annie Polk, b 2 Sep 1868 lc/o Charles Lowndes & Kate Tilghman bp 6 Oct 1868 spr Louisa Silyhian p455

LOWNDES – Catharine Mary Lowndes "(born Tilghman)", "aged 27" bp 10 Jun 1867 "baptized conditionally" Thos. Foley, priest p414

LOWRY – Charles Geales, b 7 Feb 1868 lc/o Michael Lowry & Mary O'Connor bp 12 Feb 1868 spr Ellen Ryan p433

LOWRY – Martin, b 23 Apr 1862 lc/o John Lowry & Bridget Collins bp 27 Apr 1862 spr John Collopy & Eliza Collopy p280

LUBY – Thomas Sylvester, b 2 Jan 1860 lc/o Thomas Luby & Rosanna Riley bp 29 Jan 1860 spr Sylvester & Mary Ann Donovan p213

LUCAS – Bertha Eliza, b 31 Aug 1857 lc/o William Francis Lucas & Mary Roberts bp 15 Sep 1857 spr Rev. James Dolan & Harriet Lucas p134

LUCAS – John Carrell, b 18 Feb 1859 lc/o William F. Lucas & Mary Roberts bp 10 Mar 1859 spr Thomas White & Carrie Scott p184

LUCAS – William Francis, b 20 Aug 1854 lc/o William Francis Lucas & Mary Robert bp 21 Sep 1854 spr Edward V. Warde & Harriet Warde p24

LUDWELL – Beulah Maria, b 12 Feb 1857 lc/o David F. W. Ludwell & Margaret Peckocheeke bp 31 May 1857 spr Beulah Peckocheeke p122

LUG – Elmira Virginia, b 9 apr 1860 lc/o Peter Lug & Catharine Miller bp 6 May 1860 spr Elizabeth Surgeon p221

LUIS – Joseph, b 6 Sep 1862 lc/o Dominic Luis & Mary Zinge bp 28 Sep 1862 spr Joachim Silva & Caroline Newcome p290

LURGAN – Margaret, b 7 Dec 1864 lc/o John Lurgan & Hannah Tuohy bp 11 Dec 1864 spr Michael McConnell & Ellen Crotty p345

LUTTS – Albert W. Lutts, "aged fourteen years" lc/o _____ Lutts & _____ Lutts bp 17 Jun 1865 witness: Mrs. Elizabeth Porterfeld p359

LYMAN – Christopher Thomas, b 9 Oct 1869 lc/o John Lyman & Hannah Connor bp 17 Oct 869 spr William Moran & Mary Wagner p486

LYNCH – Catharine, b 17 Feb 1867 lc/o Dennis Lynch & Ellen McTague bp 8 Mar 1867 spr Hugh McTague & Margaret McTague p407

LYNCH – Charles, b 9 Jun 1854 lc/o Matthew Lynch & Bride Gillan bp 25 Jun 1854 spr Thos. Lynch & Rosa McDermott p16

LYNCH – Daniel, b 17 Nov 1854 lc/o Danl. Lynch & Ann Barrett bp 16 Jan 1855 spr Joanna Grady p34

LYNCH – Honora Theresa, b 14 Feb 1857 lc/o Francis Lynch & Mary A. O'Sullivan bp 31 Jan 1861 spr Harriet Spalding p241

LYNCH – James, b 2 Apr 1856 lc/o Denis Lynch & Ellen McTagne bp 13 Apr 1856 spr Jas. Patrick McKeever & Magaret Carr p79

LYNCH – Mary Ann, b 9 Dec 1855 lc/o Martin Lynch & Bridget Gillings bp 16 Dec 1855 spr Michael Reilly & Catherine Lynch p68

LYNCH – Mary Ellen, b 2 Dec 1865 lc/o Michael Lynch & Emily Stevens bp 14 Mar 1866 spr Mary Reardon p377

LYNCH – Peter Simon, b 2 Apr 1856 lc/o Denis Lynch & Ellen McTagne bp 13 Apr 1856 spr Jos. Judge, & Mary Leonard "I supplied the ceremonies…previously baptized by Dr. Chatam" H. B. Coskery, priest p79

LYNN – Bernard Thomas, b 28 May 1862 lc/o Charles Lynn & Mary Flynn bp 8 Jun 1862 spr Felix McLavey & Bessie Kennan p283

LYNN – John Edward, b 16 Nov 1860 lc/o Charles Lynn & Mary Flynn bp 23 Nov 1860 spr Laurence Flynn & Sarah Flynn p236

LYONS – Catharine Margaret, b 24 Oct 1867 lc/o John Lyons & Catharine Lloyd bp 28 Nov 1867 spr Dennis Collins & Mary McNamara p428

LYONS – Mary Helena, b 6 Dec 1864 lc/o William Lyons & Ella Daley bp 13 Dec 1864 spr Jno. Dorsey & Hanorah Dorsey p346

LYONS – Thomas Henry, b 29 Nov 1865 lc/o John Lyons & Catharine Lloyd bp 10 Dec 1865 spr Patk. Connell & Margaret Ann Gallagher p371

LYONS – William Patrick, b 17 Mar 1863 lc/o John Lyons & Kate Lloyd bp 5 Apr 1863 spr Edw. Lloyd & Mary O'Connell p305

MACKEN - Anna Rosalin, b 10 Oct 1855 lc/o Michael Macken & Mary Ann Simmons bp 10 Nov 1855 spr Simmons _____ & Elizabeth N. A. Simmons p64

MACKENHAMMER – Ida Mary, b *ndg* lc/o Frederick Mackenhammer & Catharine Baughman bp 19 May 1859 spr Kate Reilly p190

MACKENHAMMER – Mary, b *ndg* lc/o Frederick Mackenhammer & Catharine Baughman bp 4 Jun 1859 spr Kate Reilly p192

MACKIN – Elizabeth Virginia Lucy, b 13 Dec 1868 lc/o Michael Mackin & Mary Ann Timmons bp 13 Jan 1869 spr John Clark & Ann Lynch p463

MACKIN – George Henry, b 5 Nov 1859 lc/o Michael Mackin & Mary Ann Simmons bp 30 Nov 1859 spr Anne Lynch p207

MACTAVISH - Charles Carroll, b 31 Mar 1857 lc/o Charles Carroll Mactavish & Ella Scott bp 2 Apr 1857 spr Thomas Foley & Elizabeth Stafford p116

MACTAVISH – Emily Carroll, b 25 Oct 1855 lc/o Charles Carroll Mactavish & Ella Scott bp 1 Nov 1855 spr Thomas Foley & Emily Mactavish p63

MACTAVISH – Francis Osborne, b 19 Oct 1857 lc/o Alexander S. MacTavish & Ellen Gilmore spr Emily MacTavish, "proxy for the Duchess of Leeds, the Duke of Leeds, nominal sponsor" p139

MACTAVISH – Paul Winfield Scott, b 23 Jul 1860 lc/o Charles Carroll Mactavish & Ella Scott bp 29 May 1861 spr Rev. J. J. Genistimani & Emily Mactavish, "proxy for Louisa Catharine Osborne, Duchess of Leeds" "I supplied the ceremonies for baptism…who was baptized privately by Rev. B. S. Piet at the Folly" Thos. Foley, priest p253

MACTAVISH – Virginia, b *ndg* Jan 1859 lc/o Charles Carroll Mactavish & Ella Scott "baptized privately, see page 189" Thos. Foley, priest p181

MACTAVISH – Virginia, lc/o Carroll Mactavish & Ellen Scott bp 10 May 1859 spr. Col. Henry Lee Scott & Cornelia Scott "I supplied the ceremonies of baptism…baptized privately by me 4th February this year, see page 181" Thos. Foley, priest p189

MADDEN – James, b 23 Mar 1856 lc/o William Madden & Bridget Dennison bp 30 Mar 1856 spr Thomas Coleman & Mary Harvey p78

MADDEN – Mary Ann, b 9 Oct 1857 lc/o William Madden & Bridget Denison bp 9 Oct 1857 spr John Ford & Rosanna McCaffey p137

MADDOX – Mary Ann Helen Augusta, b 3 Feb 1854 lc/o August Maddox & Virgin Warnly bp 23 Oct 1854 spr John Noel & Margaret Ann Dobson (all c) p27

MADEN – James, b 6 May 1854 lc/o Henry Maden & Jane Boyd bp 10 Nov 1855 spr Mary _____ "baptized conditionally" H. B. Coskery, priest p64

MAGEE – Mary, b 18 Feb 1856 lc/o Abraham Magee & Mary Graham bp 2 Mar 1856 spr Patk. Ratty & Ellen Curtis p74

MAGILLY – James Foley, b 7 Oct 1861 lc/o James Magilly & Mary Riley bp 15 Dec 1861 spr Catharine Quinn p269

MAGNAN – Ellen, b 28 Feb 1854 lc/o John Magnan & Catherine Ward bp 8 Mar 1854 spr Pat. Magnan & Cath. Magnan p7

MAGNAN – Joseph, p 18 Sep 1857 lc/o Michel Magnan & Ann Fitzpatrick bp 27 Sep 1857 spr John Flannigan & Margaret McAdams p136

MAGRAW – Charles Philips Geo. b 21 Aug 1870 lc/o James Magraw & Catharine McKenna bp 1 Sep 1870 spr Catharine O'Neill p507

MAGRAW – Mary Alice, b 18 May 1864 lc/o Michael Magraw & Bridget Enright bp 29 May 1864 spr Martin & Mary Ann Shanahan p333

MAGRUDER – George Henry, b 6 Feb 1854 lc/o John Magruder & Mary South bp 19 Feb 1854 spr Margaret Hunt p5

MAGRUDER – Jacob Thomas Magruder, b *ndg* 1835 bp 25 Sep 1856 spr Margaret Jones p96

MAGUIRE – Alexander, b 14 Jan 1864 lc/o Patrick Maguire & Mary Duffy bp 17 Jan 1864 spr Solomon Maguire & Mary Ingles p324

MAGUIRE – Charles, b 7 Sep 1854 lc/o Thomas Maguire & Jane Kelly bp 10 Dec 1854 spr Mary Norton p31

MAGUIRE – Julia, b 7 Oct 1864 lc/o Michael Maguire & Mary Fitzgerald bp 9 Oct 1864 spr Geoffrey Fitzgerald & Julia McGran p341

MAHER – Mary Elizabeth, b 11 Feb 1857 lc/o Edward Maher & Elizabeth Murray bp 22 Feb 1857 spr Wm. Mahar & Mary Martin p111

MAHONEY – John, b 25 Feb 1854 lc/o Michael Mahoney & Ellen Donahue bp 25 Feb 1854 spr James Sullivan & Cath. Dacy p6

MALATESTA – John Baptist, b 23 Jan 1861 lc/o Benedict Malatesta & Livia Arata bp 28 Jan 1861 spr John Cella & Philomena Cella p241

MALLAGAN – Mary A. Mallagan (c), "age about 70 years" bp 26 Oct 1854 "baptized conditionally" H. B. Coskery, priest p27

MALONE – Francis James, b 18 Jan 1857 lc/o Gerald Malone & Mary A. McCormick bp 15 Feb 1857 spr John McCormick & Mary McCormick p110

MALONE – Patrick, b 7 Aug 1855 lc/o James Malone & Mary Brown bp 8 Aug 1855 spr Pat. Flynn & Ann Duffy p54

MALONEY – Mary Ann Melissa, "about six months old" lc/o _____ _____ & Mary Ann Maloney bp 29 Apr 1855 spr Mary Ann _____ p45

MALONEY – Michael, b 9 Jun 1859 lc/o Thomas Maloney & Bridget Barrett bp 13 Jun [sic] 1859 [*ed. note: the baptism entry month, Jun, was listed in the July entries of the Baptism Register, thus the baptism mostly likely took place on 13 July,1859*] spr Patk. Connelly & Ann Irwin p195

MANIAN – John, b 31 Dec 1854 lc/o Patrick Manian & Catherine Homes bp 14 Jan 1855 spr Martin Homes & Ann Finnity p34

MANION – Catherine, b 17 Apr 1856 lc/o John Manion & Catherine Ward bp 20 Apr 1856 spr Henry Manion & Cath. Keogh p80

MANION – John, b 6 Jun 1861 lc/o John Manion & Catharine Ward bp 9 Jun 1861 spr John Hogan & Bridget Kelly p253

MANION – John, b 7 Sep 1863 lc/o John Manion & Margaret Daley bp 13 Sep 1863 spr John Tully & Bridgit Manion p315

MANION – Mary Catherine, b 19 Jun 1858 lc/o John Manion & Bridget Leaghy bp 27 Jun 1858 spr Michael Manion & Mary Fritz p161

MANNING – James Bartholomew, b 6 Apr 1857 lc/o James Manning & Catherine Golden bp 17 May 1857 spr Timothy Kelly & Eliza King p120

MANNING – Joseph, b 26 Jan 1857 lc/o Henry Manning & Margaret Flynn bp 1 Feb 1857 spr Joseph Manning & Catharine Royal p109

MANNING – Richard Augustus, b 24 Nov 1854 lc/o James Manning & Cate Golden bp 2 Jan 1855 spr Jane Kelly & Rose Fyoloca p33

MANNION – Bedelia, b 18 Dec 1865 lc/o John Mannion & Margaret Daley bp 31 Dec 1865 spr John Coulahan & Ellen Tully p373

MANNION – Bridget, b 18 Aug 1857 lc/o John Mannion & Catherine Ward bp 20 Sep 1857 spr Wm. & Honora Hofour p135

MANNION – Emily, b 2 Jun 1856 lc/o Michael Mannion & Ann Fitzpatrick bp 12 Jun 1856 spr Emily Wycoff p85

MANNION – James, b 3 Oct 1863 lc/o John Mannion & Bridget Lakes bp 11 Oct 1863 spr Michael Freeze & Ann Freeze p317

MANNION – Mary, b 17 Aug 1857 lc/o John Mannion & Catherine Ward bp 20 Sep 1857 spr Martin & Ellen Mannion p135

MANNION – Mary, b 7 Oct 1860 lc/o Michael Mannion & Ana Fitzpatrick bp 24 Oct 1860 spr Owen Martin & Julia Irwin p232

MANNUEL – Elizabeth Ann, b 27 Nov 1854 lc/o Michael Mannuel & Ann Fitzpatrick bp 3 Dec 1854 spr John Nevin & Emma Michael p31

MARION – Alfonse Victor Alfred, b 30 Oct 1866 lc/o Alfred Marion & Victorine Devonges bp 26 Nov 1866 spr Alfonse Devonges & Lucilla T. Dandelet p399

MARION – Arthur Gustave, b 12 Jul 1868 lc/o Alfred Marion & Victorine Devonges bp 17 Sep 1868 spr Gustave Dandelet & Julia Dandelet p453

MARRON – John, b 13 Dec 1868 lc/o William Marron & Mary Wallach bp 18 Dec 1868 spr Wm. Lewis & Ellen Willeux p461

MARSHALL – Joseph, b 21 Aug 1868 lc/o Spencer Marshall & Anna Marshall (c) bp 23 Aug 1868 spr Charlotte Chester p452

MARSHALL – Mary Elizabeth, b 4 Jul 1866 c/o Charles Marshall & Mary Frances Johnson (c) bp 17 Aug 1866 spr Anne Green p392

MARTIN – Albert Ashton, b 9 Dec 1855 lc/o Ashton Alexander Martin & Martha Ann Monsanier bp 19 Jun 1856 spr Louisa Leppler p86

MARTIN – Catharine, b 5 Mar 1865 lc/o Eugene Martin & Ginny Wade bp 12 Mar 1865 spr John & Margaret Wade p353

MARTIN – Charles Joseph, b 10 Jun 1858 lc/o Patrick C. Martin bp 20 Jun 1858 spr N. Kennedy Jenkins & Caroline Wynn p160

MARTIN – Charles, b 9 Sep 1858 lc/o Ashton Martin & Anna Mommonier bp 18 Nov 1858 spr Charles Mommonier & Ellen Taylor p174

MARTIN – Emma Virginia, b 20 Jun 1865 lc/o Francis Martin & Catharine Rodoval bp 6 Aug 1865 spr Elizabeth Martin p361

MARTIN – Francis de Sales, b 29 Jan 1856 lc/o Patrick C. Martin & Mary Ann Simmons bp 10 Feb 1856 spr Harriet White p72

MARTIN – Henry Charles, b 6 Jul 1854 lc/o James Henry Martin & Annie F. Watson bp 19 Jul 1854 spr Je_____ Valette & M. Victorina Page p18

MARTIN – James, b 6 Mar 1863 lc/o Owen Martin & Jane Wade bp 15 Mar 1863 spr James Martin & Jane Wade p303

MARTIN – James Henry, b 21 Nov 1860 lc/o James Henry Martin & Anne F. Watson bp 31 Dec 1860 spr Gengels Bruner & Josephine Nalette p238

MARTIN – James Patrick, b 16 Mar 1857 lc/o David Martin & Rosaina Dugace bp 22 Mar 1857 spr William Dugace & Ellen Dugace p115

MARTIN – James, b 6 Dec 1867 lc/o James Martin & Ann McDonald "(born McCoy)" bp 12 Dec 1867 spr Pat. O'Neal & Mary Brennan p429

MARTIN – John Michael, b 14 May 1855 lc/o Michael Martin & Sarah Walsh bp 20 May1855 spr Catherine Garvey p47

MARTIN – John Nichols Martin "of Maryland", b 29 Sep 1870 bp 9 Sep 1870 "baptized conditionally" H. B. Coskery, priest p511

MARTIN – John Wilson, b 12 Sep 1867 lc/o John Martin & Emily Jane Wilson bp 12 Apr 1868 spr Michl. & Margaret Callaghan p439

MARTIN – Lucy Elvira, b 20 Aug 1857 lc/o James Henry Martin & Anna F. Watson bp 17 Sep 1857 spr Louis Merceret & Zoe E. Armstrong p135

MARTIN – Mary, b 20 May 1867 lc/o Eugene Martin & Mary Wade bp 9 Jun 1867 spr Jas. Naughton & Marg. Wade p414

MARTIN – Mary Ann, b 2 Aug 1858 c/o Mary Ann Martin & James Hughes bp 11 Aug 1858 spr Mary Kane p166

MARTIN – Mary Edith, b 29 Apr 1866 lc/o David A. Martin & Sara Jane Thompson bp 28 May 1866 spr Juliana Flaherty p385

MARTIN – Matthew, b 13 May 1869 lc/o Owen Martin & Eugenia Wade bp 23 May 1869 spr James Murphy & Kate O'Brien p472

MARTIN – Richard Alburn, b 6 July 1857 lc/o Richard Martin & Elizabeth Smith bp 1 Mar 1857 spr Jno. Mullacy & Maria Mullacy p113

MARTIN – Thomas, b 23 Nov 1854 lc/o William Martin & Bridget Dennison bp 26 Nov 1854 spr Thomas Burns & Margaret Burns p29

MARTIN – Thomas Fowler, b 8 Dec 1854 lc/o John Martin & Elizabeth Idlespear bp 25 Feb 1855 spr Mary Veymar p38

MARTIN – William Henry, b 5 May 1855 lc/o William Martin & Mary Clark bp 5 Sept 1855 spr Frances Shipney p57

MARTIN – William Watson, b 21 Apr 1859 lc/o James Henry Martin & Annie M. Watson bp 16 Jun 1859 spr Olivia E. Caperon p192

MARTIN – Zoe Marie, b 2 Jan 1856 lc/o Henry Martin & Annie F. Watson bp 4 Mar 1856 spr Jennie Vallete & Zoe E. Armstrong p74

MARTINEZ – Eugenia, b 27 May 1867 lc/o Antonio Martinez & Mary Hite bp 7 Jun 1870 spr Laura Hite "I supplied the ceremonies" John Daugherty, priest p503

MARTINEZ – Mary Ultima, b 20 Sep 1867 lc/o Antonio Martinez & Mary Hite bp 7 Jun 1870 spr Louis Martinez & Teresa Jenkins p503

MASON – Ann Clementine, b 16 Feb 1855 lc/o Joseph Mason & Clementine Roberts (all c) bp 7 Mar 1855 spr Rachel Brooks (c) "baptized conditionally" H. B. Coskery, priest p39

MASON – Caroline Douglass, b 6 Mar 1866 lc/o John F. Mason & Carolina L. Rodriguez bp 4 Nov 1866 Carrie Mason, "proxy for Emily Harper" p398

MASON – Caroline Mason (c), "forty-three years old today" bp 12 Apr 1857 spr Ann Green p117

MASON – Geo. Alexander (c), b 18 Oct 1859 lc/o James & Susan Mason bp 12 Feb 1860 spr Joseph Watson & Ann Holly (c) "I supplied the ceremonies" "This child had been previously baptized by a well intentioned lay person" H. B. Coskery, priest p214

MASON – Hon. John Thompson Mason, "aged 48 years" bp 7 Aug 1863 "baptized conditionally" H. B. Coskery, priest p313

MASON – William Jackson, b 7 Jan 1859 lc/o Joseph Mason & Clementine Robinson bp 9 Jun 1859 spr Elizabeth Roberts p192

MASON – William Mason (c), "six months old" lc/o Joseph L. Mason & "his wife" bp 9 Oct 1869 p485

MASON- Mary Louisa (c), b *ndg* Oct 1854 lc/o Joseph Wilson & Clementine Roberts (all c) bp 11 Aug 1854 spr Mary Roberts p20

MATLOCK – Mary Euphemia, b 3 Jun 1857 lc/o Robert Matlock & Mary Ann Egan bp 12 Jul 1857 spr Sarah Rooney p127

MATTHEWS – Henry W., b 18 Sep *ndg* lc/o James Matthews "of New England" & Anna Corbin "of County Cavan, Ireland" bp 15 Oct 1870 spr Susan Daiger p514

MATTHEWS – Mary Ann Elizabeth (c), b *ndg* c/o Lesley Matthews & Martha Ann Queen bp 22 Apr 1855 spr Angela Queen p44

MATTHEWS – Mary Teresa Matthews, "aged about 15 years" bp 29 Nov 1865 spr Susan Matthews p370

MATTHEWS – Sally Talbot, b 21 *ndg* 1865 lc/o Edw. T. Matthews & Jane E. Faherty bp 13 Dec 1865 spr Maggie Faherty p371

MATTINGLY – Mary Boury, b 25 Dec 1861 lc/o John Mattingly & Mary F. Boury "both residents of Washington, D. C." bp 12 Jan 1862 spr Mary Enge Broadbent p271

MAUSER – Mary Catharine, b 15 Oct 1862 lc/o Godfrey S. Mauser & Mary Catharine King bp 26 Oct 1862 spr Eugene Daley & Caroline King p292

MAXVILLE – Catharine Maxville (c), "aged about 22 years" bp 16 Aug 1860 spr Josephine Drummond (c) "baptized conditionally" H. B. Coskery, priest p229

MAXWELL – Margaret Rebecca, b 9 Nov 1854 lc/o John Maxwell & Bridget Quinlin bp 28 Dec 1854 spr Noah Donelson & Elizabeth Randolph p32

MAXWELL – Mary Elizabeth, b 9 Nov 1854 lc/o John Maxwell & Bridget Quinlin bp 28 Dec 1854 spr Matt Lyons & Ellen Lyons p32

MAY – Charles May, b 12 Nov 1854 lc/o Patrick May & Mary Highland bp 9 Apr 1855 spr Edward Evans & Ellen Dougherty p42

MAY – Eleanor Rozier, b 20 Mar 1857 lc/o Henry May & Henrietta DeCourcy bp 14 May 1857 spr William H. DeCourcy & Mary Carroll, "proxy for Ellen Dangerfield" p120

MAY – Eva, b 20 May 1868 lc/o Dominic May & Mary Libby bp 8 Jun 1870 spr Mary Holmes p503

MAY – George May, b 7 Apr 1855 lc/o Henry May & Henrietta DeCourcey bp 2 May 1855 spr George May & Catherine Elder p45

MAY – Henry May, "aged 50 years" bp 20 Sep 1866 "baptized conditionally" Thos. Foley, priest p396

MAY – Julia, b 16 Oct 1860 lc/o Henry May & Henrietta DeCourey bp 1 Nov 1860 spr Richardson Wilson & Rosalie May p235

MAY – Julian, b 15 May 1865 lc/o Dominic May & Mary Libby bp 8 Jun 1870 spr Mary Holmes p503

MAY – Mary Ella, b 23 May 1869 lc/o Joseph May & Sarah Parker bp 14 Jul 1869 spr Mary Allen p476

MAYATTE – Flora Johanna, b 6 Dec 1869 lc/o Aytons Mayatte & Josephine Hamma bp 11 Jan 1870 spr Johanna Killmyer p491

MAYER – Francis Patterson, b 23 Mar 1860 c/o Peter Augustine Mayer & Jemina Manger bp 14 Apr 1860 g - Anne Cropper p219

MAYNES – John, b 22 Jan 1855 lc/o James Maynes & Ann McMahon bp 28 Jan 1855 spr Thomas McMahon & Biddy Curley p35

MCABEE – Catharine, 11 "inst" 1865 [*ed. note: probably should be* ult, *that is, June, as the baptism is dated 2 Jul 1865*] lc/o John McAbee & Julia Donovan spr Mary McAbee p359

MCABEE – Charles, b 7 Oct 1866 lc/o John T. McAbee & Julie Donovan bp 25 Dec 1866 spr John Broderick & Mary McAbee p402

MCABEE – John Thomas, b 19 Feb 1864 lc/o John Thomas McAbee & Julia Donovan bp 25 Mar 1866 spr Emily Crabbs p329

MCABEE – Julia Isabella, b 28 Mar 1862 lc/o John T. McAbee & Julia Donovan bp 23 Jun 1862 spr Josephine Morris p284

MCALLISTER – William McAllitster, "aged 24 years" bp 24 Apr 1864 "baptized conditionally" Thos. Foley, priest p331

MCBEE – Anne Paulina, b 9 Feb 1868 lc/o Thomas J. McGee & Anne Thomas bp 16 Feb 1868 spr Daniel Sheehan & Anne McGee p434

MCBRIDE – John Andrew, b 18 Mar 1856 lc/o John McBride & Mary Toner bp 20 Mar 1856 spr Wm. McHenry & Eliz McBride p76

MCCABE – Elizabeth, b 28 Jun 1857 lc/o John McCabe & Elizabeth Crawford bp 1 Jul 1857 spr Peter Fox & Bridget Farrell p125

MCCADDEN – Thomas, b 19 Mar 1865 lc/o William McCadden & Catharine Waldron bp 26 Mar 1865 spr John Connell & Ann Flately "baptized conditionally" Thos. Foley, priest p354

MCCAFFERTY – Arthur, b 18 Mar 1867 lc/o Arthur McCafferty & Eliza Cardwell bp 25 Mar 1867 spr John McCafferty & Clara Parker p408

MCCAFFERTY – Elizabeth James, b 10 Jul 1854 lc/o Arthur McCafferty & Margaret Carr bp 3 Sep 1854 spr Edward McPhelan & Ann Owens p22

MCCAFFERTY – Ella Mary Matilda, b 15 Jun 1858 lc/o Arthur McCafferty & Eliza Cardell bp 19 Jun 1858 spr Mary Cardell p160

MCCAFFERTY – Samuel Jackson, b 15 Dec 1856 lc/o Arthur McCafferty & Elizabeth Cardwell bp 25 Dec 1856 spr Edward Brown & Frances Brown p105

MCCAFFERTY – Sarah Theresa, b 7 Oct 1865 lc/o Arthur McCafferty & Eliza Cardwell bp 22 Oct 1865 spr Emile Bastien & Mary Theresa Bastien p368

MCCAFFNEY – Arthur Edward, "5 years old" lc/o Francis McCaffney & Mary Ann Sheehan bp 28 Oct 1862 spr Daniel & Mary I. Broderick p292

MCCAFFREY – Alice Carmichael, b 15 Mar 1869 lc/o George McCaffrey & Susannah Connolly bp 29 Mar 1869 spr Michael Connolly & Catharine Dorsey p467

MCCAFFREY – Sally McCaffrey "(born Burrows)", "aged 25 years" bp 25 Mar 1868 spr Ann McCaffrey p436

MCCALL – Francis, b 5 Jul 1861 c/o Samjel Levering & J. McCall bp 12 Jul 1861 spr Isabella McCall [*ed. note: last name is listed both as Levering or McCall in record*] p256

MCCALLA – James, b 28 Jul 1863 lc/o William McCalla & Catharine Waldron bp 2 Aug 1863 spr Thos. Barry & Bridget Infant p312

MCCANLY – Charles William, b 16 Nov 1858 lc/o Charles McCanly & Mary Ann Magraw bp 21 Nov 1858 spr Wm. & Bridget McCanly p174

MCCANN – Anna, b 30 Jun 1860 lc/o Alexander McCann & Mary A. Gatch bp 23 Apr 1861 "baptized privately" Thos. Foley, priest p249

MCCANN – Clara Elizabeth, b 5 Jul 1855 lc/o Charles McCann & Catherine Mulligan bp 6 Jul 1855 spr James Gallagher & Mary J. Gallagher p51

MCCANN – Eugenia Mary, "about 17 years of age" lc/o William McCann & Catharine, "his wife" bp 20 Oct 1861 spr Fannie Clarke p264

MCCANN – Frances, b 18 Jun 1856 lc/o Thomas McCann & Esther Donnelly bp 24 Jun 1856 spr Ann Sullivan p87

MCCANN – George Bernan, b *ndg* lc/o Mich. McCann & Mary McCann bp 8 Oct 1854 spr Margaret McCann p25

MCCANN – Gustave Beauregard, b 29 Dec 1861 lc/o Daniel McCann & Mary Biddle bp 17 Jan 1862 spr Maria Bogue p272

MCCANN – James Michael, b 25 Jun 1856 lc/o Michael McCann & Mary McCann bp 29 Jun 1856 spr Henry Murphy & Bridget McCann p88

MCCANN – Margaret, b 19 Feb 1839 lc/o Henry McCann & Augusta Monk bp 1 Mar 1860 spr Sallie Kennedy p216

MCCANN – Mary Harney, b 5 Oct 1857 lc/o Alexander McCann & Mary A. Gatch bp 23 Apr 1861 "baptized privately" Thos. Foley, priest p249

MCCANN – Mary Virginia, b 6 Apr 1864 lc/o Alexander McCann "(dec)" & Mary Ann Gatch bp 16 Aug 1864 spr Anna Gatch p338

MCCANN – Robert, p 2 Jul 1856 lc/o Michael McCann & Louisa Wade bp 13 Jul 1856 spr Patrick Cloud & Anna McGann p89

MCCANN – Thomas Robert, b 5 Feb 1857 lc/o Thomas McCann & Rosanna Marwood bp 22 Feb 1857 spr Patk. Nolan & Rose Hanlon p111

MCCANN – William Thomas, b 15 Oct 1858 lc/o Michael McCann & Louisa Welch bp 20 Oct 1858 spr Sally McCann p172

MCCANN – William, b 3 Jul 1861 lc/o William McCann & Catharine Waldron bp 27 Jul 1861 spr Mary Conroy p257

MCCARDELL – Ann Maria, b 30 Dec 1854 lc/o Samuel McCardell & Mary Jane Addison bp 12 Jan 1855 spr Ann Maria McCardell p34

MCCARDLE – Agnes Jane, b 22 May 1858 lc/o Samuel McCardle & Mary Jane Ellison bp 3 Jun 1858 spr Sarah Blondell p158

MCCARDLE – Anastasia, b 3 Apr 1861 lc/o Samuel McCardle & Mary Jane Ellison bp 14 Apr 1861 spr Margaret McCormick p249

MCCARDLE – John Thomas, b 27 Nov 1867 lc/o Samuel McCardle & Mary Jane Ellison bp 8 Dec 1867 spr Jos. McCardle & Mary Or_____ p429

MCCARDLE – Sarah Elizabeth, b 9 Aug 1864 lc/o Samuel McCardle & Mary Jane Ellison bp 21 Aug 1864 spr Julia Burns p338

MCCARNEY – James Felix, b 31 Jan 1860 lc/o John McCarney & Mary Lanbert bp 5 Mar 1860 spr Maria McBlair p216

MCCARNEY – John Joseph, b 2 Sep 1854 lc/o John McCarney & Mary Cautly bp 1 Oct 1854 spr Robert B. Dentry & Cath. Dentry p25

MCCARNEY – Thomas Patrick, b 20 Jul 1857 lc/o John McCarney & Mary Colton bp 23 Jul 1857 spr Mary C. Lambert p128

MCCARNLEY – Catherine, b 5 Dec 1861 lc/o Charles McCarnley & Mary Ann McGraw bp 8 Dec 1861 spr Philip McGraw & Catharine McGraw p269

MCCARRAHER – Michael Henry, b 19 Aug 1854 lc/o _____ McCarraher & Mary O'Rourk bp 27 Aug 1854 spr Jackson McQuaid & Bridgett Slattery p21

MCCARTHY – Bridget, b 25 Nov 1854 lc/o Peter McCarthy & Catherine Curley bp 11 Dec 1854 spr Patk. & Mary Curley p31

MCCARTHY – Catharine Maria, b 19 Nov 1856 lc/o John McCarthy & Mary Kennedy bp 26 Feb 1857 spr Kate England p113

MCCARTHY – Clarence Albins, b 22 Oct 1861 lc/o John McCarthy & Mary E. Kenney bp 20 Nov 1861 spr Margaret O'Hare p267

MCCARTHY – Francis Joseph, b 29 Apr 1860 lc/o John McCarthy & Mary Elizabeth Kenny bp 28 May 1860 spr Rev. Jeremiah McCarthy & Margaret Lynch p222

MCCARTHY – Henry, b 16 Dec 1869 lc/o Timothy McCarthy & Alice Nolan bp 2 Jan 1870 spr Danl. McCarthy & Bridget Nolan p490

MCCARTHY – Joanna Mary, b 3 Oct 1855 lc/o Timothy McCarthy & Alice Nolan bp 14 Oct 1855 spr James Sullivan & Ann Nolan p61

MCCARTHY – Joseph Edward, b 19 Mar 1866 lc/o Jeremiah McCarthy & Sarah Ward bp 6 May 1866 spr J. Torby & Mary Keirnan p 383

MCCARTHY – Martin, b 30 Sep 1866 lc/o Michael McCarthy & Bridget Welsh bp 17 Nov 1866 spr Michael Welsh & Ann Delaney p399

MCCARTHY – Peter, b 31 Jan 1858 lc/o Andrew McCarthy & Ellen Maher bp 3 Mar 1858 spr Mary Mullan p149

MCCARTHY – Viriginia, b 29 Oct 1865 lc/o John McCarthy & Virginia Jones bp 17 Dec 1865 spr Joseph & Teresa McCarthy p371

MCCARTHY- John Gerome, b 2 Dec 1867 lc/o Timothy McCarthy & Alice Nolan bp 26 Dec 1867 spr John J. Fuller & Joanna McCarthy p430

MCCARTY – Charles, b 16 Jan 1859 lc/o Jeremiah McCarthy & Sarah Ward bp 17 Apr 1859 spr James McFadden & Margaret Keenan p187

MCCARTY – Charles <u>Horace</u>, b 15 Oct 1857 lc/o Timothy McCarty & Alice Nolan bp 25 Oct 1857 spr Bryan Nolan & Kate Nolan p139

MCCARTY – John, b 12 Feb 1857 lc/o Peter McCarty & Catherine Curley bp 22 Feb 1857 spr Jeremiah Ryan & Bridget Mannion p111

MCCARTY – Margaret Ann, b 4 Mar 1855 lc/o Jeremiah McCarty & Sarah Kard bp 13 May 1855 spr John Maguire & Catherine Maguire p46

MCCARTY – Theresa, b 20 Jul 1855 lc/o Denis McCarty & Henora Welch bp 29 Jul 1855 spr John Gorman & Mary Welch p53

MCCARTY – Willet Cecilia, b 8 Dec 1864 lc/o Wm. B. McCarty & Lucilla Lily Oliver bp 8 Jan 1865 spr Dr. Felix Jenkins & "lady" p348

MCCATCHEY – Ann Elizabeth, b 29 Apr 1860 lc/o Robert McCatchey & Elizabeth Ann Smith bp 6 May 1860 spr Saml. Hurdy & Catharine Naughton p221

MCCAUGHY – William, b 19 Mar 1856 lc/o James McCaughy & Catherine Flanelly bp 28 Mar 1856 spr John McCaughy & Mary Mae p77

MCCHRISTAL – Margaret Elizabeth, b 1 Jul 1858 lc/o Patrick McChristal & Bridget McGuirk bp 25 Jul 1858 spr Terence McMahon & Mary Horan p164

MCCHRISTAL – Rosa, b 15 Mar 1856 lc/o Patrick McChristal & Bridget McGurk bp 30 Mar 1856 spr Pat. McMahan & Mary Nichols p78

MCCLAYTON – Eugene Francis, b 13 Nov 1854 lc/o John McClayton & Mary I. Williams bp 28 Jan 1855 spr Rose Williams p35

MCCLAYTON – Eugene Francis, b 8 Aug 1865 lc/o John McClayton & Josephine Williams bp 23 Aug 1865 spr Mrs. Harriet Dugan p363

MCCLAYTON – Mary Agnes, b 3 Feb 1863 lc/o John R. McClayton & Mary J. Williams bp 11 Mar 1863 spr Rosa Williams p303

MCCLAYTON – Rose, b 13 Oct 1868 lc/o John McClayton bp 23 Oct 1868 spr Jos. Dugan & R_____ Williams p456

MCCLELLAN – Elizabeth McClellan, "about 15 years" bp 31 Jan 1868 spr Anne Doughert "baptized conditionally" James Gibbons p433

MCCLELLAN – Francis Edward, b 14 Dec 1867 lc/o Geo. McClellan & Frances Doughert bp 17 Dec 1867 spr Catharine Doughert p430

MCCLELLAN – George Washington, b 7 Jun 1864 lc/o George W. McClellan & Frances Daugherty bp 10 Jun 1864 spr Anna Daugherty p334

MCCLELLAN – Hannah Theresia, b 15 Jan 1865 lc/o George McClellan & Frances Dougherty bp 19 Jan 1866 spr Hannah Dougherty p374

MCCLELLAN – Rose Catharine, b 25 Nov 1867 lc/o Michael McClellan & Catharine Fullerton bp 31 Aug 1868 spr Vincent Lally & Mary Lally p452

MCCLOSKY – Emily, b 4 Nov 1857 lc/o Thomas McClosky & Catherine More bp 3 Jan 1858 spr James Burn & Margaret Murphy p146

MCCLURE – Mary Cecilia, b 2 Sep 1862 lc/o William McClure & Mary Ann Gillespie bp 11 Sep 1862 spr Mary T. Bastino p290

MCCLUSKY – Catherine, b 13 May 1858 lc/o Thomas McClusky & Mary Russell bp 13 Jun 1858 spr John Mannion & Ann Delaney p159

MCCLUTCHY – Jane, b *ndg* lc/o Robert McClutchy & Elizabeth Ann Smith bp 7 Jul 1861 spr John Manly & Julia Fletcher p255

MCCLUTCHY – John Francis, b 15 Aug 1862 lc/o Robert McClutchy & Elizabeth Ann Smith bp 12 Aug 1862 "I supplied the ceremonies…the child had been privately baptized" H. B. Coskery, priest p288

MCCOLGAN – Edward Beauregard, b 23 Aug 1861 lc/o Michael McColgan & Mary Ann O'Brien bp 25 Aug 1861 spr Patrick & Catharine Maguire p259

MCCOLGAN – Mary, b 28 Dec 1854 lc/o Davis McColgan & Ann Campbell bp 7 Jan 1855 spr Cornelius McLaughlin & Rose McColgan p33

MCCONNELL – Anna, b 2 Aug 1866 lc/o Thomas McConnell & Margaret Anderson bp 4 Aug 1866 spr Maggie McConnell p391

MCCONNELL – Anna, b 8 Dec 1862 lc//o John McConnell & Mary Jane Fisher bp 12 Dec 1862 spr Matt Gorman & Ann McConnell p297

MCCONNELL – Emily Jane, b 23 Nov 1854 lc/o Hugh McConnell & Elizabeth Falkinbridge bp 24 Dec 1854 spr Thos. McConnell & Ann Hall p32

MCCONNELL – Francis [sic] Mary, b 16 Jul 1866 lc/o Francis McConnell & Mary Fortune bp 26 Jul 1866 spr Thos. Foley & Elizabeth Fortune p389

MCCONNELL – James McConnell, b 27 Oct 1868 lc/o John F. McConnell & Mary J. Fisher bp 8 Nov 1868 spr Nicholas Creamer & Mrs. Susan Gilday p457

MCCONNELL – Jane, b 25 Jun 1866 lc/o John F. McConnell & Mary Jane Fisher bp 1 Jul 1866 spr Bernard J. Gorman & Margaret Barry p387

MCCONNELL – John Francis, b 24 Aug 1864 lc/o John F. McConnell & Mary J. Fisher bp 4 Sep 1864 spr Thomas J. Griffin & Bridget Connolly p339

MCCONNELL – Mary Agnes, b 18 Jul 1861 lc/o John Francis McConnell & Mary Jane Fisher bp 21 Jul 1861 spr John Gorman & Theresa McConnell p256

MCCONNELL – Theresa, b 5 Sep 1867 lc/o John J. McConnell & Mary J. Fisher bp 14 Sep 1867 spr Jas. Gibbons & Maggie Gorman p421

MCCONNELL – Thomas Mary, b 20 Jul 1868 lc/o Francis McConnell & Mary Fortune bp 3 Aug 1868 spr Joseph Eleoch & Katy Moore p449

MCCONNELL – William, b 2 Jul 1870 lc/o John F. McConnell & Mary J. Fisher bp 17 Jul 1870 spr Nora Barry & Thomas S. Lee p506

MCCORMICK – Anna Catherine, b 19 Apr 1855 lc/o James McCormick & Sarah Wall bp 8 May 1855 spr Pat. Cahile & Ann Wall p46

MCCORMICK – Esther Ann, b 13 Feb 1858 lc/o William McCormick & Bridget Moemella bp 14 Mar 1858 spr James McCormick & Rose McCormick p150

MCCORMICK – Michael, b 23 May 1854 lc/o John McCormick & Mary Smith bp 6 Aug 1854 spr John Smith & Margaret Smith p19

MCCOY – Charles Maury, b 8 May 1862 lc/o Chas. N. McCoy & Lucretia Bartlett bp 23 Jul 1866 spr Agnes Dougherty p390

MCCOY – Hugh, b 4 Mar 1857 lc/o Daniel McCoy & Georgiana McCauley bp 2 Apr 1857 spr I. Veazy p116

MCCOY – Susanna, b 13 Apr 1854 lc/o William McCoy & Susan Davis bp 10 Jan 1856 spr Daniel McCoy & Georgina McCoy p70

MCCOY –Mary Ellen, b 10 Feb 1854 lc/o Daniel McCoy & Georginna McCallan bp 26 Feb 1854 spr Antony McCallan & Joanna Hill p6

MCCRISTAL – Mary Ann, b 13 Apr 1854 lc/o Patrick McCristal & Bridget McGurk bp 2 Apr 1854 spr Lawrence McKagan & Bridget McGurk p9

MCCUBBIN – Mary Ellen, b 3 Apr 1864 lc/o William McCubbin & Ann Gorman bp 25 Apr 1864 spr Ellen McKenna p332

MCCULLOUGH – Henry, b 9 May 1866 lc/o John M. McCullough & Catharine Kennedy bp 3 Jun 1866 spr Felix Kennedy & Kate Hume p385

MCCULLOUGH – Lucy Mary, b 6 May 1863 lc/o Dr. J. Haines McCullough & Maria Tubman bp 3 Jun 1863 spr Eugene & Julia Tubman p308

MCCULLOUGH – Thomas, b 4 Apr 1861 lc/o John McCullough & Mary Ann Coleman bp 21 Apr 1861 spr Thos. McCullough & Mary Dwyer p249

MCCULLOUGH – William Ambrose, b 12 Nov 1862 lc/o John McCullough & Catharine Kennedy bp 30 Nov 1862 spr Brian Down & Sally Bell p296

MCCURLEY – Isadora Pamelia, b 19 Oct 1858 lc/o James McCurley & Susan Vansant bp 16 Oct 1859 spr Thomas _____ & Amelia Brown p202

MCCUSKER – William Alexander, b 10 Apr 1862 lc/o Thomas McCusker & Catharine Moore bp 22 Apr 1862 spr Mary J. Dorsey p279

MCDERMOTT – Eliza Jane, b 28 Sep 1862 lc/o Patrick McDermott & Jane Carr bp 27 Oct 1862 spr Pa_____ H. Carr & _____ Carr p292

MCDERMOTT – Joseph, b 8 Nov 1856 lc/o Cornelius McDermott & Mary Murray bp 15 Nov 1856 spr Margaret Kane p101

MCDERMOTT – Mary Ann, b 27 Jan 1860 lc/o Patrick McDermott & Jane Carr bp 5 Feb 1860 spr Thos. Foley & Ann Farrell p213

MCDEVITE – Edward, b 12 Oct 1854 lc/o Edward McDevite & Elizabeth Morris bp 29 Oct 1854 spr Susanne Morice & John Veiley p28

MCDIVIT – Sarah, b 10 Jan 1857 lc/o Edward McDivit & Elizabeth Murray bp 25 Jan 1857 spr Wm. Clark & Ann Riley p108

MCDONALD – Charles William, b 4 Feb 1855 lc/o William McDonald & Ann Price bp 14 Feb 1857 spr Mary Matluck p110

MCDONALD – Charles, b 24 Jan 1864 lc/o Michael McDonald & Ann McCall bp 26 Jan 1864 spr John McSoley & Mary McCall p325

MCDONALD – Charles, b 31 Aug 1856 lc/o Laurence McDonald & Lavinia Kriket bp 1 Feb 1857 spr Mary Ann Hanley p109

MCDONALD – Elizabeth Ann, b 2 Aug 1856 lc/o John McDonald & Catherine Malone bp 24 Aug 1856 spr James Brown & Joanna McCarthy p93

MCDONALD – John, b 15 Nov 1859 lc/o John McDonald & Catharine Maloney bp 18 Dec 1859 spr John Farrar & Johanna Casey p208

MCDONALD – Margaret, b 1 Sep 1862 lc/o Michael McDonald & Ann McCall bp 10 Sep 1862 spr Alice Gallaghar p289

MCDONALD – Margaret, b 15 Dec 1869 lc/o Thomas McDonald & Margaret Hemely bp 26 Dec 1869 bp Patk. Hoar & Catharine Manning p490

MCDONALD – Margaret M., b 3 Sep 1854 lc/o Patk. McDonald & Mary Smith bp 17 Sep 1854 spr Denis Tierney & Ann Donahoe p23

MCDONALD – Mary Ann, b 8 Mar 1855 lc/o Hugh McDonald & Ann Slattery bp 5 Apr 1855 spr James Barry & Catherine McDonald p41

MCDONALD – Mary Elizabeth McDonald, "12 years old" bp 25 May 1861 spr Bridget McCormick "baptized at St. Mary Asylum" Thos. Foley, priest p252

MCDONALD – Mary Ellen, b 20 Dec 1857 lc/o Michael McDonald & Ann McCaul bp 20 Dec 1857 spr Michl. McCabe & Teresa Mahony p144

MCDONALD – Maurice, b 20 Feb 1868 lc/o Thomas McDonald & Margaret Hennessy bp 22 Mar 1868 spr John Connors & Mary Glaster p437

MCDONALD – Teresa, b 26 Dec 1855 lc/o Patrick McDonald & Mary Smith bp 30 Dec 1855 spr Chas. ______ & Ann ______ [*ed. note: faint record*] p69

MCDONNELL – Mary Eugene DeLoury, *ndg* lc/o Eugene McDonnell & Mary E. DeLoury bp 3 Nov 1864 spr P. A. McCarthy & Mary A. McDonnell p344

MCDONNELL – Michael James, b 19 Nov 1859 lc/o Michael McDonnell & Ann McCaul bp 22 Nov 1859 spr Dan. McCaul & Theresa Blondell p205

MCDONNELL – Thomas, b 11 Jul 1860 lc/o John McDonnell & Bridget Sevanick bp 22 Aug 1860 spr Mary Sevanik p229

MCDOUGALL – Frances Pamelia, b 7 Aug 1842 lc/o Dr. Charles McDougall, USA and Maria, "his wife" bp 23 Jun 1859 spr Anne M. Foley p193

MCELROY – Anthony Brown, b 10 Mar 1862 lc/o James N. McElroy & Mary C. Bonn bp 12 Apr 1862 spr Samuel I. Donaldson & Margaret J. Hop____ p278

MCELROY – Catharine Grey, b 10 April 1868 lc/o James H. McElroy & Mary C. Brown bp 26 May 1868 spr Michael A. Mullin & Susan McCaffrey p443

MCELROY – Ernest Spalding Lanahan, b 9 Oct 1866 lc/o James M. McElroy & Kate Bonn bp 13 Nov 1866 spr J. F. Broadbent & Raphael Sullivan p399

MCELROY – James Millitop, b 25 Mar 1870 lc/o James N. McElroy & Catharine Brown bp 25 Jun 1870 spr Daniel Coakley & Nellie Passan "I supplied the ceremonies" Thomas Foley, priest p504

MCELROY – James W., b 25 Mar 1870 lc/o James W. McElroy & Mary Catharine Bonn bp 9 May 1870 spr "by proxy" Michl. Coakley "baptized privately" "ceremonies supplied by B. P. Foley, June 25, 1870" H. B. Coskery, priest p501

MCELUCE – Catherine, b 18 Jun 1855 lc/o William McEluce & Mary Ann Gillespie bp 30 Jul 1855 spr Margaret Maxwell p54

MCELWEE – Mary Ann, b 2 Jan 1854 lc/o William McElwee & Mary Ann Gillespie bp 19 Jun 1854 spr Elizabeth Power p15

MCELWEE – Thomas Foley, b 28 May 1864 lc/o William McElwee & Mary Ann Gillespie bp 9 Jun 1864 spr Margaret Breen p334

MCELWELL – Mark, b 8 Sep 1860 lc/o William McElwell & Mary Ann Gillespie bp 23 Sep 1860 spr Wm. J. Doyle & Isabella M. Gillespie p231

MCEWELL – Sophia, b 26 Feb 1858 lc/o William McEwell & Mary Ann Gillespie bp 24 Mar 1858 spr John & Catherine Donovan p152

MCFADDON – Francis Patrick, b 6 Dec 1868 lc/o Francis Patrick McFaddon "and his wife" Kate Cassiday bp 8 Jan 1869 spr John M. Travers & Maria G. Cassiday p462

MCFALY – Elizabeth, b 3 Jan 1860 lc/o Edward McFaly & Mary Gill bp 29 Jan 1860 spr Robt. Martin & Margaret Donnelly p213

MCFAUL – Blandy, b 27 Aug 1861 lc/o Daniel McFaul & Mary Unkle bp 13 Oct 1861 spr John McFaul & Virginia Maughrey p263

MCFAUL – Charles Alexander, b 31 May 1856 lc/o Alexander McFaul & Elizabeth Martin bp 31 May 1861 spr Anna Walton p253

MCFAUL – Josephine, b 14 Oct 1855 lc/o John McFaul & Eliza Ann Cartavine bp 3 Feb 1856 spr Danl. McFaul & May Ann Ward p71

MCFEELEY – William John, b 27 Aug 1857 lc/o Edward McFeely & Mary Gill bp 11 Oct 1857 spr John Thompson & Magdalene Whistle p137

MCGANN – James, b 8 Sep 1859 lc/o Thomas McGann & Margaret McCadden bp 11 Sep 1859 spr George McGann & Elizabeth McCann p200

MCGARRITY – John, b 26 Oct 1855 lc/o John McGarrity & Susan Walsh bp 4 Nov 1855 spr Henry McNally & Catherine Lennan p63

MCGEE – Abel Augustine, b 19 Nov 1854 lc/o Abel McGee & Mary Graham bp 17 Dec 1854 spr Jas. McGuigan & Elizabeth O'Neal p32

MCGEE – Agnes, b 5 Nov 1860 lc/o Abel McGee & Mary Graham bp 17 Feb 1861 spr Rebecca Diggs p244

MCGEE – Edward Thomas, b 4 Mar 1870 lc/o Thomas McGee & Ann M. Thomas bp 20 Mar 1870 spr Peter J. Reilly & Joanna Stanton p497

MCGEE – Emily, b 1 Feb 1866 lc/o Edward McGee & Anna Cook bp 30 Aug 1866 spr Margaret McGee p394

MCGEE – Eugene, b 30 Apr 1858 lc/o Abell McGee & Mary Graham bp 27 Jun 1858 spr Maria Bush & Mary McCarn p161

MCGEE – Rebecca, b 25 Apr 1848 lc/o Miles McGee & Rachel Smith bp 28 Nov 1855 spr Margaret McGee p66

MCGEEHAN – Thomas Augustus, b 3 Apr 1864 c/o Margaret McGeehan bp 21 Sep 1864 spr Virginia McGeehan p340

MCGILL – Elizabeth, b 30 Dec 1866 lc/o John McGill & Eliza Smith bp 27 Jan 1867 spr Mary Clark p404

MCGILLAN – Mary Catharine, b 17 Aug 1863 lc/o James McGillan & Mary [sic] bp 6 Oct 1863 spr Catharine Quinn p317

MCGILLEY – Sarah Alice, b *ndg*Jun 1859 lc/o James McGilley & Mary Reilly bp 3 Jul 1859 spr Arthur Stewart & Sarah Maring p194

MCGILLY – Anna Suvinia, b 9 Jun 1869 lc/o James McGilly & Mary Reilly bp 1 Aug 1869 spr Arthur Stewart & Mary E. Sribel p478

MCGILLY – William Abbott, b 7 Jun 1865 lc/o James McGilly & Mary Reilly bp 16 Jun 1865 spr Jane Hagan & Catharine Quinn p359

MCGINNIS – Ellen, b 29 Jun 1857 lc/o Jeremiah McGinnis & Ann Gallan bp 30 Jun 1857 spr Thos. Carroll & Ellen Drane [twin of Mary McGinnis] p125

MCGINNIS – Mary, b 29 Jun 1857 lc/o Jeremiah McGinnis & Ann Gallan bp 30 Jun 1857 spr John Tinan & Maria Small [twin of Ellen McGinnis] p125

MCGINNITY – George Thomas, b 9 Nov 1860 lc/o Felix McGinnity & Elizabeth O_____ bp 20 Jan 1861 spr Alexander McCabe & Ann Reilly p240

MCGIVIN – Bridget Ann, b 11 Aug 1865 lc/o Patk. McGivin & Mary Lyon bp 19 Aug 1865 spr Mary Ann Ennis p362

MCGLONE – Charles Adam, b 15 Aug 1860 lc/o John McGlone & Sarah Jane Reed bp 10 Sep 1860 spr Elenora McGlone p231

MCGLONE – James Patrick, b 27 Sep 1865 lc/o Patrick McGlone & Ellen McKenna bp 5 Oct 1865 spr Pat. McCann & Ann McKenna p366

MCGLONE – Mary Jeannetta, b 20 Mar 1859 lc/o Thomas McGlone & Margaret Heard bp 28 Mar 1859 spr John F. McGlone & Mary McGlone p185

MCGORMAN – Joseph, b 30 Jan 1858 lc/o James McGorman & Catherine Riley bp 7 Feb 1858 spr Frederick Scriggins & Josephine Uhlhorn p148

MCGOVERN – David, b 12 Oct 1854 lc/o James McGovern & Catherine Dix bp 15 Oct 1854 spr David McGovern & Sarah Dix p26

MCGOVERN – Mary, b 25 Sep 1856 lc/o James McGovern & Catherine Dixon bp 1 Oct 1856 spr Sally Dixon p98

MCGOWAN – Frances Theresa, b 14 Mar 1866 lc/o Henry McGowan & Mary A. Bevans bp 15 Apr 1866 spr Jeremiah Bradley & Frances S. Bevans p382

MCGOWAN – George Vincent, b 28 Sep 1860 lc/o Henry McGowan & Mary Bevans bp 11 Nov 1860 spr George McGowan & Mary Heggerty p235

MCGOWAN – Henry May, b 1 Mar 1858 lc/o Henry McGowan & Mary Bevans bp 28 Mar 1858 spr Thomas Bevans & Susan McGowan p152

MCGOWAN – James, b 6 Dec 1853 lc/o John McGowan & Catherine Feeney bp 19 Mar 1854 spr James Bradley & Mary Egan "supplied ceremonies-previously baptized" H. B. Coskery, priest p8

MCGOWAN – James Lee, b 27 Apr 1864 lc/o Henry McGowan & Mary Bevans bp 29 May 1864 spr Wm. J. Bevans & Mary G. Golden p333

MCGOWAN – Margaret Jane McGowan, b 21 Oct 1868 lc/o Geo. McGowan & Ellen Drane, bp 8 Nov 1868 spr Jno. Kelly & Ellen Dohoney p457

MCGOWAN – Martha Jane, b 1 Apr 1856 lc/o George McGowan & Martha Connolly bp 11 May 1856 spr Henry McGowan & Bridget Kelly p82

MCGOWAN – William John, b 8 Jun 1856 lc/o Henry McGowan & Mary Ann Bevans bp 20 Aug 1854 spr John McGowan & Bridget McGill p20

MCGRANE – Julia, b 7 Aug 1867 lc/o Francis McGrane & Bridget Road bp 29 Aug 1867 spr Jas. Road & Mary McGrane p420

MCGRATH – Mary Catharine, b 21 Aug 1865 lc/o Michael McGrath & Margaret Donoho bp 23 Aug 1865 spr Pat. Murphy & Joanne Monaghan p362

MCGREEVY – George Clinton, b 28 Oct 1867 lc/o Hamilton R. McGreevy & Mary E. Frailey bp 20 Nov 1867 spr J. A. Walter & Mary Clare McGreevy p427

MCGREEVY – Mary Elzina, b 24 Sep 1869 lc/o Archibald Hamilton McGreevey & Mary Emily Fraily bp 18 Oct 1869 spr Marshall M. Fraily & Maria C. McGreevey p486

MCGREGOR – Joseph William McGregor, b 29 Nov 1867 bp 7 Jan 1868 spr Eliz. McConnell p431

MCHENRY – Helen Forrest, b 20 Jan 1856 lc/o William R. McHenry & Frances M. Goswell bp 25 Feb 1856 spr Henrietta Eichelberger p73

MCHERRY – Mary Loretta, b 25 May 1858 lc/o John Andrew McSherry & Clementine Villers bp 4 Jul 1858 spr Peter Foudrial, "proxy for James Shaw", & Eliza Shaw p162

MCINTIRE – Henry Thomas, b 20 May 1855 lc/o Peter McIntire & Catherine Banan bp 3 Jun 1855 spr Eduard McIntire & Catherine Donoghue p48

MCINTYRE – James Dessauser, b *ndg* Mar 1859 lc/o Captain James B. McIntyre, USA & Jane Amanda Selkirk bp 25 Nov 1865 spr Hugh McIntyre & Sarah Ann Addison p369

MCINTYRE – John Thomas, b 7 Mar 1857 lc/o James McIntyre & Mary Donaho bp 8 Mar 1857 spr John McIntyre & Mary McIntyre p114

MCINTYRE – Mary Bel, b 19 Jul 1857 lc/o Captain James B. McIntyre, USA & Jane Amanda Selkirk bp 25 Nov 1865 spr Hugh McIntyre & Sarah Ann Addison p369

MCINTYRE – Patrick, b 25 Jul 1855 lc/o Patrick McIntyre & Maria Kelly bp 29 Jul 1855 spr John Kelly & Mary McIntyre p53

MCINTYRE – Thomas Jefferson, b 15 Jun 1862 lc/o Edward McIntyre & Bridget Kells bp 22 Jun 1862 spr Thomas McIntyre & Kate <u>Sillivay</u> p284

MCINTYRE – William Eduard, b 5 Jun 1857 lc/o Owen McIntyre & Catherine Kelly bp 7 Jun 1857 spr Patrick McIntyre & Ellen Kelly p123

MCKEAN – John George, b 22 Oct 1855 lc/o William Henry McKean & Margaret E. <u>Thize</u> bp 26 Mar 1856 spr Mary O'Brien p77

MCKEEVER – Charles Bradley <u>Keyworth</u>, b 28 May 1864 lc/o Joseph McKeever & _____ <u>Keyworth</u> bp 1 Jul 1864 "baptized privately" Thos. Foley, priest p336

MCKEEVER – Edward, b 28 Oct 1862 lc/o Joseph Edw. McKeever & Ann Isabelle Keyworth bp 13 Feb 1863 spr John Grayson, Jr. & Mary Dorsey p301

MCKELUP – Mary Catherine, b 29 Nov 1857 nc/o Ann McKelup ("father unknown") bp 13 Dec 1857 spr Elizabeth Ann Phipps p143

MCKENEN – Margaret, b 8 Sep 1859 lc/o Arthur McKenen & Ellen Fahey bp 18 Sep 1859 spr Peter Murray & Mary McNally p200

MCKENNA – William, b 5 Jun 1856 lc/o James McKenna & Catherine Boaque bp 8 Jun 1856 spr William Boaque & Eliza McKenna p84

MCKENNA – Alexander, "2 weeks old" lc/o Joseph A. McKenna & Jane Forsyth bp 5 Aug 1863 "baptized privately" Thos. Foley, priest p312

MCKENNA – Catharina, b 18 Mar 1860 lc/o Thomas James McKenna & Mary Ann Sullivan bp 25 Mar 1860 spr Eugene Sulliavan & Bridgit Holland p217

MCKENNA – Daniel, b 6 Oct 1867 lc/o Patrick McKenna & Mary McFaul bp 13 Oct 1867 spr James Campbell & Mary Grogan p423

MCKENNA – Mary Ann, b 17 Jul 1861 lc/o James McKenna & Mary Ann Sullivan spr Eugene Sullivan & Alice Riley "I supplied the ceremonies in the case of…previously baptized properly" H. B. Coskery, priest p259

MCKENNA – Mary, b 5 Jul 1869 lc/o Thomas McKenna & Anna McCain bp 15 Aug 1869 spr John & Susan Considine p480

MCKENNA – Robert, b 15 Mar 1854 lc/o Patrick McKenna & Mary Finley bp 19 Mar 1854 spr. Fr. Daley & Susan Finley p8

MCKENNA – Rosanna, b 13 Nov 1863 lc/o Clarence McKenna & Mary Ann Sullivan bp 8 Nov 1863 spr Francis Dowling & Cartharine Mallon p320

MCKENNA – Rosanna, b 28 Nov 1855 lc/o Patrick McKenna & Mary Sisley bp 2 Dec 1855 spr? [*ed. note: faint record*] p67

MCKENNA – Sarah Ann, b 23 Jun 1855 lc/o Patrick McKenna & Catherine McMahon bp 8 Jul 1855 spr Patrick Graham & Ann O'Neil p51

MCKENNA – Sarah, b 13 Mar 1863 c/o Anna McKenna bp 18 May 1863 p307

MCKENNEY – Margery Catharine, b 22 Nov 1865 lc/o Bernard McKenney & Mary McKenna bp 3 Dec 1865 spr Pat. Daley & Jane McKenna p370

MCKERNAN – James, b 23 Jan 1854 lc/o Hugh McKernan & Isabella McCaghan bp 5 Feb 1854 spr Francis McCaghan & Mary Keogh "I gave ceremonies to James, prev. baptized" Thos. Foley, priest p4

MCKERR – Bridget-Emily, b 11 Jan 1854 lc/o William McKerr & Ellen Manion bp 22 Jan 1854 spr Lauren Gleen & Ellen Hughes p3

MCKEWN – Margaret, b 2 May 1862 lc/o Arthur McKewn & Ellen Fahey bp 8 May 1862 spr Robert Gibbons & Margaret Gibbons p281

MCKILLUPS – Daniel, b 24 Sep 1859 nc/o Ann McKillups bp 26 Sep 1859 spr Catharine Scanlan p201

MCKIM – John, b 11 Sep 1854 ("age about 5 weeks") lc/o John McKim & Avarilla Barney (all c) bp 10 Oct 1854 spr Ann Brodigan (w) p26

MCKINSTRY – Mary S. McKinstry, "aged 22 years" bp 28 Nov 1867 spr Mary Smith "baptized conditionally" Thos. Foley, priest p428

MCKNEW – Mary Joanna, "aged 21 years" bp 2 May 1867 spr Mary Clare Burk p411

MCLANAHAN – Mary, b 1 May 1858 lc/o James McLanahan & Margaret Fitzpatrick bp 16 May 1858 spr Geo. Kehoe & Ann Gaitley p156

MCLAUGHLIN – Alice Augusta Maud, b 20 Mar 1865 lc/o Philip S. McLaughline & Agnes C. Lipp bp 27 April 1865 spr Alfred Reey & Laura Lipp p355

MCLAUGHLIN – Charles Irvin, b 7 Aug 1858 lc/o Joseph McLaughlin & Mary Rebecca Daley bp 18 Oct 1858 spr Eliza I. Anderson p171

MCLAUGHLIN – Clara Elizabeth, b 24 Jan 1867 lc/o Peter McLaughlin & Julia Dennison bp 17 Feb 1867 spr Rebecca Bloss p406

MCLAUGHLIN – Frances Virginia, b 14 Jun 1858 lc/o Philip S. McLaughlin & Agnes C. Lipp bp 4 Aug 1858 spr Thos. I. McLaughlin & Susanna F. McLaughlin p165

MCLAUGHLIN – Joseph Jacob, b 12 May 1828 lc/o Irvin McLaughlin "of Havre de Grace, Maryland" & Rosa A. Christopher "of Harford County, Maryland" bp 6 Dec 1870 "baptized conditionally" John Dougherty, priest, p516

MCLAUGHLIN – Mary Catharine, b 21 Feb 1856 lc/o Joseph McLaughlin & Mary Rebecca Daley bp 1 Jun 1856 spr Catharine Bears p83

MCLAUGHLIN – Mary Josephine, b 30 May 1861 lc/o Joseph McLaughline & Rebecca Daly bp 18 July 1861 spr Susanne Daly p256

MCLAUGHLIN – Michael, b 1 Jun 1854 lc/o Michael McLaughlin & Jane Connolly bp 11 Jun 1854 spr John McLaughlin & Alice Kelly p14

MCLAUGHLIN – Peter Frances, b 13 Nov 1865 lc/o Peter McLaughlin & Julia Dennison bp 3 Dec 1865 spr Rebecca Bloss p370

MCLAUGHLIN – Virginia Tucker "born in Winchester, Va", b 20 Aug 1869 c/o J. Fairfax McLaughlin & Virginia Tucker Brooke bp 12 Oct 1869 spr Judge T. Parkin Scott & Juliana Scott p485

MCLAUGHLIN – William Morris Beauregard, b 22 Aug 1863 lc/o Joseph McLaughlin & Rebecca Dales bp 29 Sep 1863 spr Louisa J. Hevener p316

MCMAHON – Catherine, b 10 Nov 1855 lc/o Sylvester McMahon & Mary Branagan bp 16 Nov 1855 spr James McMahon & Bridget Carey p65

MCMAHON – Catherine Welch, b 23 Dec 1854 c/o Michael S. McMahon & Catheine Welch bp 7 Jan 1855 spr Patk. McMahon & Sarah Mary Heron p33

MCMAHON – Hannah Elizabeth Mary, b 6 Jul 1859 lc/o Michl. McMahon & Anna Conroy bp 6 Jul 1859 spr Hannah & Bridget Henchy p194

MCMAHON – James Donald, b 3 Feb 1864 lc/o Michael McMahon & Ann Conroy bp 14 Feb 1864 spr Lizzie Henry p326

MCMAHON – Joseph Patrick, b 19 Mar 1862 lc/o Michael McMahon & Hannah Conlan bp 23 Mar 1862 spr Thomas Conroy & Margaret Conroy p276

MCMAHON – Mary, b 6 Jul 1859 lc/o Michl. McMahon & Anna Conroy bp 6 Jul 1859 spr Hannah & Bridget Henchy p194

MCMAHON – Matthew Patrick, b 1 Dec 1856 lc/o Michael S. McMahon & Catherine Welsh bp 28 Dec 1856 spr Daniel Curley & Sarah C______ p106

MCMAHON – Matthew Stephen, b 16 Oct 1866 c/o Michael McMahon & "his lawful wife" Hanna L. Gregory bp 28 Oct 1866 spr Michl. Long & Mary Consedine p398

MCMAHON – Michael John, b 23 Jun 1857 lc/o Michael McMahon & Hannah Conroy bp 28 Jun 1857 spr Mary Keating "baptized conditionally" H. B. Coskery, priest p125

MCMAHON – Michael, b 23 Jun 1862 lc/o John McMahon & Catharine O'Reilly bp 13 Jul 1862 spr John & Mary Riley p285

MCMAHON – Rosa, b 26 May 1860 lc/o Sylvester McMahon & Mary Brannigan bp 13 Jun 1860 spr Timothy Loftus & Bridget Daley p224

MCMAHON – Sylvester, b 30 Aug 1861 lc/o Sylvester McMahon & Mary Branigan bp 8 Sep 1861 spr James Branigan & Ann Welch p260

MCMANUS – Catharine, b 28 Jul 1866 lc/o John McManus & Sarah Rainey bp 8 Aug 1866 spr John S. Fox & Mary Fox p391

MCMANUS – Felix Robert, b 18 Jul 1869 lc/o Frederick McManus, M.D. & Florence Wier bp 24 Jul 1869 spr Thomas Foley & Phi_____ McManus p477

MCMANUS – George Thomas, b 5 Mar 1860 lc/o James McManus & Elizabeth Kenscher bp 22 Apr 1860 spr Frances McCormick & Ellen Kelly p219

MCMANUS – Helena, b 3 May 1854 lc/o Felix McManus M.D. & Julia Ann Shultz bp 12 May 1854 spr _____ McManus p12

MCMANUS – Margaret, b 16 Oct 1869 lc/o John McManus & Susan Raney bp 31 Oct 1869 spr Robt. Raney & Margaret Hampshire p487

MCMULLAN – Florence Rebecca, b 14 Sep 1863 lc/o John McMullan & Margaret Parsons bp 18 Oct 1863 spr Mary E. Reilly p318

MCNAHAN – John Thomas, b 24 Jun 1855 lc/o Michael McNahan & Hannah Conroy bp 1 Jul 1855 spr Jno. Rudden & Cath. Mack p50

MCNALLY – Henry, b 18 *nmg* 1855 lc/o James McNally & Bridget Murray bp 19 Oct 1855 spr Francine _____ & Catherine Daugherty p61

MCNALLY – Henry, b 26 Jan 1864 lc/o Henry McNally & Louisa Ducatel bp 6 Feb 1864 spr Rich. C. Wilson & Polyannia Ducatel p325

MCNALLY – John Henry, b 21 Jan 1856 lc/o John McNally & Mary Campbell bp 3 Feb 1856 spr O. ______Tine & Mary Magee p71

MCNALLY – John Thomas, b 10 Oct 1857 lc/o James McNally & Bridget Murray bp 22 Nov 1857 spr Thomas Gehagan & Bridget Gehagan p141

MCNALLY – Mary, b 12 Mar 1862 lc/o James McNally & Bridget Mulroy bp 13 Sep 1862 spr Mary Cassady p290

MCNALLY – Peter, b 25 Jan 1854 lc/o John McNally & Mary Campbell bp 5 Feb 1854 spr P. McNally & B. Masine "I gave ceremonies to Peter prev. baptized" Thos. Folley, priest p4

MCNANAY – Mary Ann, b 9 Jan 1858 lc/o Joseph McNanay & Margaret Doon bp 13 Mar 1858 spr John Nespy & Bridget May p150

MCNEAL – Arthur, b 5 Feb 1867 lc/o Peter McNeal & Catharine McConvinn bp 17 Feb 1867 spr Arthur Monaghan & Isabelle Kelly p 406

MCNEAL – Catharine, b 16 Nov 1869 lc/o Peter McNeal & Catharine McConnell bp 25 Nov 1869 spr Catharine Carroll p488

MCNEAL – James Buchanan, b 10 Aug 1856 lc/o Hugh McNeal & Elizabeth Parsons bp 24 Aug 1856 spr John Bannan & Bridget M. Rooney p93

MCNEAL – Lewis, b 3 Mar 1861 lc/o Hugh McNeal & Elizabeth Parsons bp 31 Mar 1861 spr John Brady & Margaret McNeal p247

MCNEAL – Mary Ann, b 28 Apr 1860 lc/o James McNeal & Catharine Hamil bp 7 May 1860 spr Dominic & Ann Hogan p221

MCNEAL – Mary Jane, b 5 Nov 1863 lc/o James McNeal & Catharine Hammel bp 12 Nov 1863 spr Hugh O'Hara & Mary Hobain p320

MCNEAL – Peter, b 8 Oct 1864 lc/o Peter McNeal & Catharine McConnell bp 23 Oct 1865 spr Dennis Clarke & Rose Fitzpatrick p342

MCNEAL – Sarah Jane, b 29 Mar 1862 lc/o James McNeal & Catharine Hammer bp 6 Apr 1862 spr Michael Hogan & Mary Hogan p278

MCNEAL – Thomas, b 1 May 1862 lc/o Peter McNeal & Catharine McConnille bp 4 May 1862 spr Patrick McManus & Anne Rial p280

MCNEILL – Margaret, b 8 Aug 1865 lc/o James McNeill & Catharine (Hamil) McNeill bp 15 Aug 1865 spr Michael Kelly & Sarah Kelly p362

MCNICHOLAS – Elizabeth, b 1 Mar 1866 lc/o Richard McNicholas & Bridget Miskell bp 2 Apr 1866 spr Thos. McNicholas & Sara L. Glenn p380

MCNULTY – Mary McNulty, "aged 70 years" bp 12 Oct 1865 spr Jane Duffy p367

MCNULTY – Thomas Francis, b 9 Sep 1857 lc/o Thomas McNulty & Eliz. Dailey bp 20 Sep 1857 spr Ellen McNulty p135

MCPHAIL – Agnes, b 21 Feb 1865 lc/o Edward McPhail & Mary J. Gill bp 2 Apr 1865 spr Joseph Voll & Virginia Voll p354

MCPHELEY – George Hay, b 14 Sep 1854 lc/o Edw. McPheley & Mary Jane Gill bp 8 Oct 1854 spr Arthur McCafferty & Bridget Norton p25

MCPHERSON – Caroline, b 27 Sep 1861 lc/o Alexander McPherson & Martha McPherson (c) bp 3 Nov 1861 spr Maria A. Joseph p266

MCPHERSON – Catharine Rosella McPherson, b 19 Mar 1866 c/o Samuel Tobias McPherson & Anna Hack "(born Thompson)" spr Catharine Wentz p383

MCPOLAND – Charles Henry, b 28 Mar 1859 lc/o Daniel McPoland & Bridget Rodan bp 21 Jan 1860 spr Lizzie Slade p212

MCQUAID – Francis "twin", b 10 Mar 1970 lc/o Charles McQuaid & Rose McGee bp 20 Mar 1870 spr Frances McGinness & Eliza Garrity p497

MCQUAID – Mary "twin", b 10 Mar 1970 lc/o Charles McQuaid & Rose McGee bp 20 Mar 1870 spr James McDonald & Mary McDonald p497

MCSHANE – Hannah Rosalie, b 24 Oct 1865 lc/o Henry McShane & Catharine Denny bp 18 Nov 1865 spr John McShane & Mary King p369

MCSHANE – Henry, b 28 Sep 1861 lc/o Henry McShane & Catharine A. Denny bp 25 Oct 1861 spr Thos. Foley & Mary McGlone p264

MCSHANE – Julian Gibbney, b 29 Aug 1868 lc/o Henry McShane & Kate Dennie bp 29 Sep 1868 spr J. Gibbney & Rose Dennie p454

MCSHANE – Mary Catharine, b 23 Dec 1869 lc/o Edward McShane & Catharine McKenna bp 1 Jan 1870 spr Peter McKenna & Mary Harris p490

MCSHANE – Mary Catharine, b 27 Feb 1859 lc/o Henry McShane & Catharine Dennis bp 26 Apr 1859 spr Edwin Bailey & Mary Ann Ryan "I supplied the ceremonies of baptism" "baptized by Rev. B. I. McManus" Thos. Foley, priest p187

MCSHANE – Mary Catherine, b 10 Nov 1857 lc/o Charles McShane & Bridget Sa_____ bp 22 Nov 1857 spr John Jennings & Rose Boyle p141

MCSHANE – William James, b 27 Jun 1863 lc/o Henry McShane & Catharine Denny bp 18 Jul 1863 spr John C. Drury & Ellen Elwood p311

MCSHERRY – Edward Norris, b 3 Jan 1861 lc/o Dr. Richard McSherry & Catharine Wilson bp 19 Jan 1861 spr Col. J. G. Mathias & Mary, "his wife" p240

MCSHERRY – Francis Holmes Courand, b 28 May 1856 lc/o Dr. Richard McSherry & Catherine S. Wilson bp 21 Jun 1856 spr Mon. Rev. F. P Kenrich & Harriet Spalding p86

MCSHERRY – Francis Oliver, b 24 Jn 1856 lc/o John A. McSherry & Clementine Villens bp 24 Feb 1856 spr Wm. Norbeck & Eliza Shaw p73

MCSHERRY – George Allan, b 28 May 1854 lc/o Dr. Richard McSherry & Catherine Wilson bp 29 Jun 1854 spr Lieut. Augustus Kelly USN & Mary Kelty "proxy for Ellen Schu_____" p16

MCSHERRY – Mary Helena, b 19 Jun 1858 lc/o Dr. Richard McSherry & Catherine Summerville Wilson bp 20 Jun 1858 spr Alfred Jenkins & _____ _____ p160

MCSHERRY – Thomas Eugene, b 7 Sep 1860 lc/o John Andrew McSherry & Clementine Villers bp 23 Sep 1860 spr Wm. Joseph Flavilla & Ann Kreist p231

MEAGHER – Josephine, b 20 May 1860 lc/o John Meagher & Ann Fitzbannon bp 6 Jul 1860 spr Mary A. Kilduff p225

MEEKS – Edward Valentine, b 22 Dec 1856 c/o Edward Chs. Val. Meeks & Sarah C. Webb bp 15 Feb 1857 spr Henry Meeks & Eliza A. Meeks p111

MEEKS – Mary Ellen, "4 years old" lc/o Adam Meeks & Mary Ellen McFaul bp 12 Jan 1865 spr Mabel Meeks p348

MEEKS – Susan Meeks, b 10 Jun 1842 lc/o William P. Meeks & Mary Jane Sh_____ bp 28 Oct 1859 spr Mary Carrese "I made their abjuration of Prot. before baptism" Thos. Foley, priest [*ed. note: 'their' references all four individuals the priest baptized that day*] p202

MENAGÉ – Ann Catherine, b 5 Oct 1853 lc/o Firnian Menagé & Annie Richard bp 19 Oct 1856 spr Cath. Sullivan p99

MENAGÉ – Clara Josephine, b 4 Oct 1856 lc/o Firnian Menagé & Annie Richard bp 19 Oct 1856 spr Jos Gunter & Clara Duplix p99

MERCERET – Anna Maria, b 17 Nov 1859 lc/o Louis Merceret & Rebecca L. Baltzell bp 24 Nov 1859 spr Basil T. Elder & Josephine M. Elder p206

MERCERET – Francis Jules, b 20 Nov 1862 lc/o Louis Merceret & Rebecca L. Baltzell bp 11 Dec 1862 spr Julia Baldwin & Jules and Alex Merceret p297

MERCERET – Francis Louis, b 24 Apr 1857 lc/o Francis Merceret & Amélie Picquet bp 30 Apr 1857 spr Louis Merceret & Marie Alice Merceret "for Cleophie Picquet" p118

MERCERET – George Heighe, b 29 Dec 1863 lc/o Louis Merceret & Rebecca Baltzell bp 20 Jan 1864 spr Ephraim F. Baldwin & Amelie Merceret p324

MERCERET – John Henry, b 5 Jun 1865 lc/o Louis Merceret & Rebecca L. Baltzell bp 22 Jun 1865 spr Robert Hickly & Mary Adele Merceret p359

MERCERET – Maria Nathalie, b 5 Sep 1855 lc/o Francis Merceret & Amelie Picquet bp 13 Sept 1855 spr Basil I. Elder & Nathalie Merceret p58

MERCERET – Mary Alice, b 2 May 1858 lc/o Louis Merceret & Rebecca C. Baltzell bp 13 May 1858 spr Matthew J. Foley & Mary Natalie Merceret p155

MERCERET – Rebecca Ludenberger Merceret "(born Baltzell)", "age about 29" bp 9 Nov 1855 spr Mary Katherine Merceret "baptized conditionally" Thos. Foley, priest p64

MERCERET– Louis Ferdinand, b 23 Oct 1850 lc/o Louis Merceret & Rebecca L. Baltzell bp 1 Nov 1856 spr Basil T. Elder & Alice Merceret p100

MEREDITH – Annie Lee Meredith, b 5 Aug 1857 bp 8 Dec 1866 spr Mary Conroy p401

MEREDITH – Caroline Meredith, b 23 Nov 1855 bp 8 Dec 1866 spr Louise O'Connor p400

MEREDITH – Evyline Meredith, b 12 Apr 1859 bp 8 Dec 1866 spr Bridget McCormick "baptized conditionally" Jas. Gibbons, priest p401

MERETTI – Charles Andrew, b 24 Dec 1856 lc/o Anthony Meretti & Catherine Meretti bp 26 Feb 1857 spr Anthony Russo & Maria Cunia p112

MERRILL – Virginia Gertrude, b 31 Jan 1844 lc/o Mary Catharine Merrill bp 2 Nov 1864 spr Bridget Johns "baptized conditionally" Thos. Foley, priest p343

MERRITT – Alfred Clifton, b 19 Nov 1860 lc/o Isaac Merritt & Ellen [*sic*] bp 23 Jan 1861 spr John Devlin & Kate Dolan p240

MERRITT – Charles Tinis, b 8 Jun 1856 lc/o Isaac H. Merritt & Ellen Shehan bp 20 Jul 1856 spr John G. Fledderman & Elizabeth Fledderman p 91

MERRITT – Emma Underwood, b 25 Nov 1854 lc/o William Merritt & Mary Ann Jenkins bp 4 Feb 1855 spr Mary A. Kane p36

MERRITT – Eva Howlaine, b 27 Dec 1862 lc/o Isaac Merritt & Ellen Shane bp 31 Jan 1863 spr Thos. Foley & Obistia Colston p300

MERRITT – George Washington, b 5 Jul 1858 lc/o Isaac Merritt & Ellen Sheahan bp 12 Jul 1858 spr Rev. John McNally & Mary Merritt p162

MERRITT – William Sydney, b 6 Feb 1854 lc/o Isaac H. Merritt & Ellen Shawe bp 10 Mar 1854 spr Thos. Foley & Marion T. Devlin p7

MERRYWEATHER – Hester Merryweather "(alias Brown)", b *ndg* bp 27 Apr 1857 "baptized conditionally" Francis Patrick, Archb. p117

MESSONIER – Hortense Lucile Jeanine, b 27 Apr 1864 lc/o Felix Marie Messonier & Marie Hortense Cayé bp 31 May 1864 spr Jean Fenillant & Lucille Fayset p333

MICHIE – Dr. James William Michie "of Charlottesville, Va", "aged about 48 years" bp 17 Jun 1868 spr Jonathan Mullan & Josephine Placide p446

MICKLE – Henry, b 28 Jul 1859 lc/o Robert Mickle & Stephanie Laurentrie bp 22 Aug 1859 spr Charles & Ann Williamson p198

MIDDLETON – Arthus Soth_____, b 2 Oct 1862 lc/o James F. S. Middleton & Evelyn Norr_____ bp 10 Nov 1862 spr Mary E. Heaton p293

MIDDLETON – Joseph, b 4 Jan 1867 lc/o Ignatius L. Middleton & Ann Rebecca Mills "(born Hooper)" bp 25 Jan 1867 spr J. D. Padgett & Maria Conie p403

MIDDLETON – Mary Rosina, b 17 Jan 1868 lc/o John D. Middleton & Eliza Miles bp 10 Feb 1868 spr Dr. Felix R. McManus & Sara G. McManus p433

MIDDLETON – Mary, b 21 Jul 1865 lc/o Ignatius Middleton & Nannie R. Mills "(born Hooper)" bp 15 Aug 1865 spr Jeremiah Dyer & "(Mrs. Padget, proxy for)" Nellie Diggs p362

MILABAN – Ellen, b 4 Jun 1857 lc/o Cornelius William Milaban & Ann Donohue bp 7 Jun 1857 spr Daniel Sullivan & Catherine Walsh p123

MILAN – James Michael, b 23 Jun 1860 lc/o John Milan & Mary Mitchel bp 6 Jul 1860 spr Danl. & Cath. Carroll p226

MILES – Bernard, b 12 Sep 1856 lc/o John Miles & Elizabeth McGowan bp 28 Sep 1856 spr John Goodwin & Bridget Goodwin p97

MILES – Eleanor Ashton, b 15 May 1856 lc/o Dr. Ashton Miles, USN & Mary Jennie Stewart bp 29 Jul 1856 spr James Miles & Eleanor Miles p91

MILES – George Henry, b 12 Jul 1859 lc/o John Miles & Elizabeth McGovern bp 22 Aug 1859 spr Mary Costello p198

MILES – John William, b 19 Feb 1859 lc/o Robert Miles & Eliza Ann Trego bp 26 Nov 1860 spr Martha Donnelly p236

MILES – Lemuel, b 23 Aug 1862 lc/o John Miles & Elizabeth McGovern bp 5 Oct 1862 spr George McGovern & Bridget Reilly p291

MILES – Mary Ann Rebecca (c), b 29 Nov 1863 c/o Jacob Miles & Henrietta McClure bp 9 May 1864 spr Mary Matthews p332

MILLBURN – Elijah Milburn, "40 years old" bp 1 Mar 1857 spr Lucy Hall p113

MILLER – Ann Elizabeth, b 8 Feb 1869 lc/o Joseph Miller & Nancy O'Leary bp 1 Mar 1869 spr Elizabeth Arnold p466

MILLER – Charles Ulysses S. Grant, b 9 Feb 1869 lc/o Charles Miller & Annie Hayes bp 2 Aug 1869 spr Mary A. Valiant p478

MILLER – Eliza Virginia Miller "(born Peters)", "aged 27 years" bp 3 Jul 1867 "baptized conditionally" Thos. Foley, priest p416

MILLER – John Henry, b *ndg* Nov 1854 lc/o Henry Miller & Barbara Miller bp 19 Apr 1855 spr Mary Lewis p43

MILLER – Mary Anne Miller, "aged 34 years" bp 7 Nov 1867 spr Anne Garmendia "baptized conditionally" James Gibbons, priest p426

MILLER – Mary Anne Miller, "aged about 7 years" bp 12 Dec 1867 spr Mary Anne Courly & Winifred Conroy p429

MILLER – no name given, "22 years old" bp 29 Apr 1864 "previously baptized by a minister" Thos. Foley, priest p331

MILLER – Rufina Anna Miller, "an orphan in St. Mary's Asylum" "about 11 years old" bp 4 Jun 1864 spr Rose McFarlan - Thos. Foley, priest p334

MILLIS – Mary Catharine Millis, "born in 1839" lc/o James & Ann Jane Millis bp 28 Oct 1859 spr Eliza Donelan "I made their abjuration of Prot. before baptism" Thos. Foley, priest [*ed. note: 'their' references all four individuals the priest baptized that day*] p203

MILLS – Laura Caroline, "aged 22" lc/o John L. Mills & Cecilia Pathain bp 15 Dec 1864 spr Mary Mullan p347

MINCHI/MITCHELL – Eliza Virginia, b 23 Oct 1853 lc/o John Minchi (or) Mitchell & Ann Jane Braden bp 19 Oct 1858 spr Rosanna A. Campbell p171

MINCHI/MITCHELL – Lelia Emma, b 8 Jul 1857 lc/o John Minchi (or) Mitchell & Ann Jane Braden bp 19 Oct 1858 spr Mary Grady p171

MINCHI/MITCHELL –John Franklin, b 24 Apr 1855 lc/o John Minchi (or) Mitchell & Ann Jane Braden bp 19 Oct 1858 spr Elizabeth Carroll p171

MINOR – Sophia Virginia, "born 5 weeks ago" lc/o Eduard Minor & Josephine Dugan bp 5 Jul 1857 spr Sophia Sabbs p126

MIRAFER – Margaret Mirafer, "aged 25 years" bp 13 Apr 1862 spr Martha Logue p279

MISKELL – Anna, b 27 Mar 1858 lc/o Michael Miskell & Mary Dolan bp 4 Apr 1858 spr John Miskell & Margaret Roberts p153

MISKELL – Laurence, b 19 Feb 1856 lc/o Michael Miskell & Mary Dolan bp 24 Feb 1856 spr John Dolan & Mary Miskell p73

MISKILL – William, b 9 Jan 1854 lc/o Michael Miskill & Mary Dolan bp 12 Feb 1854 spr John O'Dee & Bridget McMahen p5

MITCHELL – Fanny Ann Elizabeth Mitchell, b 2 Jul 1854 "a child abandoned by her mother who called herself Mrs. Mitchell" bp 29 Apr 1855 spr Rosanna McCormick p45

MOALE – Anna Margaretta, b 20 Jul 1863 lc/o Henry Moale & Maggie Elder bp 4 Aug 1863 spr Francis N. Elder & Matilda M. Elder p312

MOALE – Annie, b 14 Sep 1864 lc/o Edward Moale "Lt. __ S. Vol." & Jannie Wilson bp 19 Sep 1864 spr Henry Moale & Nannie Wilson p340

MOALE – Frances Elver, b 30 Nov 1867 lc/o Henry Moale & Margaretta Elder bp 8 Dec 1867 spr Ambrose A. White & Mary Hazzard p429

MOALE – Henry, b 17 Nov 1865 c/o Henry Moale & Margaret Elder, "his wife" bp 17 Mar 1866 spr T. P. Scott & Augusta Moale "I supplied the ceremonies" "previously baptized by Dr. Chatard" H. B. Coskery, priest p378

MOALE – William Travers, b 14 Sep *ndg* [*ed. note: most likely 1870*] lc/o Henry Moale "of Baltimore" & Margaret Elder "of Baltimore" bp 24 Sep 1870 spr Ephraim Baldwin & Anna M. Smith p510

MONAGHAN – James, b 8 Apr 1868 lc/o John Monaghan & Mary Shail bp 14 May 1868 spr John Shail & Kate Lambert p442

MONAHAN – John Patrick, b 23 Sep *ndg* [*ed. note: most likely 1870*] lc/o Peter Monahan "of County Roscommon, Ireland" & Anna Melwood "of the same place" bp 25 Sep 1870 spr Cath. Melwood & John Monahan p510

MONAHAN – John, b 6 Mar 1866 lc/o John Monahan & Mary <u>Sheil</u> bp 22 Mar 1866 spr John McCarney & Alice McCarney p378

MONAHAN – William Charles, b 5 Dec 1858 lc/o John Monahan & Kate Coughlin bp 2 Jan 1859 spr Joseph Kuhn & Margaret McCullough p178

<u>MONAHU</u> – Francis Henry, b 23 Jan 1861 lc/o John <u>Monahu</u> & Catharine Coughlan bp 25 Mar 1861 spr Jane Coughlan p247

MONAHUE – Mary Celestrina, b 11 Aug 1863 lc/o John Monahue & Catharine Coughlin bp 27 Sep 1863 spr Danl. McCoy & Ellen Noonan p316

MONTEVERDE – John Antonio, b15 Jan 1860 lc/o John Monteverde & Magdalen Guio bp 16 Jan 1860 spr Josep L. Costa & Mary Monteverde p211

MONTEVERDE – Louis Joseph, b 19 Dec 1856 lc/o Luiz Joseph Montaverde & Maria Magdalene Goia bp 4 Jan 1857 spr Martin Cumber & Sarah Cumber p107

MOONEY – James Henry, b 13 Feb 1855 lc/o John Mooney & Mary A. Hanlan bp 27 Feb 1855 spr Pat. Hanlan & Mary Boyle p38

MOONEY – Mary Ellen, b 16 Jun 1861 lc/o Thomas Mooney & Margaret O'Donnell bp 26 Jun 1861 spr John Smith & Ann E. Mooney p255

MOORE – Joseph Thomas, b 1 Mar 1856 lc/o John Thomas Moore & Ellen Sullvan bp 2 Mar 1856 spr Luke Kerney & Mary Shea p74

MOORE – Sara, b 7 Nov 1856 lc/o William Moore & Rose Reilly bp 28 Dec 1856 spr Thomas Harvey & Susan Moore p106

MOORE – Thomas, b 24 Feb 1868 lc/o Thomas Moore & Ellen Reilly bp 30 Mar 1868 spr George Kidd & Kate Fagan p438

MOORE – William Patrick, b 23 Oct 1865 lc/o Thomas Moore & Ellen Reilly bp 3 Dec 1865 spr John May & Maggie Moore p370

MORAN – Denis, b 10 Dec 1868 lc/o William Moran & Ann Gannon bp 12 Dec 1868 spr John _____ & Mary Ann Nugent p460

MORAN – Ellen, b 6 May 1867 lc/o William Moran & Anna Gannon bp 9 May 1867 spr Hugh McCoy & Georgianna McCoy p412

MORAN – Sarah, b 24 Mar 1864 lc/o William Moran & Honora Gannon bp 3 Mar 1864 spr John Gannon & Ellen Moran p327

MORAN – William John, b 23 Dec 1870 lc/o William Moran "of County Galway, Ireland" & Ann Gannon "of County Roscommon, Ireland" bp 28 Dec 1870 spr John Lynam & Mary Moran p517

MOREHOUSE – Joseph Henry, b 17 Jan 1866 lc/o John Morehouse & Margaret Brown bp 3 Dec 1866 spr Mary McCarron p400

MORGAN – Ann Maria, b 1 Aug 1861 lc/o Richard Morgan & Ann Connolley bp 28 Aug 1861 spr Francis & Mary Morgan p259

MORGAN – Anna, b 6 Apr 1865 lc/o Thos. Morgan & Anna "(Gannon)" bp __ Apr 1865 spr Thos.Nally & Cath. _____ [*ed. note: no baptism day recorded, but entry was between 11 & 16 April*] p354

MORGAN – Ardinia Mary Morgan (c), "aged about 13 years" bp 21 Oct 1867 spr Elizabeth Cassidy p424

MORGAN – Charles Henry, b 6 Sep 1856 lc/o William Morgan & Susanah McClellan bp 14 Sep 1856 spr Joseph & Johanna Martz p95

MORGAN – Eliza Ann, b *ndg* Jan 1854 lc/o John Morgan & Margaret Stresgreen bp 15 Jan 1854 spr Louis Dunsblow p2

MORGAN – George Washington, b 29 Apr 1856 lc/o ______ Morgan & Mary Ann Moffitt bp 3 May 57 spr M. Moffitt p 118

MORGAN – John Louis, b 29 Dec 1860 lc/o John L. Morgan & Julia Taylor (c) bp 12 Jan 1861 spr Caroline Pratt p239

MORGAN – Mary Ellen, b 14 Mar 1867 lc/o Thomas Morgan & Bridget Harney bp 31 Mar 1867 spr Dennis Callaghan & Mary Harney p409

MORGAN – Mary Estella, b 11 Dec 1858 lc/o William Morgan & Susan McClellan bp 26 Dec 1858 spr Francis C. Klunk & Louisa Klunk p177

MORGAN – William Edward, b 29 Jul 1854 lc/o William Morgan & Susan McClellan bp 6 Aug 1854 spr Michael Albert & Amanda Cook p18

MORGAN – William Henry, b 5 Oct 1859 lc/o Benjamin Morgan & Dolly Clayton (c) bp 24 Nov 1859 spr Cecilia Hollins p206

MORIARTY – Catherine, b 8 Nov 1856 lc/o Michael Moriarty & Catherine Casey bp 10 Nov 1856 spr Bridget Caranaugh & John Caranaugh p101

MORIARTY – Francis Patrick, b 16 Jan 1859 lc/o Michael Moriarty & Catharine Casey bp 30 Jan 1959 spr Terence McManus & Ann McManus p 180

MORRELL – Ellen Morrell, "aged 22 years" bp 30 Oct 1865 spr Maggie Barron p368

MORRELL – Jeremiah, b 13 Aug 1860 lc/o Patrick Morrell & Hannah Connelly bp 16 Aug 1860 "baptized conditionally" "privately baptized by a midwife whose testimony was not forthcoming" Francis Patrick, Archb. p229

MORRIS – Mary Ellen, b 4 May 1858 lc/o William Morris & Julia A. McDonald bp 13 Jun 1858 spr Edward Mitchell & Mary __ Mitchell p159

MORRISON – Annie Morrison, "aged 21 years" bp 28 Sep 1868 spr Clara Parker p455

MORRISON – Ellen, b 22 Aug 1858 lc/o James Morrison & Mary McCormick bp 10 Sep 1858 spr Catherine Morrison p169

MORROW – Mary Rosina, b 20 Feb 1855 lc/o Samuel Morrow & Mary Elizabeth Foyes bp 3 Jul 1855 spr Rosina Agnes Foyes & Jno. McNally p51

MORROW – Robert Morrow, "aged 62 years" bp 17 Mar 1863 "baptized conditionally" Francis Patrick, Archb. p304

MORTON – John, b 3 Dec 1858 lc/o Patrick Morton & Mary McCoy bp 10 Dec 1858 spr James Boylan & Catharine Boylan p176

MORTON – Mary Ellen, b 6 May 1859 lc/o John Morton & Mary More bp 13 Jun 1859 spr Thomas & Mary Martin p192

MORTON – Patrick, b 2 Nov 1860 lc/o Patrick Morton ("deceased 22 July") & Mary McCoy, "his wife" bp 6 Nov 1860 spr Michael Morton & Ellen Boylan p235

MOSS – Agnes Celia, b 9 Sep 1856 lc/o James Moss & Ann Reilly bp 12 Oct 1856 spr James McLoughlin & Ann Reilly p99

MOSS – Ann Maria, b 28 Dec 1853 lc/o James Moss & Ann Riley bp 22 Jan 1854 spr James Conburgan & Mary McCoffy p3

MOYCE – Sophia, b 23 Oct 1857 lc/o Stephen Moyce & Sarah McGlone bp 15 Nov 1857 spr Eleanora McGlone p140

MUCI – Mary Honora, b 17 Dec 1867 lc/o Robert Muci & Joanna Maloney bp 16 Feb 1868 spr Daniel Kenley & Mary Kenf p434

MULDOON – Peter Jerome Ignatius, b 9 Dec 1856 lc/o James Muldoon & Sarah Hitselberger bp 4 Jan 1857 spr Peter Hitselberger & Kate McNulty p107

MULGROW – John, b 9 Jan 1855 lc/o John Mulgrow & Martha Miles bp 22 Jan 1855 spr Michl. Murphy & Jane Mag__ p35

MULLAN – Ann Elizabeth, b 15 Aug 1855 lc/o Arthur William & Sarah Welsh bp 9 Sep 1855 spr John Carroll & Mary A. McWilliams p57

MULLAN – Charles Ignatius, b 3 Jul 1857 lc/o John Mullan & Maria McKenna bp 28 Aug 1857 spr Bernard Finnian & Gulia Guthrie p132

MULLAN – Edith Virginia, b 11 Jul 1864 lc/o Samuel Mullan & Matilda Harrimer bp 27 Jul 1854 spr Jonathan Mullan & Louisa Harrimer p337

MULLAN – James Cornelius, b 29 Sep 1865 lc/o John Mullan & Mary Elizabeth McAleer bp 15 Oct 1865 spr James Mullan & Bridget Shannon p367

MULLAN – John, b 10 Feb 1861 lc/o William Mullan & Elizabeth Henry bp 21 Feb 1861 spr Arthur Henry & Bridget N. Henry p244

MULLAN – John, b 23 Jun 1860 c/o Patrick Mullan & Margaret Daley bp 12 Jul 1860 spr Cath. Collins "I supplied the ceremonies.... This child had been baptized by a colored woman, said to be quite intelligent." H. B. Coskery, priest p226

MULLAN – Laura Virginia, b 28 May 1860 lc/o John Mullan & Margaret Parsons bp 22 Apr 1860 spr John Bannon & Marg. Riley p220

MULLAN – Lawrence John, b 30 Jan 1857 lc/o John Mullan & Ann Derbin bp 8 Feb 1857 spr Henry Gibbon & Ellen Lane p109

MULLAN – Margaret Jane, b 10 Dec 1856 lc/o John Mullan & Margaret Parsons bp 11 Jan 1857 spr John Coyle & Ann E. Rooney p107

MULLAN – Maria Elizabeth, b 18 Oct 1856 lc/o Thomas Mullan & Maria Smith bp 23 Nov 1856 spr Andrew Russell & Maria Brady p102

MULLAN – Mary Ann William, b 8 Mar, 1854 lc/o John William & _____ _____ Terclarn bp 19 Mar 1854 spr John Terclarn & Jane Healey p8

MULLAN – William John, b 19 Dec 1854 lc/o Thomas Mullan & Maria Smith bp 11 Feb 1855 spr Jos. McIntyre & Mary Ann Leonard p36

MULLAN –Thomas Foley, b 25 Dec1853 lc/o John P. Mullan & Sarah Jane Geddes bp 1 Jan 1854 spr Thomas Foley, Mary Mullen p1

MULLANEY – Ellen, b 4 Sep 1869 lc/o Matthew Mullaney & Bridget Lyon bp 12 Sep 1869 spr Dennis Lyon & Julia Lyon p483

MULLEN – William Henry, b 5 May 1869 lc/o Wm. Mullen & Mattie Jordan bp 30 May 1869 spr Mary Mullen & Charles Jordan p473

MÜLLER – Mary Elizabeth, b 23 Dec 1868 lc/o John Müller & Mary Ann "his wife" bp 3 Jan 1869 spr Rose Fitzpatrick p462

MULLIN – Anna Mary, b 3 Dec 1861 lc/o John Mullin & Mary E. McAleer bp 22 Dec 1861 spr John F. McAleer & Sarah Mullin p270

MULLIN – Frances August, b 9 Nov 1870 lc/o John P. Mullin "of Baltimore, Maryland" & Emily Susanne Adams "of the same place" bp 29 Nov 1870 spr Wm. G. R. Mullin & Maria E. Mullin p516

MULLIN – Helen Theresa, b 2 Dec 1866 lc/o William H. Mullan & Martha Ann Jordan bp 9 Dec 1866 spr Wm. L. Brady & Mary Blondell p401

MULLIN – John Francis, b 8 Feb 1860 lc/o John Mullin & Mary E. McAleer bp 8 Feb 1860 spr Elizabeth Mullin p214

MULLIN – William John, b 1 Apr 1859 lc/o William Mullin & Elizabeth Henry bp 6 May 1859 spr Margaret Ledin p189

MULRANNAN – John Thomas, b 4 Nov 1858 c/o Edward Mulrannan & Ellen Dulaney, "his wife" [twin of John Mulrannan] bp 21 Nov 1858 spr Thomas Cullen, Mary McAllister, John Lyons & Mary Lyons, "I supplied the ceremonies of baptism for Martin & Thomas John Mulrannan, who were privately baptized by me on the 11 inst and entered on the preceeding page" Thos. Foley, priest p174

MULRANNAN – John, b 11 Nov 1858, c/o c/o Edward Mulrannan & Ellen Dulaney, "his wife" bp 11 Nov 1858 [twin of Martin Mulrannan] p173

MULRANNAN – Martin, b 11 Nov 1858 c/o Edward Mulrannan & Ellen Dulaney, "his wife" bp 11 Nov 1858 [twin of John Mulrannan] p173

MULRANNAN – Martin, b 4 Nov 1858 c/o Edward Mulrannan & Ellen Dulaney, "his wife" [twin of John Mulrannan] bp 21 Nov 1858 spr Thomas Cullen, Mary McAllister, John Lyons & Mary Lyons "I supplied the ceremonies of baptism for Martin & Thomas John Mulrannan, who were privately baptized by me on the 11 inst. and entered on the preceeding page" Thos. Foley, priest p174

MULRENNON – Edward Michael, b 17 Jun 1856 lc/o Edward Mulrennon & Ellen Delany bp 6 Jul 1856 spr Mark & Bridget Meagher "I supplied the ceremonies…previously baptized by Rev. Thos. Foley" H. B. Coskery, priest p89

MUMFORD – Georgianna Mary Mumford, "aged about 15 years" bp 23 Dec 1867 spr Helen Turner "baptized conditionally" James Gibbons, priest p430

MUNCKS – William, b 23 Aug 1864 lc/o William Muncks & Margaret Martin bp 11 Sep 1864 spr Eugene Martin & Jane Martin p340

MUNNIGAN – Mary Teresa, b 13 Oct *ndg* [*ed. note: most likely 1870*] lc/o John Munnigan "of Baltimore" & Mary Shields "of Dublin, Ireland" bp 3 Oct 1870 spr Cecilia Danley p511

MURPHY – Anna Eululia, b 9 Apr 1864 lc/o John Murphy & Margaret E. Donaho bp 14 Apr 1864 spr Frances H. Brennan & Elizabeth Donaho p330

MURPHY – Catharine, b 20 Oct 1867 lc/o Owen Murphy & Catharine Johnston bp 10 Nov 1867 spr Patrick Johnston & Mary McElroy p426

MURPHY – Catharine, b 26 Sep 1859 lc/o Michl. Murphy & Jane McGlone bp 9 Oct 1859 spr Hugh Smith & Bridget Kelly p202

MURPHY – Cecilia, b 22 Dec 1856 lc/o John Murphy & Margaret O'Donohue bp 31 Dec 1856 spr Edward Roth & Sarah Quigley p106

MURPHY – Daniel, b 4 Oct 1857 lc/o Michael Murphy & Jane Maglone bp 11 Oct 1857 spr James Donnelly & Bridget Ford p 137

MURPHY – Edward, b 18 Sep 1866 lc/o Thos. Murphy & Catharine Tobin bp 22 Oct 1866 spr Mrs. Mary Quinn p398

MURPHY – Francis Matthew, b 8 Jul 1856 lc/o Pierce Murphy & Margaret Doyle bp 13 Jul 1856 spr John S. McEnnis & Ann Denaho p89

MURPHY – Francis S. Thomas, b 5 Jul 1855 lc/o Owen Murphy & Catharine Johnson bp 14 Jul 1855 spr Bridget Murphy p52

MURPHY – Francis, b 6 Aug 1859 son of John (Johanis) Murphy & Margaret Donohue bp 20 Aug 1859 spr John Foley & Kate Donohue Smith p198

MURPHY – George David, b 24 Aug 1862 lc/o Owen Murphy & Catharine Johnston bp 31 Aug 1862 spr Thomas Rooney & Julia Trainer p289

MURPHY – James, b 12 Dec 1853 lc/o Michael Murphy & Jane Maglone bp 8 Jan 1854 spr James Donnelly & Cath. McGovern p2

MURPHY – James Clarence, b 9 Apr 1862 lc/o John Murphy & Margaret E. Donoghue bp 23 Apr 1862 spr Daniel J. Foley & Anne M. Foley p279

MURPHY – James Murphy, b 9 Mar 1859 lc/o James Murphy & Eliza Meagher bp 28 Mar 1859 spr Edward McGlenian & Ann O'Neill p185

MURPHY – John, b 6 May 1857 lc/o Bernard Murphy & Alice Gray bp 24 May 1857 spr John Gray & Mary McElroy p121

MURPHY – Joseph Aloysius, b 21 Jun 1854 lc/o Pierce Murphy & Margaret Doyle bp 25 Jun 1854 spr Robert Rickets & Cecilia Donahue p15

MURPHY – Margaret, b 7 Oct "or 8" 1869 lc/o Owen Murphy & Cath. Johnstone bp 23 Oct 1869 spr Francis Thomas Murphy & Ann Murphy p486

MURPHY – Mary, b 9 Apr 1854 lc/o Thomas Murphy & Mary Hughes bp 9 Apr 1854 spr Michael Hughes & Bridget Clarke p10

MURPHY – Mary Alice, b 20 Jun 1869 lc/o John Murphy & Margaret E. Donoho bp 9 Jul 1869 spr F. Matthew Lancaster & Anne Euthalia Lancaster "proxies for" John A. Murphy & Anne Murphy p476

MURPHY – Mary Ann, b 6 Dec 1856 lc/o Owen Murphy & Catharine Johnson bp 7 Dec 1856 spr Bernard Trainer & Ann Trainer p103

MURPHY – Mary Catharine, b 5 Dec 1862 lc/o Michael Murphy & Catharine Boylan bp 8 Dec 1862 spr Patk. McQuaid & Ellen Boylan p297

MURPHY – Mary Ellen, b 11 Feb 1865 lc/o Owen Murphy & Catharine Johnston bp 19 Feb 1865 spr Francis Trainer & Rose Murphy p351

MURPHY – Mary Ellen, b 16 Jun 1854 lc/o Owen Murphy & Catherine Johnson bp 16 Jun 1854 spr Wm. Shaw & Mary Ann Trainor p14

MURPHY – Mary Georgiana, b 5 Jun 1868 lc/o Edwd. Murphy & Margaret McGary bp 24 Jun 1868 spr Annie Christie p447

MURPHY – Mary Jane, b 26 Oct 1855 lc/o Michael Murphy & Jane McGlone bp 4 Nov 1855 spr Andrew Keith & Joanna Toole p63

MURPHY – Mary Louise, b 5 Jul 1855 lc/o John Murphy & Margaret Donaghue bp 6 Jul 1855 spr Florence Donaghue & Sarah Donaghue p51

MURPHY – Mary Lydia, b 22 Jan 1862 lc/o Bartholomew Murphy & Margaret Dorsey bp 2 Feb 1862 spr John S. Dorsey & Mary Wallace p273

MURPHY – Mary Sarah, b 14 Mar 1859 nc/o Adeline Murphy bp 25 Mar 1859 spr Julia Greatfield p184

MURPHY – Rosa, b 12 Jul 1858 lc/o Owen Murphy & Catharine Johnson bp 15 Aug 1858 spr Francis Cassidy & Catharine Baldwell p167

MURPHY – Terrence, b 25 Mar 1860 lc/o Owen Murphy & Catharine Johnson bp 15 Apr 1860 spr Francis Shaw & Mary McShane p219

MURPHY – Thomas, b 11 May 1855 lc/o Bernard Murphy & Alice Grady bp 20 May 1855 spr Patrick Murphy & Bridget Grady p47

MURPHY – William, b 27 Sep 1865 lc/o Patrick Murphy & Margaret Tierney bp 1 Oct 1865 spr Ann Fitzgerald p365

MURRAY – Catharine, b 21 Aug 1860 lc/o Peter Murray & Catharine Feehely bp 26 Aug 1860 spr Edward Dunn & Bridget Feehely p229

MURRAY – Francis Patrick, b 30 Oct 1861 lc/o Hubert Murray & Anna Buckley bp 10 Nov 1861 spr John Slavin & Mary Buckley p266

MURRAY – George, b 9 Nov 1857 lc/o Patrick Murray & Ann Holten bp 9 Nov 1857 "baptized privately in sickness" H. B. Coskery, priest p140

MURRAY – George, b 9 Nov 1857 lc/o Patrick Murray & Ann Holton bp 29 Dec 1857 spr Louisa Ducatel p145

MURRAY – James, b 1 June 1857 lc/o James Murray & Ann McElroy bp 7 June 1857 spr Hugh Smith & Catherine Murray p123

MURRAY – John Bernard, b 23 Jun 1859 c/o James Murray & Ann McElroy, "his wife" bp 20 Nov 1859 spr Upensors Hubert Murray & Catherine Coleman p205

MURRAY – John Lewis, b 21 May 1856 lc/o John Murray & Mary Jane Dignam bp 8 Jun 1856 spr Mary Dwyer p84

MURRAY – Margaret, b 31 Mar 1855 lc/o James Murray & Ann McElroy bp 9 Apr 1855 spr Edward Campbell & Bridget Hayley p42

MURRAY – Mary Ann, b 5 Feb 1867 lc/o James Murrray & Ann McElroy bp 10 Feb 1867 spr Terence Murphy & Margaret Honovan p405

MURRAY – Mary Ann, b 7 Aug 1858 lc/o John Murray & Bridget Lynn bp 12 Aug 1858 spr Patrick Lynn & Mary Langan p166

MURRAY – Thomas Havier, b 7 Dec 1863 lc/o Thomas Murray & Catharine Tolen bp 1 Jan 1864 spr Ellen Brady p323

MURRAY – William, b 18 Aug 1861 lc/o James Murray & Ann McElroy bp 21 Aug 1861 spr Catharine Clusky p259

MUSE – Elizabeth Adelaide Muse "(born Bailey)", "aged 37", db 9 Jan 1854 spr Mr. & Mrs. Elliott p2

MUSE – Jonas Alexander Bailey, "aged twenty-one years" lc/o Joseph E. Muse & Ann Bailey "late of Cambridge, Md" bp 25 Feb 1857 "baptized conditionally" H. B. Coskery, priest p112

MUSE – Joseph Muse "age 43 yrs" bp 26 Feb 1854 p6

MYERS – Emma Maria, "about 2 weeks old" lc/o James Myers & Joanna T. Brooks bp 20 Feb 1870 spr Christopher Tandry & Annie Nagts p494

MYERS – George, b 26 Dec 1862 lc/o Fred. K. Myers & Caroline Owens bp 31 Jan 1863 spr Mary Harriet Leonar p300

MYERS – Mary Frances, "5 months old" lc/o Genge Myers & Christiana Marshall bp 6 Jun 1860 spr Fanny Hurst p224

MYERS – Mary Myers, "aged 22" register date: 27 Oct 1865 "previously baptized by Rev. F. Baker" Thos. Foley, priest p368

MYERS – William Thomas, b 24 Jul 1862 lc/o Jacob Myers & Ann Maria Slater (c) bp 27 Jul 1862 spr Sophy Jenkins p286

NAFF – Margarita, b *ndg* bp 20 Mar 1861 spr Mary White "baptized conditionally" H. B. Coskery, priest p246

NASH – Elizabeth, b 3 Jan 1857 lc/o William Nash & Elizabeth Miller (c) bp 29 Jan 1857 spr Minty LeCompte p109

NASH – Matilda, b 11 March 1854 lc/o William Nash (c) & Elizabeth Miller (c) bp 18 Mar 1854 spr Eliza Butler p8

NASH – Patrick Thomas, b 12 Nov 1858 lc/o William Nash & Elizabeth Miller (c) bp 18 Nov 1858 spr Matilda Miller p174

NASH – William Fabius, b 12 Jul 1855 lc/o William Nash & Elizabeth Miller (all c) bp 20 Jul 1855 spr Letitia Sorrichs p53

NEAL – Mary Rosa, b 17 Nov 1851 lc/o John Neal & Adelaide Armstrong bp 30 Aug 1866 spr Sister Mary of St. Bernard Barron "baptized conditionally" Thos. Foley priest p394

NEALE – Aloysius, "9 years old" lc/o Charles Neale & Eliza Adams (c) bp 19 Jan 1870 spr Fanny Sniffias p491

NEALE – Joseph John, "4 months old" lc/o Charles Neale & Eliza Adams (c) bp 31 Mar 1869 spr Bridget O'Rourke p467

NEALE – Mary Louisa, "3 years & 6 months old" lc/o Charles Neale & Eliza Adams (c) bp 19 Jan 1870 spr Fanny Sniffias p491

NEEDHAM – Anne, b 17 Dec 1867 lc/o Michael Needham & Bridget Kelly bp 27 Jan1868 spr Mary Anne Kilduff p433

NEEDHAMMER – Lewis Galt, b 5 Aug 1867 lc/o Lewis Saml. Needhammer & Mary Virginia Bailey bp 12 Oct 1867 spr Susan Piet p423

NEEDUM – Ellen, b 18 Dec 1865 lc/o Michael Needum & Bridget Tosnay bp 8 Jun 1866 spr Mary A. Kilduff p385

NEELY – Elizabeth Neely, "aged 22 years" bp 27 Jun 1867 spr Catharine McDonald "baptized conditionally" Jas. Gibbons, priest p415

NEGLIS – Joseph Augustine, b 15 Oct 1862 lc/o Augustine Neglis & Louise LaMere bp 2 Nov 1862 spr Mr. Dandelet & Mrs. Lucile Dandelet p293

NEIL – Margaret, b 26 Dec 1854 lc/o Matthew Neil & Ellen Cullen bp 4 Feb 1855 spr Patrick Stack & Sarah Ennis p36

NEILLISE – Eugenie Leonida, b 28 May 1860 lc/o Auguste Neillisse & Louisa Lerner bp 11 Jul 1860 spr Eugenie Guerand & Leonida Guerand p226

NELSON – Augusta, b 24 Jan 1856 lc/o James Nelson & Maria E. Cain bp 24 Mar 1856 spr Mary Nelson p77

NELSON – Mary Cora, b 12 Jan 1858 lc/o James Nelson & Mary Elizabeth Cain bp 10 Sep 1859 spr Lucille Nelson p199

NELSON- Laurence, b 11 Nov 1853 lc/o James Nelson & Mary E. Cain bp 4 Jan 1854 spr F. H. Lipp & Mary E. Clark p1

NEVILLE – Sarah, b 12 May 1858 lc/o Matthew Neville & Ellen Murphy bp 27 May 1858 spr Sarah Nicholson p157

NEVIN – Elizabeth Ann, b 14 Dec 1856 lc/o Eduard Nevin &______ ______ bp 25 Dec 1856 p105

NICHOLAS – Henry Moale, b 28 Apr 1869 lc/o Wilson Carey Nicholas & Augusta Moale bp 20 May 1869 spr T. P. Scott, & Fannie Gibbons p471

NICHOLAS – John Patterson, b 7 Aug 1867 lc/o Wilson C. Nichols & Augusta Moale bp 4 Sep 1867 spr Henry & Margaret Moale p420

NICHOLLS – Henry, b 4 Jun 1862 c/o James McGinnis & Mary Nicholls bp 11 Jun 1862 spr Hannah Nicholls p283

NICHOLLS – Thomas Nicholls, "aged 67 years" bp 31 May 1860 "baptized conditionally" Thos. Foley, priest p223

NICHOLSON – Edith Goldsborough, b 20 Apr 1863 lc/o Charles G. Nicholson & Emma Goldsborough bp 13 Jun 1863 spr Annie Goldsborough, w - Gustavus Nicholson p309

NICHOLSON – James Cormicke, b 28 Jul 1857 lc/o Michael Nicholson & Georgiana Betson bp 21 Mar 1858 spr Hannah Dougherty p151

NICKERSON – Pamelia Ann Nickerson, "aged 60" bp 22 May 1867 spr _____ Martin p413

NOFF – Franklin Noff, "aged about 31 years" bp 27 Dec 1859 "baptized privately" H. B. Coskery, priest p209

NOLAN – Catherine Ann, b 21 Aug 1854 lc/o John Nolan & Ellen Nolan bp 3 Sep 1854 spr Michl. & Mary O'Shea p22

NOLAN – Eliza, b 15 Mar 1859 lc/o William Nolan & Catharine Kane bp 20 Mar 1859 spr Wm. Blondell & Honora S. Blondell p184

NOLAN – James, b 20 Jul 1865 c/o Thomas Nolan & Cath. Reilly Nolan bp 30 Jul 1865 spr John Ford & Mary McCourt p361

NOLAN – John Hines, b 28 Jan 1860 lc/o Martin Nolan & Margaret Fahey bp 5 Feb 1860 spr [*ed note: cannot read names*] p213

NOLAN – Julian, b 15 Apr 1860 lc/o Thomas Nolan & Catharine Riley bp 22 Apr 1860 spr James Cornell & Anne Dunn p220

NOLAN – Margaret, b 23 Jan 1861 lc/o Thomas Nolan & Catharine Reilly bp 2 Feb 1862 spr John Bradley & Rose Finnegan p273

NOLAN – Margaret Ann, b 13 May 1862 lc/o Martin Nolan & Margaret Fahey bp 23 Mar 1862 spr Martin Fahey & Ann Hartman p276

NOLAN – Mary, b 25 Dec 1856 lc/o Dennis Nolan & Eliza Kane bp 19 Feb 1857 spr Owen Byrne & Mary Kane p111

NOLAN – Mary, b 21 Apr 1858 lc/o Martin Nolan & Margaret Fahey bp 25 Apr 1858 spr Eduard Coullahan & Mary Burke p154

NOLAN – Mary Elizabeth, b 10 Sep 1854 lc/o Thos. Nolan & Catherine Riley bp 17 Sep 1854 spr Patk. Barry & Eliza Coakley p24

NOLAN – Thomas, b 30 Jul 1856 lc/o Thomas Nolan & Catherine Riley bp 10 Aug 1856 spr Christopher Retten & Annie Beady p92

NOLAN – William Joseph Aloysius, b 8 Dec 1861 lc/o William Nolan & Catharine Kane bp 22 Dec 1861 spr John Handshaw & Ann Kane p270

NOONAN – Francis Joseph, b 19 Nov 1856 lc/o John Noonan & Catherine Malloney bp 23 Nov 1856 spr Patrick H. Riordan & Elizabeth Reilly p102

NOONAN – Francis Thomas, b 9 Aug 1855 lc/o Jno. Noonan & Catherine Maloney bp 19 Aug 1855 spr Chas. Callahan & Kate Borland p56

NOONAN – James, b 18 Apr 1854 lc/o Robert Noonan & Alice Murphy bp 30 Apr 1854 spr William Blondell & Sarah Sinnott p11

NOONAN – John, b 10 Mar 1856 lc/o Robert Noonan & Alice Murphy bp 16 Mar 1856 spr James Fitzsimmons & Catherine Gallagher p75

NOONAN – Thomas, b 22 Jun 1858 lc/o Robert Noonan & Alice Murphy bp 4 Jul 1858 spr James Kane & Rosa Kelly p162

NOONAN – Wm. Patrick, b 25 Jun 1861 lc/o Robert Noonan & Alice Murphy bp 7 Jul 1861 spr Malachy Blondel & Mary Riley p255

NOONEY – Mary Ann, b 25 Jul 1854 lc/o Mathias Nooney & Mary Patterson bp 10 Aug 1854 spr Julia Patterson p19

NORBECK – Julia Anna Norbeck "(born Wilson)", "aged about 33 years" bp 2 Apr 1860 "baptized conditionally" Thos. Foley, priest p218

NORBECK – Mary Philomena Norbeck "(nee Fields)", "aged 35 years" bp 27 May 1858 spr Jane E. Foudriat p157

NORDHUFF – William Henry, b 29 Oct 1863 lc/o William F. Nordhuff & Mary Kleffman bp 18 Nov 1863 spr Fanny Hurst p321

NORRIS – Charles Emmanuel, b 5 Dec 1868 lc/o Charles Solomon Norris & Margaret Ann Harris bp 13 Dec 1868 spr Eleanora Harris (all c) p460

NORRIS – Mary Norris, "aged 31 years" bp 3 Oct 1869 "baptized conditionally" Thos. Foley, priest p485

NORRIS – William Brown Ignatius, b 31 Oct 1856 lc/o Patrick Norris & Elizabeth Norris, "his wife" bp 2 Aug 1857 spr Ann Scantlebury p129

NORRIS – William Sterritt Norris (c), "30 years of age" bp 28 Jul 1857 p129

NORTON – Ann, b 27 Sep 1869 lc/o Andrew Norton & Bridget Kane bp 3 Oct 1869 spr Patrick Reilly & Eliza Norton p484

NUGENT – Julia Ann, b 20 Mary 1863 lc/o Thomas Nugent & Mary Landers bp 8 Mar 1863 spr John & Ann Landers p303

NUNES – Eliza Nunes, "adult", b *ndg* 26 bp 26 Mar 1855 spr H. B. Coskery "baptized conditionally" H. B. Coskery, priest p40

NUNES – William Wing Loring, b 14 Oct 1847 lc/o Albert Angel Nunes & Eliza Loring bp 26 Oct 1854 spr H. B. Coskery & Ellen Schmunck p27

NUNEZ – Mary, b 1 Apr 1846 lc/o Albert Nunez & Eliza Loring bp 27 Nov 1854 "I supplied the ceremonies in the case of Mary…previously baptized" H. B. Coskery, priest p30

NUSS – George Henry, b 19 Dec 1853 lc/o George A. Nuss & Margaret Myers bp 14 Mar 1854 spr Margaret McCormick p7

O'BRIAN – Florence, b 29 Mar 1868 lc/o Daniel O'Brian & Mary E. Curran bp 9 Apr 1868 spr J. S. Houlahan & George Marriott p439

O'BRIAN – Thomas, b 8 Mar 1868 lc/o Jas. O'Brian & Mary McCann bp 10 Mar 1868 spr Eliza Gibney p435

O'BRIEN - Margaret June, b 24 Feb 1854 lc/o John O'Brien & Susan Simmons bp 5 Mar 1854 spr James Qurid & Bridget Road p7

O'BRIEN – Cecilia Helen, b 16 Feb 1865 lc/o Patrick O'Brien & Frances Fink bp 1 Mar 1865 spr Mary O'Brien p352

O'BRIEN – Charles, b 13 Aug 1870 lc/o Patrick O'Brien & Frances Fink bp 17 Aug 1870 spr Francis O'Brien & Emma O'Brien p506

O'BRIEN – Clara Louisa, b 11 Apr 1863 lc/o Patrick O'Brien & Frances Fink bp 21 Apr 1863 spr Mary O'Brien p306

O'BRIEN – Elizabeth Frances, b 15 Mar 1858 lc/o Patrick O'Brien & Elizabeth McElroy bp 25 Apr 1858 spr John Riley & Catherine Branigan p154

O'BRIEN – Emily Jane, b 8 Jun 1858 lc/o Edward O'Brien & Rachel Anderson bp 18 Aug 1858 spr Elizabeth Upton p167

O'BRIEN – Francis Patrick McHenry, b 29 Jun 1856 lc/o Patrick O'Brien & Frances Fink bp 3 Aug 1856 spr Owen Murphy & Margaret Fitzgerald p92

O'BRIEN – George Patrick, b 4 Sep 1860 c/o James O'Brien & "his lawful wife Margaret McCann" bp 6 Sep 1860 spr George McCann & Alice Morris [*ed. note: twin of James O'Brien*] p230

O'BRIEN – Grace Agnes, "aged about 22 yrs" bp 1 Apr 1869 spr Margaret M______ "baptized privately" H. B. Coskery, priest p468

O'BRIEN – Honora Frances, b 15 Jan 1857 lc/o James O'Brien & Ann Rebecca McLaughlin bp 11 Apr 1858 spr Michael Roche & Mary Roche p153

O'BRIEN – James Christopher b 25 Nov 1854 lc/o James O'Brien & Ellen O'Connor bp 8 Dec 1854 spr Wm. Connor p31

O'BRIEN – James O'Brien, b 31 Jan 1855 lc/o James O'Brien & Rebecah _____ bp 10 Jun 1855 [*ed. note: faint record*] p49

O'BRIEN – James, b 4 Sep 1860 c/o James O'Brien & "his lawful wife Margaret McCann" bp 6 Sep 1860 spr Thomas McKenna & Mary Dooley [*ed. note: twin of George Patrick O'Brien*] p230

O'BRIEN – John, b 19 March 1854 lc/o Cornelius O'Brien & Bridgit Sharon bp 19 Mar 1854 spr John & Ellen Sharon "baptized conditionally" Thos. Foley, priest p8

O'BRIEN – John, b 2 Aug 1862 lc/o James O'Brien & Margaret McCann bp 7 Aug 1862 spr Sarah Robinson p287

O'BRIEN – John, b 28 Oct 1856 lc/o John O'Brien & Susan Simmons bp 16 Nov 1856 spr Alban Marr & Mary Martin p101

O'BRIEN – John Christopher, b 26 Oct 1869 lc/o John O'Brien & Grace Agnes, "his wife" bp 4 Oct 1869 spr Wm. Noonan & Mary Sharkey p487

O'BRIEN – John James, b 6 Jun 1858 lc/o James O'Brien & Margaret McCann bp 20 Jun 1858 spr Thomas McCann & Margaret McCadden p160

O'BRIEN – Joseph Henry, b 3 Oct 1860 lc/o Edward O'Brien & Rachel Anderson bp 2 Dec 1860 spr Mary Henry p237

O'BRIEN – Marian Genevieve, b 7 Jun 1870 lc/o Daniel O'Brien "of County Wexford, Ireland" & Mary E. Curran "of Baltimore" bp 19 Oct 1870 spr Cecilia Foley p512

O'BRIEN – Mary Catherine, b 4 Sep 1856 lc/o Patk. O'Brien & Elizabeth McElroy bp 5 Oct 1856 spr Arthur Keaney & Mary Hart p98

O'BRIEN – Richard, b 8 Oct 1855 lc/o Richard O'Brien & Sarah Gosslin "(born Becroft)" bp 4 Nov 1855 spr Martin & Hester Kelly p63

O'BRIEN – Rosetta, May, b 14 Apr 1869 lc/o Daniel O'Brien & Mary Elizabeth Curran bp 6 May 1869 spr Michael Sheehan & Cecilia Fahey p470

O'BRIEN – Sarah Frances, b 17 Oct 1860 lc/o Patrick O'Brien & Frances Fink bp 28 Oct 1860 spr John Nugent & Mary Corcoran p233

O'BRIEN – Sarah, b 17 May 1858 lc/o Richard O'Brien & Sarah Ann Whereaft bp 14 Jun 1858 spr George Kelly p159

O'BRIEN – Thomas, b 12 Jul 1856 lc/o William O'Brien & Mary Scanlon bp 20 Jul 1856 spr Peter Hollohan & Mary Scanlon p90

O'BRIEN – Thomas Joseph, b 7 Oct 1867 lc/o Patrick O'Brien & Frances Fink bp 14 Oct 1867 spr Elizabeth O'Brien p424

O'BRIEN – William George, b 12 Feb 1854 lc/o Edward O'Brien & Rachel Anderson bp 20 Aug 1854 spr Ellen Dalton p21

O'BRIEN –Timothy John, b 13 Apr 1856 lc/o Edward O'Brien & Catherine Pope bp 20 Apr 1856 spr Timothy O'Brien & Ellen O'Brien p81

O'CONNELL – David, b 24 Nov 1862 [*sic*] [*ed. note: since the baptism took place on 10 Feb 1862, the birth year is recorded incorrectly*] lc/o Patrick Donnelly & Julia O'Connell bp 9 Feb 1862 spr John Tangney & Ann Tierney p273

O'CONNELL – Edward Elliott, b 5 Sep 1862 lc/o Columbus O'Donnell & Caroline Jenkins bp 30 Oct 1862 spr Reginald & Martha Jenkins p293

O'CONNOR – Abbie Sarah, b 29 Nov 1861 lc/o Edward O'Connor & Ann O'Connor bp 1 Dec 1861 spr James O'Neal & Mary Henrick p268

O'CONNOR – Ellen O'Connor, "aged 8 years" bp 8 Dec 1866 spr Alice Goldsborough p401

O'CONNOR – Francis, b 29 Sep 1861 nc/o Elliot Johnson & Johanna O'Connor bp 9 Oct 1861 spr Mary O'Connor [*ed. note: last name is listed both as either Johnson or O'Connor in record*] p262

O'CONNOR – Franklin St. Mary Louisa O'Connor, b *ndg* 1854 "an orphan" lc/o Laurence O'Connor & Mary Louisa Jones bp 23 May 1866 spr Susan McGarry p384

O'CONNOR – George Henry, b 23 Sep 1869 lc/o John O'Connor & Rosanna Coulter bp 6 Mar 1870 spr Elizabeth Coulter "I supplied the ceremonies" "This child had been privately baptized by Rev. Matthew O'Keefe at Norfolk, Va." H. B. Coskery, priest p495

O'CONNOR – Harriet, 17 May 1857 lc/o Edward O'Connor & Ann Connor bp 31 May 1857 spr Terence Murray & Mary Reilly p122

O'CONNOR – James, b 22 Apr 1858 lc/o James O'Connor & Mary Plunkett bp 2 May 1858 spr John King & Catherine Ferguson p155

O'CONNOR – John, b 16 Aug 1859 lc/o Edward O'Connor & Ann O'Connor bp 18 Aug 1859 spr Margaret Dormity p198

O'CONNOR – Joseph Aloysius, b 10 May 1857 lc/o Matthew O'Connor & Maria Barrett bp 24 May 1857 spr Luke Barry & Mary Victory p121

O'CONNOR – Laura, "aged 9 years" bp 8 Dec 1866 spr Alice Goldsborough "baptized conditionally" Jas. Gibbons, priest p401

O'CONNOR – Margaret Kelena O'Connor, b 6 Jun 1859 lc/o Timothy O'Connor & Amanda, "born Moon" bp 16 Dec 1859 p208

O'CONNOR – Margaret, b 26 Aug 1854 lc/o John O'Connor & Margaret McDonald bp 19 Nov 1854 spr Cath. Burris p29

O'CONNOR – Mary Ann, b 14 Oct 1865 lc/o James O'Connor & Mary Plunkett bp 22 Oct 1865 spr Philip Callahan & Ann Omeara p368

O'CONNOR – Mary Elizabeth, b 27 Aug 1854 lc/o John O'Connor & Charlotte Carlton bp 2 Sep 1854 spr Mary Clementine Ahmer, "proxy for Mary Hester" p22

O'CONNOR – Mary Ellen, b 28 Nov 1859 lc/o John O'Connor & Mary Murray bp 24 Jan 1860 spr Charles O'Connor & Brid. Murray p212

O'CONNOR – Michael, b 16 Jan 1857 lc/o John O'Connor & Murray ______ bp 3 May 1857 spr George O'Connor & Bridget O'Connor p119

O'CONNOR – Rosanna, b 2 Sep 1855 lc/o Charles O'Connor & Mary McGuire bp 9 Sep 1855 spr James Parsons & Ann Ward 57

O'CONNOR – William, b 7 May 1868 lc/o James O'Connor & Mary Plunkett bp 7 Jun 1868 spr Daniel Ber_____ & Catharine Flynn p444

O'DAIRE – Mary, b 25 Dec 1854 lc/o Samuel O'Daire & Catherine Emelia bp 11 Aug 1856 spr Eugene Sullivan & Mary Ann Sullivan p92

O'DAY – Michael, b 28 Oct 1859 lc/o Edward O'Day & Bridget Coughlan bp 6 Nov 1859 spr Michl. McGovern p204

O'DENCHAL – James Felix, b 10 Jul 1860 lc/o John O'Denchal & Rosalie Bobee bp 12 Jul 1860 spr Matilda W. Cook p226

O'DONNELL – Caroline, b *ndg* lc/o John Edw. O'Donnell & Elenora Adams bp 8 Nov 1857 spr William Butler & Margaret Butler "was baptized by Rev. John S. Foley" Thos. Foley, priest p140

O'DONNELL – John, b 22 May 1868 lc/o Charles Oliver O'Donnell & Helen Carroll bp 1 Jun 1868 spr H. B. Coskery & S. C. Read, "proxy for Dr. Eleseo Costa" & Mary Acola p444

O'DONNELL – John Columbus, b 30 Oct 1858 lc/o Columbus Edward O'Donnell & Mary Caroline Jenkins bp 4 Nov 1858 spr Charles Oliver O'Donnell & Luizina O'Donnell p172

O'DONNELL – Lewis Courtney, b 26 Feb 1860 [*ed note: the birth date is recorded as "26 inst.", but this could not be correct as the baptism was performed on 6 Feb 1860*] lc/o Columbus O'Donnell & Caroline Jenkins bp 6 Feb 1860 spr Sol. & Emily Hillen p214

O'DONNELL – Margaret Elizabeth, b 2 Feb 1862 lc/o James O'Donnell & Margaret E. Thompson bp 1 Apr 1862 spr Mary Mullan p278

O'DONNELL – Mary Acosta, b 8 Aug 1869 lc/o Charles Oliver O'Donnell & Helen Carroll bp 8 Sep 1869 spr Rev. Thomas S. Lee & Mary Lee p482

O'DONNELL – Mary Elenor, b 17 May 1861 lc/o Edward Columbus O'Donnell & Mary Caroline Jenkins bp 25 May 1861 spr Thomas & Cecilia Jenkins p252

O'DONNELL – Michael, b 23 Jun 1866 lc/o Thomas O'Donnell & Margaret Hennessy bp 4 Jul 1866 spr Patrick Connor & Mary Conner p387

O'DONNELL – Sarah, b 15 Oct 1830 lc/o Benjamin Tombs & Elizabeth Fisher bp 13 Sep 1854 spr Euphenia Blenkins "baptized conditionally, Thos. Foley, priest p23

O'DONOVAN – Charles, b 9 Sep 1858 lc/o John H. O'Donovan & Maria Louisa Clagett bp 22 Aug 1859 spr Phebe O'Donovan "I supplied the ceremonies of baptism…and baptized as recorded page 171" Thos. Foley, priest p198

O'DONOVAN – Charles, b 9 Sep 1858 lc/o John Henry O'Donovan & Maria Louisa Clagett bp 16 Oct 1858 "see page 198" [O'Donovan] p171

O'DONOVAN – Elie Claggett, b 10 Oct 1861 lc/o John O'Donovan & Maria Claggett bp 3 Dec 1861 spr Cecilia Barry p268

O'DONOVAN – Francis, b 18 Feb 1868 [sic] [*ed. note: probably should be 1869*] lc/o John O'Donovan & Louise Claggett bp 9 Mar 1869 spr Mary Brady p466

O'DONOVAN – Henrietta Jenkins, b 13 Nov 1865 lc/o Charles O'Donovan & Henrietta Jenkins bp 2 Jul 1866 spr Phebe O'Donovan p387

O'DONOVAN – John Henry, b 23 Oct 1867 lc/o Charles O'Donovan & Henrietta Jenkins bp 22 Jun 1868 spr Phoebe O'Donovan p446

O'DONOVAN – John Henry, b 31 May 1856 lc/o John Henry O'Donovan & Maria Louisa Clagett bp 20 May 1856 spr Charles O'Donovan & Phebe O'Donovan p83

O'DONOVAN – Mary Louisa, b 15 Feb 1864 lc/o John O'Donovan & Louisa Clagett bp 5 May 1864 spr Joseph Berry & Cecilia Berry p332

O'DONOVAN – Robert Lee, b 30 Aug 1866 lc/o John O'Donovan & Louisa Clagett bp 22 Sep 1866 spr Mary Maguire p396

O'FARRELL – Victorine, b 21 Sep 1869 lc/o Charles O'Farrell & Eugenie Devonges bp 18 Oct 1869 spr Alphonse Devonges & Theresa O'Farrell p486

O'KEEFE – Thomas, b 27 Feb 1861 lc/o John O'Keefe & Mary O'Leary bp 6 Oct 1861 spr John O'Leary & Margaret Keeley p262

O'LEARY – Catharine, b 30 Dec 1862 lc/o Arthur O'Leary & Bridget McCullough bp 5 Jan 1863 spr Michael O'Keefe & Anne O'Leary p299

O'LEARY – Johanna, b 13 Feb 1860 lc/o James O'Leary & Catharine McCullough bp 14 Feb 1860 spr John & Johanna McCullough p215

O'NEAL – Ann, b 12 Dec 1862 lc/o William O'Neal & Ann James bp 19 Jan 1862 spr James O'Neal & Mary Kelly p272

O'NEAL – Ann, p 17 Sep 1856 lc/o James O'Neal & Isabel Carr bp 12 Oct 1856 spr John Graham & Ann O'Neal p98

O'NEAL – Anna Virginia, b 16 Mar 1855 lc/o Charles O'Neal & Louisa Cornprobt bp 22 Mar 1855 spr Catherine Cornprobt p40

O'NEAL – Elizabeth, b 22 Dec 1857 lc/o Michael O'Neal & Ellen Burns bp 27 Dec 1857 spr Owen O'Neal & Margaret Burns p145

O'NEAL – Isabella O'Neal, "age about nineteen years" bp 23 Apr 1854 "conditional baptism" H. B. Coskery, priest p10

O'NEAL – James, b 22 Aug 1857 lc/o James O'Neal & Catherine McGurke bp 6 Sep 1857 spr John McNally & Mary Campbell p134

O'NEAL – James, b 22 May 1856 lc/o Michael O'Neal & Ellen Burns bp 25 May 1856 spr Dennis Burns & Margaret O'Neal p83

O'NEAL – John Charles, b 22 Mar 1866 lc/o Michael O'Neal & Cecilia Gilcrist bp 1 Apr 1866 spr Thomas Gilcrist & Catharine Rafferty p380

O'NEAL – John Owen, b 20 Feb 1855 lc/o John Owen O'Neal & Ellen O'Neal bp 11 Mar 1855 spr James Quaid & Margaret O'Neal p39

O'NEAL – Joseph, b 25 Oct 1855 lc/o Daniel O'Neil & Catherine McGuirk bp 28 Oct 1855 spr Peter Canlis & Ann Carney p62

O'NEAL – Joseph, b 31 Jan 1855 lc/o John O'Neal & Bridget Derennis bp 16 Mar 1856 spr Michael Griffin & Brid. McNamara p75

O'NEAL – Julia Lyvia, b 20 Sep 1854 c/o James O'Neal & Mary Ann Wise bp 7 Jan 1855 spr Julia McElroy p33

O'NEAL – Margaret, b 23 Aug 1866 lc/o Wm. O'Neal & Ann James bp 2 Sep 1866 spr Christopher Riley & Mary McCarthy p394

O'NEAL – Mary Ann, b 4 Aug 1861 lc/o Daniel O'Neal & Catharine McGurk bp 11 Aug 1861 spr Mary Velden p258

O'NEAL – Mary, "in her 9th year" lc/o Wm. H. O'Neal & Mary Green bp 29 Nov 1865 spr Columbus G. Shriver p370

O'NEAL – Michael, b 18 Feb 1860 lc/o Michael O'Neal & Ellen Burns bp 26 Feb 1860 spr Michael Gallagher & Julia O'Neal p215

O'NEAL – Patrick, b 20 Jan 1857 lc/o Thomas O'Neal & Margaret O'Neal bp 25 Jan 1857 spr Dennis Daley & Bridget Fenton p108

O'NEAL – Thomas, b 3 Sep 1861 lc/o Michael O'Neal & Ellen Burns bp 15 Sep 1861 spr John Farrell & Bessie O'Neal p260

O'NEAL – William, b 19 Nov 1864 lc/o William O'Neal & Anna Jane bp 20 Nov 1864 spr Patrick McHanna & Catharine Defley p345

O'NEIL – Francis Joseph, b 22 Apr 1856 lc/o Charles O'Neil & Rose McCann bp 27 Apr 1856 spr James Lang & Mary Mathers p81

O'NEIL – Mary, b 15 Aug 1858 lc/o Charles O'Neil & Rosa McCann bp 21 Aug 1858 spr Patrick Lamb & Mary Hughes p168

O'NEILL – Eliza, b 9 Apr 1863 lc/o William O'Neill & Ann James bp 19 Apr 1863 spr Luke Carney & Alice Morrison p306

O'NEILL – Jane, b 17 Jun 1854 lc/o James O'Neill & Isabelle Carr bp 2 Jul 1854 spr Mary McGee p16

O'NEILL – Joseph Maurice, b 4 Dec 1867 lc/o Michael O'Neal & Cecilia Gilcrist bp 15 Dec 1867 spr Edward Hanaway & Mary Gilcrist p429

O'NEILL – Mary Cecilia, b 13 Jun 1870 lc/o Michael O'Neill & Cecilia Gilcrist bp 23 Jun1870 spr Francis Gildea & Mary J. Gildea p503

O'NEILL – Ralph, b 24 Jan 1859 lc/o Howard D. O'Neill & Alice N. McManus bp 21 Feb 1859 p182

O'ROOK – Catharine, b 5 Mar 1856 lc/o Morid O'Rook & Margaret McTweely bp 23 May 1856 spr Denny McTweely & Ann D. Elany p76

O'ROURK – John Walter, b 29 Nov 1868 lc/o Wm. O'Rourk & Cather [sic] Fletcher bp 6 Dec 1868 spr James O'Rourk & Catharine Roach p459

O'ROURKE – George William, b 21 Nov 1856 lc/o Luke O'Rourke & Mary Wright bp 10 Dec 1856 spr Hannah Maddox p104

O'SHAUGHNESSY – Malachy Martin, b 4 Nov 1862 lc/o Thomas O'Shaughnessy & Mary Holmes bp 9 Nov 1862 spr Patrick Fitzpatrick & Catharine Holmes p293

O'SHEA – Hannah Ann, b 1 Sep 1854 lc/o James O'Shea & Bridget Joyce bp 3 Sep 1854 spr Michael O'Shea & Hester Flannigan p22

O'SHEA – James, p 14 Jul 1856 lc/o James O'Shea & Bridget Joyce bp 20 Jul 1856 spr Ann McLaughlin & Ellen Moore p91

ODENSCHAL – James Sebastian, b 7 Aug 1861 lc/o John Odenschal & Rosalee Bobee bp 31 Aug 1861 spr Sebastian Odenschal & Elizabeth Tackenberg p260

OHLENDORF – Francis Theodore, b 22 Aug _____ lc/o Willliam G. Ohlendorf & Margaret Eschbach bp 28 Aug 1866 spr Margaret Eschbach [*ed. note: year of birth is not written, however, it most likely was 1866*] p393

<u>OLDRICHK</u> – Eliza Ann, b 15 Dec 1853 lc/o Michael <u>Oldrichk</u> & Mary McKelligan bp 20 May 1855 spr Eliza A. Buck p47

ORENDORFF – Marie Louise, b 3 Sep 1869 lc/o John S. M. Orendorff & Maria Forest Bohrer bp 27 Sep 1869 spr Michael J. Brown & Maria Ohrendorff p484

ORENDORFF – Mary Catharine <u>Matthai</u>, b 17 Aug 1870 lc/o John F. M. Ohrendorff & Maria Bohrer bp 25 Aug 1870 spr Mrs. Bohrer p507

ORR – Andrew, b 1 Sep 1870 lc/o David Orr "of Ireland" and Helen Carr "of Ireland" bp 2 Oct 1870 p511

ORR – Ellen, b 15 Oct 1864 lc/o David Orr & Ellen Carr bp 15 Nov 1864 spr Jane Kelly p345

ORR – James Alexander, b 15 Feb 1860 lc/o David Orr & Ellen Carr bp 8 Apr 1860 spr Edw. Martin & Acy Orr p218

ORR – Lucy Ida Jane, b 29 Oct 1860 lc/o Thomas Orr "(deceased)" & Francina Strausbaugh bp16 Jan 1868 spr Florence Strausbaugh & Annie Strausbaugh p432

ORR – Lucy, b 29 Dec 1862 lc/o David Orr & Ellen Carr bp 25 Jan 1863 spr Owen McGowan & Lucy Orr p300

ORR – Mary Louisa, b 14 Sep 1858 lc/o Thomas Orr "(deceased)" & Francina Strausbaugh bp16 Jan 1868 spr Florence Strausbaugh & Annie Strausbaugh p432

ORR – Mary, b 31 May 1858 lc/o David Orr & Ellen Carr bp 18 Jul 1858 spr John Deany & Cath. Finn "I supplied the ceremonies" "this child had previously been baptized by F. S. Coskery, M.D." H. B. Coskery, priest p163

OSBORNE – Elvira Annn Osborne, "aged about 40 yrs" bp 26 Nov 1867 spr Elizabeth A. Jenkins "baptized conditionally" H. B. Coskery, priest p428

OSBORNE – Elvira Osborne, b *ndg* bp 28 Mar 1867 spr Mary McLaughlin p408

OSBORNE – William Osborne, "aged 14 years" lc/o Wm. & Elvira Osborne bp 10 Jan 1868 spr Chas. Renahan & Virginia Osborne p432

OSBORNE – William Osborne, "aged about 50 years" bp 26 Nov 1867 spr Jonathan Mullan "baptized conditionally" H. B. Coskery, priest p428

OULAHAN – Sarah Ellen, b 19 Mar 1864 lc/o John Oulahan & Ann Hylan bp 12 Mar 1864 spr Margaret Sullivan [*ed. note: see also Ullahan*] p328

OULAHAN – Theresa, b 8 Nov 1866 lc/o John Oulahan & Ann Hyland bp 24 Nov 1866 spr Mary Kelly [*ed. note: see also Ullahan*] p399

OULLAHAN – Catharine, b 9 Dec 1861 lc/o John Oullahan & Ann Hyland bp 19 Jan 1862 spr Wm. Hyland & Catharine Rourk [*ed. note: see also Ullahan*] p272

OWENS – Edward William, b 13 Aug 1859 lc/o John Owens & _____ _____, "his wife" bp 14 Aug 1859 spr James <u>Connor</u> & Bridget McDonald p197

OWENS – Harriet, b 20 May 1850 lc/o Helmsley Owens & Harriet Lecourt bp 14 Jun 1858 spr Mary Ann <u>Heines</u> & Jno. McCally p159

OWENS – Mary Ida (c), b 5 Jun 1863 lc/o Richd. Owens & Eliza Cook bp 19 Jul 1863 spr Mary Cook (c) p311

OWENS – Michael, b 22 May 1859 lc/o James Owens & Bridget Melany bp 29 May 1859 spr Patk. Nolan & Ann McLaughlin p191

OWINGS – Louis Richard, b 5 Jan 1861 lc/o Richard Owings & Elizabeth Cook (c) bp 17 Feb 1861 spr John A. Cook & Mary A. Peter p244

OXFORD – Moses, "servant of John E. Toole", b 24 May 1863 lc/o Henry & Fanny Oxford (c) bp 27 Mar 1864 spr Elizabeth A. Harris p329

OXLEY – Sarah Oxley, "age about 58 yrs" bp 27 Apr 1856 spr Mary Burke "conditional baptism" H. B. Coskery, priest p81

PAGE – Natalie Caroline "L. B." b 22 Sep 1863 lc/o Francis M. Page & Marie Victorine Vallette bp 2 Dec 1864 spr Emma Vallette p346

PAGET – William Henry, b 25 Apr 1855 lc/o William A. Paget & Maria T. Curray bp 21 Oct 1855 spr Mary Mackin "I supplied the ceremonies of the baptism of …and baptized in danger death by Rev. A. D. Elder" Thomas Foley, priest p62

PAINI – George Lucian Anthony, b 19 Sep 1860 lc/o Joseph Paini & Frances Daley bp 21 Oct 1860 spr George Webb & Lucie M. Dandelet p233

PAINI – Victorine, b 27 Oct 1856 lc/o Joseph Paini & Frances Daley bp 14 Dec 1856 spr Victorine Guene p104

PALMER – Sarah Mary, "16 years old" lc/o Thomas Palmer & Eliza Sullivan bp 26 Sep 1858 spr Margaret Dillon p169

PARK – John Jennings Park, "aged 26 years" bp 5 May 1860 "baptized conditionally" Thos. Foley, priest p220

PARKER – Ann Elizabeth, "3 years old" lc/o James Parker & Elizabeth Tilghman (c) bp 27 Jul 1857 spr Minty LeCompte p129

PARKER – Charles William Joseph, b 11 May 1859 lc/o Charles Parker & Sarah Kane bp 7 Sep 1859 spr Mary A. McDermott p199

PARKER – Clara Parker, b 10 Oct 1844 lc/o John & Mary Parker bp 11 Nov 1864 spr Mary S. Robey p344

PARKS – Mary Elizabeth, "born about the middle of December 1854" lc/o Nicholas Parks & Elizabeth Brown bp 13 Dec 1854 spr John McNally & Elizabeth LeCount p32

PARKS – Mary Rebecca Parks, "in her …" bp 13 Apr 1855 spr Mary Carter p43

PARSONS – John Hardesty, b 19 Oct 1857 lc/o Joseph Parsons & Priscilla Hardesty bp 3 Jan 1858 spr John Banan & Margaret Parsons p146

PARSONS – Margaret, b 28 Feb 1855 lc/o Joseph Parsons & Priscilla Hardesty bp 13 Apr 1855 spr Mary Ann Gallanay p43

PASSAGNO – James, b 25 Jun 1856 lc/o Francis Passagno & Catherine Berletta bp 28 Jun 1856 spr James Passagno & Teresa Passagno p87

PASSANO – Amelia Alice, "26 years of age" lc/o Joseph & Rosina Passano bp 26 Oct 1860 spr Matilda Lanahan p233

PASSANO – Henrietta Gertrude, "24 years of age" lc/o Joseph & Rosina Passano bp 26 Oct 1860 spr Matilda Lanahan p233

PASSANO – Joseph, b 22 Jan 1860 lc/o G_____ Passano & Catharine Passano bp 25 Jan 1860 spr Lucia Passano & Ant. Passano p213

PASSANO – Joseph Antony, b 23 Sep 1861 c/o James Passano & Catharine Passano, "his lawful wife" bp 27 Sep 1861 spr Joseph Peregino & Rosa Cella p261

PASSANO – Maria Magdelena, b 10 Apr 1860 lc/o Anthony Passano & Theresia Passano spr Giocomo Passano & Maria Magdelena Monteverde "I supplied the ceremonies" "baptized by a mid-wife in presence of her father, who fully testified to it" Frances Patrick, Archb. p218

PATTEN – Joseph Henry, b 17 Apr 1862 lc/o George Patten & Mary Martin bp 6 Jul 1862 spr Helen Gallagher p285

PATTEN – Mary Barbara, b 10 May 1864 lc/o George Patten & Mary Martin bp 17 Jul 1864 spr Margaret Dietrich p336

PATTERSON – Ann, b 13 Aug 1856 lc/o James Patterson & Catherine Dunn bp 13 Oct 1856 spr Susan Wallis p99

PATTERSON – Helen Maria, b 23 Dec 1866 lc/o Martin L. Patterson & Maria Chambers bp 18 Mar 1867 spr Theresa Jenkins p408

PATTERSON – Mary Chambers, b 16 Feb 1869 lc/o Martin L. Patterson & Maria Chambers bp 4 May 1869 spr Mary Chambers p470

PAUL – Agnes Ann Carter, b 10 Apr 1863 lc/o Jennings Park & Agnes Ann Thompson bp 19 Jul 1863 spr E. Sprague & Maria Grahan p311

PAUL – James Wallace, b 1 Feb 1867 lc/o Jennings Paul & Agnes A. Thompson bp 5 Aug 1867 spr Robert & Maria A. Dow p418

PAUL – Lucian Horsby, b 7 Jan 1862 lc/o Jennings Paul & Agnes Thompson bp 9 May 1862 spr Robert McGraham, Maria A. Graham & Terese Van Shalenyck, "proxy" p281

PAUL – Mary Corinne, b 8 Dec 1868 lc/o Jennings Paul & Agnes Thompson bp 10 Feb 1869 spr James L. Barroh & Maryln Barroh p465

PAUL – Robert Graham, b 10 May 1865 lc/o Jennings Paul & Agnes Thompson bp 26 Jul 1865 spr Victor Sirata & Minnie Sirata p360

PAYNE – Joseph Alfonso, b 23 Jul 1865 lc/o James Payne & Henrietta Hopkins (c) bp 9 Aug 1865 spr Anna Callender p362

PEAKE – Charles Davis Peake, "23 years old today" bp 9 Apr 1866 p381

PEASE – William Lee, b 19 Mar 1869 lc/o Charles Pease & Mary Gardner bp 22 Apr 1867 spr John H. Haupt & Sophy Tingle p411

PEIRCE – Madeleine Peirce, "in the sixteenth year of her age" bp 17 April 1858 spr M. Sheppard p154

PERDUE – Mary Elizabeth, b 30 Nov 1833 lc/o John Perdue & Sarah, "his wife" bp 23 Mar 1855 spr Elizabeth Slade "baptized conditionally" Thos. Foley, priest p40

PERKINS – Eugene Theodore, b 22 Mar 1839 lc/o _____ Perkins & Eliza, "his wife" bp 30 Oct 1860 spr Jonathan Mullan p234

PERKINS – Francis Joseph, b 8 Dec 1855 lc/o John & Cecilia Perkins bp 9 Dec 1855 spr Pat. O'Gorman & Cecilia O'Gorman p67

PERKINS – Lucy Virginia, b 27 Oct 1868 lc/o Eugene Perkins & Elizabeth Wheatley bp 20 Dec 1868 spr Joseph Blackley & Mary Blackley p461

PERKINS – Mary Rosanna, b 4 Aug 1866 lc/o Eugene Perkins & Elizabeth Weakley bp 26 Oct 1866 spr Mary Hughes p398

PERKINS – Thomas Eugene, b 7 Mar 1864 lc/o Eugene Perkins & Elizabeth Wheatley bp 24 Apr 1864 spr Sarah Palmer p331

PERKINS – William Henry, b 11 Aug 1862 lc/o William Henry Perkins & Laura Packon bp 22 Sep 1862 spr Charles Packon & Margaret Murphy p290

PERNELL – John Mellville, b 12 Dec 1856 lc/o William P. Pernell & Mary Louise Lawson bp 15 May 1858 spr Jane Lawson p156

PERRINE – Joseph Edmonson, b 29 Aug 1869 lc/o Richard Perrine & Elizabeth Stans bp 14 Sep 1869 spr Wm. F. Brady & Mary Blundell p483

PETERS – Margaretta (c), b 1 Feb 1853 lc/o John Peters & Margaret Peters (c) bp 19 Jun 1854 spr Eliza Dunn p15

PFISTERER – Ida Louisa, b 5 Oct 1868 lc/o Joseph Pfisterer & Carry Noah bp 26 Nov 1868 spr Cath. Pfisterer p458

PHELPS – Jane Phelps "aged 17 years" bp 8 Feb 1868 p433

PHELPS – Josephine, b *ndg* lc/o Adoran & Emily Phelps bp 7 May 1865 spr Mary Jordan "baptized conditionally" Thos. Foley, priest p356

PICART – Mary Frances Antoinette Du Sablat b 31 Mar 1856 lc/o Francis Anthony Picart & Maria Louisa Du Sablat bp 23 May 1856 spr Maria Antoinette Du Sablat p83

PIET – John, b 14 Mar 1855 lc/o John B. Piet & Mary Floyd bp 26 Mar 1855 spr John & Sarah Piet p40

PIET – Olesin Mary, b 22 Jun 1858 lc/o John B. Piet & Mary Floyd bp 4 Jul 1858 spr Ambrose Emory & Mary I. Emory, "proxy for Olivia Floyd" p162

PINKNEY – Charles Lewis, b 11 May 1861 ic/o Lewis Pinkney & Ann Butler bp 23 Jun 1861 spr Ann Hammond (all c) [*ed. note: last name is listed both as Pinkney or Butler in record*] p254

PINKNEY – Mary Emily, b 4 Aug 1839 lc/o Lieut. Henry Pinkney, U.S.N. & Maria Sperry, "both dead" bp 19 Feb 1859 spr Ann N. Foley p182

PIQUETT – Clara Edith, b 27 Sep 1865 lc/o Daniel Piquett & Mary Ann Christopher bp 28 Nov 1865 spr Mary Helen Dempster p370

PISANI – Elizabeth Jane, b 25 Oct 1865 lc/o Antonio Pisani & Margaret Hanan bp 31 Dec 1865 spr F. Mondinari & Mary Castor p373

PISANI – Peter Julius, b 21 Mar 1864 lc/o Antonio Pisani & Margaret Harman bp 24 Jul 1864 spr Massimo Pasani & Ann Meagher p337

PITTMAN – George Stewart Brown, b 11 Oct 1857 lc/o Edward Pittman & Alvira Barrett bp 17 Nov 1857 spr Felix Jenkins & Julia Pittman p141

PITTMAN – Mary Harriet, b 2 Apr 1863 lc/o Eduard Pittman & Alvira Barrett bp 27 Apr 1863 spr Julie Pittman p306

PLACIDE – Henry Hart, b 29 Apar 1869 lc/o Paul Placide & Louisa Hartgens bp 25 Apr 1869 spr Christopher & Mary Hartgens p469

PLATER – Johanna Plater (c), "aged about 29 years" bp 29 Sep 1866 spr Ann Green (c) "baptized conditionally" H. B. Coskery, priest p397

PLATER – John Thomas, b 16 Aug 1867 lc/o John Plater & Joanna Johnson bp 30 Aug 1867 spr Cath. Grooms (all c) p420

PLATER – William Martin, b 29 Jun 1869 lc/o John Plater & Frances Johnson (c) bp 8 Jul 1869 spr Anne Bowling p476

PLOWMAN – Harriet Ann, "aged 23 years" lc/o Edward & Eliza Plowman bp 10 Nov 1862 "baptized conditionally" Thos. Foley, priest p294

PLUNKETT – Joseph Higgins, b 15 Mar 1861 lc/o James Plunkett & Anna Higgins bp 31 Mar 1861 spr Isaac C. & Mary A. Hildreth p247

PLUNKETT – Mary Higgins, b 9 Apr 1863 lc/o James Plunkett & Ann Higgins bp 24 May 1863 spr John Rosenteel & Amande Bishop p307

POLLS – Mary Ellen Polls, "about 17 years old" (c) bp 6 Jun 1855 spr Annette Bartlett "baptized conditionally" Thos. Foley, priest p48

PONTIER – Mary Ann Pontier "(born Chestnut)", "aged 43 years bp 14 Nov 1867 spr Mary Stuart p426

PORTER – Joseph Lernmon, b 6 Jan 1853 nc/o Henry Moore & Mary Porter (c) bp 18 Jun 1854 spr Ann Connolly p14

PORTERS – Ellen, b 21 Feb 1857 lc/o David Porters & Margaret Mooney bp 13 Mar 1857 spr Mary McTague p114

PORTERS – James, b 22 May 1859 lc/o David Porters & Maryann Mooney bp 2 Jun 1859 spr Mary Flanigan p191

PORTERS – Thomas Kennith, b 30 Nov 1860 lc/o David Porters & Margaret Mooney bp 16 Dec 1860 spr Martha Logue p237

POWELL – Catherine, b 28 Sep 1857 lc/o John Powell & Mary Kernan bp13 Oct 1857 spr James L. Kernan & Mary Duane p138

POWELL – Daniel Aloysius, b 21 Jun 1856 lc/o John Powe. & Mary Kernan bp 16 Jul 1856 spr James Kernan & Mary Duane p90

POWELL – George Francis, b 17 May *ndg* [*ed. note: year not written, probably 1869*] lc/o Robert M. Powell & Elizabeth Grace bp 3 Jun 1869 spr The Marquise of San Carlo, Rosa Sciele p473

POWELL – John James, b 17 Nov 1862 lc/o John Powell & Mary Kernan bp 25 Nov 1862 spr Eugene Kernan & Mary J. Lorham p296

POWELL – Mary Anastasia, b 30 Mar 1855 lc/o John Powell & Mary Kernan bp 20 Apr 1855 spr Peter Duane p43

POWER – John Thomas, b 30 Nov 1860 lc/o Michael Power & Ann Stapleton bp 2 Dec 1860 spr Wm. Ryan & Catharine Stapleton p237

POWERS – Joseph, b 19 Mar 1854 lc/o John Powers & Margaret Matthews bp 9 Apr 1854 spr Nicholas Powers & Margaret Powers p10

PRATT – Amelia Pratt (c), "aged 102 years" bp 14 Jan 1856 p70

PRESTON – John Patrick, b 2 Dec 1855 lc/o Timothy Preston & Margaret Harrington bp 13 Dec 1855 spr Pat. Preston & Martha Wilson p68

PRICE – Mary Justine, b 1 Jul 1851 lc/o Alfred Price & Charlotte Pyfer (c) bp 12 Nov 1862 spr Juliana Needs p294

PRICHARD – Mary Elizabeth, b 30 Jun 1855 lc/o William Prichard & Julia Peters bp 30 Jun 1856 spr Ann Hammond p88

PRINCE – Martha Jenkins, b 19 Sep 1862 lc/o William B. Prince & Mary Elizabeth Lee bp 22 Sep 1862 spr H. B. Coskery & Martha Ann Lee p290

PROCTOR – Esther Isabella, b 17 Feb 1857 lc/o Robert Proctor & Oleria Grooms (all c) bp 30 Mar 1857 spr Caroline Bullen p116

PROCTOR – Rosa Elizabeth, b 15 Jul 1855 lc/o Robert Proctor & Olivia Grooms (c) bp 16 Sep 1855 spr Daniel I. Mays & Eliz Grooms p58

PURCELL – Eliza, b 8 Jul 1855 c/o Nicholas Purcell & Catherine Farrell bp 23 Aug 1855 g Ann Purcell p56

PUSEY – Mary J. Corinthia Pusey, "aged 26 years" lc/o John & Mary Pusey bp 14 May 1857 "baptized conditionally" Thos. Foley, priest p412

PUTSCHE – Ann Eliza, b 30 Oct 1863 lc/o Frederick Putsche & Bridget Manning bp 8 Nov 1863 spr Thomas H. Smith & Margaret Manning p319

PUTSCHE – Edward, b 7 Apr 1835 lc/o George Putsche & Catherine Sieberhein bp 28 Dec 1857 spr Thos. Foley p145

PUTSCHE – George Henry, b 9 Oct 1865 lc/o Frederick Putsche & Bridget Manning bp 15 Oct 1865 spr George Henry Rush Williams p367

PUTSCHE – John George, b 9 Aug 1861 lc/o Edward Frederick Putsche & Bridget Manning bp 18 Aug 1861 spr Thomas Walsh & Mary Manning p259

PUTSCHE – Thomas, b 28 Dec 1859 lc/o Edward Frederick Putsche & Bridget Manning bp 8 Jan 1860 spr T. Foley & Annie Manning p210

PYFER – Rachel Elizabeth, b 11 Sep 1840 lc/o William Pyfer & Hannah Pyfer bp 16 Aug 1858 spr C. Mary Hickley p167

QUEEN – Charlotte Ann, b 22 Jan 1858 lc/o Daniel Queen & Charlotte A. Netherburg (c) bp 4 Nov 1858 spr Mary A. Gannon p172

QUIGLEY – Catharine Quigley, "aged 42 years" bp 21 Jun 1868 p446

QUIGLEY – Catherine, b 24 Sep 1854 lc/o Edw. Quigley & Mary Ellen Hayln bp 8 Oct 1854 spr Jno. Dixon & Cath. Doyle p25

QUIGLEY – Edward, b 21 Jul 1858 lc/o Edward Quigley & Mary Ellen Staylor bp 1 Aug 1858 spr John Quigley & Mary A. Quigley p165

QUILLAN – Michael, b 13 Sep 1855 lc/o Thomas Quillan & Rose Commisky bp 16 Sep 1855 spr James Powers & Bridget Smith p58

QUIN – Henrietta Elizabeth, b 22 Dec 1853 lc/o Daniel Quin & Charlotte Ann Leatherberry bp 16 Aug 1855 spr Angela Quin p55

QUINLAN – James, b 19 Jan 1854 lc/o Michael Quinlan & Ellen Daley bp 19 Feb 1854 spr John Custy & Ann Quinlan p5

QUINLAN – Margaret Ann, "about 7 years old" lc/o John & Rebecca Bullen "(married Quinlan)" bp 8 Oct 1858 spr Eleanor Foy "baptized conditionally" Thos. Foley, priest p170

QUINLAN – Mary Belle, b 6 Jul 1860 lc/o Joseph Quinlan & Margaret Bullon bp 15 Aug 1860 spr Thos. Foley & Mary Stuart p228

QUINN – John, b 29 Apr 1866 lc/o William Quinn & Catharine Kane bp 27 May 1866 spr Dennis Gould & Marcella Rehan p385

QUINN – William, b 22 Jun 1864 lc/o William Quinn & Catharine Kane bp 24 Jan 1864 spr Maurice Duggan & Martha Marshall p324

RABILLON – Henry Franklin Lence, b 16 Jul 1857 lc/o Peter Lewis Lence Rabillon & Mary Zoe Caroline LeFort bp 20 Aug 1857 spr Henry Vermot, "French Consul" & Eliza Chatard p131

RACKERMANN – Robert, b 9 Feb 1859 lc/o Joseph Rackermann & Eve Altwine bp 28 Feb 1860 spr Marie Scheib p216

RADIGAN – James, b 6 Apr 1855 lc/o Edward Radigan & Mary Doyle bp 12 Apr 1855 spr David Ward & Margaret Ward p43

RAFFERTY – Anna Maria, b 27 Jun 1856 lc/o John Rafferty & Margaret Barry bp 29 Jun 1856 spr Nichs. Berry & Johanna Rassiter p88

RAFFERTY – Jacob Sebastian, b 12 Mar 1857 lc/o Pat. Rafferty & Mary Dalton bp 22 Mar 1857 spr Sebastian Sullivan & Margaret Ruthbert p115

RAFFERTY – John William, b 26 Jun 1854 lc/o Patrick Rafferty & Mary Dalton bp 7 Jul 1854 spr Bridget Costolay p17

RAGAN – Martin, b 12 Jan 1854 lc/o Martin Ragan & Mary Ragan bp 15 Jan 1854 spr Thos. Quillan & Bridget Ragan p2

RAGAN – Patrick, b 18 Dec 1855 lc/o Martin Ragan & Mary Ragan bp 22 Dec 1855 spr Cath. & Rose Riley p69

RAINEY – Anna, b 17 Oct 1864 lc/o Edward J. Rainey & Mary Helen McDermott bp 6 Nov 1864 spr Geo. N. Haupt & Mary Dunn p344

RAINEY – Henry, b 21 Feb 1861 lc/o Robert Rainey & Margaret Green bp 24 Feb 1861 spr John Rainey & Sarah Racing p244

RAINEY – John, b 23 Nov 1866 lc/o Edward Rainey & Mary Helen McDermott bp 2 Dec 1866 spr Thos. J. Smith & Hannah Johnson p400

RAINEY – Mary Catharine, b 20 May 1859 lc/o Robert Rainey & Margaret Green bp 22 May 1859 spr Lewis O'Neill & Margaret Rainey p190

RAINEY – Mary, b 11 Aug 1869 lc/o Edward Rainey & Mary McDermott bp 29 Aug 1869 spr Francis M. Johnson & Bridget Johnson p481

RANDALL – Mary Stella, b 18 Apr 1857 lc/o John K. Randall & Ruth Harper bp 13 May 1857 spr James Randall & Mary Lucas p120

RANDALL – Mary, b 5 Jun 1855 lc/o George B. Randall & Elizabeth Boyle bp 22 Jun 1855 spr Elizabeth Grace p49

RANDOLPH – Eliza Randolph, "aged 73 years" bp 16 May 1868 spr Mary Greatfield p442

RAPHEL – Stephen Amedee, b 16 Apr 1864 lc/o Stephen Amedee Raphel & Louisa White bp 23 Apr 1864 spr T. Parkin Scott & Juliana Scott p331

RASIN Mary Clare, "two months old" lc/o Alfred Rasin & Mary Hook bp 7 Mar 1867 spr Mary Hook p407

RATTLIATI – Gaspero, b 15 Jul 1860 lc/o Antonio Rattaliati & Celetina Cernio bp 16 Jul 1860 spr Carlo & Teresa Rattaliati p227

RATTY – Christopher, b 14 Feb 1864 lc/o Patrick Ratty & Mary McGee bp 28 Feb 1864 spr Michael Smith & Sarah N. McGee p327

RATTY – Henry, b 16 Oct 1861 lc/o Patrick Ratty & Mary McGee bp 27 Oct 1861 spr John Kelly & Bridget Moran p265

RATTY – Michael James, b 28 Oct 1859 lc/o Patrick Ratty & Mary McGee bp 9 Nov 1859 spr Christopher Ratty & Mary Mactier p204

RATTY – Patrick Henry, b 10 Dec 1865 lc/o Patrick Ratty & Mary McGee bp 24 Dec 1865 spr Michael Murphy & Catharine McGee p372

RATTY – William, b 21 Dec 1868 lc/o Patrick Ratty & Mary McGee bp 10 Jan 1869 spr John Reilly & Tilly O'Keeffe p463

RAWLEY – Sarah Sylvania, b 30 Oct 1867 lc/o Saml. Rawley & Clara Booth bp 14 Oct 1868 spr Sarah Booth p455

RAWLINGS – Adeline Elizabeth, b 11 Oct 1847 lc/o George A. Rawlings & _____ J. Woodcock bp 30 Aug 1865 "baptized conditionally" Thos. Foley, priest p363

RAWLINGS – Amelia Rebecca, b 16 Nov 1848 lc/o George & Elmira Rawlings bp 20 May 1866 spr Sallie Tenine p384

RAY – Hugh, b 5 Jul 1864 lc/o John Ray & Bridget McLaughlin bp 7 Aug 1864 spr Francis McLaughlin & Jane Gallagher p338

READ – Florence Mary, b 10 Apr 1863 lc/o Wm. Geo. Read & Elizabeth A. Howard "(born Waters)" bp 19 Mar 1863 spr Charles Carroll & Mary Rebecca Howard p307

REARDON – Catharine, b 8 Jan 1863 lc/o Philip Reardon & Mary Reardon bp 18 Jan 1863 spr Timothy Harngan & Catharine Costello p300

REARDON – Dennis, b 19 Jan 1868 lc/o Daniel Reardon & Catharine Costello bp 26 Jan 1868 spr Cornelius & Ellen Reardon p433

REARDON – Honora, b 10 Jun 1866 lc/o Philip Reardon & Mary Reardon bp 24 Jun 1866 spr Maurice Dean & Margaret Reardon p386

REDMOND – Mary, b *ndg* Sep 1867 lc/o Henry Redmond & Eliz. Holly (c) bp 29 May 1868 spr Jane Blackstone (c) p443

REED – Emma Estelle, b 9 Jan 1870 c/o Sarah Reed bp 17 Feb 1870 spr Minan Millen p494

REESE – Thomas Hilton Orville, b 14 May 1869 l/co Henry O. Reese & Emma Watkins bp 26 May 1869 spr Dr. Ferdinand Chatard, Sr. & Mary Watkins p472

REILLY – Bridget, b 1 May 1869 lc/o John Reilly & Ann Shaughnessy bp 23 May 1869 spr Martin Connor & Winifred Manning p472

REILLY – Charles Henry, b 17 Oct 1860 c/o Charles Reilly & Wilhemina J. Leyburn bp 27 May 1862 spr Mary Reilly p282

REILLY – Charles, b 16 Jan 1856 lc/o John Reilly & Hannah Morris bp 27 Jan 1856 spr Philip Johnson & Susan McDenis p70

REILLY – Cornelius Antony, b 8 Sep 1863 lc/o Thomas Reilly & Catharine Conlan bp 13 Sep 1863 spr Samuel Baker & Mary Conlan p315

REILLY – Edwin, b 24 Sep 1869 lc/o Patrick Reilly & Margaret Bradley bp 30 Sep 1869 "baptized privately" Thos. Foley, priest p484

REILLY – Frances, b 12 Feb 1856 lc/o Peter Reilly & Bridget Fitzpatrick bp 28 Mar 1856 spr Ann Maddin p77

REILLY – George Laurence, b 9 Jul 1868 lc/o Patrick Reilly & Sarah McDonald bp 25 Jul 1868 spr John Reilly & Mina Reilly p449

REILLY – Henry Myers, b 5 Oct 1865 lc/o John Reilly & Mary Hack bp 29 Jul 1866 spr Eliza Comp_____ p390

REILLY – James Foley, b 3 Aug _____ lc/o Patrick Reilly & Elizabeth McDonald bp 19 Aug 1866 spr Edward Reilly & Mary Rial [*ed. note: year of birth is not written, however, it most likely was 1866*] p393

REILLY – John Foley, b 29 Sep 1861 lc/o Patrick Reilly & Margaret Bradley bp 20 Oct 1861 spr James Reilly & Annie McWilliams p264

REILLY – Joseph William, b 21 Mar 1856 lc/o James Reilly & Mary McDonald by 13 Apr 56 spr Patrick Reilly & Rose McDonald p79

REILLY – Mary Ellen, b 10 Feb 1863 lc/o Charles Reilly & Wilhemina T. Leyburn bp 22 Feb 1863 spr John Reilly & Mary Moore p302

REILLY – Mary Ellen, b 17 Jul 1857 lc/o John Reilly & Ann Morice bp 26 Jul 1857 spr Bernard Donahue & Eliza McDevill p128

REILLY – Wilhemina Theresa Reilly "(born Leyburn)", b 5 Aug 1844 lc/o William & Mary Leyburn bp 20 May 1862 spr Mary Reilly "baptized conditionally" Thos. Foley, priest p281

REILLY – William Joseph, b 3 Nov 1870 c/o Patrick Reilly "of Baltimore" & Sarah McDonald "of the same place" bp 15 Nov 1870 spr Joseph Reilly & Catharine Reilly p514

REINWICK – Mary Alice, b 8 Feb 1855 ic/o John Reinwick & Mary B___ridge bp 29 Jun 1855 spr Mary Je____ "I supplied the ceremonies" Jno. McNally, priest p50

RENEHAN – John Foley, b *ndg* 1863 lc/o William Renehan & Augusta Benzinger bp 13 Oct 1863 spr Mathias Benzinger & Elizabeth Benzinger p317

RENEHAN – Josephine Cecilia, b 31 May 1868 lc/o William Renehan & Margaret August Benzinger bp 8 Jun 1868 spr Mathias J. Benzinger & Cath. C. Benzinger p444

RENEHAN – Mary Aloysius, b 3 Dec 1865 lc/o Willian Renehan & Margaret Augusta Benzinger bp 8 Dec 1865 spr Aloysius L. Grey & Mary Benzinger p371

RENNAR – William John, b 26 Oct 1864 lc/o Francis Rennar & Maria Gosnell bp 16 Dec 1864 spr Elizabeth Rennar p347

RENNER – George Washington, b 12 Sep 1860 lc/o Francis Renner & Maria Gosnell bp 17 Oct 1860 spr Elizabeth Renner p233

RENNER – Lemuel Francis, b 11 Feb 1859 lc/o Francis Renner & Maria Gosling bp 4 Mar 1859 spr Elizabeth Renner p183

RENNER – Thomas, b 11 Sep 1862 lc/o Francis Renner & Maria Gosnell bp 13 Nov 1862 spr Ann Hammond p294

RENNICK – Edward, b 7 Jun 1857 lc/o Francis Rennick & Maria Gosnell bp 13 Jul 1857 spr Elizabeth Rennick p127

RENWICK – John Alonzo, b 11 Aug 1861 lc/o John Adam Renwick & Mary Jane Bottomer bp 14 Aug 1862 spr Helen Berger p287

RENWICK – Mary Isabell, b *ndg* 1859 lc/o John A. Rennick & Mary I. Bottomer bp 13 Aug 1862 spr Matilda Sanders p287

RETALIATA – Maria Louisa, b 22 Jan 1860 lc/o John Baptist Retaliata & Teresa Retaliata bp 22 Jan 1860 spr John Baptist & Maria Louisa Retaliata p212

REVERE – Col. Joseph Revere, USA, "age about 48 years" bp 19 Oct 1862 "baptized conditionally" H. B. Coskery, priest p292

REY – Francis Henry, b 11 Oct 1854 lc/o Francis Rey & Mary Ann Elder bp 5 Jul 1855 spr Catherine Elder p51

REY – John Joseph, b 26 Jul 1856 lc/o James Rey & Charlotte Tuff bp 24 Aug 1856 spr Christopher Gibbon & Bridget Hughes p93

REYNOLDS – Ann, b 30 Oct 1861 lc/o William Reynolds & Alice McCann bp 30 Oct 1861 spr Ann Cosgore p265

REYNOLDS – Catharine, b 6 Jul _____ lc/o John Reynolds & Catharine Campbell bp 22 Jul 1866 spr Jon Gaitly & Rose Gaitly [*ed. note: year of birth is not written, however, it most likely was 1866*] p389

REYNOLDS – Eliza Augusta, b 29 Jan 1855 lc/o Valentine deWitt C. Reynolds & _____ Aiken bp 6 Mar 1855 spr Mary Ann Kennedy p39

REYNOLDS – Elizabeth, b 5 Nov 1868 lc/o John N. Reynolds & Catharine Campbell bp 25 Nov 1868 spr Bernice Campbell & Annie Carter p458

REYNOLDS – Ida Virginia, b 1 Apr 1868 lc/o Howard Reynolds & Bridget Smith bp 10 May 1868 spr Lizzy McGilly p441

REYNOLDS – Robert Aiken, b 20 Aug 1857 lc/o V. Clinton Reynolds & Rebecca Aitkin bp 17 Sept 1857 spr Ellen Matthews p135

RIAL – Jane Rial "(born McMahon)", "aged 26 years" bp 30 Apr 1858 spr Jane _____ p154

RIAL – Julia Elizabeth, b 28 Dec 1853 lc/o James Rial & Mary Corbill bp 12 Feb 1854 spr Francis Fiddon & Ann Rial p5

RIAL – Thomas Foley, b 6 Mar 1855 lc/o James Rial & Mary Corbitt bp 18 Mar 1855 spr Patrick Rial & Margaret Henderson p40

RICE – James Jefferson Beauregard bp 16 Mar 1862 lc/o Stephen Rice & Margaret Freeze bp 29 Mar 1862 spr Mary J. Loughran p277

RICE – Margaret Ann, b 26 Jun 1867 lc/o Robert Rice & Catharine Clancy bp 7 Jul 1867 spr Peter Kelly & Mary Toomay p417

RICE – Mary Catharine, b "about" 19 Dec. 1864 lc/o Robert Rice & Catharine Clancy bp 8 Jan 1865 spr Wm. Butler & Kate Norton p348

RICE – Mary Catharine, b 13 Mar 1868 lc/o Peter Rice & Mary Friese bp 31 Mar 1868 spr Michl. Friese & Rosa Ray p438

RICHARDS – Margaret Richards "(alias Hunter)", "aged 23" "born 11 April 1835" bp 14 Jan 1858 "Validly baptized by infusion by a Presbyterian minister as her father attests." "…I gave her conditional baptism on Jan 20." Francis Patrick, Archb. p146

RICHARDSON – Joseph, b 17 Sep 1853 lc/o William Richardson & Isabel Knight bp 17 Jul 1857 spr Elizabeth Knight p127

RICHARDSON – Mary Elizabeth, b 29 Jun 1859 lc/o William H. Richardson & Isabella Knight bp 11 Jul 1859 spr Elizabeth Knight p195

RICHARDSON – William (c), b 21 Jan 1870 c/o Richard Richardson & Anne O'Donnell bp 22 Feb 1870 spr Annie Mary Freshline p494

RICHARDSON (or SMITH) – George Henry, b 10 Feb 1861 nc/o Henry Smith & Nannie Richardson (both c) bp 6 Jan 1864 spr Mary Matthews (c) "baptized conditionally" H. B. Coskery, priest p323

RICHFIELD – Joseph Octavus, b 11 Apr 1855 lc/o Octavus Richfield & Mary <u>Mucky</u> bp 18 May 1855 spr Mary <u>Mucky</u> p46

RICHFIELD – Mary Ann Theresa (c), b 7 Nov 1863 lc/o Richard Richfield & Mary Moquette bp 11 Nov 1863 spr Mary Moquette [*ed. note: same name recorded for mother & sponsor*] p320

RICHMOND – Ferdnanda Agnes, b 11 Apr 1855 lc/o Ferdinand Richmond & Mary Agnes Richmond bp 15 Aug 1855 spr Sarah Richmond p55

RICHTER – Charles Richter, b 11 Nov 1851 bp 22 Mar 1870 spr Mrs. Coakley "baptized conditionally" John Dougherty, priest p498

RICKETTS – Virginia Ricketts, "aged about 18 years" bp 24 Oct 1859 spr Mary Tubman "baptized conditionally" Thos. Foley, priest p202

RIDGAWAY – Mary Elizabeth, "aged 18 years" lc/o James A. & Elizabeth A. Ridgaway "of Talbot County" p366

RIDGLEY – Lewis Augustus, b *ndg* Apr 1868 lc/o Neil Ridgley & Delia Magnose_____ (all c) bp 4 Jul 1869 spr Wm. Willyams p475

RIDGLEY – Sarah Zelia, b *ndg* Apr 1868 lc/o Neil Ridgley & Delia Magnose_____ (all c) bp 4 Jul 1869 spr Wm. Willyams p475

RIDGLEY – Victor, b 10 Feb 1869 lc/o Augustus Ridgley & Sara Belt bp 10 Apr 1869 [*ed. note: this record was inserted between baptism records dated 6 May and 14 May respectively*] spr Teresa Thomas (all c) "baptized privately" H. B. Coskery, priest p471

RIGGINS – Mary Louisa, b 6 Nov 1855 lc/o Francis Riggins & Elizabeth While bp 23 Dec 1855 spr Ignatius Watts & Eliza Small (all c) p69

RIGGS – Mary Ellen, b 5 Jul 1865 lc/o John Riggs & Ellen Clark bp 24 Jul 1865 spr Maggie Rourke p360

RILEY – Ann, b 6 Sep 1856 lc/o James Riley & Mary Herron bp 14 Sep 1856 spr Jno. C. Coskery & Mary Riley p95

RILEY – Charles Thomas, b 25 Feb 1855 lc/o Daniel Riley & Elizabeth Nugent bp 9 Apr 1855 spr Frederick Nugent & Mary Nugent p42

RILEY – Edward, b 13 Dec 1868 lc/o Edward & Margaret Riley bp 27 Dec 1868 spr Patk. & Margaret Riley p461

RILEY – Elizabeth Bridget, b 16 Jan 1857 lc/o Patk. Riley & Mary Quinn bp 25 Jan 1857 spr Patk. Henry & Ann Quinn p108

RILEY – Ellen Jane, b 14 Feb lc/o Peter Riley & Bridget Fitzpatrick bp 15 Mar 1854 spr Hugh Fitzpatrick & Mary Smith p7

RILEY – John Ambrose, b 14 Sep *ndg* [*ed. note: most likely 1870*] lc/o Carl Riley "of County Armagh, Ireland" & Nina Leyburn "of Ireland" bp 2 Oct 1870 p511

RILEY – John, b 15 Mar 1860 lc/o James Riley & Catharine Griffin bp 18 Mar 1860 spr Maurice Riley & Mary Riley p217

RILEY – Mary, b 4 Jan 1869 lc/o John Riley & Elizabeth Nolan bp 24 Jan 1869 spr Bernard Gardiner & Kate Riley p464

RILEY – Thomas, b 21 Oct 1867 lc/o John Riley & Anoia Schackensie bp 27 Oct 1867 spr Patk. Renderfast & Julia Ryan p425

RILOR – William George, b 7 Aug 1857 lc/o William Rilor & Elizabeth Turner bp 30 Aug 1857 spr Mary Ann Collier p132

RINGGOLD – John Perigrin, b 24 Nov 1868 lc/o William Ringgold & Fanny Smith bp 13 Feb 1869 spr Louisa Ringgold p465

RINGGOLD – Mary Louisa, b 6 Jan 1869 lc/o Charles Fredk. Ringgold & Sarah Virginia Wiles bp 11 Feb 1869 spr Mary Roberts p465

RINN – Isabel, b 4 Sep 1870 lc/o John S. Rinn & Sarah Burns bp 18 Sep 1870 spr James Keenan & Mrs. Mary Keenan p509

RIORDAN – Edward, b 19 Jul 1866 lc/o Daniel Riordan & Cath. Costello bp 22 Jul 1866 spr Wm. Curtin & Mary Riordan p389

RIORDAN – Mary Ellen, b 17 Jan 1865 lc/o Danl. Riordan & Catharine Costello bp 22 Jan 1865 spr Thos. & Mary Costello p349

RITAGLIATI – John Baptist, b 17 Apr 1860 c/o Joseph Ritagliati & Cathraine Gar_____, "his wife" bp 18 Apr 1860 spr Andrew Ritagliati & Catharine Ritagliati p219

RITUE – Amelia, b 7 May 1855 lc/o Wm. Ritue & Elizabeth Turner bp 11 Nov 1855 spr Ellen Broderick p65

RIVERS – William Charles, b 7 Dec 1859 lc/o Jonathan Rivers & Bridget Hopkins bp 19 Jan 1860 spr Mary A. Hopkins p211

ROACH – Ann, b 20 Aug 1863 lc/o Michael Roach & Emily Irvin bp 23 Sep 1863 spr H. B. Coskery & Mary Cormell p315

ROACH – John Henry, b 12 Jan 1860 lc/o Michael Roach & Emily Irvin bp 16 Jan 1860 spr Wm. Roach & Elizabeth Fortune p211

ROACH – Mary, b 6 Nov 1861 lc/o Michael Roach & Emily Irvin bp 10 Nov 1861 spr Edward McAdams & Adele Dubernard p266

ROACH – Mary Bridget, b 11 Nov 1856 lc/o James Roach & Mary Ann Brady bp 23 Nov 1856 spr Michael Roach & Bridget Roach p102

ROACH – Richard Beauregard, b 15 Sep 1867 lc/o P. J. Road & Hettie G. Jones bp 18 Sep 1867 spr Gen. G. T. Beauregard & Mary A. Roach p421

ROBB – Mary Ann, b 29 May 1862 lc/o Duncan Robb & Margaret Smith bp 23 Jul 1862 spr Bridget Melaney p286

ROBERSON – James, b 27 May 1859 lc/o Rezin Roberson & Louisa Shea bp 30 May 1859 spr Bridget Mitchell p191

ROBERTS – Charles Francis, b 23 Nov 1868 lc/o Augustus Roberts & Elizabeth Brooks bp 16 Apr 1869 spr Susan Roberts "I supplied the ceremonies" Thos. Foley, priest p468

ROBERTS – Charles Francis, b 23 Nov *ndg* [*ed. note: probably 1868*] lc/o Daniel Augustine Roberts & Susan Elizabeth Brooks (c) bp 14 Dec 1868 spr Susan Roberts p460

ROBERTS – George (c), "four months old" lc/o William Roberts &______ ____ bp 7 Jul 1857 spr Teresa Mahony (c) p126

<u>ROBERTS</u> – Mary Louisa Walker <u>Roberts</u>, "aged 34 years bp 25 Jul 1869 spr Mrs. Middleton p477

ROBERTS – Rachel Ann, b 2 Jan 1862 lc/o Augustus Roberts & Elizabeth Brookes (c) bp 2 Mar 1862 spr Elizabeth Colbert p277

ROBERTS – Theresa Mary Virginia, b *ndg* 1848 lc/o Charles Roberts & Virginia Lusby bp 22 May 1855 spr Louisa Lusby p47

ROBINE – Margaret Jane, b 17 Feb 1854 lc/o Timothy Robine & Mary Burke bp 26 Feb 1854 spr James Conaughton & Margaret Kinne p6

ROBINSON – Eliza, b 12 May 1840 lc/o William Robinson & Mary "his wife" bp 6 Feb 1854 p4

ROBINSON – Henry Owen, b 30 Jun 1869 lc/o Wm. J. Robinson & Mary Hanley bp 28 Jul 1869 spr Ellen Hanley p478

ROBINSON – James, b 11 Dec 1953 lc/o William Robinson & Mary, "his wife" bp 6 Feb 1854 "baptized conditionally" H. B. Coskery, priest p4

ROBINSON – Mary Ann Robinson, b *ndg* 1814 "in England" bp 26 Jun 1859 p193

ROBINSON – Mary Elizabeth Robinson, "about 16 years old" bp 9 Jun 1860 spr Jane Duffy p224

ROBINSON – Sylvester, b 3 Jun 1856 c/o Henrietta Robinson (c) bp 30 Jun 1856 spr Mary C. Robinson p88

ROCK – Mary Rebecca, b 24 May 1854 lc/o Patk. Rock & Ann Tye bp 28 May 1854 spr Jno. & Ellen Tye p13

ROGERS – Alice, b 13 Feb 1868 lc/o Patrick Rogers & Margaret Sharkey bp 21 Feb 1868 spr Mary Cleary & Catharine Poe p434

ROGERS – John, b 10 Sep 1863 lc/o Patrick Rogers & Margaret Sharkey bp 3 Oct 1863 spr Cath. Gibbon p316

ROGERS – Mary, b 13 Feb 1868 lc/o Patrick Rogers & Margaret Sharkey bp 21 Feb 1868 spr Mary Cleary & Catharine Poe p434

ROONEY – Charles Edgar Rooney, b 25 Jan 1866 lc/o _____ Rooney & _____ _____ bp 2 Feb 1866 spr J. McBride & Mary Trainor p375

ROONEY – Ellen, b 6 Feb 1856 lc/o Thomas Rooney & Ellen Martin bp 17 Feb 1856 spr Patrick Mullan & Annie McPhilip p72

ROONEY – John Thomas, b 21 Mar 1859 lc/o James Rooney & Ann O'Brien bp 10 Apr 1859 spr James McCourt & Bridget McCourt p186

ROONEY – John William, b 28 Nov 1859 lc/o Thomas Rooney & Ellen Martin bp 13 Dec 1859 spr John Mannion & Ann Cassidy p207

ROONEY – Margaret Ann, b 15 Jul 1862 lc/o Thomas Rooney & Ellen Martin bp 12 Aug 1862 spr Ellen Jenkins p287

ROOT – Helen Isadore, b 20 Apr 1863 lc/o Henry R. Root & Elizabeth B. Slater bp 12 May 1863 spr George & Emma Slater p307

ROOT – Henry Slater, b 21 Feb 1860 lc/o Henry Root & Betty Slater bp 12 Apr 1860 spr Geo. Slater & Wm. Geo. Slater p219

ROOT – Joseph Banks, b 19 Dec *1866* [lc/o Henry R. Root & Elizabeth V. Slater bp 31 Dec *1866* [*ed. note: obviously there was a recording error in the year of birth and baptism as the previous and subsequent register entries are Jan & Feb 1866*] "I supplied the ceremonies" "this child had been baptized by a competent lay" H. B. Coskery, priest p375

ROOT – Mary Lota, b 30 Dec 1861 lc/o Henry Root & Betty Slater bp 2 Jan 1862 spr Mary Ann Greenwell "baptized privately (ceremonies supplied June 27, 1862)" H. B. Coskery, priest p271

ROSE – Anne, "aged about 65 years" bp 5 Jul 1867 p416

ROSE – Catherine, b 2 Nov 1853 lc/o William Rose & Elizabeth McCrodan bp 8 May 1854 spr Catherine McCrodan p12

ROSE – Henry Johnson, b 30 Jan 1832 lc/o George Rose & Eliza Brines bp 1 Dec 1856 spr Matt Shannon p103

ROSE – Mary Catharine, b 28 Nov 1864 lc/o Anthony Rose & Catharine Tiernan bp 20 Feb 1865 spr Josephine Farrell p351

ROSS – Letitia, "2 months old" lc/o Thomas Ross & Sarah Pinkney (c) bp 16 Sep 1868 spr Harriet Johnson p453

ROSSITER – Lewis Henry, b 7 Jul 1857 lc/o John Rossiter & Mary Courtney bp 7 Sep 1857 spr Margaret Beltz "privately baptized, being dangerously ill" H. B. Coskery, priest p134

ROTE – Elizabeth Knipe, b 3 May 1870 lc/o John Rote & Rosalie Knipe bp 16 Jun 1870 spr Charles Aloysius Dennigan & Eliabeth Knipe p503

ROTE – John S. Rote, "aged 27 years" bp 20 Jun 1869 p475

ROUGH – Mary, b Jan 1857 "day not known by parents" lc/o Frederich Rough & Isabella Shealla bp 11 May 1857 spr Mary Shealla p120

ROUSE – Ann Maria, b 21 Aug 1865 lc/o Henry H. Rouse & Joanna Dahoney bp 29 Dec 1865 spr Mary Dahoney p372

ROUSE – Joseph Rouse, "7 days old" c/o Elmira Redding bp 2 Nov 1866 "baptized privately" Thos. Foley, priest p398

ROUSSELOT – Francis Thompson, b 12 Apr 1856 lc/o Charles A. Rousselot & Bridget Longhan bp 15 Jun 1856 spr Michael J. Grady & Fredericka Rousselot p85

ROVAN – Richard James, b 8 Jul 1856 lc/o Timothy Rovan & Margaret Burch bp 16 Jul 1856 spr Patrick Gallarin & Margaret McLanan p90

ROWE – Francis Stewart, b 18 Feb 1869 lc/o Harry Hoffman Rowe & Johanna Doheny bp 6 Sep 1869 spr Francis Patk. Luppin & Kate McTeeney p482

RUCKEL – Ann Rebecca, b 9 Mar 1855 lc/o George Ruckel & Ann Hollins bp 26 Mar 1855 spr Michael Kagan p40

RUCKLE – Margaret Ellen, b 29 Oct 1858 lc/o George Ruckle & Ann Hollin bp 7 Nov 1858 spr Denis O'Brien & Ellen Welsh p173

RUCKLE – Mary Elizabeth, b 7 Nov 1855 lc/o George Ruckle & Ann Hollin bp 22 Feb 1857 spr Eliza C_____ p112

RUCKLES – George, b 12 Oct 1832 bp 26 Feb 1854 spr James Allen p6

RUFF – Clara, b 7 Mar 1854 lc/o Frederick Ruff & Isabell Sheeler bp 22 May 1854 spr May Sheeler p13

RUSSELL – Anna, b 22 Dec 1869 lc/o David C. Russell & Anna Boland bp 16 May 1870 spr Mary Boland p501

RUSSELL – Mary Ann, b 20 Dec 1857 lc/o Andrew Russell & Margaret Brady bp 10 Jan 1858 spr Thos. Cooney & Alice McEver p146

RUSSELL – Thomas Russell, "aged 40 years" bp 15 Oct 1862 "baptized conditionally" Thos. Foley, priest p291

RUTLEDGE – Joseph, b 19 Mar 1860 lc/o John Rutledge & Kate McCaffey bp 3 Jun 1860 spr Mary Martin p223

RUTLEDGE – Thomas John, b 3 Aug 1870 lc/o Charles William Rutledge & Jane Poole bp 12 Sep 1870 spr Martha Dorsey p508

RUTTER – Mary Julia Rutter, "aged 23" bp 8 Feb 1857 spr John McWalls "baptized conditionally" Jno. McNally, priest p110

RYAN – Anastasia, b 30 Apr 1854 lc/o Thomas Ryan & Anastasia Butler bp 15 May 1854 spr Maurice Henrilam & Ann Keswick p12

RYAN – John Francis, b 5 Aug 1870 lc/o James Ryan & Mary Sweeney bp 4 Sep 1870 spr Michl. Quinn & Maggie Sweeney p508

RYAN – John Henry Augustus, b 5 Mar 1864 lc/o Wm. Ryan & Bridget Cannon bp 3 Apr 1864 spr Wm. Cannon & Anne Burrick p330

RYAN – Joseph, b 19 Oct 1855 lc/o James Ryan & Mary Kennidy bp 28 Oct 1855 spr Pat Ryan & Maria Bonlice p62

RYAN – Margaret, b 21 Aug 1862 lc/o James Ryan & Mary Ann Carroll bp 31 Aug 1862 spr Philip Quirk & Catharine Ryan p288

RYAN – Mary, b 26 Feb 1857 lc/o Edward Ryan & Bettie Whelan bp 8 Mar 1857 spr Michael Whelan & Catherine Ryan p114

RYAN – Mary, b 1 Mar 1858 lc/o James Ryan & Mary Carroll bp 7 Mar 1858 spr John Quinn & Ellen Kelly p150

RYAN – Mary Catharine, b 26 Oct 1859 lc/o John Ryan & Catharine Healey bp 30 Oct 1859 spr Michael Riordan & Mary Harnaby p203

RYAN – Patrick Henry, b 21 Nov 1859 lc/o James Ryan & Mary Ann Carroll bp 27 Nov 1859 spr Patk. Connoughty & Mary Leland p206

SALE – Lucy Sale, "aged about 48 years" bp 19 Feb 1866 p376

SALINAS – Carlos, b 28 Feb 1861 lc/o Carlos Hernandez Salinas & Ann Elphin bp 24 Sep 1861 spr Diego Palacios Suarez & Sallie Ross p261

SANDERS – Anna Catharine, b 18 Aug 1870 lc/o Andrew Sanders "of Germany" & Helen Burns "of Ireland" bp 15 Oct 1870 spr Rosanna Sanders p512

SANDERS – Beverly Constantine, b 28 Jul 1854 lc/o Beverly C. Sanders & Elizabeth E. Hillen bp 6 Sep 1854 spr S. Hillen Hunter & Robina Roper p23

SANDERS – Clara Virginia, b 22 May 1864 lc/o William Sanders & Cecilia Coulter bp 30 Jun 1864 spr Sarah Coulter p335

SANDERS – James Arthur, b 1 Feb 1870 lc/o James Sanders & Julia Frederica Hammer bp 20 Mar 1870 spr Nich. Holahan & Eliza Hammer p497

SANDERS – Jeremiah, b 30 Dec 1857 lc/o John Sanders & Bridget Cashmiere bp 3 Jan 1858 spr Veronica Cashmiere & Julia McDonogh p146

SANDERS – John, b 6 Dec 1835 lc/o William & Nancy Sanders (c) bp 23 Sep 1856 spr Mary A. Hams p96

SANDERS – Laura Frances, b 22 Aug 1861 lc/o Alexander Sanders & Ann McLeif bp 16 Sep 1861 spr Margaret Neider p261

SANDERS – Louisa (c), b 8 Jan 1856 lc/o William Andrew Sanders & Sarah Smith bp 25 Apr 1856 spr George Andrew Hall & Mary Ann Pierce p81

SANDERS – Sophia Sanders, "about 10 yrs old" lc/o William Sanders & Ann Mahan (c) bp 19 Oct 1855 spr Susanna Sanders [*ed. note: faint record*] p61

SANDERS – William Horton Richard, b 29 Jan 1860 lc/o Alexander Sanders & Ann McLeif bp 16 Sep 1861 spr Richard Schnapp p261

SANDERS – William Russell, b 20 Aug 1865 lc/o William R. Sanders & Mary Ellen Staylor bp 10 Sep 1865 spr Ella Quigley p364

SANDERS – William Sanders (c), b 28 Mar 1812 bp 1 Sep 1870 "baptized conditionally" John Dougherty, priest p507

SANDERSON – Mary Frances, b 9 Jul 1838 lc/o John Sanderson & Elizabeth Simms bp 9 Jul 1854 spr Rebecca Whelan p17

SANFORD – Mary Grace, b 23 Aug 1863 lc/o Edward Sanford & Elizabeth McGowan bp 14 Oct 1863 spr Ellen Kenney p318

SANTIMYER – Lewis Allen, "aged __ years" [*ed. note: number unclear*] lc/o Louis A. Santimyer & _____, "his wife" bp 18 Jul 1860 p227

SANTUCCI – Angelo Antonio David, b 3 Mar 1861 c/o Isadore Santucci & Angela Teresa Ripetto, "his lawful wife" bp 12 Mar 1861 spr John Andrew Ripetto & Angela Ripetto p246

SANTUCCI – Catarina Giosifina, b 17 Nov 1858 lc/o Isidor Santucci & Teresa Repetto bp 22 Nov 1858 spr Joseph Santucci & Gertrude Repetto p 174

SARGENT – James Carroll, b 4 Aug 1868 lc/o Henry Sargent & Ida Loveday bp 18 Sep 1868 spr Charles & Anne Loveday p453

SATTERFIELD – William Robinson, b 20 Feb 1854 lc/o John Satterfield & Jane McNulty bp 28 Mar 1854 spr Mary Lewis p9

SAUNER – Francis, b 29 Nov 1865 lc/o Wm. Sauner & Jane Buzza bp 17 Dec 1865 spr E. T. Saheey & Martha Burk p371

SAUNER – Wm. Valentine, b 14 Feb 1868 lc/o Wm. F. & Virginia Sauner bp 8 Mar 1868 spr Anna Kline p435

SAURRET – Elie Pierre Gustave, b 20 Jul 1859 lc/o Pierre Saurret & Anna Marie Revert bp 21 Aug 1859 spr Peter Foudriat & Elizabeth Foudriat p198

SAWNER – Ida Elizabeth, b 1 Apr 1864 lc/o William F. Sawner & Jane Jamison "(born Huzza)" bp 17 Apr 1864 spr Alice Bell p331

SAXTON – Mary Jenkins, b 21 May 1869 lc/o Wm. H. Saxton & Mary Armor Jenkins bp 1 Jun 1869 spr George & Lydia Jenkins p473

SAXTON – Mary, b 17 Nov 1854 lc/o Alexander Saxton & Alice Hand bp 29 Nov 1854 spr William Saxton & Ann Hand p30

SCALLAN – Catherine, b 29 Mar 1856 lc/o Andrew Scallan & Ellen Broderick bp 30 Mar 1856 spr Wm. & Cath. Broderick p78

SCANLON – Daniel, b 26 Mar 1855 lc/o Michael Scanlon & Catherine Keogh bp 28 Mar 1855 spr Wm. Kirk & Mary Myles p41

SCANNELL – John, b 2 Oct 1860 lc/o Andrew Scannell & Ellen Broderick bp 7 Oct 1860 spr Michael & Mary Scannell p223

SCARF – George S. Scarf, "age about 40 years" bp 4 May 1855 p46

SCHULTZE – Ann Elizabeth, b 3 Jan 1869 lc/o Frederick W. Schultze & Winifred Halpin bp 22 Jan 1869 spr M. Collins & Sarah Collins p464

SCHULTZE – Mary Florence, b 29 Oct 1867 lc/o Frederick Schultze & Winifred Halpin bp 14 Nov 1867 spr Eliza Halpin & Francis Judge p426

SCOTT – Edward Laurence Carey, b 19 Jan 1855 lc/o Henry C. Scott & Caroline Baird bp 30 Jan 1855 spr William P. Scott & Mary H. Scott p35

SCOTT – Geroge James, b 12 Dec 1867 lc/o Charles Scott & Mary Deal bp 6 Apr 1868 spr _____ W. Rasin & Alice Sweeney p439

SCOTT – Harriet Augusta Scott, "aged about 34 years" bp 20 Apr 1867 spr Sophia C. Read "baptized conditionally" Jas. Gibbons, priest, p410

SCOTT – Henry Chatard, b 5 Oct 1861 lc/o Henry C. Scott & Lassie Baird bp 15 Oct 1861 spr Dr. Ferdinand Chatard & Eliza Chatard p264

SCOTT – Ida Frances, b 31 Dec 1860 lc/o Wilkins Scott & Celestia Welsh (c) bp 8 Apr 1861 spr Elizabeth Colbert p248

SCOTT – John Gordon Scott, "aged about 8 years" lc/o John Scott & Harriet Augusta Cuskie bp 2 Jan 1868 spr Jas. Gibbons "baptized conditionally" Jas. Gibbons, priest p431

SCOTT – John Scott "(of Virginia)", b 22 Apr 1820 bp 4 Apr 1866 spr Chas. Tiernan p380

SCOTT – Julianna Mary, b 7 Oct 1856 lc/o Henry C. Scott & Carrie A. Baird bp 11 Oct 1856 spr John M. Scott & Jul. M. Scott p98

SCOTT – Mary Henrietta, b 24 May 1869 lc/o Channing M. Scott & Mary E. Taylor bp 26 May 1869 spr Joseph Dillon & Jane Taylor "(in proxy)" p473

SCOTT – Nina Massey, b 14 Sep 1869 "(born in Greensborough, E. S. of Maryland)" lc/o John M. Scott & Anne M. Massey bp 13 Oct 1869 spr Judge T. Parkin Scott & Juliana Scott p485

SCOTT – Otho Scott, "aged 68 years" bp 22 Jan 1864 p324

SCOTT – Thomas Parlein, b 22 Aug 1860 lc/o Henry C. Scott & Annie Baird bp 29 Aug 1860 spr T. Parlein Scott & Catherine Jenkins p230

SCOTT – William Henry (c), "3 months old" c/o Thomas Scott & Anna Young bp 25 Feb 1867 spr Maria Bonley p407

SEANALL – Cornelius Andrew, b 13 Aug 1858 lc/o Andrew Seanall & Ellen Broderick bp 15 Aug 1858 spr Thomas Broderick & Mary Marie p167

SEANTELBURG – Charles Edmund, b 26 May 1854 lc/o Charles C. Seantelburg & Ann D. Seantelburg pb 10 Jun 1854 spr Clementina Aldermer p14

SEARFF – Charles Lee, b 4 Mar 1868 lc/o Wm. Searff & Alice Woodward bp 26 Mar 1868 spr Mary Francis Woodward p437

SEEGERMAN – William Henry, b 3 Apr 1869 lc/o William Henry Seegerman & Agnes Divine bp 16 Apr 1869 spr S_____ Nelson p469

SEIM – Mary Estelle Houston, b 5 Aug 1868 lc/o Henry Seim & Annie Wright bp 7 Jun 1869 spr Elenna Foy p474

SEIM – William Frederick, b 1 Nov 1854 lc/o Henry Seim & Mary Jane Smith bp 2 Jul 1869 spr Mrs. Walbach "I supplied the ceremonies of baptism" Thomas S. Lee, priest p475

SEIP – Margaret Amanda, b 21 Mar 1864 lc/o Robert C. Seip & Maggie A. Dermott bp 25 Mar 1864 spr Edmonde C. & Marie C. Lifener "baptized privately" "supplied ceremonies July 3rd" Thos. Foley, priest p329

SELK – Mary Ann, b 12 Nov 1857 lc/o Michael Selk & Mary Farrell bp 15 Nov 1857 spr James & Catherine Duffy p140

SELLENS – Mary Frances, b 21 Nov 1867 lc/o John Sellens & Mary Lewis bp 24 Nov 1867 spr James Garney & Jane Garney p427

SEURRET – Marie Pauline, b 22 Jun 1857 lc/o Gustave Seurret & Annie Sevère bp 7 Aug 1858 spr Marie Brun p166

SEWEL – Elizabeth, b 5 Mar 1861 nc/o James Sewel & Rose Harris bp 29 Apr 1861 spr Ann Phipps [*ed. note: last name is listed both as Sewel or Harris in record*] p250

SEWELL – Charles Lee, b 1 Sep 1859 c/o John M. Sewell & Rosa Carr bp 17 Jan 1860 spr Eliza Phipps p211

SEYERMAN – Bessie, b 11 Mar 1867 lc/o William Seyerman & Alice Devine bp 1 Apr 1867 spr Mary O. Fields p409

SHADE – George, b 23 Jul 1868 lc/o John Shade & Susan Weeks bp 4 Dec 1868 spr Caroline Menzies "baptized (*sine ceremonis*)" Thomas S. Lee, priest p459

SHALER – Armantine Souli Marie, b 1 Feb 1850 lc/o Thomas Shaler & Adelaide Talbode bp 1 May 1857 spr Elizabeth L. Goldsmith p118

SHALER – Thomas, b 21 Aug 1847 lc/o Thomas Shaler & Adelaide Talbode bp 1 May 1857 spr Elizabeth L. Goldsmith p118

SHANDLEY – Sarah Jane, b 24 Dec 1854 c/o William Shandley & Sarah Griffin bp 7 Jan 1855 spr Joh. Bottornee & Catherine McCarty p33

SHANKS – Joseph Aloysius, b 11 Mar 1857 c/o John Shanks & Mary Brennan bp 19 Mar 1857 spr Patrick Miles & Kate O'Neal p115

SHANNON – James Thomas, b 12 Jul 1855 lc/o Matthew Shannon & Bridget Ann Dougherty bp 22 Jul 1855 spr Edward D. Evans & Lucy Hall p53

SHARPE – Mary, b 9 Dec 1825 bp 6 May 1854 spr Thos. Foley & Mary S. Roby p12

SHARPS – Mary Sharps (c) "aged 13 years" bp 1 May 1866 spr Rose Williams p383

SHAUGHNESSY – Margaret, b 4 Sep 1870 lc/o Jos. Shaughnessy & Mary Holmes bp 17 Sep 1870 spr John Murphy & Sarah Lornagan p509

SHAUGHNESSY – Thomas, b 31 Oct 1867 lc/o Thomas Shaughnessy & Mary Holmes bp 3 Nov 1867 spr Thomas Holmes & Catharine Holmes p425

SHAW – Bernard Lee, b 4 Jan 1864 lc/o Bernard Shaw & Susan C. Cook bp 24 Feb 1864 spr Lotty Evans p327

SHAW – Francis, b 27 May 1857 lc/o James Shaw & Anne Carroll bp 12 Jul 1857 spr Francis & Mary Shaw "baptized conditionally" H. B. Coskery, priest p126

SHAW – Gillis James, b 1 Nov 1856 lc/o Bernard Shaw & Susan Cook bp 18 Feb 1857 spr Henrietta Cook p111

SHAW – James Henry, b 28 Jul 1859 lc/o James Shaw & Anna Carroll bp 7 Aug 1859 spr Patk. Johnson & Mary McElroy p197

SHAW – John Franklin Pierce, b 30 May 1855 lc/o Bernard Shaw & Susan Cook bp 9 Jun 1855 p49

SHAW – Mary Alice, b 26 Jan 1859 lc/o Bernard Shaw & Susan Cook bp 4 Feb 1859 spr Mary Kildey p181

SHAW – Susan Mary Shaw "(born Cook)", b 19 Nov 1836 lc/o John & Rosetta Cook bp 3 Mar 1855 spr Helen Scott "baptized conditionally" Thos. Foley, priest p41

SHAW – Thomas Jefferson Jackson, b 26 Aug 1862 lc/o Bernard Shaw & Susan C. Cook bp 29 Sep 1862 spr Ann Brus____p291

SHEA – Heather Ambrosa, b 9 Apr 1865 lc/o Ambrose Shea & Elizabeth Smith bp 11 Apr 1865 spr Lizzie Carroll p354

SHEA – Joseph Michael, b 25 Dec 1856 lc/o John Shea & Teresa Dunn bp 13 Jan 1857 spr Roger & Honora Kavanaugh p108

SHEARER – Mary, b 12 May 1864 lc/o Thomas Shearer & Harriet Fox bp 1 Jun 1864 spr Cath. Bordley p333

SHEEDY – Michael John, b 23 Jul 1855 lc/o Michael Sheedy & Margaret Floyd bp 15 Aug 1855 spr Sarah Gallagher p55

SHEEHAN – Timothy, b 29 Aug 1854 lc/o Timothy Sheehan & Catherine Caton bp 1 Sep 1854 spr Mary White p22

SHEEHY – Mary Martha, b 19 Jan 1855 c/o James Sheehy & Catherine Walsh bp 4 Mar 1855 spr Rosa Keegan p38

SHEEHY – William Thomas, b 28 July 1858 lc/o James Sheehy & Catherine Welsh bp 24 Oct 1858 spr John Creesim & Kate Haig p172

SHEESLEY – Daniel Sheesley, b 30 Mar 1836 bp 13 Sep 1861 "baptized conditionally" Thos. Foley, priest p260

SHEETS – Henry John, b 14 Jun 1855 lc/o Henry Sheets & Maria Fitzpatrick bp 1 Jul 1855 spr Michl. & Bridget Conly p50

SHEETS – William Albert, b 28 Feb 1857 lc/o Henry Sheets & Maria Fitzpatrick bp 26 Jul 1857 spr Jane McClenan & Bernard McClenan p128

SHEHAN – Joseph Strahan, b 10 Jul 1858 lc/o Patrick Shehan & Ann Whelan bp 1 Aug 1858 spr Ellen Kilduff p164

SHEHAN – Michael, b 7 May 1854 lc/o Michael Shehan & Mary Shields bp 15 May 1854 spr Pat. Killian & Mary Shields p12

SHELLEY – Mary Martha Serena, b 21 Feb 1869 lc/o John Shelley & Josephine Addison (c) bp 9 Mar 1869 spr Mary Brady p466

SHEPHERD – Marie Louise, b 18 May 1870 lc/o Nicholas Shepherd & Louisa Mead bp 2 Sep 1870 spr Louisa Josephine Dugan p508

SHEPPARD – Emma Lee, b 4 Dec 1855 lc/o William H. Sheppard & Augusta Moffit bp 17 Jul 1856 spr Louisa Hevener p90

SHEPPARD – Mary, b 14 Mar 1860 lc/o Nicholas C. Sheppard & Emily Louisa Meade bp 18 Mar 1860 "baptized privately" Thos. Foley, priest p217

SHEPPARD – Ursula Jane Hevener, b 7 Nov 1854 lc/o William H. Sheppart & Augusta Moffit bp 17 Jul 1856 spr Louisa Hevener p90

SHEPPERD – Elise Hamtranck "of Shepperdstown, Va", b 11 Feb 1868 lc/o James H. Shepperd & Ann Florence Hamtranck "both of Va" bp 10 May 1868 spr Thomas Foley & Mary D. G_____ p441

SHERAN – Ann, b 8 Feb 855 lc/o James Sheran & Mary Campbell bp 29 Apr 1855 spr Wm. Hughes & Mary Kerison p45

SHERDEN – Annie, b 29 Mar 1855 lc/o James Sherden & Maria Fitzsimmons bp 29 May 1855 spr N. Hughes & Mary A_____ p47

SHERMAN – Genivieve Blanche, b *ndg* Nov 1863 lc/o William Sherman & Mary Coldscot bp 24 Feb 1864 spr Catharine Loftus p327

SHERRACE – Mary Ellen, b 8 Nov 1857 lc/o James Sherrace & Mary Simmons bp 13 Sep 1857 spr Grace Riley p143

SHERWOOD – William Edward, b 19 Dec 1864 lc/o William B. Sherwood & Sarah C. Winsett bp 28 May 1867 "I supplied the ceremonies" "previously baptized in danger by Rev. J. S. Foley" Thos. Foley, priest p413

SHINKS – Margaret Jane, "age some few weeks" lc/o John Shinks & Mary Bramion bp 23 Oct 1854 spr Michl. Larkin & Ann Guttrow p27

SHORTER – Joseph Edward (c) b 29 Sep 1862 lc/o Edward Shorter & Mary J. Butler (c) bp 4 Mar 1863 spr Josephine Minor p303

SHORTER – Mary Frances (c), b 25 Jan 1854 lc/o Alexander Shorter & Mary Cook (c) bp 10 May 1854 spr Harriet Smith p12

SHORTER – Mary Virginia, b 11 Sep 1867 lc/o Isaac Shorter & Eliz. Squaggins (c) bp 28 Dec 1867 spr Mary Williams p430

SHRIVER – Alfred Jenkins, b 5 Jan 1867 lc/o Albert Shriver & Anna Jenkins "of Alfred" bp 14 Jun 1867 spr Columbus Shriver & A. Rosa Jenkins p415

SHRIVER – Joseph William, b 3 Nov 1869 lc/o Albert Shriver & Annie Jenkins "of Alfred" bp 10 Nov 1869 spr Robert Jenkins & Sallie Shriver p487

SHRIVER – Mary Josephine, b 21 Jun 1864 lc/o William Shriver & Roberta C. Lyon bp 29 Jun 1864 spr John Shriver & Elizabeth Myer p335

SHRIVER – Robert Lyon, b 7 Mar 1861 lc/o William Shriver & Cecilia Roberta Lyon bp 25 Mar 1861 spr Thomas Foley & Sarah C. Shriver p247

SHRIVER – Susan Wilson, b 3 Feb 1868 lc/o William Shriver & Cecilia Lyon bp 18 Feb 1868 spr Susan Wilson p434

SHRIVER – Thomas Foley, b 15 Aug 1862 lc/o William Shriver & Cecilia Roberta Lyon bp 21 Aug 1862 spr Theresa J. Meyer & Mary Hamilton p287

SHRIVER – William Shriver, "aged 72 years" bp 19 Apr 1869 p469

SHRIVER – William, b 26 Jun 1866 lc/o William Shriver & Roberta Cecilla Lyon bp 5 Jul 1866 spr Ann Keiser Shriver & Emma J. Shriver p388

SHULTZ – Louisa, b 14 Nov 1867 lc/o Gerard Shultz & Sarah McEwen bp 6 Jan 1868 spr Louisa Freedberger p431

SHULTZ – Mary Clara, b 24 Aug 1861 lc/o Garrett Shultz & Sarah McKewin bp 13 Oct 1861 spr John Hogan & Bridget Vaughan p263

SIBLEY – John Thomas Rufus, b 28 Jul 1854 lc/o Robert Sibley & Sarah Laskey bp 5 Jun 1855 spr Eliza Hayden p48

SILK – Frances, b 7 Jun 1854 lc/o Michael Silk & Mary Farrell bp 11 Jun 1854 spr Pat. Burke & Cath. Malden p14

SILK – John, b 6 Feb 1868 lc/o Michael Silk & Mary Farrell bp 23 Feb 1868 spr John King & Fanny Silk p435

SILK – Peter, b 3 May 1860 lc/o Michael Silk & Mary Farrell bp 13 May 1860 spr William McCann & Cecilia Fitzmorris p222

SILK – Thomas, b 18 Jan 1862 lc/o Michael Silk & Mary Farrell bp 26 Jan 1862 spr Anthony Griffen & Catharine Infant p272

SILK – Thomas, b 29 Feb 1856 lc/o Michael Silk & Mary Farrell bp 9 Mar 1856 spr Hugh Cofield & Ellen Cofield p75

SIMMONS (Hendix) - Anne, b 12 Jun 1864 nc/o John Simmons "white" & Jane Hendix (c) bp 18 Jun 1864 spr Maria Lowry (c) p335

SIMMS – Elizabeth, b 8 Dec 1861 c/o Elizabeth Simms (c) bp 29 Dec 1861 spr Ann Hammond p271

SIMMS – Margaret Ellen, b 29 Jun 1855 lc/o Robert A. Simms & Margaret J. Mitchell bp 14 Apr 1862 spr Margaret Simms p279

SIMMS – Robert Franklin, b 5 Sep 1857 lc/o Robert A. Simms & Margaret J. Mitchell bp 14 Apr 1862 spr Margaret Simms p279

SIMMS – William Albert, b 21 Dec 1859 lc/o Robert A. Simms & Margaret J. Mitchell bp 14 Apr 1862 spr Margaret Mitchell p279

SIMON – Mary Lucia, "11 months old" lc/o Charles Simon & Amanda Lerner bp 17 Jun 1860 spr Joe Paini & Mary Kelly p225

SIMONIN – Josephine, "aged 20 years" lc/o Charles F. A. Simonin & Sarah, "his wife" bp 27 Mar 1866 spr Margaret Fox p379

SIMONSON – Martha Jane, b 12 Sep 1861 lc/o John Simonson & Mary Ann Norman bp 26 Dec 1861 g – Mary Elizabeth Norman "baptized condit." "doubtfully bapt. by Caroline Norman" Francis Patrick, Archb. p270

SINCLAIR – Margaret Priscilla, b 18 Mar 1870 lc/o P. Sinclair & Elizabeth Pugh bp 3 Apr 1870 spr Denis Shea & Catharine Shea p499

SINGLETON – Elizabeth Singleton (c), "about 15 years old" bp 10 Jun 1855 spr Mary R. Spelman p49

SINGLETON – Emma Mary Singleton (c), "40 years old" bp 6 Nov 1859 spr Anna Green p204

SINNOTT – Alexander Nicholson, b 30 Sep 1855 lc/o Patrick Sinnott & Mary Bulger bp 1 Oct 1855 spr Richard & Sarah Sinnott p60

SINNOTT – Alexander, b 26 Nov 1858 lc/o Patrick Sinnott & Catharine Henry bp 12 Dec 1858 spr Thomas Cousins & Elizabeth Mullan p176

SINNOTT – Alexander, b 30 May 1862 lc/o Patrick Sinnott & Catharine Henry bp 22 Jun 1862 spr Wm. Doyle & Mary Pender p283

SINNOTT – Michael, b 20 Oct 1860 lc/o Patrick Sinnott & Catharine Henry bp 4 Nov 1860 spr Michl. Henry & Rosa McWilliams p234

SINNOTT – William Robert, b 19 Nov 1870 lc/o Jocob Sinnott "of County Wexford, Ireland" & Maria Heinhan "of County Galway, Ireland" bp 27 Oct 1870 spr Robert Noonan & Catharine Heinhan p515

SISCO – Theresa Lucinda, b 29 Aug [*ed. note: year not written, probably 1868*] lc/o Dennis Sisco & Martha Ann Queen (c) bp 13 Sep 1868 spr Theresa Queen p453

SKINNER – Caroline Goldsborough Skinner, "aged about 46 years" bp 24 Jun 1868 spr Mother Mary Vincent "for whom Mrs. Middleton acted as proxy" "baptized conditionally" James Gibbons, priest p447

SLADE – Belinda Mary Slade, b 10 Oct 1842 bp 17 Aug 1866 spr Lizzie Slade "baptized conditionally" Thos. Foley, priest p392

SLADE – Henry Montrose, b 14 Jan 1861 lc/o William Augustus Slade & Belinda Slade, "his wife" bp 3 Aug 1868 spr Rosalie Wise p450

SLADE – Mary, b 12 Jul 1862 lc/o Wm. A. Slade & Belinda Slade, "his wife" bp 3 Aug 1868 spr Lizzie Slade p450

SLADE – Olvier Slade, "aged 22 years" bp 12 Jun 1868 spr Elizabeth Slade p445

SLATER – Helen Anna, b 10 Aug 1856 lc/o George Slater & Catherine Cunningham bp 22 Sep 1856 spr George & Betty Slater p96

SLATER – Thomas Wm., b 10 Aug 1870 lc/o Thomas Wm. Slater & Mary Ann Leyd__ bp 22 Aug 1870 spr John Dougherty & Lizzie Sanders p507

SLATER – Virginia Roberta Slater, "aged about 14 years" bp 28 Mar 1867 spr Nannie Emory "baptized conditionally" H. B. Coskery, priest p409

SLATTERY – David Patrick, b 28 Mar 1868 lc/o John Slattery & Kate Pollard bp 5 Apr 1868 spr Thomas Smith & Catharine Whelan p438

SLATTERY – Mary Catharine, b 28 Dec 1866 lc/o John Slattery & Kate Rolland bp 30 Dec 1866 spr Jas. Fitzsimmons & Margaret Murray p 402

SLECK – Emma Teresa, b Mar *ndg* lc/o Joseph Sleck & Annette Laughlin bp 1 Apr 1855 spr Josh. _____ & Mary _____ [*ed. note: faint record*] p41

SLEVIN – John, b 9 Aug 1864 lc/o Michael Slevin & Margaret McDonnell bp 10 Aug 1864 spr Michael Egan & Ann Ryan p338

SLOAN – Emily Jane, b 4 Feb 1860 lc/o Michael Sloan & Mary Granger bp 29 Feb 1860 spr Susan Gildea p216

SLOAN – Joseph Alexius, b 21 May 1856 lc/o Michael Sloan & Mary Granger bp 2 Jul 1856 spr Sophia Granger p88

SLOAN – Mary Agnes, b 25 Aug 1854 lc/o Michael Sloan & Mary Granger bp 5 Oct 1854 spr Sophia Granger "I supplied the ceremonies of Baptism. …The child had been previously baptized by an intelligent Catholic woman." H. B. Coskery, priest p25

SLOAN – William C. Sloan, "aged 2 years" bp 5 Feb 1867 spr Pat Brady & M. S_____ p405

SLOBOL – Robert, b 15 Dec 1867 lc/o Robert Slobol bp 25 Dec 1867 spr John Butler & Mary McDonald p430

SMALL – Anna Virginia, "some few days old" lc/o John Small & Ann Walsh bp 5 Mar 1854 spr James T. Small & Theresa Toomey p7

SMALL – William C. Small, "about 33 years old" bp 25 Mar 1858 p152

SMITH - Andrew Thomas, b 16 Jul 1857 lc/o Owen Smith & Maria Lecompte (c) bp 6 Aug 1857 spr Loretta Lewis p129

SMITH – Agnes Valentine Smith, b 13 Feb 1857 nc/o Henry Thomas & Harriet Smith (c) bp 26 Feb 1857 spr Elizabeth Gans p113

SMITH – Amelia, b 3 Jun 1866 lc/o Monroe Smith & Catharine Jordan bp 3 Sep 1866 spr Maggie Griffith p394

SMITH – Ann, b 22 Jan 1855 lc/o Andrew Smith & Catherine Cox bp 4 Feb 1855 spr Michl. & Mary O'Farrell p36

SMITH – Ann, b 12 Jan 1855 lc/o Dr. Berwick B. Smith & Nanny Moale bp 19 Feb 1855 spr Henry Pike & Nancy Moale p37

SMITH – Ann, b 20 Jan 1867 lc/o John Smith & Ann Barrett bp 27 Jan 1867 spr Patk. Barrett & Mary Ward p404

SMITH – Ann Maria Louisa Smith (c), "aged about 18 years" bp 20 Jun 1859 "baptized privately & conditionally" H. B. Coskery, priest p192

SMITH – Anne Smith, "aged about 21 years" "parents unknown to her" bp 7 Mar 1866 spr Thos. Sullivan & Joanna Lynch "baptized conditionally" James Gibbons, priest p377

SMITH – Daniel Wm., b 2 Dec 1869 lc/o Jno. Smith & Ella Harrison (all c) bp 6 Jan 1870 spr Ellen Hall p491

SMITH – Daniel, b 5 Jun 1863 lc/o Philip Smith & Catharine Burke bp 14 Jun 1863 spr James O'Connor & Susan Urbrook p309

SMITH – Elizabeth Rosanna, b 9 Sep 1859 nc/o Thomas Smith & Nancy Richardson bp 29 Jan 1864 spr Mary Matthews (all c) "baptized conditionally" H. B. Coskery, priest p325

SMITH – Frances Smith "née Hillier", "aged 22 years" lc/o Joseph Hillier & Charlotte, "his wife" bp 24 May 1869 spr Margaret Foy p472

SMITH – Francis, b 11 Dec 1868 lc/o Owen Smith & Maria LeCompte (c) bp 14 Jul 1869 spr Elizabeth Denny p476

SMITH – George Greene, b 27 Jul 1856 lc/o George Smith & Margaret Green bp 21 Sep 1856 spr Mary Sanders p96

SMITH – George Henry (c), "aged about 12 years" bp 18 Apr 1858 spr Mary Martin "baptized conditionally" H. B. Coskery, priest p154

SMITH – George Thomas, b 16 May 1869 lc/o Alonzo Smith & Gertrude Dempsey bp 1 Nov 1869 spr Mary Martha Dempsey p487

SMITH – Jesse, b 22 Dec 1862 lc/o George Smith & Margaret Green bp 2 Mar 1863 spr Margaret Schley p303

SMITH – John, b 19 Dec 1856 lc/o Peter Smith & Mary Coffee bp 11 Jan 1857 spr Laurence Murphy & Mary Henaghan p107

SMITH – John Andrew, b 2 Nov 1854 c/o John Smith & Mary Rush bp 5 Nov 1854 spr Thos. Cravan & Mary Ann Brandy p28

SMITH – John James, b 3 Jan 1868 lc/o Alonzo Smith & Gertrude Dempsey bp 18 Mar 1868 spr Beula Hall p436

SMITH – John Newton, b 6 Nov 1858 lc/o George Thomas Smith & Margaret Ann Green of Towson Town, B. Co." bp 2 Feb 1859 spr Eliza C. Green p180

SMITH – John Smith (c), "aged about 18 years" 28 Feb 1859 spr Wm. Kilduff "baptized conditionally" H. B. Coskery, priest p183

SMITH – John Thomas, b 24 Sep 1854 lc/o Michl. Smith & Bridget McCullough bp 9 Oct 1854 spr Bridget Hipsley p26

SMITH – Margaret Ann, b 10 Apr 1868 lc/o John Smith & Ellen Harris (c) bp 23 Apr 1868 spr Mary E. Elvert p440

SMITH – Mary, b 4 Feb 1858 lc/o Patk. Smith & Mary O'Brien bp 7 Feb 1858 spr Martin Burns & Margaret O'Brien p148

SMITH – Mary Ann Robinson, b 16 Jan 1861 lc/o Owen Smith & Maria LeCompte (c) bp 29 Jan1861 spr Sidney Matthews p241

SMITH – Mary Catharine, b 18 May 1870 c/o Barbay Smith bp 21 Jul 1870 spr Mrs. Julia Lehigh p506

SMITH – Mary Eliza, b 20 Feb 1857 c/o Harriet Smith (c) bp 17 Aug 1856 [(*sic*) *ed note: should be 1857*] spr Hannah Brown p130

SMITH – Mary Elizabeth, b *ndg* lc/o Philip Smith & Catharine Burke bp 19 Mar 1866 spr Mary Fitzpatrick p378

SMITH – Mary Frances, b 17 Jan 1858 nc/o Kelly & Frances Smith (all c) bp 25 Mar 1858 spr Ann Eliza Howard (c) p152

SMITH – Mary Frances, b 23 Feb 1861 lc/o Thomas Smith & Mary Sullivan bp 20 Mar 1861 spr Alice M. Carney p246

SMITH – Mary Henrietta (c), b 10 Apr 1864 lc/o Owen Smith & Maria Lecompte bp 5 May 1864 spr Henrietta Brown p332

SMITH – Mary Virginia, b 2 Feb 1860 c/o Cornelius Smith & Jane Johnson (c) bp 7 May 1861 spr John Castor & Fanny Castor [*ed. note: last name is listed both as Smith or Johnson in record*] p251

SMITH – Michl., b 22 Jul 1869 lc/o John Smith & Mary McAvery bp 1 Aug 1869 spr Peter McAvery & Bridget Quin p478

SMITH – Oliver Campbell, b 8 Nov 1860 lc/o George Smith & Margaret Green bp 21 Jan 1861 spr Mary Green p240

SMITH – Owen Augustus, b 23 Mar 1866 lc/o Owen Smith & Maria Lecompte (c) bp 27 Apr 1866 spr Lizzie Colbert p383

SMITH – Telulah Mary, b 11 Jul 1868 lc/o William A. Smith & Massey O. Smith bp 17 Sep 1869 spr Maria Smith p483

SMITH – Thomas, b 28 Jan 1854 lc/o James Smith & Alice McNamee bp 22 Feb 1854 spr Pat. Neale & Rose Gallagher p6

SMITH – Thomas, b 3 Apr 1855 lc/o Peter Smith & Mary Coffee bp 15 Apr 1855 spr Michael Smith & Mary Coffee p43

SMITH – Thomas Jefferson, b 4 Jul 1857 lc/o Francis Smith & Mary Alnay bp 25 Jan 1858 spr Mary A. Hanley p147

SMITH – William Kerry, b 31 Jan 1850 c/o Coles Smith & Mary Coffee, "his wife" bp 1 Jan 1859 spr Michael Brady & Bridget Brady [*ed. note: birth year looks like 1850, but it could have been 1859*] p210

SMITH – William Starr Smith, "aged 4 years" lc/o Thomas Smith & Ann Clifton bp 20 Apr 1869 "I baptized privately" Thos. Foley, priest p469

SMITH (or RICHARDSON) – George Henry, b 10 Feb 1861 nc/o Henry Smith & Nannie Richardson (both c) bp 6 Jan 1864 spr Mary Matthews (c) "baptized conditionally" H. B. Coskery, priest p323

SNEERINGER – Mary Caroline, b 10 Mar 1869 lc/o Wm. James Sneeringer & Mary B. _____ bp 24 Mar 1869 spr Isabel N. Guise p467

SNOWDEN – Emily Jane (c), b 1 Sep 1863 lc/o Caleb Snowden & Mary Gannon (c) bp 7 Oct 1863 spr Elizabeth Singleton p317

SNYDER – Henry Stalker Snyder "aged 19 yrs." bp 9 Jun 1867 "baptized conditionally" Thos. Foley, priest p414

SNYDER – Joseph, b 26 Dec 1861 nc/o Ann Snyder, "father unknown" bp 13 Jan 1862 spr Julia Gratefield (c) p272

SNYDER – Julie Snyder, "aged 45 years" bp 7 Feb 1867 "baptized privately in danger of death" Thos. Foley, pries p405

SOLAN – Francis, b 22 Nov1861 lc/o Michael Solan & Ellen O'Neal bp 1 Dec 1861 spr Lanty Ryan & Mary A. Mack p268

SOLAN – Mary Ellen, b 5 Apr 1863 lc/o Michael Solan & Ellen O'Neal bp 29 Apr 1863 spr Bridget Powers p306

SOMERS – Agnes Elizabeth, b 16 Apr 1860 lc/o Charles Somers & Maria, "his wife" (c) bp 22 May 1860 spr Elizabeth Gaines p222

SOMERS – Mary Ellen, b 24 Oct 1868 lc/o Andrew Somers & Ellen Burns bp 28 Nov 1868 spr Bridget O'Neill p458

SOMERVILLE – Mary Frances (c), "4 weeks old" c/o Frances Somerville (c) bp 6 Jan 1856 spr Priscilla Jenkins p70

SÖTBÖRG – Joseph Augusta, b 13 Aug 1856 lc/o Joseph Maria Sötbörg & Mary Jane Rankin bp 1 Dec 1856 spr Eugene Janisky & Elizabeth Coughlin p103

SPALDING – James Thomas, b 2 Mar 1870 lc/o James Spalding & Susan Gordon bp 15 Apr 1870 (all c) p500

SPANGLER – Rebecca, b 2 Jul 1859 lc/o Allen Spangler & Julia Keilkotty bp 17 May 1861 spr Susanna Spangler p251

SPECIE – Catharine, b 29 Jun 1858 "daughter of Francis Specie & Maria Valente, "his lawful wife" bp 30 Jun 1858 spr Joseph Ceregina & Mary Ceregina "I supplied cer. of bap. for infant duly baptized by Margaret Ceregina" Francis Patrick, Archb. p161

SPENCER – David Williamson, b *ndg* Jul 1865 lc/o Jervis Spencer & Juliana Williamson bp 21 Jul 1865 spr Rebecca Young p360

SPIES – Catharine Spies "(born King)", "aged 53 years" bp 11 Jul 1867 p417

SPIES – Charles Albert, b 11 Aug 1859 lc/o Charles L. Spies & Mary Catharine bp 25 Mar 1863 spr Julia M. Spies p304

SPIES – Julia Mary, b 25 Jul 1843 lc/o Charles L. Spies & Mary Catharine "his wife" spr Elizabeth Hensler "baptized conditionally" Thos. Foley, priest p277

SPINDLER – Charles, b 17 Aug 1858 lc/o Henry Spindler & Ellen Boyle bp 26 Sep 1858 spr Mary McDermott p169

SPINDLER – Henry, b 18 Apr 1863 lc/o Henry Spindler & Ellen Boyle bp 26 Apr 1863 spr Ann Waldron p306

SPINDLER – Mathias, b 16 Nov 1860 lc/o Henry Spindler & Ellen Boyle bp 25 Nov 1860 spr Peter Spindler & Alice Quinn p236

SPRADLEY – Alice Elizabeth, b 16 Feb 1864 lc/o John Spradley & Catharine Kelly bp 18 Apr 1864 spr Ellen Dolan p331

SPRADLEY – Mary Ann, b 7 May 1862 lc/o John Spradley & Catharine Kelly bp 31 May 1862 spr Margaret Rodgers p282

SPRIG – Felix Sargeant Vanlear, b 20 Mar 1868 lc/o J. R. L. Sprig & Sossia Brunot bp 6 Nov 1867 spr Maria Snowden "proxy for" Eugenie Duchein p487

SPRIG – Henry Bayne, b 20 Jul 1869 lc/o R. L. Sprig & Sophia B_____ bp 14 Oct 1869 spr "by proxy" Louisa Charnal "baptized without the ceremonies Nov. 6 1869" H. B. Coskery, priest p486

STACK – Honora, b 28 Nov 1859 lc/o Patrick Stack & Catharine Picket bp 8 Dec 1859 spr Wm. O'Keefe & Ellen Kelly "baptized privately" "ceremonies supplied Oct 24, 1860" H. B. Coskery, priest p207

STACK – Joseph Simon, b 15 Jul 1858 lc/o Garrett Stack & Elizabeth Kelly bp 6 Aug 1858 spr Elizabeth O'Neal p165

STACK – Mary, b 15 Sep 1857 lc/o Patrick Stack & Catherine Picquett bp 16 Sep 1857 spr Samuel & Catherine Drury [Robert Stack's sister] p134

STACK – Robert, b 15 Sep 1857 lc/o Patrick Stack & Catherine Picquett bp 16 Sep 1857 spr John Picquett & Mary Drury [Mary Stack's brother] p134

STACK – Thomas Patrick, b 15 Sep 1855 lc/o John Stack & Ann Kelly bp 30 Sep 1855 spr Jas. & Mary Ann McGioney [*ed. note: faint record*] p60

STAKES – Henry, b 11 Jan 1853 lc/o Patrick Stakes & Catherine Piquet bp 12 Jan 1855 spr William Connolly & Honora McNamee p34

STANFIELD – Helen, b 14 Dec 1845 lc/o William & Elizabeth Stanfield bp 26 Nov 1866 p399

STANLEY – John Stanley (c), "about fifty years old" bp 18 Apr 1857 spr M. Dorsey p117

STANSBURY – Henrietta Stansbury (c), "aged 16 years" bp 18 Jul 1865 "baptized conditionally" Thos. Foley, priest p360

STANSBURY – Martha Amelia, b 6 Aug 1855 lc/o John Stansbury & Amelia Maguire bp 20 Feb 1862 spr Mary Bell p274

STARKEY – Agnes, b 16 Sep 1858 lc/o John Starkey & Margaret Harvey bp 1 Oct 1858 spr James Thomas Starkey & Rose McDevit p170

STARKEY – Ann Harvey, b 30 Jul 1860 lc/o John Starkey & Margaret Harvey bp 15 Aug 1860 spr Peter & Mary Starkey p229

STARKEY – Catherine Teresa, b 28 Sep 1856 lc/o John Starkey & Margaret Harvey bp 20 Oct 1856 spr Basil T. Elder & Alice Merceret p100

STARKEY – Charles, b 2 Jul 1854 lc/o John Starkey & Margaret Harvey bp 19 Oct 1854 spr Jno. & Cath. Hinley p26

STARKEY – Rosa, b 28 Jul 1863 lc/o John Starkey & Margaret Harvey bp 12 Aug 1863 spr Joseph Starkey & Eunice O'Brien p313

STARR – Matilda Starr, "aged 19 years" bp 3 Mar 1870 spr Ann Stansbaugh p495

STAUB – Carol Edward, b 3 Sep *ndg* [*ed. note: most likely 1870*] lc/o John F. Staub "of Martinsburg, Virginia" & Maria R. Blondel "of the same place" bp 24 Sep 1870 spr Henry Clark & Anna Clark p509

STAUB – William Henry, b 13 May 1867 lc/o John F. Staub & Mary R. Staub bp 5 Jun 1867 spr John H. Blondell & Caroline Blondell p414

STAUF – John Stauf, b *ndg* bp 6 Jun 1866 "baptized conditionally" Thos. Foley, priest p385

STAYLOR – Ellen Staylor, "age about 65 years" bp 9 Dec 1856 "baptized conditionally" H. B. Coskery, priest p104

STAYLOR – Frances Catherine, b 3 Jul 1857 lc/o George Staylor & Washington [*sic*] bp 13 Dec 1857 spr Catherine McNulty "I supplied the ceremonies. Baptized privately by a competent lay person." Jno. McNally, priest p143

STAYLOR – George Edwin, b 3 May 1858 lc/o George Staylor & Mary Washington bp 1 Jun 1858 spr Margaret Carroll p158

STEDMAN – Daniel, b 31 Jul 1861 lc/o John Stedman & Margaret Lawlor bp 27 Aug 1861 spr Mary A. Kilduff p259

STEDMAN – Edward, b 4 May 1863 lc/o John Stedman & Margaret Lalor bp 2 Jun 1863 spr Bridget Kilduff p308

STEELE – Mary Cora, b 3 Nov 1846 lc/o James Steele & Elizabeth Richardson bp 7 Jun 1855 spr Mary Sipple p48

STEFFIN – William Charles, b 13 Mar 1866 lc/o Ely C. Steffin (or Cheffin) & Arabella C. Dempsey bp 3 Apr 1866 spr Mary A. Dempsey & John F. Dempsey p380

STEMMA – Elizabeth Stemma, "aged 19 years" register date: 18 Jan 1866 "privately baptized by a minister" "I received the profession of Catholic faith" Thos. Foley, priest p374

STEPHENS – Catherine Elizabeth, b 2 Mar 1855 lc/o Theodore Stephens & Mary Min____ bp 4 Jul 1855 spr <u>Sophia</u> <u>Sabbs</u> (all c) [*ed. note: faint record*] p50

STEPHENS – Mary Jane, b 28 Jul 1855 lc/o Anthony Stephens & Mary <u>Conlan</u> bp 12 Aug 1855 spr Thos. _____ & Mary Costello [*ed. note: faint record*] p55

STEPPER – Mary Elizabeth, b 4 May 1860 lc/o Andrew Stepper & Cecilia Chenowith bp 12 Oct 1860 spr James Staris p232

STEWARD – Annie Eliza, b 13 Jan 1857 lc/o William Steward & Clara <u>Shirply</u> bp 2 Aug 1857 spr Annie <u>Moony</u> p129

STEWARD – Clara Augusta, b 11 Feb 1855 lc/o William Steward & Clara Shadden bp 23 Apr 1855 spr Mary Quigley p44

STEWART – Alexander Thomas, b 13 Nov 1857 lc/o Arthur Stewart & Ann King bp 26 Nov 1857 spr Pat. Griely & Rose Henry p141

STEWART – Ann Elizabeth, b 25 Jan 1859 lc/o Arthur Stewart & Ann King bp 6 Feb 1859 spr George A. Kurtz & Mary C. King p181

STEWART – Arthur B., b 17 May 1864 lc/o William Stewart & Ann King bp 26 Jun 1864 spr Luke Quinn & Sarah Brown p335

STEWART – Charlotte Stewart (c), "aged 82 years" bp 30 Jun 1865 "baptized conditionally" Thos. Foley, priest p359

STEWART – Edward Stewart, "aged 22 years" bp 18 Nov 1863 p321

STEWART – George Vincent, b 31 Mar 1860 lc/o Arthur Stewart & Ann King bp 15 Apr 1860 spr Hugh Drogan & Bridget Silk p219

STEWART – Georgiana Stewart "(born Gist)", "aged about 19 years" bp 12 Apr 1857 spr Mabel Stewart p117

STEWART – Henry Robert, b 1 Nov 1862 lc/o Arthur Stewart & Ann King bp 9 Nov 1862 spr Michael McMahon & Mary Norris p293

STEWART – John Hollingsworth Warfield, b 4 Nov 1852 lc/o William Stewart & Clara Thittey bp 8 Oct 1854 spr Dora Yeasb p25

STEWART – Mary Rose Stewart, "aged 14 years" bp 28 Jul 1868 spr Mary Banon p449

STEWART – Maud Juliana, b 19 Jul 1870 lc/o Charles Glenn Stewart & Mary Elizabeth Rosensteel bp 28 Jul 1870 spr Michl. & Susanna Connolly p506

STILES – Sarah Stiles (c), "aged 24 years" bp 15 May 1867 p412

STIRLING – Mary Ellen, b 1 Jan 1869 lc/o John Stirling & Maria Shipley bp 28 May 1869 spr Maria Hooper p473

STODDARD – Henry Calvert, b 6 Apr 1859 lc/o Albert Stoddard & Kate Menzies bp 12 Apr 1859 spr Wm. Chs. Kelly p186

STONE – John Lewis, b 16 Oct 1867 lc/o Lewis Stone & Martha Mahoney (c) bp 2 Jan 1868 spr Harriet Brown p431

STONE – Thomas Walter, b 10 Oct 1859 lc/o Walter Stone & Jane Carland bp 5 Feb 1861 spr Mary Carroll p242

STONESIFER – Charles Amos, "18 months old" lc/o Amos Stonesifer & Fannie, "his wife" bp 20 May 1864 "baptized privately" Thos. Foley, priest p333

STRAHAN – Anna Strahan, "1 year old," bp 8 Feb 1854 "baptized privately" Thos. Foley, priest p4

STRAHAN – William Lewis, b 11 Jan 1857 lc/o Edward Strahan & Mary A. Hanna bp 8 Feb 1857 spr John Strahan & Margaret Floyd p110

STRANEY – John Henry, b 24 Mar 1860 lc/o Edw. Straney & Mary Ann Hannah bp 27 May 1860 spr Lewis & Ann Straney p223

STRAUSBAUGH – Mary Ida, b 1 Feb 1860 lc/o Jacob W. Strausbaugh & Sarah Ann, "his wife" bp 13 Feb 1860 spr Elizabeth Heuislet p215

STREET – Mary Street, "aged 25 years" bp 25 Jan 1870 spr Sarah Jenkins "baptized conditionally" H. B. Coskery, priest p492

STRONG – Elizabeth Strong, "aged 27 years" bp 8 Sep 1863 "previously baptized by an Episcopal Minister & competent to testify to the validity of her baptism" Thos. Foley, priest p314

STRYDER – Joseph Martin, b 19 Nov 1866 lc/o George Stryder & _____ Conlan bp 20 Apr 1867 spr Mary Conlan p410

STUART – Charles William, b 12 Jul 1866 lc/o Charles Stuart & Martha Wilson bp 30 Jul 1866 spr George Barrenger & Emma Bolton p391

STUART – George Paul Ludger, b 26 Mar 1869 lc/o Charles G. Stuart & Mary E. Rosensteel bp 10 Apr 1869 spr George Rosensteel & Ellen Wells p468

STUART – Laura Rosalie, b 18 Nov 1868 lc/o John F. Staub & Mary R. Blondel bp 19 Jan 1869 spr Samuel Rhinehart & Susan Piet p464

STUART – Marie, b 31 Aug 1864 lc/o Edward V. Stuart & Jeannette Sanders bp 8 Sep 1864 spr Thomas "proxy for Sol. Hellen" & Emily Hillen p339

STUMP – William, b 7 Dec 1829 lc/o John W. Stump & Sarah B. Bias bp 13 May 1856 spr Carrie Scott p82

SULLIVAN – Dennis, b 6 Jul 1868 lc/o Daniel Sullivan & Elizabeth Gibson bp 15 Aug 1868 spr Mary Melcher p451

SULLIVAN – Eugene Thomas, b 23 Sep 1855 lc/o James Sullivan & Elizabeth Calwell bp 31 Oct 1855 spr Eug. Sullivan & Mary Sullivan p62

SULLIVAN – Eugene, b 29 Aug 1855 lc/o Ralph Sullivan & Ann Donnelly bp 23 Sep 1855 spr Denis & Mary Sullivan [*ed. note: faint record*] p59

SULLIVAN – Frances de Chantal, b 29 Jul 1865 lc/o Thos. E. Sullivan & Mary R. Dunleavey bp 19 Sep 1865 spr Rosanna McGinnis p365

SULLIVAN – James, b 28 Feb 1863 lc/o James Sullivan & Sarah Denis bp 12 Apr 1863 spr Mary Jane McCarthy p305

SULLIVAN – Joseph Dallas, b 5 Mar 1854 lc/o Henry Sullivan & Martha Vansant bp 23 Apr 1854 spr Mary Ellen Beacham p11

SULLIVAN – Marie Agnes, b 30 Aug 1870 lc/o Danl. Sullivan & Nora McVille bp 3 Sep 1870 spr James Quinn & Bridget McVille p508

SULLIVAN – Mary, b 12 Jul 1860 lc/o Radolphus (sic) Sullivan & Ann Donnelly bp 15 Jul 1860 spr John M_____ & Mary Tornity p226

SULLIVAN – Mary Ellen, b 23 Jun 1864 lc/o Patrick Sullivan & Honora Hearns bp 11 Jul 1864 spr Mary Hook p336

SULLIVAN – Mary Frances, b 10 Jan 1867 lc/o James Sullivan & Ellen Kelly bp 14 Feb 1867 spr Mary Ann Butl_____ p406

SULLIVAN – Mary Virginia, b 27 Aug 1859 lc/o Daniel Sullivan & Susan Luxero bp 28 Jan 1860 spr Rosa Sullivan p213

SULLIVAN – Milford Henry, b 22 Oct 1855 lc/o Henry Sullivan & Martha Vansant bp 13 Nov 1855 spr Mary Ellen Beacham p65

SULLIVAN – Nancy Ellen, b 3 Feb 1870 lc/o James Sullivan & Ellen Kelly bp 9 Feb 1870 spr Kate Hutchinson p493

SULLIVAN – Patrick Rudolph, b 4 Nov 1858 lc/o Rudolph Sullivan & Ann Donnelly bp 14 Nov 1858 spr John Mack & Bridget Fail p173

SULLIVAN – Thomas, b 17 Dec 1853 lc/o James Sullivan & Mary Elizabeth Caldwell bp 8 Nov 1854 spr Eugene Sullivan & Mary Ann Sullivan p29

SULLIVAN – William Henry, b 8 Sep 1867 lc/o Joseph Robert Sullivan & Sarah Worley bp 12 Sep 1867 spr Mary Concannon p421

SULLIVAN – William Patrick, b 28 Oct 1869 lc/o Pat. Sullivan & H. Ahern bp 13 Nov 1869 spr Mary O'Connor p488

SUMMERS – Mary Catharine, b 17 Apr 1868 lc/o Joseph Summers & Margaret Seymour Greenwell bp 28 May 1868 spr Mary Hughes p443

SUTTLE – Frances Suttle, "75 years old" bp 26 Feb 1869 "baptized conditionally" Thomas S. Lee, priest p465

SUTTON – Frances Marian, b 28 Jun 1869 lc/o Alfred Wesley Sutton & Mary Ellen Grant bp 20 Jan 1870 spr Lan_____ Granger p492

SWAGLER – Alice Walker, b 24 Oct 1867 lc/o Peter Joseph Swagler & Judith Teresa Murphy bp 1 Dec 1867 spr John Casper Brady & Mary M. P. Brady p428

SWAN – Margaret Jane, b 11 Aug 1854 c/o John Swan & Catherine Garrity bp 20 Aug 1854 spr Wm. Kelly & Margaret Smith p21

SWAN – Mary Alberta, b 19 Oct 1866 c/o Cornelius Swan & Sarah Jane Brown bp 6 Oct 1867 spr Susan Briscoe (all c) p423

SWANN – Mary, b 5 Dec 1856 lc/o John Swann & Catherine McGarrity bp 11 Jan 1857 spr James Smith & Ann O'Neal p107

SWAREN – Ann Mary Swaren, "about 50 years old" bp 19 May 1855 p47

SWEENEY – Catharine, b 29 Jul 1866 lc/o David Sweeney & Ellen Ward bp 5 Aug 1866 spr Michael Hanly & Bridget Sweeney p391

SWEENEY – Charles Henry, b 2 Apr 1854 lc/o Patrick Sweeney & Ellen Holton bp 16 Apr 1854 spr Michl. Holton, Rosa Blake p10

SWEENEY – Elizabeth, b 7 Aug 1861 lc/o David Sweeney & Ellen Ward bp 18 Aug 1861 spr John Ward & Sarah Somers p258

SWEENEY – George, b 3 Apr 1864 lc/o David Sweeney & Ellen Ward bp 17 Apr 1864 spr Martin Ward & Mary Ellen Ward p331

SWEENEY – Mary Isabel, b 12 Sep 1855 lc/o Jared Sweeney & Louisa Waltrom bp 23 Sept 1855 spr Mary L. Sweeney p59

SWEENEY – Mary Julia, b 15 Aug 1867 lc/o Peter Sweeney & Julia Cook "(born Bevan)" bp 18 Aug 1867 spr Edward Sweeney & Alice Sweeney p419

SWEENEY – Mary Maude, b 1 Sep 1862 lc/o Peter Sweeney & Margaret Hart bp 15 Sep 1862 spr Daniel Coakley & Ann J. Coakley p290

SWEFLER – Robert, b 25 Aug 1866 lc/o Peter Swefler & Teresa Murphy bp 30 Sep 1866 spr John & Dora Brady p397

SYKES – Mary Jenny Sykes "(born McCrea)", "35 years old" bp 12 Dec 1866 "baptized conditionally" Thos. Foley, priest p402

SYNOT – John Thomas, b 17 May 1857 lc/o Patrick Synot & Mary Bulge bp 31 May 1857 spr John Fogarty & Catherine Henry p122

SYNOT – William Edward, b 17 Jul 1855 lc/o William Synot & Margaret Grady bp 5 Aug 1855 spr Mary Teresa Wheeler & Jno. McNally p54

TAABS – Mary Taabs (c), "aged 40 years" bp 28 Oct 1869 "baptized conditionally" Thos. Foley, priest p487

TAFFIE – Joseph, b 6 Dec 1869 lc/o Joseph Taffie & Virginia Seeber bp 1 Jan 1870 spr Victor Coster & Mary Hipsley p490

TAGGART – Patrick Taggart, "aged about 60 years" bp 19 Oct 1867 p424

TAMMAN – William Hyje, b 27 Jun 1857 c/o John Frederick Tamman & Anna Clantice, "his lawful wife" bp 3 Aug 1857 g Margaret Clantice p129

TARR – Henry Thomas, b 19 Sep 1855 lc/o Wesley B. Tarr & Margaret I. Casey bp 28 Sep 1855 spr George F. Hartman & Margaret E. Holden p59

TASKELLY – Catharine Taskelly (c), "13 years old" bp 1 Nov 1864 spr "Justine" p343

TAWD – William, b 17 Jan 1856 lc/o Willam Tawd & Ann Scanlon bp 2 Mar 1856 spr Andrew Miller & Catherine Doras p74

TAYLOR – Charles Morris Giddleman, b 17 May 1859 c/o Geo. A. Taylor & Mary A. Jordan, "his lawful wife" bp 29 May 1859 spr Anthony Russo & Catharine Merietti p191

TAYLOR – Charlotte, "aged about 3 years" lc/o Wm. Taylor & Maria Ann Cannon bp 27 Nov 1868 spr Georgianna Jones p458

TAYLOR – Emma Virginia, b 27 Dec 1857 lc/o Isaac Taylor & Ellen Fawcett (c) bp 13 Jan 1858 spr Fanny Castor p146

TAYLOR – Henry Levi, b 19 Aug 1866 lc/o Isaac C. Taylor & Ellen Fawcett (c) bp 6 Sep 1866 spr Mary Jane Danson p395

TAYLOR – Isabella Celestine, b 5 Jan 1865 lc/o Joseph P. Taylor & Theresia (Murphy) Taylor bp 29 Jan 1865 spr Francis R. Coleman & Isabella C. Murphy p349

TAYLOR – Joseph Wilson Sumner, b 13 Feb 1862 lc/o Isaac Taylor & Ellen Foussett (c) bp 29 May 1862 spr Mary A. Eames p282

TAYLOR – Martha Mixen, b 18 Mar 1869 lc/o Wm. & Fannie E. Carter bp 4 Apr 1870 spr Mrs. Burrier "baptized *sine cerem*" Thomas S. Lee, priest p499

TAYLOR – Mary Ellen, b 15 May 1855 lc/o Isaac Taylor & Ellen Faucet (c) bp 1 Oct 1855 spr Minty LeCompte p60

TAYLOR – Mary Taylor, "aged about 17 years" c/o Milton N. Taylor bp 12 Jun 1868 spr Anne Brady p445

TAYLOR – Maurice Albert, b 19 Apr 1864 lc/o Isaac Taylor & Ellen Fawcett (c) bp 27 May 1864 spr Annie Sanders p333

TAYLOR – William Carroll, b 30 Dec 1859 lc/o Isaac Taylor & Ellen Fancett (c) bp 20 Apr 1860 spr William Oliver & Emily L. Ford p219

TAYLOR – William Howard Irvin, b 26 Nov 1868 lc/o Isaac Taylor & Ellen Fawcett (c) bp 26 May 1869 spr Amelia Greer p472

TEAL – Ella Scott, b 21 Sep 1860 lc/o George McK. Teal & Mary A. Clark bp 14 Feb 1861 spr Louis Berry p244

TEMPLE – William, b 5 Nov 1868 lc/o William Geo. Temple & Emma Virginia Robert bp 6 Jan 1869 spr Tho. Foley & Ann Louisa Amat p462

TENISON – James Joseph, b 28 Oct 1857 lc/o William Tenison & Catherine Tenison bp 18 Nov 1857 spr Mary A. Bittaker p141

TENNISON – John, b 1 Oct 1859 lc/o William Tennison & Catharine McDillon bp 29 Oct 1859 spr Mary Bittiger p203

TENNISON – Rose, b 28 Mar 1869 lc/o William Tennison & Catharine _____ bp 30 Mary 1869 spr James Tennison & Mary McCamhay p467

TENNISON – William Henry, b 20 Jun 1856 lc/o James Tennison & Catharine Gillam bp 5 Jul 1856 spr Ellen Nolan p88

TERLS – Mary Ann, b 8 Mar 1855 lc/o John Terls & Johanna Tracy bp 23 Mar 1856 spr James Moran & Mary Multrone p76

TERRELL – Mary Catharine, b 24 Mar 1862 lc/o John Terrell & Ann Dronay bp 30 Mar 1862 spr Patrick Greeley & Catharine Hankin p277

TETZIN – John Jorgan, b 25 May 1855 lc/o John Tetzin & Ann O'Donnell bp 10 Jun 1855 spr Jas. O'Donnell & Mary I. O'Donnell p49

THOMAS – Laura Virginia, b 11 May 1856 lc/o Daniel Thomas & Rosetta McMaclin bp 14 Aug 1856 spr John Simmons & Mary McAtee p92

THOMAS – Lewis Napoleon Thomas, b 14 Jan 1854 c/o Lewis Thomas & Matilda Johnson bp 20 Aug 1854 spr Clare Wheeler (all c) "I supplied the ceremonies…previously baptized by one of the Redemptorist Fathers" H. B. Coskery, priest p21

THOMAS – Lewis Stephen Thaddeus, b 10 Mar 1868 c/o Robert Thomas & Mary Queen bp 4 May 1868 spr Mary Harris p441

THOMAS – Lewis Thomas Carroll (c), "age about 29 years" bp 16 Mar 1854 spr Thos. Foley p8

THOMAS – Maria Susette, b 13 Mar 1861 lc/o Philip Evan Thomas & Susette de Marrigery bp 23 May 1861 spr Charles Claiborne & Mary Matilda Elder p252

THOMAS – Mary Ann (c), b 10 Mar 1854 lc/o Paul Thomas & Elizabeth Roberts (c) bp 2 May 1855 spr Elizabeth Harris p45

THOMAS – Paul Thomas, "about 26 years old" lc/o Philip & Mary Thomas (c) bp 9 Aug 1854 spr Eliza Harris p19

THOMAS –James, b 16 Jul 1857 lc/o Paul Thomas & Elizabeth Roberts (c) bp 20 Jul 1857 spr Annie Thomas p127

THOMAS– Mary Elizabeth (c), [*ed note: surname is Williams or Thomas*] b 10 Jul 1854 ic/o Edward Thomas & Ann Williams bp 6 Sep 1854 spr Sarah O'Donnell p23

THOMPSON – Agnes Eliza, b 16 Mar 1855 lc/o Thomas Thompson & Ann Courtney bp 20 Apr 1855 spr Mary E. Gallagher p44

THOMPSON – Ann, 6 May 1856 lc/o Danl. Thompson & Elizabeth Williams bp 8 Jun 1856 spr Jas. Thompson & Mary McGuigan p84

THOMPSON – Anna Maria, b 19 Oct 1854 lc/o James Thompson & Anna Philips bp 26 Nov 1854 spr Daniel Thompson & Elizabeth Donnelly p30

THOMPSON – Annie Elizabeth Thompson "(born Miles)", "aged 35 years" bp 17 May 1858 spr Mary Michael p156

THOMPSON – Charlotte Elizabeth, b 3 Mar 1862 lc/o Isaac Thompson & Eliza Butler bp 20 Mar 1862 spr Susan Butler p276

THOMPSON – Isaac Thompson (c), "aged 37 yrs" bp 19 Nov 1857 spr Jonathan Mullan "baptized conditionally" H. B. Coskery, priest p141

THOMPSON – John Robert, b 16 Oct 1859 lc/o Daniel Thompson & Elizabeth Williams bp 30 Oct 1859 spr John Thompson & Agnes Thompson p203

THOMPSON – Margaretta Virginia, b 26 Jul 1858 lc/o Daniel Thompson & Elizabeth Williams bp 15 Aug 1858 spr John Thompson & Rachel Thompson p166

THOMPSON – Mary Thompson, "aged 56 years" bp 12 Jun 1864 p334

THOMPSON – Mary Agnes, b 6 Mar 1859 lc/o Isaac Thompson & Eliza Butler bp 12 Mar 1859 spr Annette Bartlett (all c) p184

THOMPSON – Mary Catharine Thompson, "aged about 15 years" bp 8 Jun 1866 spr Ann Martin "baptized conditionally" H. B. Coskery, priest p386

THOMPSON – Mary Magdalen, "18 years old" lc/o William Thompson & Mary Bunn bp 21 May 1866 spr Mary Barron p384

THOMPSON – Thomas, 5 Feb 1854 lc/o Thomas Thompson & Eliz. A. Courtney bp 7 Mar 1854 spr Margaret Gallagher p7

THOMPSON – William Edward, b *ndg* Dec 1850 lc/o Edward Thompson & Mary Kilgore bp 16 Nov 1855 spr Ellen _____ [*ed. note: faint record*] p65

THORNTON – David Stephen Thornton, b *ndg* June 1844 bp 10 May 1870 spr Augustus Robbins & Elizabeth Robbins (all c) "baptized (*sub cer*)" John Dougherty, priest p501

THRUSDIN – Mary, b 8 May 1855 lc/o John Thrusdin & Catharine Morris bp 21 Sep 1855 spr Mary Ann Killduff "I supplied the ceremonies… This child had been previously baptized by Rev. M. Foley" H. B. Coskery, priest p58

TIEGEN – Jacob Augustine, b 19 Sep 1857 lc/o John Tiegen & Ann Cecilia O'Donnell bp 9 Oct 1857 spr Philip Jacobs & Margaret O'Donnell p137

TIERNAN – Robert, b 28 Jan 1854 lc/o Robert Tiernan & Cath. Flynn bp 15 Feb 1854 spr Rose McCormick p5

TIERNEY – James Dominic, b 6 Jan 1854 lc/o John Tierney & Ann Willis bp 22 Jan 1854 spr Thos. Hickey& Johanna Gaban p3

TILGHMAN – Louisa Tilghman, "41 years old" bp 7 Nov 1866 "baptized conditionally" Thos. Foley, priest p398

TINDALL – Robert, b 20 Jun 1869 lc/o William Tindall & Sophia Miller bp 31 Jul 1869 spr Helen Chabot p478

TINDEN – Mary Catharine, b 25 Jul 1866 lc/o William Tinden & Sophie Miller bp 20 Aug 1866 spr Anne M. Shedell p393

TIRRELL – John Joseph, b 30 Sep 1863 lc/o John Tirrell & Ann Droney bp 4 Oct 1863 spr John Slane & Margaret Dunn p316

TODD – Isabella Sarah Jane, b 14 Dec 1857 lc/o Thomas H. Todd & Lucy A. Magill bp 23 May 1859 spr Kate Reilly p190

TOLBERT – Geo. W., b 23 Dec 1862 lc/o Arthur Tolbert & Emma Miles bp 4 Jan 1863 spr John & Sarah Dorsey p299

TOLDRIDGE – Elizabeth Augusta, b 16 Jul 1861 lc/o William H. Toldridge & Margaret Frances O'Loughlin bp 1 Aug 1865 spr Julia O'Loughlin p361

TONLER – Mary Agnes, "10 years of age" lc/o Henry & Margaret Tonler bp 21 May 1866 spr Kate Barron p384

TOOTEL – Elizabeth Tootel, "aged about 45 years" bp 15 Apr 1867 spr Lucy Henkel "baptized conditionally" Jas. Gibbons, priest p410

TORMEY – Alfred Jenkins, b 3 Sep 1865 lc/o Leonard J. Tormey & Ellen Jenkins bp 8 Sep 1865 spr Anna Jenkins & M. J. Spaulding, Archb. Balto. p364

TORMEY – Catherine Johanna, b 11 Mar 1854 lc/o Michael Tormey & Bridget Fitzpatrick bp 28 Mar 1854 spr Cath. Doyle p9

TORMEY – John Lee, b 7 Sep 1870 lc/o Francis Dominic Tormey "of Frederick, Maryland" and Sarah Flannigan bp 24 Sep 1870 spr John M. Tormey & Barbara Tormey p509

TORMEY – Mary Elizabeth, b 10 Apr 1864 lc/o Leonard Tormey & Ellen Jenkins bp 14 Apr 1864 spr Alfred Jenkins & Lizzie Jenkins p330

TORMEY – Mary Helen, b 26 Sep 1861 lc/o Leonard J. Tormey & Ellen Jenkins bp 3 Oct 1861 spr Alfred Jenkins & Elizabeth Jenkins p262

TORMEY – Mary Rosalie, b 26 Mar 1863 lc/o Leonard Tormey & Ellen M. Jenkins bp 4 Apr 1863 spr John M. Tormey & Rosa Jenkins p305

TORNEY – John Edward, b 25 Mar 1856 lc/o Michael Torney & Bridget Fitzpatrick bp 13 Apr 1856 spr Mary McGraw p79

TOUHY – Cartherine Maria, b 5 Jun 1858 lc/o Patrick Touhy & Bridget Kering bp 27 Jun 1858 spr Joseph _____ & Bridget McNamara p160

TOULES – Anna Frances, b 29 Jan 1854 lc/o John Toules & Julia Lowe bp 28 Feb 1854 spr Cath. Elder p6

TOULON – Emma Lydia, b 13 Feb 1857 lc/o John Toulon & Julia Anne Lowe bp 11 Mar 1857 spr Harriet Lowe p114

TOULON – Grace Elder, b 23 Apr 1868 lc/o John Toulon & Julia Ann Louise bp 14 May 1868 spr Mary Toulon p442

TOWNSEND – Phebe Mary Townsend (c), "aged about 30 years" bp 4 Jun 1859 spr Wm. Quinn p192

TRACEY – Mary Ellen, b 25 Feb 1855 lc/o John Tracey & Emily Miller bp 23 Sep 1855 spr Mary J. Derry p59

TRAIN – Margaret Jane, b 22 Dec 1855 lc/o James Train & Margaret Rice bp 20 Jan 1856 spr Daniel Moore & Ann Dixon p70

TRAINER – Emily Maria, b 8 Jun 1856 lc/o Bernard Trainer & Hannah Trainer bp 22 Jun 1856 spr Thos. & Ann Clark p87

TRAINER – Francis Patrick, b 20 Dec 1861 lc/o Owen Trainer & Julia Holmes bp 29 Dec 1861 spr James Trainer & Catharine Trainer p271

TRAINER – Martin Denis, b 14 Oct 1866 c/o Owen Trainer & "his lawful wife" Julia Holmes bp 28 Oct 1866 spr John Daley & Hannah Elizab. Trainer p398

TRAINOR – Emily Maria T., b 31 May 1855 lc/o Bernard Trainor & Hannah Trainor bp 10 Jun 1855 spr John _____ & ______ p49

TRAINOR – Mary Catharine, b 13 Mar 1864 lc/o Owen Trainor & Julia Holmes bp 20 Mar 1864 spr Pat Millanus & Margaret A. McManus p328

TROCOCK – Francis Trocock, "age 8 years" bp 7 Dec 1854 "a native of California…of the Mono Tribe" p30

TROP – Susan Elizabeth, b 2 Jan 1854 lc/o William Trop & Ellen McMaster bp 2 Apr 1854 spr John & Mary McCoy p9

TUBMAN – Benjamin Lynn Lacklaw, b 5 Dec 1858 lc/o Benjamin G. Tubman & Margaret Jane Thompson bp 3 Mar 1859 spr Susan Tubman p183

TUBMAN – Francis Joseph, b 12 Mar 1867 lc/o F. Eugene Tubman & Caroline Coskery bp 13 Apr 1868 spr H. B. Coskery & Louise Gwynn "supplied the ceremonies" "previously baptized by Dr. Doyle" H. B. Coskery, priest p439

TUBMAN – Martha Emily, b "Easter Sunday" 1865 lc/o Charles Henry Tubman & Mary Lytia Anne (James) Tubman bp 11 Jun 1865 spr Anne G_____ p357

TUBMAN – Mary, b *ndg* May 1870 lc/o Eugene F. Tubman & Caroline Coskery bp 24 May 1870 spr H. B. Coskery & Catharine May Preston "baptized privately" "ceremonies supplied June 8, 1870" H. B. Coskery, priest p502

TUBMAN – William Billingslee Keene, b 8 Jan 1857 lc/o Benjamin G. Tubman & Mary J. Thompson bp 17 Jun 1857 spr Mary Tubman "I baptized, near Cambridge, Md…." H. B. Coskery, priest p124

TUCKER – Ada Cornelia, b 14 Sep 1868 lc/o Enod G. Tucker & Mary C. Henderson bp 25 Sep 1868 spr Amarett Lorinda Mary Tucker p454

TUCKER – Amaresh Lorinda Mary, b 31 Jan 1857 lc/o Enoch Green Tucker & Mary C. Alenderson bp 6 Jul 1862 spr Henry McGowan & Ellen Thompson p284

TUCKER – John Claude Thomas, b 7 Jan 1860 lc/o Enoch Green Tucker & Mary C. Alenderson bp 6 Jul 1862 spr Henry McGowan & Ellen Thompson p284

TUCKER – Mary, b 24 May 1846 lc/o Thomas Tucker & Emma W. Ropes bp 11 Oct 1865 spr Julia Baldwin p366

TULLEY – Rose Anna, b 23 Apr 1869 lc/o Mark Tully & Bridget Riley bp 14 May 1869 spr Hugh O'Connor & Mary McInroe p471

TULLY – Catharine, b 6 Sep 1860 lc/o Patrick Tully & Margaret Smith bp 23 Sep 1860 spr Wm. Blondel & Mary Carroll p231

TULLY – Francis Patrick, b 5 Oct 1856 lc/o Patrick Tully & Margaret Smith bp 26 Oct 1856 spr Eugene & Mary A. O'Connor p100

TULLY – James, b 14 Nov 1854 lc/o Patrick Tully & Margaret Smith bp 3 Dec 1854 spr James Saxton & Mary Clarke p31

TULLY – Mark, b 18 Apr 1863 lc/o Patrick Tully & Margaret Smith bp 14 May 1863 spr Wm. Barrow & Mary McInrone p307

TULLY – Mary, b 18 Sep 1858 lc/o Patrick Tully & Margaret Smith bp 29 Sep 1858 spr Philip & Mary Tully p170

TURNER – Cath. Marie Agnes, b 7 Sep 1870 lc/o Joseph H. Turner, Jr. & Virginia A. Mumford bp 17 Sep 1870 spr J. J. Turner, Sr. & Mrs. Turner p509

TURNER – Emma Jane, b 1 Sept 1857 lc/o Charles T. Turner & Margaret Ann Crough bp 18 Apr 1858 spr Mary Jane Crough p154

TURNER – George Henry, b 14 Jul 1854 lc/o John Thomas Turner & Margaret Jane Davis (all c) bp 10 Aug spr Jno. McSweeney p19

TURNER – George Washington, b 15 Jun 1862 lc/o George N. Turner & Elizabeth Renner bp 23 Jul 1862 spr Eliz. Renner p286

TURNER – John Turner, "aged 53 years" bp 2 Oct 1862 "baptized conditionally" Thos. Foley, priest, p291

TURNER – Joseph James, b 17 Oct 1868 lc/o Joseph Joshua Turner & Jenny Mumford bp 5 Nov 1868 spr Olivia Turner & M. J. Spalding, Archb. p456

TURNER – Joseph Turner, "aged 56 years" bp 16 Jun 1866 "baptized conditionally" Archb. _____, priest p386

TURNER – Joseph, b 18 Mar 1855 lc/o Henry Turner & Ellen Turner (c) bp 22 Mar 1855 spr Catherine Hammond p40

TURNER – Mary Arabella, b 3 Jan 1857 lc/o Reyston Turner & Adeline Brown (c) bp 5 May 1857 spr Jane Patterson p119

TYREL – Mary Joanna, b 18 Jan 1858 lc/o John Tyrel & Joanna Tracy bp 24 Jan 1858 "I supplied the ceremonies. The child received private baptism from the Rev. Thos. Foley" Jno. McNally, priest p147

TYRRELL – Margaret, b 1 Mar 1861 lc/o John Tyrrell & Ann Dronay bp 3 Mar 1861 spr John W. H. Stone & Maria Tyrrell p245

ULLAHAN – Ann Maria, b 30 Jun 1859 lc/o John Ullahan & Ann Hylan bp 17 Jul 1859 spr Augustus & Louisa Nideless [*ed. note: see also Oulahan, Oullahan*] p196

URDMAN – John William, b 22 Sept 1854 lc/o John Urdman & Sarah Elizabeth Bamberger bp 8 Nov 1854 spr Sarah McDonald Bamberger p28

VALENTINE – John Joseph, b 13 Mar 1862 lc/o Henry Valentine & Caty Cerichina bp 16 Mar 1862 spr A. Cicirella & John A. Cerichina p276

VALENTINE- Sarah Elizabeth, b 16 Jul 1853 lc/o John Valentine & Sarah Hartzell bp 1 Jan 1854 spr John Murphy & Anastasia Powell p1

VALK – Margaret, b 11 Nov 1855 lc/o Francis Valk & Elizabeth Ryan bp 1 Jan 1856 spr Josephine Ryan p69

VANBIBBER – Helen, b 28 May 1862 lc/o Dr. W. Chew VanBibber & Mary Josephine Chatard bp 7 Jun 1862 spr John VanBibber & Kate Chatard p282

VANDANAKER – Elizabeth Vandanaker "age about 25 years" bp 4 May 1855 spr Rose Riley "baptized conditionally" H. B. Coskery, priest p46

VANDEPEER – Joseph, "aged 26 years" bp 10 Nov 1864 "baptized conditionally" Thos. Foley, priest p344

VAUGHN – Catharine Agnes, b 25 Sep 1860 lc/o James Vaughn & Maria Catharine Dorsey bp 7 Oct 1860 spr Margaret Murphy p232

VAUGHN – Emma Frances, b 2 Jun 1843 lc/o James Vaughn & Maria Catharine Dorsey bp 14 Jun 1863 spr Martha Dorsey p309

VAUGHN – Maria Louisa, b 3 May 1865 lc/o James H. Vaughn & Mary C. Dorsey bp 29 May 1865 spr Margaret Murphy p357

VAUGHN – Thomas Joseph, b 22 Jan 1862 lc/o James Vaughn & Catharine Dorsey bp 2 Feb 1862 spr Thomas Dorsey & Mary J. Dorsey p273

VEHRMEYR – George Augustus, b 24 Nov 1861 lc/o Henry John Vehrmyer & Mary Ann Sibley bp 27 Jan 1862 spr Mary Jane Miller p272

VEYMAR "(or Vehmyer)" – John Franklin, b 29 Nov 1854 lc/o John H. Veymar or "Vehmyer" & Mary Jane Sibley bp 25 Feb 1855 spr Catherine Welch p38

VICKERS – Mary Susanna, b 2 Aug 1856 lc/o Theodore Vickers & Mary Agnes Hall bp 26 Jul 1857 spr Lucy Hall p128

VICKERS – William George, b 9 Jun 1860 lc/o Theodore Vickers & Mary Agnes Hall bp 10 Jul 1860 "I baptized in sickness…" H. B. Coskery, priest p226

VINCELLINI – Giovanna Elisabetha Maria, b 18 Sep 1864 lc/o Geovani Rossazza Vincellini "(of Genoa, Italy)" & Rosacilla Avanti "(of Piedmont)" bp 2 Oct 1864 spr Antonio Belsagno & Elizabetta Cella p341

VINCENT – Mary Ann, b 4 Aug 1854 lc/o Henry Vincent & Margaret Yinger bp 2 Jan 1855 spr Cath. Young p33

VOLK – George Edwin, b 4 Mar 1854 lc/o George R. Volk & Catherine McCroden bp 9 Aug 1854 spr Mary E. McCroden p19

VOORHEES – Elizabeth Voorhees "(born Hunter)", "aged 34 years" bp 3 Jan 1860 spr Frances Guyton p210

WADE – John Edward, b "26 inst" 1863 [*ed. note: this would seem a recording error of the month; prob. 26 Oct*] lc/o Michael Wade & Ellen Naughton bp 1 Nov 1863 spr John & Mary Wade p319

WADE – Rachel Ann, b 4 Oct 1858 lc/o Emanuel Wade & Eleanora Ridgway bp 27 Dec 1865 spr Mary Cook p372

WAITZ – Mary Thomasaine Laura Waitz, "aged 15 years" lc/o John & Mary Waitz bp 8 Mar 1866 spr Kate Barron p377

WALKER – Ellen Jane, b 3 Apr 1863 lc/o John H. Walker & Eliza Smith (c) bp 2 Oct 1863 spr Martha A. Cole p316

WALL – Mary Jessie Wall, "aged 20 years" bp 17 Aug 1869 spr Harriet Spalding "baptized conditionally" H. B. Coskery, priest p480

WALLACE – Elizabeth Wallace, "born in 1839" lc/o Capt. Wm. Wallace & Sarah, "his wife" bp 4 Apr 1861 "baptized conditionally" Thos. Foley, priest p247

WALLACH – Mary De Barth, b 27 May 1868 lc/o John De Barth Wallach bp 20 Aug 1868 spr Louis Gardner & Nellie Jenkins p451

WALLIS – Arthur James Wallis, "11 months old" nc/o Isaac Brown & Rosanna Wallis (c) bp 16 Nov 1859 spr Mary E. Singleton p205

WALLIS – Catharine Mary, b 2 Mar 1859 lc/o Robert Wallis & Elizabeth Heyburn bp 15 Jun 1860 spr Jane Corbitt p224

WALLIS – Frances Elizabeth Wallis "(born Hromas)", "aged 23 years" bp 15 Jul 1861 "baptized conditionally" Thos. Foley, priest p256

WALLIS – Martin, b 20 Feb 1859 lc/o John Wallis & Frances Thomas bp 8 Mar 1859 spr Martin Wallis & Catharine Wallis p183

WALLIS – Rose Wallis (c), "aged 20 years" bp 15 Aug 1863 "baptized conditionally" Thos. Foley, priest p313

WALSH – Caius Walter, b 22 Apr 1861 lc/o Matthew Walsh & Mary Ann Scanlon bp 15 May 1861 spr James McElroy p251

WALSH – Ellen, b 22 Mar 1856 lc/o Jeffrey Walsh & Sarah Cain bp 27 Apr 1856 spr Timothy Sheehan & Mary Walsh p 81

WALSH – Francis Patrick, b 5 Jan 1856 lc/o Philip Walsh & Catherine O'Rourke bp 25 Feb 1856 spr James E. Rooney & Margaret J. Eschbach p73

WALSH – Geoffrey Jerome, b 20 Jan 1858 lc/o Geoffrey Jerome Walsh & Sarah King bp 7 Feb 1858 spr Ann Lynch & James Walsh p148

WALSH – Helen Stewart, b 13 Oct 1862 lc/o Jeffrey Walsh & Sarah King, bp 10 Nov 1862 spr James Walsh & Cecilia Brown p294

WALSH – Mary Alice, b 29 Nov 1860 lc/o James M. Walsh & Mary I. Walsh bp 8 Sep 1861 spr Benjamin J. Correy & Eliza Devlin p260

WALSH – Mary, b 16 Dec 1853 lc/o Jeffrey Walsh & Mary King bp 22 Jan 1854 spr Thos. Walsh & Mary Louglan p3

WALSH – Victoria Eugenia, b 25 May 1859 lc/o James Walsh & Mary Isabella Walsh bp 18 Dec 1859 spr Louisa Devlin p209

WALSH – William Vincent Harold, b *ndg* lc/o John Carroll Walsh & Sarah Amanda Lee bp 14 Apr 1858 p153

WALTER – Ernest Aloysius, b 21 Jun 1869 lc/o Joseph M. Walter & Emily Magrassan bp 24 Jun 1869 spr Mary Water p475

WALTER – Joseph Matthews, b 26 Jan 1867 lc/o Joseph M. Walter & Emily Eliz. Magauran bp 30 Jan 1867 spr Mary Walter p404

WALTER – Julia <u>Guthson</u>, b 11 Jul 1854 lc/o Joseph U. Walter & Emily <u>Maganian</u> bp 6 Aug 1854 spr Judy <u>Guthson</u> p18

WALTER – Mary Emily Anthony, b 30 Apr 1860 lc/o Joseph M. Walter & Elizabeth <u>Maguran</u> bp 6 May 1860 spr Margaret Dowd p221

WALTER – Mary Emma Emily, b 13 Apr 1858 lc/o Joseph Walter & Emily Maguarn bp 18 Apr 1858 spr Anna <u>Gurtraio</u> p154

WALTER – Mary Helen, b 18 Nov 1864 lc/o Joseph M. Walter & Emily "(Magannan)" bp 22 Nov 1864 spr Mary D. Walter p345

WALTER – Mary Lewis, b 19 Nov 1861 lc/o Joseph M. Lewis & Emily E. <u>McGauran</u> bp 25 Nov 1861 spr Lewis C. Gross & Mary C. McGreevy p267

WALTERS – John Switzer, b 25 Feb 1854 lc/o William C. Walters & Margaret Rise bp 15 May 1854 spr Jeremiah McCartey & Cath. Harvey p12

WARD – Ann, b 4 Jun 1858 lc/o Michael Ward & Catherine Burns bp 7 Jun 1858 spr Ann Burnes p158

WARD – Charles Edward Ward (c), "about 45 years old" bp 17 Sep 1870 "baptized privately *sine cer*" John Dougherty, priest p509

WARD – Edward Lee, b 26 Jun 1863 lc/o Davis Ward & Bridget Doyle bp 5 Jul 1863 spr Edward Rattigan & Eliza Owens p310

WARD – Frederick Chatard, b 17 Jul 1864 lc/o William Ward & Kate Chatard bp 26 Jul 1864 spr Fred. D. Chatard & Mary Jos. VanBibbler p337

WARD – Jane Mary, b 20 Jan 1858 lc/o Henry Ward & Josephine Dugan bp 29 Jan 1858 spr Pierce C. Dugan & Harriet Buchanan "baptized by The Rev. John F. Hickey" Thos. Foley, priest p148

WARD – John, b 22 Jul 1855 lc/o Patrick Ward & Catharine Cooney bp 29 Jul 1855 spr Ann Mooney p53

WARD – Margaret Agnes, b 10 Oct 1864 lc/o Michael Ward & Cath. Garry bp 6 Nov 1864 spr Pat. Byrne & Agnes McCoy p344

WARD – Margaret, b 10 Oct 1864 lc/o Michael Ward & Catharine McGarry bp 24 Oct 1864 "baptized privately" Thos. Foley, priest p343

WARD – Mary Ann Eliza, b 16 Oct 1854 nc/o George Harper & Anna Ward bp 20 Aug 1854 spr Eliza Phipps p21

WARD – Mary Catherine, b 7 Sep 1857 lc/o Patrick Ward & Margaret McGlenan bp 4 Oct 1857 spr Thomas McGlenan & Catherine McGlenan p136

WARD – Mary Jane, b 28 Feb 1856 lc/o Bernard Ward & Mary Durr bp 2 Mar 1856 spr Jas. Ward & Mary McDonogh p74

WARD – Maurice, b 24 May 1854 lc/o Michael Ward & Catherine Byrne bp 4 Jun 1854 spr Thomas & Mary Hackett p13

WARD – Mgt. Ward "(born Butler)", "aged 35 years" bp 4 Mar 1870 spr Ann Summers "baptized conditionally" Thomas S. Lee, priest p495

WARD – Michael Owen, b 2 Sep 1857 lc/o Thomas Ward & Mary Kelly bp 3 Feb 1858 spr Thomas Simmons & Hannah Kelly p148

WARD – Michael, b 19 Oct 1860 lc/o Michael Ward & Catharine Byrne bp 21 Nov 1860 spr Patrick Keogh & Martha Donnelly p236

WARD – Michael, b 4 Jun 1856 lc/o Michael Ward & Catherine Burn bp 27 Jul 1856 spr John Ward & Ann O'Day p91

WARD – Sarah Jane, b 6 Jan 1858 lc/o Robert Ward & Catherine Holbrook bp 25 Jan 1858 spr Nicholas N. Holbrook & Mary Duff p147

WARTZ – Mary Catharine, b 28 Apr 1861 lc/o Henry Wartz & Catharine Carroll (c) spr John Castor & Mary Mitchell p250

WASHINGTON – John Henry Washington (c), "aged 33 years" bp 4 Jan 1866 p373

WASHINGTON – Mary Ann, b 1 Jan 1865 lc/o John Henry & Felicia Washington (c) bp 4 Jan 1866 p373

WATEN – John Arnold, b 8 Aug 1867 lc/o Wm. Waten & Susan Incs (c) bp 6 Jun 1870 spr Fannie Griffiss "baptized (*sub cer*)" John Daugherty, priest p502

WATERS – Eliza June (c), b 6 Jan 1854 nc/o Thomas Mason & Mary Waters (c) bp 6 Jul 1854 spr John Noel p17

WATERS – Susan Waters, "aged about 55 years" bp 5 May 1864 "baptized privately" H. B. Coskery, priest p327

WATKINS – Frances Caroline, b 28 Feb 1862 "names of parents unknown" bp 24 Mar 1862 spr Eliza Phipps p277

WATKINS – Isaac Daniel, b 5 Jan 1859 lc/o Isaac Daniel Watkins & Elizabeth Jones (c) bp 17 Apr 1859 spr Elizabeth Jones p187

WATKINS – Mary Emma, b 31 Mar 1867 lc/o William O. Watkins & Winifred Burke bp 15 May 1867 spr Emma Watkins p412

WATKINS – Sarah Catharine Watkins, "aged 24 years" bp 26 Aug 1867 p420

WATSON – Frances Ann Watson (c), "about 20 years old" bp 19 Jun 1854 spr Ellen Mahoney p15

WATSON – Joshua Watson, "aged 68 years" bp 10 Feb 1860 p214

WATTS – Charles Edgar, b 21 Jan 1865 lc/o John Watts & Harriet Brown bp 13 Jun 1865 spr Elizabeth D. Buley p358

WATTS – Matilda, b *ndg* May 1866 lc/o Hanson Watts & Adline Duck (c) bp 25 Nov 1867 spr Jane Blackson p427

WEBSTER – John Francis, "21 months old" lc/o John Webster & Eliza Francis (c) bp 26 Jul 1863 spr Gustav Morris p311

WEEKLY – Catherine Ann Weekly, "about 20 years" "of Virginia" bp 27 Dec 1857 spr Catherine Clark p145

WEEKS – Mary Virginia, b 28 Feb 1856 lc/o Charles Weeks & Sarah C. Wells bp 29 Feb 1856 spr Mary V. Wells p73

WEEMS – Mary Catharine, b 2 Dec 1858 lc/o James Weems & Matilda Turbott bp 23 Jan 1859 spr Jane Duffy p179

WEIDHAMMER – John Nashby, b 28 Jun 1867 lc/o George Weidhammer & Catharine Shaw bp 11 Jul 1867 spr Mary Fitch p417

WEIGH – Rose Ann, b 7 Jan 1870 lc/o John Weigh & Rose Anne Riley bp 6 Feb 1870 spr Thos. Luby & Margaret Killen p493

WEISON – Jacob Albert, b 1 Dec 1858 lc/o Jacob Weison & Mary Duering bp 6 Mar 1859 spr Mary Sloan p183

WELB – Louis, b 7 Aug 1864 lc/o Francis Welb & Mary Postley bp 16 Feb 1865 spr Fannie Welb p350

WELCH – Catherine Jane, b 6 Sep 1854 lc/o John Welch & Ellen Roach bp 8 Oct 1854 spr Patk. Welch & Cath. Barry p25

WELCH – Helen Welch, "aged 42 years" bp 11 Apr 1859 spr Mary Jenkins "baptized conditionally" H. B. Coskery, priest p186

WELCH – Henrietta Welch, "aged about 36 years" bp 11 Apr 1859 spr Mary Jenkins "baptized conditionally" H. B. Coskery, priest p186

WELCH – Robert Aloysius, b 21 Jun 1861 lc/o Thomas J. Welch & Mary Doddrell bp 21 Aug 1861 spr Dr. Robert Welsh & Genevieve Welch p259

WELCH – Sarah Doddrell, b *ndg* Jun 1858 lc/o Thomas J. Welch & Mary E. Doddrell bp 2 Sep 1858 spr Mary Jenkins p168

WELD – Edith Mary, b 13 Jan 1855 lc/o Arthur Thomas Weld & Mary Sophia Rear bp 17 Feb 1855 spr Wm. Lee Rear & Cornelia Howard p36

WELD – Maria Louisa, b 25 Jan 1867 lc/o Arthur S. Weld & Mary Sophia Read bp 2 Feb 1867 spr C. Oliver O'Donnell & Cornelia Lee p404

WELSEY – Thomas William Henry, b 18 Jan 1863 lc/o Thomas M. H. Welsey & Anna Quinn (c) bp 19 Mar 1863 spr Hannah Quinn p304

WELSH – Alice Virginia, b 16 Jan 1855 lc/o James Welsh & Julia Williams bp 29 Apr 1855 spr Frances _____ p45

WELSH – Elvira Paula Welsh, b *ndg* 1821 bp 24 Jan 1860 w – Mary Jenkins, "baptized conditionally" E. Q. S. Waldron, priest p212

WELSH – Frances Welsh, "aged 26 years" bp 2 Apr 1862 p278

WELSH – Francis, b 11 Mar 1856 lc/o Francis Welsh & Mary Burns bp 21 Jun 1856 spr Ellen Nevin p86

WELSH – James Francis, b 2 Nov 1858 lc/o John Welsh & Frances Hobbs bp 5 Dec 1858 spr Louisa I. Herener p 175

WELSH – James, b 18 Aug 1856 lc/o William Welsh & Catherine Burke bp 1 Sep 1856 spr Mary Jane O'Loughlin p94

WELSH – Mary Doddrell Welsh, "aged 43 years" bp 10 May 1867 spr Eliza Randall p412

WELSH – Mary Ellen, b 2 May 1862 lc/o Robert S. Welsh & Genevieve Garcia bp 5 Jul 1862 spr Thos. Foley & Fanny Jackson p284

WELSH – Thomas J. Welsh, "aged 50" bp 6 Jan 1868 "baptized conditionally" Thos. Foley, priest p431

WELSH – Thomas Jefferson, b 10 Dec 1861 lc/o John Welsh & Frances Hobbs bp 29 Dec 1861 spr Ann Doyle p271

WERNET – Charles Thomas, b 22 Oct 1861 lc/o Joseph Wernet & Esther A. Bond bp 5 Mar 1862 spr Margaret Carman p275

WHALEN – Anna, b 4 Dec 1868 c/o Mary Ellen Whalen bp 23 Feb 1869 spr Ennis Mullan p465

WHALEN – Francis, b 27 Jan 1870 lc/o John Whalen & Catharine Higgins bp 13 Feb 1870 spr Francis Scott & Ellen Connolly p494

WHALEY – Mary Henrietta, b 23 Sep 1862 lc/o Ambrose Whaley & Mary Jane Suter bp 12 Jan 1863 spr Rachel Whaley p299

WHEATHERTON – Mary Laura (c), b 10 May 1870 lc/o John Weatherton & Caroline Lee (c) bp 24 Jun 1870 spr Annie Brisese p504

WHEELAN – Thomas, b 14 Oct 1854 lc/o Thomas Wheelan & Mary Dunnall "(born Gleek)" bp 7 Nov 1854 spr Thomas Wheelan & _____ "by proxy Mary _____" p28

WHEELER – Ann, b 5 Jul 1858 lc/o John Wheeler & Catherine Clear bp 18 Jul 1858 spr John & Robert McKernan p163

WHEELER – James, b 7 Jun 1854 lc/o John Wheeler & Catherine Clare bp 25 Jun 1854 spr Martin Cavanaugh & Mary A. McMahan p15

WHELAN – Agnes Theresa, b 15 Oct 1861 lc/o Louis N. Whelan & Rosa I. Foudriat bp 31 Oct 1861 spr Sarah A. Collins p265

WHELAN – Ann Elizabeth, b 24 Oct 1860 lc/o Alexander Whelan & Margaret Lyris bp 7 Nov 1860 spr Ignatius and Catharine Elder p235

WHELAN – Catherine Elizabeth, b 25 Apr 1858 lc/o James Brown & Catherine Whelan bp 20 Jun 1858 spr Bridget Whelan p160

WHELAN – Clara Louisa, "aged 9 months" lc/o William Whelan bp 28 Sep 1859 "baptized privately" Thos. Foley, priest p201

WHELAN – Eduard, b 7 Mar 1856 lc/o Denis Whelan & Julia Ryan bp 9 Mar 1856 spr John Wade & Mary Ruan p75

WHELAN – Francis, b 24 May 1866 lc/o John Whelan & Kate Higgins bp 3 Jun 1866 spr Patrick Colin & Margaret Henchy p385

WHELAN – George Ignatius, b 18 Aug 1860 [*ed. note this cannot be correct, the month was probably July*] lc/o Louis N. Whelan & Rose J. Foudriat bp 6 Aug 1860 spr George Whelan & Elizabeth Jenkins p228

WHELAN – James, b 27 Nov 1867 lc/o John Whelan & Kate Higgins bp 8 Dec 1867 spr Andrew Connolly & Bridget Dugan p429

WHELAN – Louisa Philomina, b 27 Nov 1858 lc/o Louis N. Whelan & Rosa J. Fondriat bp 11 Dec 1858 spr Peter Fondriat & M. Josephine Fondriat p176

WHELAN – Mary Elizabeth, b 5 Apr 1864 lc/o John Whelan & Catharine Higgins bp 17 Apr 1864 spr John Dugan & Margaret Hanley p330

WHELAN – Mary, b 7 Dec 1856 lc/o William Whelan & Henrietta, "his wife" bp 24 Jun 1857 spr Margaret Sullivan p124

WHELAN – Richard Vincent, b 1 Sep 1857 lc/o Louis N. Whelan & Rosa J. Foudriet bp 24 Sep 1857 spr Harriet Spalding, "proxy for Rt. Rev. Richard Vincent Whelan" & Harriet Spalding "This child had been privately baptized" H. B. Coskery, priest p136

WHELAN – Sarah Ellen, b 18 Nov 1861 lc/o John Whelan & Catharine Higgins bp 1 Dec 1861 spr Thomas Kane & Ellen Kelly p268

<u>WHERMEYER</u> – Charles, b 5 Jun 1857 lc/o John Henry <u>Whermeyer</u> & Mary Jane <u>Sibley</u> bp 5 Jul 1857 spr Julia Manahan p126

WHITE – Edward Nichols, b 17 Feb 1869 lc/o James Mckenny White & Martha M. Goldsmith bp 13 Apr 1869 spr Egbert Goldsmith & Eliza Goldsmith p468

WHITE – Edward, b 13 Jun 1854 lc/o John White & Aurelia Hyatt bp 24 Jul 18555 spr Ida Hyatt p53

WHITE – Eliza Henrietta, b 28 Apr 1870 lc/o James McKenny White & _____ _____ bp 25 May 1870 spr John Dougherty & Mary Elizabeth Russell p502

WHITE – George Linton, b 22 Jun 1869 lc/o William George White & Ann Maria Smith bp 8 Jul 1869 spr Mary Toulon p476

WHITE – Henry, b 15 Jun 1854 lc/o Ambrose White & Mary Hurley bp 7 Jul 1854 spr Edward Lucas & Catherine Lucas p17

WHITE – James Edward, b 6 Jan 1855 lc/o Edward & Mary White bp 3 Jun 1855 spr Elizabeth Mitchel p48

WHITE – Mary Emma, b 29 Mar 1869 lc/o John J. White & Mary Emma Carver bp 12 Apr 1869 spr Rt. Rev. J. Gibbons & Henrietta White p468

WHITE – Patrick, b 28 Feb 1859 lc/o William White & Barbara Myers bp 7 Mar 1859 spr P. Morton & Mary Morton p183

WHITE – Thomas, b 20 Nov 1863 lc/o John White & Ellen Quinlan bp 29 Nov 1863 spr Thos. Quinlan & Kate O'Brien p321

WHITEFORD – William, b 24 Sep 1863 lc/o Alfred H. Whiteford, M.D. & Elizabeth Dinkle bp 10 Jun 1864 spr Josephine Placide p334

WHITNEY – Alice, b 15 Sep 1861 lc/o George Whitney & Jane Harrison bp 19 Nov 1861 spr Daniel I. Fallon & Margaret O'Farrell p266

WHITNEY – Frances Rose, b 7 Jan 1864 lc/o George H. Whitney & Jane Harrison bp 29 Feb 1864 spr Kate Chatard Hurd p327

WHITNEY – George Henry, b 20 Sep 1866 lc/o George Whitney & Jane Harrison bp 1 Nov 1866 spr James T. Darling & Mary A. Darling p398

WHITNEY – George Whitney, "about 28 years old" lc/o George & Fanny Whitney bp 11 Nov 1855 spr Albert Man p64

WHITNEY – Jane Harrison, b 20 Jan 1865 lc/o George Whitney & Jane Harrison bp 22 Feb 1865 spr Mary E. Young p351

WHITNEY – Martha Beula, b 23 May 1868 lc/o George Whitney & Jane Harrison bp 22 Jun 1868 spr Ellen Vernon p446

WHITNEY – Mary, b 23 Aug 1869 lc/o George Whitney & Jane Harrison bp 31 Aug 1869 spr Thos. Foley & Martin McCauley p481

WHITRIDGE – Charles Luke, b 9 Nov 1855 lc/o Charles L. Flannigan & Martha Campbell bp 24 Nov 1855 spr Luke Flannigan & Elizabeth Flannigan p66

WHITTEMORE – Ann, "born February last" lc/o John Whittemore & Ann Care bp 3 Aug 1863 spr Margaret A. Trainor p312

WHITTEMORE – John Caleb, b 9 Apr 1855 lc/o Finagan Whittemore & Anne Bell bp 11 Nov 1855 spr Eliza Bell p64

WHITTEMORE – Josias, b 21 Jan 1861 lc/o John Whittemore & Ann Kerr bp 26 Jul 1861 spr Margaret A. Trainor p257

WIGGINS – Jane Frances, b 12 Jun 1854 lc/o Reuben H. Wiggins & Catherine Wiggins bp 8 Nov 1857 spr Edward Gaffey & Ellen Connolly "was baptized by Rev. John S. Foley" Thos. Foley, priest p140

WIGHT – Henry Mumford, b 30 Jan 1865 lc/o Jacob Wight & Cecilia Mumford Didier bp 20 Feb 1865 spr Maria Bogue p351

WILEY – Catharine Virginia, b 7 Nov 1855 lc/o William Wiley & Catharine Virginia, "his wife" bp 23 Feb 1857 spr Eliza C_____ p112

WILHELM – Elizabeth <u>Maud</u>, b 2 Sep 1858 lc/o John Wilhelm & Henrietta Clark bp 2 Jan 1859 spr Sarah Clark p178

WILHELM – John Henry, b 17 Jan 1861 lc/o John Wilhelm & Henrietta Clarke bp 28 May 1861 spr Mary A. Odin p252

WILKINSON – Ann Catharine, b 22 Mar 1866 lc/o John V. Wilkinson & Kate C. Travers bp 2 Apr 1866 spr John Travers & Maria Cassidy p380

WILKINSON – George Washington, b 11 Dec 1858 lc/o William & Mary Wilkinson bp 16 Oct 1860 "baptized privately" Thos. Foley, priest p233

WILKINSON – John Victor, b 24 Dec 1867 lc/o John Victor Wilkinson & Kate Travers bp 12 Jan 1868 spr John M. Travers & Mary O. Maxwell p432

WILKINSON – Margaret Ross, b 3 Mar 1861 lc/o William Wilkinson & Mary Ann Ross bp 30 Apr 1861 spr Frances Granger p250

WILKINSON – Mary Caroline, b 12 Oct 1863 lc/o John V. Wilkinson & Catharine Frances bp 26 Oct 1863 spr Mary Travers p318

WILKINSON – Mary Marcellina, b *ndg* lc/o William Wilkinson & Mary Ann Ross bp 17 Jun 1865 spr Marcellina Byrne p358

WILKINSON – Mary Wilkinson "(born Ross)", "aged 30 years" bp 10 Nov 1862 "baptized conditionally" Thos. Foley, priest p294

WILKINSON – William Wilkinson, "aged 33 years" bp 30 Apr 1861 "baptized conditionally" Thos. Foley, priest p250

WILLIAMS – Agnes Elizabeth, b 19 Nov 1848 lc/o James Williams & Martha G. Henderson (c) bp 19 Dec 1855 spr Mary A. Lewis p68

WILLIAMS – Ann Eliza, b 20 Oct 1858 lc/o N. Williams & Ellen Duggan bp 24 Oct 1858 spr Daniel Markham & Bridget Donaho p172

WILLIAMS – Ann Elizabeth, b 11 Feb 1866 lc/o James Williams & Mary Lynch bp 16 Mar 1866 spr Mary Doris p378

WILLIAMS – Ann Elizabeth, b 9 Nov 1862 lc/o Charles Williams & Elizabeth Dorsey (c) bp 27 Jul 1865 spr Susan Golden p360

WILLIAMS – Charles Francis, b 1 Apr 1863 lc/o John Williams & Adele Laroque bp 29 May 1863 spr Joseph Laroque & Isabelle Laroque p308

WILLIAMS – Edward James, b 16 Feb 1860 lc/o John A. Williams & Adele Laroque bp 14 Feb 1861 spr Frank Laroque & Mary Goddard, "proxies for Edward Laroque & Eugenia Laroque" p243

WILLIAMS – Ellen Augustus, "12 years old" c/o Jane Williams (c) bp 17 Sep 1865 spr Sally Jenkins p364

WILLIAMS – Emilia Ann Eliza, b 9 Jul 1858 lc/o George Williams & Cassandra Nevitt bp 21 Aug 1858 spr Mary Ann Williams p168

WILLIAMS – James William, b 10 Nov 1856 lc/o John Williams & Elizabeth I. Jefferson (c) bp 30 Dec 1856 spr Catherine McElroy p106

WILLIAMS – Josephine (c) lc/o Henry C. Williams & Mary Jane Butler bp 26 Oct 1864 spr Clara Clarke p343

WILLIAMS – Marcella, b 12 Sep 1859 lc/o George Williams & Ellen Duggan bp 18 Sep 1859 spr John Singleton & Mary Henchy p200

WILLIAMS – Marie Cecile, b 8 Dec 1865 lc/o John H. Williams & Marie Adele Laroque bp 13 Jan 1866 spr E. James & Alexandrine Laroque p374

WILLIAMS – Martha Ellen, b 18 Oct 1858 lc/o Henry Williams & Mary Jane Butler (c) bp 16 Apr 1859 spr Mary E. Thomas p186

WILLIAMS – Mary Ann, bp 24 May 1857 spr Margaret Ann Peters (both c) "baptized conditionally" H. B. Coskery, priest p121

WILLIAMS – Mary Elizabeth (c), [*ed note: surname is Williams or Thomas*] b 10 Jul 1854 ic/o Edward Thomas & Ann Williams bp 6 Sep 1854 spr Sarah O'Donnell p23

WILLIAMS – Mary Eugenia, b 22 Jun 1870 lc/o John A. Williams & Mary Adele Laroque bp 1 Jul 1870 spr Dr. Edward Jamet p505

WILLIAMS – Mary Frances, b 7 Nov 1860 lc/o Henry Williams & Mary Janet Butler (c) bp 18 Dec 1860 spr Mary E. Thomas p238

WILLIAMS – Mary Joseph, b *ndg* nc/o _____Williams & Elizabeth Gaines bp 28 Aug 1858 p168

WILLIAMS – Rodney Thomas (c), b 18 Aug 1857 lc/o Henry Williams & Mary L. Butler bp 5 Oct 1857 spr Mary E. Thomas p 136

WILLIAMS – Sarah Elizabeth, b 19 Oct 1862 lc/o Henry Williams & Mary J. Butler (c) bp 25 Mar 1863 spr Elizabeth Colbert p304

WILLIAMS – William Edward, b 26 Aug 1861 lc/o George Williams & Ellen Duggan bp 1 Sep 1861 spr John Singleton & Mary Kelly p260

WILLIAMSON – Florence Mary, b 14 Nov 1869 lc/o Luke Tiernan Williamson & Eliza Hamtramck bp 19 Dec 1869 spr Thomas Foley & Rebecca Young Smith p489

WILLOUGHBY – Frances, b 6 Feb 1855 lc/o Joseph D. Willoughby & Martha E. Kernan bp 2 May 1855 spr Mary Kernan p45

WILLS – Francis Moore, b 29 May 1854 lc/o Buchanan Wills & Lizzie Wetter bp 10 Jun 1856 spr Henrietta Brice & Mary J. Coale p85

WILLS – Mary Cecilia, b 22 Oct 1868 lc/o William Wills & Cecilia Theresa Hook bp 4 Nov 1868 spr Aloysius Connolly & Mary Hook p456

WILLS – Mary Emma Wills, b 16 Dec 1855 lc/o Buchanan Wills & Lizzie Wetter bp 10 Jun 1856 spr Henrietta Brice & Mary J. Coale p85

WILLS – William Frederick, b 16 Jun 1870 lc/o William H. Wills & Cecilia S. Hook bp 23 Jun 1870 spr Frederick Hook & Caroline Menzies p504

WILLS – William Wills, "aged 24 years" bp 27 Dec 1867 "baptized conditionally" Thos. Foley, priest p430

WILMERE – Sophia Ann, b 30 Mar 1870 lc/o Daniel Wilmere & Catharine Addison bp 14 Jun 1870 spr Teresa Queen (c) p503

WILSON – Alice Ann, b 21 Aug 1849 lc/o George Henry Wilson & Teresa Curley bp 11 Feb 1862 spr Hanna Dorrity "baptized conditionally" H. B. Coskery, priest p274

WILSON – Frances, "5 years and 6 months age" c/o Susan Wilson (c) bp 30 Oct 1867 spr Anna Greer p425

WILSON – Isabelle Genge Wilson, b *ndg* 1844 lc/o William & Isabelle Wilson bp 6 Jul 1868 spr Matilda N. Elder p448

WILSON – John Alexander Wilson, "aged 22 years" bp 4 Nov 1860 "baptized conditionally" Thos. Foley, priest p234

WILSON – Joseph Wilson, "born in 1786" bp 6 May 1859 p189

WILSON – Lilian Josephine, b 15 May 1867 lc/o John A. Wilson & Mary Keenan bp 25 Jul 1867 spr Tillie Keenan p418

WILSON – Lydia Elizabeth, b 5 May 1860 lc/o William Wilson & Margaret Hartley bp 27 Sep 1860 spr Mary A. Hanley p232

WILSON – Margaret Wilson, "aged 22 years" bp 11 Oct 1869 spr Alice McCarthy p485

WILSON – Mary, b 18 Feb 1866 nc/o Joanna Wilson bp 8 May 1866 spr Else Holiday p383

WILSON – Mary Agnes Wilson (c) "aged 22 years" bp 5 Jun 1868 spr Elizabeth Greatfield p444

WILSON – Mary Agnes, "15 years old" lc/o Malcolm & Mary Wilson bp 30 Aug 1866 p394

WILSON – Mary Anna, "11 months old" nc/o Sarah Wilson & _____Williams bp 3 Oct 1859 spr Catharine Scanlan p201

WILSON – Mary Charlotte, b 14 March 1854 lc/o Richard Wilson & Charlotte Ann McNally bp 10 April 1854 spr Thos. Foley & Ann Wilson p6

WILSON – Mary Eleanora, b 8 Nov 1861 lc/o John A. Wilson & Mary Keenan bp 20 Nov1861 spr Clarke Y. Davidson & Eleanora Davidson p267

WILSON – Mary Eliza, b 28 Apr 1845 lc/o Frederick & Ellen Wilson bp 21 Sep 1864 spr Josephine Placide p341

WILSON – Mary Elizabeth, b 11 Jun 1855 lc/o Robert Wilson & Margaret Lewis bp 29 Jul 1855 spr Louisa Broden p54

WILSON – Richard Wilson, "aged 62" bp 15 Feb 1857 "baptized conditionally" Jno. McNally, priest p112

WINCHESTER – Eliazabeth Independence, b 4 Jul 1863 lc/o William Winchester & Elizabeth Humphries bp 14 Jun 1867 spr Mary J. McKnew p415

WINCHESTER – Francis Herbert, b 9 Aug 1860 lc/o Oliver Augustus Winchester & Caroline Brown bp 6 Sep 1860 spr Francis A_____ Brown p230

WINCHESTER – Mary Anecy Elizabeth, b 4 Nov 1862 lc/o Oliver Winchester & Caroline Brown bp 27 Nov 1862 spr Francis Brown & Anecy Brown p296

WINCHESTER – Oliver Augustus, b 27 Oct 1864 lc/o Oliver Winchester & Caroline Breen bp 27 Nov 1864 spr Edward Breen & Anecy Breen p345

WINCHESTER – Victor Edward, b 1 Mar 1869 lc/o Oliver Winchester & Caroline Brown bp 4 Apr 1869 spr Victor Brown & Anecy Brown p468

WINCKER – Alfred Frederick, b 19 Sep 1862 lc/o George Wincker & Mary Plunkett bp 29 Oct 1862 spr Mary Feeney p292

WINN – Emily May, b 11 May 1860 c/o Joseph Roland Winn & Emily C. Gould, "his wife" bp 18 Jul 1861 g – Amanda Phillips p256

WINTERWRIGHT – Mary Elizabeth, b 5 Dec 1853 lc/o Henry Winterwright & Cath. U. Dolan bp 17 Feb 1854 spr D. Blundell & Mary E. Cassaress p5

WIREL – Henrietta, b 26 Feb 1859 lc/o William Wirel & Ruth Ann Jones bp 2 May 1859 spr Rose Dougherty p188

WISONG – Frances Augusta, b 17 Dec 1860 lc/o Jacob Wisong & Mary Jane During bp 7 Apr 1861 spr Emma Barrett p248

WOLF – Francis Aloysius, b 12 Oct 1857 lc/o Samuel L. Wolf & Adelaide M. Decombs bp 29 Nov 1857 spr Margaret A. Ward p142

WOLFE – Alcanus Bolingbrooke Augustine Wolfe, "about 52 years old" bp 4 May 1854 spr Parker Scott "baptized conditionally" Thos. Foley, priest p11

WOODLEY – William Thomas, b 3 Jul 1864 lc/o John Woodley & Martha J. Jackson (c) bp 15 May 1865 spr Lizzie Toland p356

WOODS – Alexander, b 4 Sep 1868 lc/o Alexander Woods & Elizabeth Adams (c) bp 15 Sep 1868 spr Thomas Foley & Emily Hillen p453

WOODS – Joseph, b 3 Sep 1867 lc/o Patrick Woods & Isabella Scott bp 14 Sep 1867 spr John W. Willet & Isabella Conway p421

WOODS – Lewis, b 17 Jun 1865 c/o Elizabeth Woods (c) "deceased" bp 18 Jun 1865 spr Julia Greatfield p358

WOODS – Mary Alice Rebecca b 25 May 1867 lc/o Henry Woods & Mary Jane Butler (c) bp 24 Jun 1870 spr Mary Ellen Butler p504

WOODS – Mary Ann, b 6 Apr 1859 lc/o William Woods & Winifred Hays bp 24 Apr 1859 spr Jeremiah Cashman p187

WOODWARD – Harriet Matilda, b 6 Aug 1866 lc/o Francis Woodward & _____ _____ bp 25 Sep 1866 spr Thos. Foley p396

WOODWARD – Louisa Smart, b 31 Jul 1868 lc/o Nicholas R. Woodward & Mary Francis [sic] Butler bp 25 Aug 1868 spr Mrs. Alice Scarff p452

WOODY – Amanda Elizabeth Woody, "aged 25 years" bp 3 May 1866 p383

WORTHING – Charles Hamilton, b 12 Sep 1868 lc/o Wm. Ed. Worthing & Susan Householder bp 1 Mar 1869 spr Mary Delaney p466

WORTHINGTON – Alice Mary Worthington, "aged 19 years" bp 25 Dec 1865 spr Harriet Dugan "baptized conditionally" Thos. Foley, priest p372

WORTHINGTON – Arthur Thomas, b 9 Sep 1855 c/o Nicholas Worthington & Annie O'Rourke "his lawful wife" bp 4 May 1856 spr Mrs. Mary Simons Murray p82

WRATH – Kate Lancaster, b 23 Mar 1867 c/o Edwd. Wrath & Kate Adams "(born Loring)" bp 15 Apr 1867 spr Kate Lancaster p410

WREN – Catherine, b 21 Feb 1857 lc/o Patrick Wren & Margaret Sanborn bp 2 Mar 1857 spr Julia Sullivan p113

WREN – John, "born about three weeks ago" lc/o Patrick Wren & Margaret Scanlon bp 11 Jan 1863 spr Bridget Jordan & William Glennan p299

WREN (Rain) – Ellen, b 1 Oct 1859 lc/o Patrick Wren "(or Rain)" & Margaret Scanlan bp 9 Oct 1859 spr M. Gillooly p202

WRIGHT – Eliza Jane Wright, b 9 Feb 1840 bp 25 Apr 1870 spr Annie Coskery p500

WRIGHT – Emily Jane, b 18 Jul 1861 lc/o Alfred Wright & Emily Cornish (c) bp 18 Sep 1861 spr Mary E. Singleton p261

WRIGHT – Frances Ann Augusta, b 10 Mar 1865 lc/o George S. Wright & Georgianna Burgess "his wife" (c) bp 27 Apr 1865 spr Frances Burgess p356

WRIGHT – Mary Deborah Wright, "age about 19 years" bp 8 Aug 1854 p19

WRIGHT – Mary Elizabeth (c), b 14 Mar 1862 lc/o George Wright & Georgianna Bingess (c) bp 6 Apr 1862 spr Julia A. Harris p278

WRIGHT – Rebecca Mary Wright (c), "aged 20 years" bp 13 Feb 1862 p274

WROTH – Eva Page, b 17 Jan1867 lc/o Edward W. Wroth & Louisa Clark bp 15 Mar 1867 spr Wm. H. Clark & Celinda Clark p408

WYNN – James Gould, b 7 Jan 1856 lc/o Joseph Robert Wynn & Emily Gould bp 14 Apr 1856 spr Christopher Wynn, Mary Virginia Ward & Ann Wynn p80

WYNN – Mary Ella, b 20 Dec 1857 lc/o Joseph Robert Wynn & Emily Gould bp 17 Dec 1857 spr Rev. Jno. McNally & Elleanora Wynn p144

WYNN – Robert Phil., b 1 Apr 1859 lc/o Joseph Robert Wynn & Emily Gould bp 12 Jul 1859 spr Caroline Wynn p195

WYSE – Mary August, b 7 Dec 1854 lc/o Octavius F. Wyse & Mary E. Pope bp 15 May 1855 spr ____ Wyse & Emily Harper p46

WYVIL – Mary Rose, b 22 Jan 1862, lc/o William Wyvil & Rose Jones bp 4 Jan 1863 spr Jerome Daugherty & Mary Ann Darling p299

WYVIL – Susanna, b 12 Apr 1861 lc/o William Wyvil & Ruth Ann Jones bp 12 May 1861 spr Ellen Johnson p251

WYVILL – Mary S. Wyvill, "aged 19 years" bp 28 Feb 1865 spr Mary S. Martin p352

WYVILL – Ruth Wyvill "aged 24 years" bp 17 Oct 1862 "baptized conditionally" Thos. Foley, priest p292

YALE – Thomas Yale, *ndg* Jun 1838 bp 17 Oct 1868 p456

YEATMAN – Elizabeth Yeatman, "aged 32 years" bp 18 Nov 1869 "baptized conditionally" Thos. Foley, priest p488

YERCAS – Francis, b 31 Jan 1855 c/o George Yercas & Maria Chase (c) bp 22 Jun 1856 spr Maria Williams p86

YORMAN – Francis Patrick, b 26 Jun 1856 lc/o Bryan Yorman & Christine McConnell bp 28 Jun 1856 spr John Connolly & Mary Bannon p87

YOUNG – Christiana (c), "5 months old" lc/o Thomas Young & Caroline Coleman bp 5 Mar 1867 spr Julia Blundell p407

YOUNG – Elizabeth Young (c), "age about 25 years" bp 8 Mar 1858 "baptized conditionally" H. B. Coskery, priest p150

YOUNG – Ellen Virginia, b 3 Jul 1866 lc/o Edward Young & Rosa Feenerty bp 8 Jul 1866 spr James Sullivan & Marcella Courtney p388

YOUNG – George Edward, b 10 Aug 1862 lc/o George Edward Young & Mary Keys bp 21 Aug 1862 spr Anabelle Williams p288

YOUNG – William Henry, b 7 May 1857 lc/o Michael Young & Ann Rebecca Ford (c) bp 12 Jul 1857 spr Eliza Hicks p127

YOUNGMAN – Laura Virginia, b 28 Apr 1856 lc/o John Youngman & Catherine Chapman bp 11 Jun 1856 spr Elizabeth McAvoy p86

ZANINO – Elizabeth, b 13 Apr 1856 lc/o Luke Zanino & Margaret Nova bp 20 Apr 1856 spr Wm. Jos. Kelly & Cath. Smith p80

ZELL – Catharine Virginia, b 11 Jul 1869 lc/o Wm. Zell & Rosanna Miller bp 1 Aug 1869 spr Jacob H. & Eliza Virginia Miller p478

ZELL – Mary Elizabeth, b 28 Apr 1866 lc/o William Zell & Rozanna Miller bp 3 Jun 1866 spr Amelia J. Keller p385

ZELL – Richard Donelan, b 12 Nov 1855 lc/o Bernard Zell & Julia Byrne bp 12 Dec 1855 spr Ann Gibson p67

ZELL – William Bernard, b 10 Aug 1858 lc/o Bernard Zell & Julia Burns bp 15 Aug 1858 spr Mary Burns p166

List of Maiden Names

Maiden Name, First Name, *Record Name*, Baptismal Register Page No.

Note: the page number does not refer to the page number of this book; it refers to the baptismal register page number. The record can be found in this book by looking under the ***Record Name****.*

Aburn, Sarah, *Foy,* 234
Aburn, Sarah, *Foy,* 13
Aburn, Sarah, *Foy,* 149
Aburn, Sarah, *Foy,* 201
Adams, Catharine, *Israel,* 448
Adams, Elenora, *O'Donnell,* 140
Adams, Eliza, *Neale,* 467
Adams, Eliza, *Neale,* 491
Adams, Elizabeth, *Woods,* 453
Adams, Emily, *Mullin,* 516
Addison, Appolonia, *Hart,* 403
Addison, Catharine, Wilmere, 503
Addison, Emily, *Goldsborough,* 84
Addison, Josephine, *Shelley,* 466
Addison, Lizzy, *Bray,* 134
Addison, Margaret, *Bond,* 13
Addison, Mary, *McCardell,* 34
Agle, Honora, *Carmody,* 177
Agnes, Grace, *O'Brien,* 487
Ahern, H., *Sullivan,* 488
Ahern, Sarah, *Foy,* 69
Aiken, ?, *Reynolds,* 39
Aikin, Rebecca, *Reynolds,* 135
Aitkin, Mary, *Farrell,* 135
Alenderson, Mary, *Tucker,* 284
Allman, Mary, *Daley,* 96
Alnay, Mary, *Smith,* 147
Altwine, Eve, *Rackermann,* 216
Ames, Susan, *Ames,* 11
Anderson, ?, *Conner,* 9
Anderson, Margaret, *McConnell,* 391
Anderson, Rachel, *O'Brien,* 21
Anderson, Rachel, *O'Brien,* 167
Anderson, Rachel, *O'Brien,* 237
Anderson, Sarah, *Anderson,* 199
Antonnelie, Marie, *Angelerie,* 507
Arata, Livia, *Malatesta,* 241
Arens, Valesca, *Baker,* 18
Armstrong, Adelaide, *Neal,* 394
Aroy, Mary, *Coyne,* 13
Austin, Mary, *Goss,* 158
Austin, Mary, *Goss,* 158
Austin, Sarah, *Givney,* 44
Austin, Sarah, *Gibbney,* 161
Avanti, Rosacilla, *Vincellini,* 341
Bachelor, Emma, *Kilduff,* 365
Bacon, Martha, *Huster,* 254
Bagge, Kate, *Ghee,* 208
Baggs, Kate, *Gee,* 354
Bailey, Ann, *Muse,* 112
Bailey, Mary, *Needhammer,* 423
Baird, Annie, *Scott,* 230
Baird, Caroline, *Scott,* 35
Baird, Carrie, *Scott,* 98
Baird, Lassie, *Scott,* 264
Baker, Alice, *Cadigan,* 497
Baker, Martha, *Huister,* 298
Baker, Mary, *Keys,* 118
Baker, Mary, *Cass,* 302
Ballentine, Ann, *Betts,* 13
Balloof, Matilda, *Linton,* 300
Baltzell, Rebecca, *Merceret,* 100
Baltzell, Rebecca, *Merceret,* 155
Baltzell, Rebecca, *Merceret,* 206
Baltzell, Rebecca, *Merceret,* 297
Baltzell, Rebecca, *Merceret,* 324